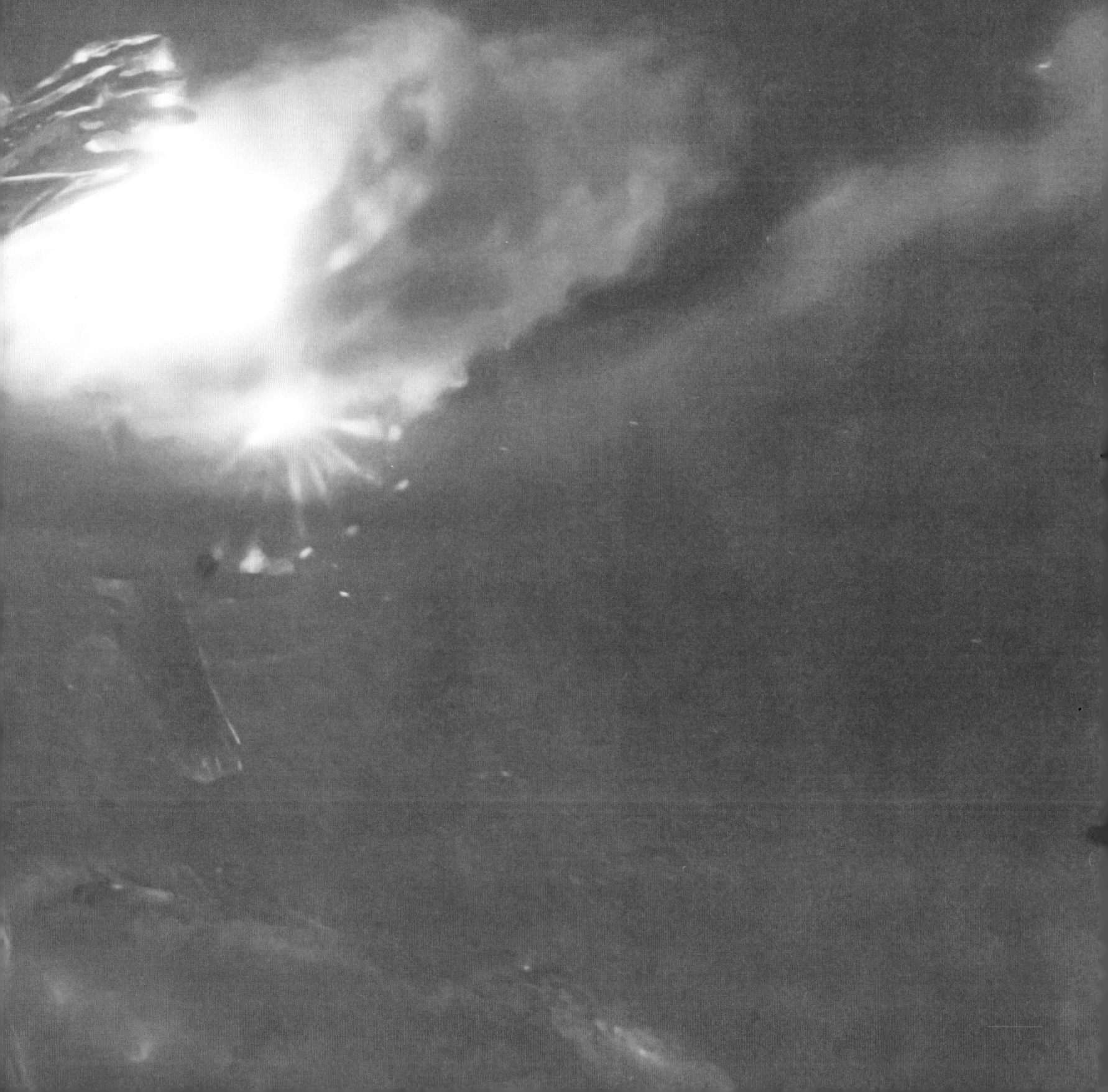

MARVEL STUDIOS

THE MARVEL CINEMATIC UNIVERSE

AN OFFICIAL TIMELINE

FOREWORD BY
KEVIN FEIGE

MARVEL STUDIOS

THE MARVEL CINEMATIC UNIVERSE

AN OFFICIAL TIMELINE

WRITTEN BY ANTHONY BREZNICAN

WITH AMY RATCLIFFE AND REBECCA THEODORE-VACHON

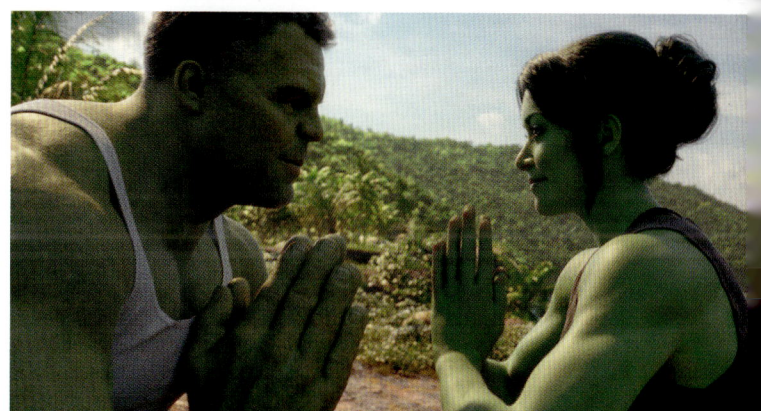

FOREWORD BY
KEVIN FEIGE

CONTENTS

FOREWORD

It is mind-boggling to think that the cinematic universe we've built at Marvel Studios justifies an entire timeline book, but after 30 films, eight series, four phases, and an Infinity Saga, it felt like the right time to attempt a project like this. More importantly, it is something our fans have been asking us for! This book is not just an in-Universe chronological order of events; this book exemplifies the thought and care that all of us here at Marvel Studios and the storytellers we work with—directors, writers, actors—have put into imagining the Marvel Cinematic Universe as it exists today.

When we were working on *Iron Man*, we didn't have a map built out that stretched all the way to the far reaches of the Multiverse. We wanted to tell a great story about one character, hoping that if it worked, we might just be able to do a few more, and if all the stars cosmically aligned, we could assemble the Avengers in a movie. That was the bet we were making when Samuel L. Jackson as Nick Fury appeared in the post credit scene on Iron Man. He could have easily been speaking directly to us when he said, "Mr. Stark, you've become part of a bigger universe. You just don't know it yet." Universes have a way of growing.

Like Marvel's comic books, the MCU is a creation of collaboration, home to hundreds of artists and storytellers. Like all of us, our onscreen heroes are all deeply human. They doubt, they grieve, they fight, and then they pick themselves back up, they forge new bonds, they celebrate. They have people they care about, and families we have watched them build, whether it's a wise-cracking raccoon and walking tree, or the sibling you're constantly at odds with, or the guy you keep lapping at the Lincoln Memorial. Across multiple movies and shows, we watch these characters come together to create something greater than the sum of their parts.

And each of these movies and shows is created to share those connections with you, making the whole bigger and grander and more dimensional. Every detail—every story beat, every piece of armor, every location—has been thought about and built by our filmmakers and the Marvel Studios team, who live in these stories sometimes for years. The result, we hope, is an immersive world that fans can return to time and again, to visit with characters they know and love, experience stories that are both exciting and moving, and explore places that are fantastical yet familiar.

As the team was pulling this book together, we went through multiple scenarios on how to present this timeline in the best possible way. We quickly realized that the real authority on these matters is the Time Variance Authority or TVA, which we introduced in *Loki*. As the guardians of the Sacred Timeline, they would be the ones who would notice when things don't quite line up. And like the real universe, the Marvel Cinematic Universe can also be a little messy in parts. Fortunately, we have Miss Minutes who will pop up throughout the book whenever we have one of those Multiversal glitches, and to provide more context.

On the Multiverse note, we recognize that there are stories—movies and series—that are canonical to Marvel but were created by different storytellers during different periods of Marvel's history. The timeline presented in this book is specific to the MCU's Sacred Timeline through Phase 4. But, as we move forward and dive deeper into the Multiverse Saga, you never know when timelines may just crash or converge (hint, hint / spoiler alert).

The Marvel Cinematic Universe continues to grow—it's growing as I write this—but for now this is the history of the MCU unraveled from end to end. It is a story I have been lucky to be a part of for over 20 years. And I am thankful for all of you reading this who are on this journey with us!

Kevin Feige
Producer and President, Marvel Studios

INTRODUCTION

Hey Y'all! I'm Miss Minutes, and welcome to the guidebook on the beings and events that make up the universe known as 616, also known as the Sacred Timeline. Here at the Time Variance Authority, our job is to keep tabs and protect the countless timelines that weave together our Multiverse. Some of these have small differences, like altered lunar cycles or events happening at slightly different times, or big ones—like everybody being made out of paint! Now, 616 may be just one thread in this vast Multiverse, but trust me, it's a wild one!

To help navigate key events along the way, when possible, we've marked them by seasons in Earth's Northern Hemisphere. Why there, y'all might ask? Because that's where the Avengers are, silly! As we make our way down the Sacred Timeline, you'll even see some folks from this reality hoppin' over to other timelines for a visit. For a long time, some of those crossovers were allowed, and we didn't interfere.

But every now and again somethin' does go wrong, and in the old days, the TVA would step in to prune the branch, restoring it to the proper flow of time. We don't do that anymore! We wanna be honest here, so now and then I'll pop in to point out temporal disruptions in the timelines! Ooo, doggy! Just remember, this isn't everything that happens in 616, much less the Multiverse—we're always trackin' this vast, evolving story. Given the fluidity of time and space, and the infinite expansion of the Multiverse—and our paperwork—we're always playing catch-up, so we appreciate y'all's patience and understanding! Maybe we'll get to the rest of it someday. Until then, sit back and enjoy!

HOW TO USE THIS BOOK

This book grants you access to all the time in the world. Feel free to skip around, moving backward or forward—however you like! The TVA has provided a few signposts along the way to label some of the most influential figures from Universe-616 and mark events that are especially meaningful.

Character Icons

The Eternals	Thor	Loki
Captain America (Steve Rogers)	The Winter Soldier	Ant-Man
S.H.I.E.L.D. /Nick Fury	Captain Marvel	
Iron Man	Black Panther	Hulk
Black Widow	War Machine	Hawkeye
The Avengers	Falcon	
Spider-Man	Wanda Maximoff/The Scarlet Witch	Pietro Maximoff
Guardians of the Galaxy	Vision	The Wasp
Doctor Strange	Captain America (Sam Wilson)	
Shang-Chi	S.W.O.R.D. /Monica Rambeau	She-Hulk
America Chavez	Moon Knight	Ms. Marvel

Events

Events in the Multiverse

Character Origin Moment

Major Villain Defeated

Major Character Dies

Major Battle

THE DISTANT PAST

Vast leaps are needed to traverse the period of time from The Big Bang to what's known on Earth as the 20th century. Vaulting forward through the chronology is part of that journey, but a degree of informed guesswork about certain events from long ago is also necessary, since the further away these incidents are, the harder it is to see them clearly.

What follows is an estimation—a mix of science, history, politics, and legend. A chronicle of powerful beings in the universe can never be especially well documented, given how often true power is shielded by secrecy. God-like beings also tend not to explain or make records of their actions for the purpose of mortal understanding. Still, moments of cosmic significance rarely go unnoticed, and even the most ancient and arcane tales have been passed down from one generation to the next, if only in whispers.

The closer one draws to the contemporary era, the more certain we are about when the timeline's major turning points occurred, where they happened, and who participated in them. In the beginning, the Celestials are a dominant sentient force, creating suns that bring light to worlds, which the gods then battle to rule. Over time, mortals, particularly human beings, will explore ways to harness new powers and abilities of their own, seizing control of their own fates.

The Distant Past

13.8 billion years ago, a universe is born. Bursts of light and energy send matter bolting away at unfathomable speeds. Galaxies sprawl, stars ignite, and clouds of debris coalesce into planets as billions of years elapse. Gradually, life evolves, and accompanying life is death. The struggle to survive will be defined by an innate sense of morality that many sentient beings possess—to protect themselves, but also others. From life, heroes will rise. This yearning to do right goes by many names: decency, honor, duty, love. All will become crucial forces that guide the destiny of this new plane of existence.

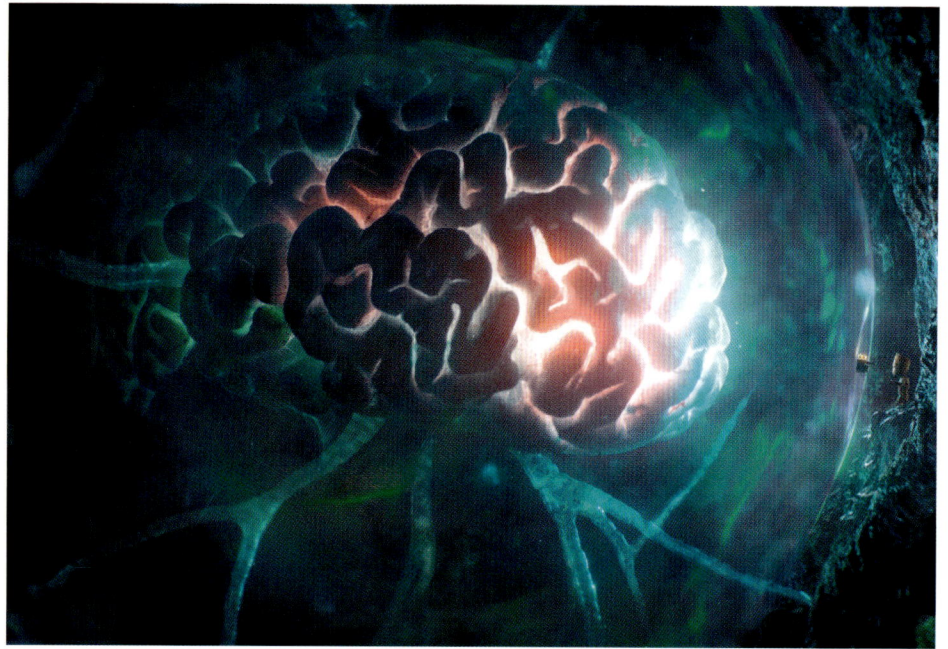

Ego's true form—the brain that lies at the core of the world that he accumulated.

Dawn of the Universe | Ego Takes Shape

Not all Celestials are born from the cores of planets. Some evolve seemingly by happenstance, like the Celestial known as Ego. At first just a spark of consciousness alone in deep space, Ego manipulates matter to construct physical neural-networks for itself in a large, brain-like receptacle, then assembles an entire planet layer by layer around that. While other Celestials exist in the form of colossal giants, Ego prefers to mimic more humble forms of life, creating avatars that look like "lesser" sentient creatures found on distant worlds.

A Celestial begins the creation of a sun.

Dawn of the Universe | The Handiwork of Celestials

Among the entities who shape the early universe are the Celestials, one of the oldest and most powerful forms of life to ever exist. These god-like beings pre-date the birth of the cosmos as well as the Infinity Stones, and use their ability to manipulate matter and energy to help construct suns that make life possible on other worlds.

Dawn of the Universe | The Six Infinity Stones

The Big Bang creates six objects of indescribable potency. Each represents a different aspect of existence: power, reality, mind, soul, space, and time. In the distant future, a being known as the Collector will describe them this way: "Before creation itself, there were six singularities. Then the universe exploded into existence, and the remnants of these systems were forged into concentrated ingots—Infinity Stones. These stones can only be brandished by beings of extraordinary strength."

All six Infinity Stones.

The Distant Past | Earth, Midgard, Terra

Known by many names, this tiny speck in the endless void of space, a blue and green world in the Yggdrasil array, will become the site of a significant number of universe-shaping events. It starts, as all worlds do, harsh and barren, but oceans form over the eons, an oxygen-rich atmosphere envelops the globe, and a vibrant array of plant and animal life blossoms on its surface. Arishem chooses Earth as the womb for a new Celestial known as Tiamut, whose seed is implanted just as intelligent life on the planet begins to thrive. One day, the human beings here will generate a high volume of powerful individuals whose actions reverberate far beyond their own solar system, sending shockwaves throughout the cosmos and even, in some cases, the Multiverse.

Arishem devises the creation of new Celestials, who in turn help create new solar systems and habitable worlds.

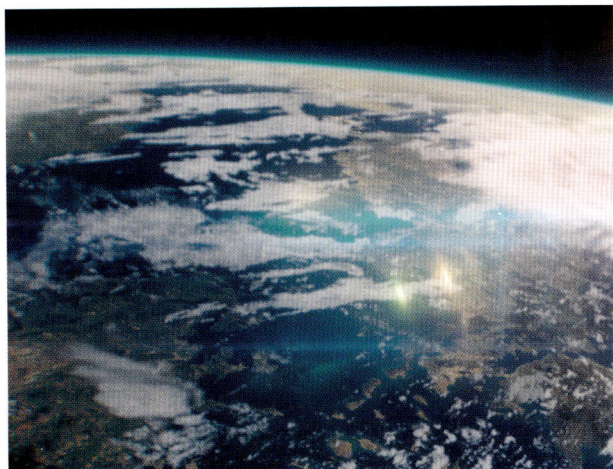

A view from above of a planet known by many names, but called by its inhabitants—Earth.

The Distant Past | Arishem

Arishem, known as the Prime Celestial, oversees a grand plan to create more of his kind. On selected planets, Celestial seeds are implanted. When large populations of sentient beings amass on those worlds, their collective lifeforce radiates the energy necessary to incubate the new Celestials, who after millions of years hatch from the center of the planets, destroying all who live on them. But they go on, in turn, to create more suns that brighten lush planets where other species of intelligent life will rise. A vast cycle of creation and destruction begins.

The Nine Realms of Yggdrasil as depicted in the Asgardian palace.

The Distant Past | The Rise of Asgard

God-like beings from the mystical kingdom of Asgard will establish an empire out of the Nine Realms of Yggdrasil, devising a means of traveling between them using a spectrum of energy they call the Bifrost. Earth is situated at the center of the tree-like Yggdrasil, earning it the name Midgard from the Asgardians as they venture between the higher and lower realms. But the Bifrost is not the only way to travel across Yggdrasil. Every 5,000 years, the Nine Realms orbit into alignment, creating wormholes through spacetime that allow passage from one realm to the next—an event known as the Convergence.

The Distant Past | The Tree of the World

Yggdrasil is the name given to an immense cosmic collection of nine worlds. It will become home to gods, mortals, giants, Dwarves, and other powerful and unique beings. Before its furnace of stars begin to shine, throwing off the light and warmth that makes such varied life possible, this cold and lightless place is home to shadow-dwellers known as "Dark Elves." These ancient beings are decimated by the emergence of light, and afterward only survive on The Dark World.

TVA ALERT!
Hey there! How long do Asgardians live? That's a great question! As Odin the Allfather will one day explain, they exist for a very long time but aren't immortal. He says they are born and die just like regular folks, but his son Loki adds: "Give or take 5,000 years." That's a whole lotta wiggle room!

The overlapping portals of the Convergence are depicted in an ancient Asgardian tome.

Prehistory

Rampaging Deviants prey on an early human civilization in Mesopotamia.

The Distant Past | The Deviant Error

Since Celestials are traditionally nurtured on the collective lifeforce of sentient beings, vast numbers of these living things are necessary to complete every new planetary incubation. Arishem and the other existing Celestials attempt to boost the volume of intelligent life on these worlds by creating ferocious Deviants to cull wild predators who might otherwise keep such populations in check. The Deviants are given the capacity to evolve, and the plan goes awry when the Deviants themselves turn against the very species the Celestials hope to propagate. A fix is required...

An Eternal is manufactured in the World Forge.

The Distant Past | The Eternal Remedy

The Celestials use the World Forge to devise even more sophisticated protectors known as Eternals to hunt the Deviants and defend sentient life on planets where new Celestials are embedded. Unlike the Deviants, the Eternals are not intended to evolve, but the emotional intelligence that makes them formidable defenders also makes them sympathetic to the populations they guard. When the time comes for a new Celestial to be born, some Eternals may be horrified by the destruction of the planet and the innocent people who inhabit it. To counter this, Arishem takes the precaution of repeatedly erasing their memories.

The Distant Past | Carving Mount Wundagore

Dark magical forces emerge on Earth, such as the demon Chthon, who carves his collection of forbidden incantations inside a temple built atop remote Mount Wundagore. It is constructed as a throne for the prophesied "Scarlet Witch," a being who will one day possess the power to bend reality to her will—or destroy it entirely.

Mount Wundagore cannot be easily reached by even the Masters of the Mystic Arts.

14

Vibranium from deep space, on a collision course with Earth.

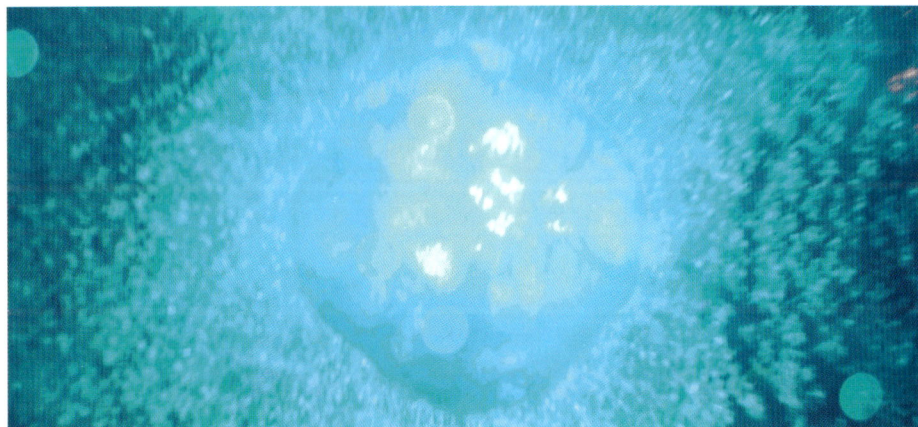

The impact will change the fates of people thousands of miles apart, but also link them together.

The Distant Past | The Vibranium Meteorite

Millions of years ago, an asteroid made of vibranium, one of the rarest and most versatile metals in the universe, strikes the planet Earth, embedding itself in the continent of Africa. The energy-absorbing properties of vibranium make the impact less destructive than ordinary meteorite strikes. At some point, vibranium also makes its way into the Atlantic Ocean. The plant life that grows around the vibranium gradually absorbs the element into its genetic structure. These enriched parts of the world await the day humans discover ways of utilizing vibranium's extraordinary potential.

The Distant Past | Ego Sows His Seeds

After spending millions upon millions of years alone, the Celestial known as Ego decides to find some company. The flesh and bone vessels he creates for himself in the forms of various mortal beings travel the galaxy, in search of connection. Underwhelmed by what he finds, Ego undertakes "the Expansion." "Over thousands of years, I implanted thousands of extensions of myself on thousands of worlds," he will one day explain. "I need to fulfill life's one true purpose—to grow and spread, covering all that exists until everything is … me."

Ego's avatar leaves the confines of his planet-body to travel the galaxy.

The Eternals known as Sersi and Ikaris look upon Earth as they arrive to safeguard the world's sentient life from the Deviants.

5000 BCE | The Eternals Arrive

A team of freshly mind-wiped Eternals is dispatched to Earth to protect humans from attacks by the Deviants and provide guidance that might further boost the population. The Eternals are prohibited from interfering in humanity's wars and catastrophes, however, since such crises often lead to life-giving forward leaps in technology.

Prehistory

The tribes of Wakanda form an alliance to stand together as a single nation, though the Jabari go their own way.

The Distant Past | The Founding of Wakanda

Five human tribes living around the vibranium impact site in Africa join together as the nation of Wakanda. The country is founded and first ruled by the warrior shaman Bashenga after he receives a vision from the panther goddess Bast, directing him to a luminous, purple flower known as the Heart-Shaped Herb. This plant has absorbed the properties of vibranium, and after consuming it Bashenga derives increased agility, strength, and acumen that enables him to lead and protect Wakanda as the regal Black Panther. Only one tribe, the Jabari, resists his rule, choosing independence from the king by isolating themselves in the country's mountain range.

The Distant Past | Withdrawal from the World

Wakanda's people devise astonishing new uses for the vibranium beneath their homeland, which quickly vaults them decades (and soon centuries) ahead of the rest of the developed world. Recognizing that the rare metal makes them susceptible to attack, colonization, and exploitation, Wakanda's rulers create an elaborate camouflage, hiding the wonders they discover by masking their country as a humble agrarian society. By closing off from the hostile world, much like the people of Talokan will later, the citizens of Wakanda focus their innovation and advancement inward.

A towering panther sculpture stands at the entrance to the vibranium mines in modern Wakanda.

The Eye of Agamotto, used by the founder of the Masters of the Mystic Arts to house the Time Stone.

Three Sanctums placed around the world serve as a supernatural shield for Earth.

The Distant Past | The Mystic Arts

The ancient people of Earth begin to dabble in magic and mysticism. Agamotto becomes one of the first humans to research and perfect these abilities, sharing his knowledge with others by founding the Masters of the Mystic Arts. This sect establishes three sanctums at locations of extraordinary power around the globe, designed to stand as watchtowers against supernatural threats. Agamotto later comes into possession of the Time Stone and creates an amulet that allows its user to manipulate the fabric of time.

2988 BCE | Dark Elves Revolt

The Convergence of the Nine Realms inspires a revolution led by Malekith of the Dark Elves. Having secured the Reality Stone in the form of the vaporous Aether, Malekith seeks to use it to return Yggdrasil (and beyond) to a state of eternal darkness. The Asgardian king Bor leads his armies in an attack against them, snatching away the Aether and hiding it before it can be used to reshape reality. An enraged Malekith sends his warships full of faithful fighters crashing into the Asgardian army in a selfish attempt to escape. He and his lieutenants go into hibernation, awaiting another chance to strike when the worlds align again.

The traditional mask of the Dark Elves.

The Distant Past | A Panoply of Gods

Deities of all kinds continue to make their presences felt on Earth, astonishing human beings who concoct elaborate mythologies to explain what they've witnessed. Some gods prefer to remain aloof from the mortals. The ruling Egyptian deities eventually banish the lunar god Khonshu for meddling in human affairs and nearly exposing the gods to the world at large. Asgardian interaction with the Nordic regions inspires local mythology, while other gods like Zeus and his pantheon become the foundation of Greek myth and faith.

The Egyptian moon deity Khonshu manifests in the form of a skeletal bird. His name translates as "Traveler."

Prehistory

The dragon known as The Great Protector.

The Distant Past | Creation of the Dark Gate

The Dweller in Darkness, a huge beast that nourishes itself on the spirits of living things, rampages through Ta Lo, a dimension adjacent to Earth. It leads an army of smaller Soul Eaters as they consume anyone in their path. An alliance of human warriors joins forces with the noble dragon they call The Great Protector to battle the monsters, imprisoning the creatures inside a mountain behind a barrier of dragonscales. A village is built for descendants of that fight to continue standing watch over the Dark Gate, protecting Earth and other worlds from the evil restrained within.

The Distant Past | The Hammer With Two Meanings

The mystical hammer known as Mjolnir is created by the giant Dwarf blacksmiths who operate a forge around the dying star Nidavellir. Odin sees it alternately as "a weapon to destroy—or as a tool to build." It's an object he will pass to his children, first his ferocious daughter Hela, who uses it to conquer, then to his son, Thor, who will be forced to prove his worthiness to wield it.

Mjolnir, the mighty hammer carried by the God of Thunder.

Hela on her father's rule of the Nine Realms: "Odin—proud to have it; ashamed of how he got it."

The Distant Past | Odin's Conquest

Odin claims the throne of Asgard from his father Bor, with ambitions to more tightly rule over the Nine Realms of Yggdrasil. He has a daughter, Hela, to whom he gives the mighty hammer Mjolnir. She wields the weapon as commander of the legions of Asgard. Together, they lead a violent takeover of the interconnected worlds, using the enslaved labor of the defeated to construct Asgard's towering royal palace.

The Distant Past | The Darkhold

The destructive spells of Mount Wundagore are transcribed into the Darkhold, a so-called "book of the damned" known to corrode the souls of those who partake of its knowledge.

The Darkhold, a book of dark magic transcribed from ancient demonic writings carved atop Mount Wundagore.

575 BCE | Expectations for Humanity

The innovator Phastos considers introducing the steam engine to the Mesopotamians, but his fellow Eternals veto the idea, insisting humans aren't ready for such technology. Pushing too hard might backfire, so an exasperated Phastos instead introduces them to the simple plow. Only their leader, Ajak, is aware that the Eternals' true purpose is to nourish the Celestial growing within the world's core—and that their work will someday lead to the planet's destruction. Based on what she has seen, Ajak asks Arishem to consider whether humans may be worthy of being spared, but he dismisses her concern.

Ajak, the leader of the Eternals, consults with the Celestial ruler Arishem atop the Hanging Gardens.

The Eternals make a stand at Babylon, one of their most pivotal battles in their mission to defend humanity.

575 BCE | The Battle for Babylon

The Eternals defeat a horde of Deviants outside the walls of Babylon, which at this point is the largest city on Earth. Mesopotamia has been the Eternals' base of operations for thousands of years, and their *Domo* starship is embedded in the ground beneath Babylon's legendary hanging gardens. This part of the world, later known as the Middle East, is the birthplace of many advancements necessary for the unfettered growth of the human population.

The Distant Past | Inspiration and Attachment

The work of the Eternals leads to a rise in several advanced societies around Earth. Their heroism becomes enmeshed with the mythology of these cultures, with the Eternals sometimes indistinguishable from gods. The storyteller of the group, Sprite, provides inspiration to the mortals by making up tales of Ikaris flying too close to the sun, or retelling the epic battles of Gilgamesh. The Eternals also develop richer bonds with each other as the centuries pass, with Ikaris and Sersi falling in love, and Druig drawing closer with Makkari.

Sprite adds constellation imagery to her stories, illustrating the Eternals' many victories for her human audience.

575 BCE | Babylon
The Deviants attempt to break through the gates of Babylon, but the Eternals fend them off. After the battle, Ajak communicates with Arishem. He warns her not to get attached to this planet.

575 BCE | Telling Tales
The Eternal known as Sprite uses her powers of illusion to weave the Eternals themselves into some of Earth's earliest legends. When the Eternals leave Babylon, Ajak reveals the truth of the Eternals' mission to Ikaris, knowing his loyalty to Arishem is strong.

5000 BCE | Dawn of Civilization
Arishem orders the Eternals to travel to Earth to protect humanity from the Deviants. However, they are forbidden from interfering in human conflict. Only their leader, Ajak, knows the true nature of their mission.

400 | Sersi and Ikaris
As Sersi and Ikaris spend more time together, they become attracted to each other and eventually fall in love. The two decide to exchange marriage vows in a lavish ceremony with all the Eternals in attendance.

The Distant Past | Creation of the Eternals
The Celestials create the Eternals, who are unaware that their true purpose is to defend a seed that will become a new Celestial, Tiamut. Tiamut's birth (known as the Emergence) will result in Earth's destruction and the end of humanity.

1521 | Tenochtitlan
Just as the Spanish invade the Aztec capital of Tenochtitlan, the Deviants attack as well. While fighting them off, Thena, suffering from an incurable mental affliction, Mahd Wy'ry, turns on her comrades and is subdued by Gilgamesh. With the last Deviants defeated, the Eternals part ways.

THE ETERNALS

The Avengers might hold the title of the Earth's Mightiest Heroes, but the Eternals have been living among humanity for thousands of years, quietly protecting Earth. Created by the Celestials, an ancient and powerful alien race, the Eternals possess a wide variety of superhuman abilities, including incredible strength, speed, regenerative abilities, flight, and near-immortality. The Eternals—Ajak, Ikaris, Phastos, Druig, Kingo, Makkari, Sprite, Sersi, Thena, and Gilgamesh—are ordered to protect humans from creatures known as Deviants. However, the Celestials' true reason for sending them to Earth is far more sinister than the Eternals could have imagined.

2024 | Rise of the Deviants
Ajak starts to have doubts about the impending Emergence, and voices them to Ikaris. Shortly after, Ikaris brings Ajak to Alaska, showing her a group of Deviants who have escaped from a melting glacier. He then pushes Ajak into the pit of Deviants, planning to use her death to distract the other Eternals until the Emergence occurs.

2024 | Ikaris' Betrayal

The other Eternals discover that Ikaris killed Ajak. He defends his actions by arguing that it is their duty to protect the Celestials so that the universe will continue to exist. Sprite leaves with Ikaris, while Thena convinces Sersi to continue Ajak's wishes and save Earth.

2024 | Defeating the Deviants

The remaining Eternals work together to prevent the Emergence but are attacked once more by Deviants. Their leader, Kro, distracts Thena by imitating Gilgamesh, but she resists his manipulation and kills him.

2024 | In the Jungle

The Eternals travel to an Amazonian village to locate their comrade Druig, in hopes he can use his telepathy to keep Tiamut dormant. They and Druig's followers soon find themselves ambushed by Deviants. The creatures are fought off, but Gilgamesh is mortally wounded.

2024 | The Uni-Mind

Ikaris battles to try and ensure the Emergence continues as planned. Linking the cosmic energy of each Eternal and Tiamut, the Uni-Mind is summoned, focusing their collective power into a single entity. Ikaris finally sees the error of his ways and apologizes to Sersi before he flies into the sun.

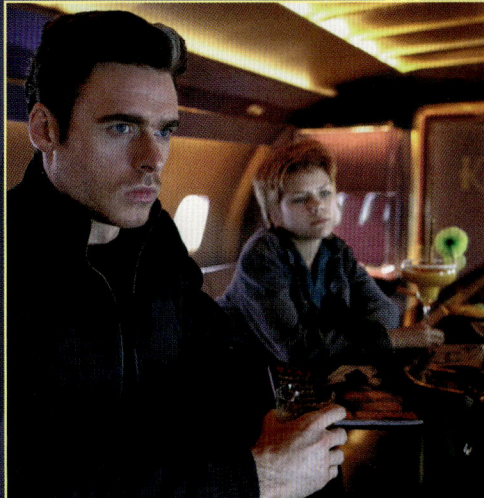

2024 | Finding Thena

Sersi and Sprite are devastated by Ajak's death, while Ikaris feigns shock about her demise. The three agree to seek out the remaining Eternals. They find Kingo, who decides to join their mission and offers the use of his private jet to find Thena and Gilgamesh in Australia.

2024 | Fallen Celestial

With the Eternals and Celestial linked in the Uni-Mind, Sersi is able to transform Tiamut's body into stone. With the Uni-Mind's leftover energy and at Sprite's request, Sersi turns Sprite into a human.

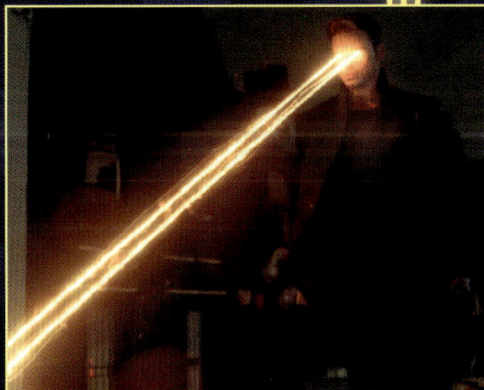

2024 | Camden

Sersi, Sprite, and the human Dane Whitman are attacked by a Deviant while heading home from a party in London. Ikaris arrives to help fight the beast. Alarmed that the Deviant can heal itself, the three Eternals head to South Dakota to seek advice from Ajak, but find her dead.

2024 | Arishem's Judgment

While Sersi enjoys a date with Dane Whitman, Arishem appears outside Earth's orbit. Arishem abducts Sersi, Phastos, and Kingo, and investigates their memories in order to form a final judgment of whether humanity is worthy to live.

The Common Era

The age that will become known as the Common Era on Earth continues to be shaped by powerful beings from other worlds. It starts approximately 2,000 years before the widespread emergence of superhumans on the planet, and the Eternals, the Asgardians, and artifacts of extraordinary power from far-off realms frequently alter the course of human events. In deep space, other worlds face similar upheaval, and shockwaves from strife in those distant places gradually make their way to Earth over the course of centuries.

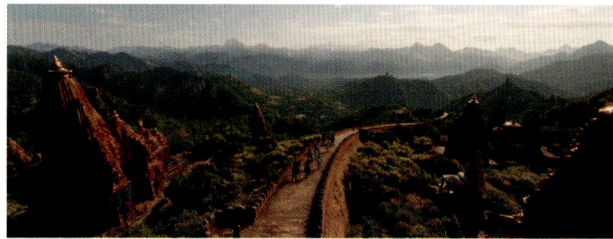

The Gupta Empire, considered a golden age in the history of India.

The happy wedding ceremony of Sersi and Ikaris is attended by the other Eternals.

400 CE | The Marriage of Sersi and Ikaris

After centuries of romance, the Eternals Sersi and Ikaris decide to pledge their love to each other in a public ceremony. While living in the Gupta Empire that sprawls across the subcontinent of India, they fulfill a tradition they picked up from humans—the ceremony of marriage. While the Eternals have had a profound influence on the Earthlings they protect, this is evidence of how humanity has affected them in return. The marriage will last for hundreds of years, but eventually the same mission that brought them together will push Ikaris and Sersi apart as the Emergence draws near.

Hela hurls her blades in battle against the Valkyrie sent to restrain her.

A single Valkyrie warrior survives the fight to return Hela to her imprisonment.

The Common Era | The Destruction of the Valkyrie

Hela breaks free. The Valkyrie, considered Asgard's greatest warriors, are virtually exterminated as they force her back into imprisonment, where she will remain locked away until Odin's death. Only one Valkyrie remains after the battle, and she spends the coming centuries in self-imposed exile, grappling with guilt over having survived when so many of the sisters she loved did not.

The Common Era | Hela's Imprisonment

After establishing Asgard's dominance, Odin refashions himself as a benevolent peacekeeper, leading to a split with his still power-hungry daughter, Hela. She turns against Odin, disgusted by what she sees as her father's weakness. Her bloodthirstiness earns her the title "Goddess of Death," and she attempts to seize the throne through a palace massacre. Since she derives her power from Asgard itself, her father banishes her to a remote, desolate realm, striking her name and image from the kingdom's art and history.

The Common Era | The Ancient One

Her precise origin is lost to time, but the beginning is not the most important detail about the Celtic woman who will rise to become the longest serving Sorcerer Supreme of the Masters of the Mystic Arts. More significant is the fact that the so-called "Ancient One" does not die for several centuries after her mortal birth, extending her lifespan by practicing forbidden rituals that draw energy from the Dark Dimension. She believes her longtime defense of Earth justifies an unnatural existence, but the hypocrisy of her actions will one day anger students who crave such longevity for themselves and their loved ones.

"Just how ancient is she?" Stephen Strange will one day ask. "No one knows the age of the Sorcerer Supreme," Karl Mordo replies.

The Common Era | The Dark Ages

This era of history remains murky, but the legendary rulers and knights of this period interact frequently with the Eternals. When Makkari begins assembling a collection of historic objects aboard their *Domo* starship, she includes Excalibur, the weapon of Arthur, who was said to have harbored romantic feelings for the Eternal swordstress Thena.

Makkari's collection of artifacts aboard the *Domo* during the early 21st century.

The Common Era

Tønsberg is a flashpoint in the longtime conflict between Asgard and the Frost Giants of Jotunheim.

965 CE | Battle in Tønsberg

When the Frost Giants of Jotunheim attack Earth, the Asgardians arrive as defenders, engaging in a pivotal battle in this Viking settlement in Scandinavia. King Laufey of the Frost Giants attacks with a weapon known as the Casket of Ancient Winters, which has the potential to create a new ice age on the planet. Aided by the Eternal warrior Gilgamesh, the Asgardian army repels the Frost Giants.

c. 965 CE | Loki

The armies of Asgard pursue the Frost Giants back to Jotunheim, where Laufey is subdued and the Casket of Ancient Winters captured. Odin also takes Laufey's abandoned child, Loki, home to Asgard to raise as his own son, hoping this will somehow establish a bond between the two realms in the future.

The Common Era | Heirs to Asgard

Odin and Frigga raise Loki alongside their own son, Thor, without revealing Loki's true origin, and the brothers establish a close but contentious relationship. With Thor the favored "firstborn," Loki counters by developing trickster tendencies. Frigga teaches Loki the power of magic and illusion, but he uses these newfound abilities to torment Thor, once turning Thor into a frog, and another time transforming himself into a snake to surprise (and stab) his gullible brother. Odin tries to teach his boys the wisdom of avoiding war and promoting peace and tranquility, but Thor is drawn to raw displays of power, such as those of the showboating Eternal Kingo.

c. 1000 CE | Galactic War Erupts

Far out in the cosmos, tensions between the Kree and the Nova Empire lead to open fighting that becomes a sprawling, multi-planetary war that drags on for a thousand years. It rages over many lifetimes, and in its final stages the conflict will be exploited by a Kree extremist known as Ronan, who will attempt to use the Power Stone to end the war in the Kree's favor, after the Kree and Nova have already signed a peace treaty.

A fleet of Starblaster ships flies above the Nova Empire capital world of Xandar, centuries after the outbreak of war.

The Common Era | Wenwu Uses The Ten Rings

In one legend retold for thousands of years, an ordinary man named Wenwu discovers ten indestructible rings that imbue him with endless life and god-like strength. Some tellings claim the rings were found in a mysterious crater, while other versions say he raided them from a tomb. All that's certain is he uses the fighting ability they grant him to seek power. He assembles an army that stretches around the globe, topples kingdoms, and changes history. He names his army after the weapons that brought him his power—The Ten Rings.

The mighty warlord Wenwu.

Wenwu unleashes his mysterious rings in a battle against a seemingly insurmountable army.

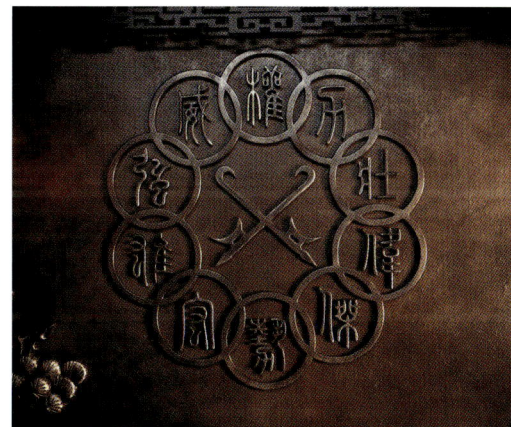
The symbol of Wenwu's Ten Rings organization—sometimes stolen by others seeking to shift blame onto the clandestine group.

A replica of the Tesseract was placed in this tomb to confuse would-be plunderers.

The Common Era | Tesseract Hidden on Earth

At an undetermined time, and for unknown reasons, the Tesseract cube that contains the Space Stone is hidden inside a medieval church in Tønsberg, Norway, the location of one of Odin's proudest battles against King Laufey of the Frost Giants. Once the most cherished object in Odin's vault, the Tesseract is tucked into a hidden drawer inside a wooden carving that depicts Yggdrasil as "the Tree of the World." It goes unseen for centuries. A counterfeit Tesseract is added to the nearby sarcophagus to confuse any would-be thieves.

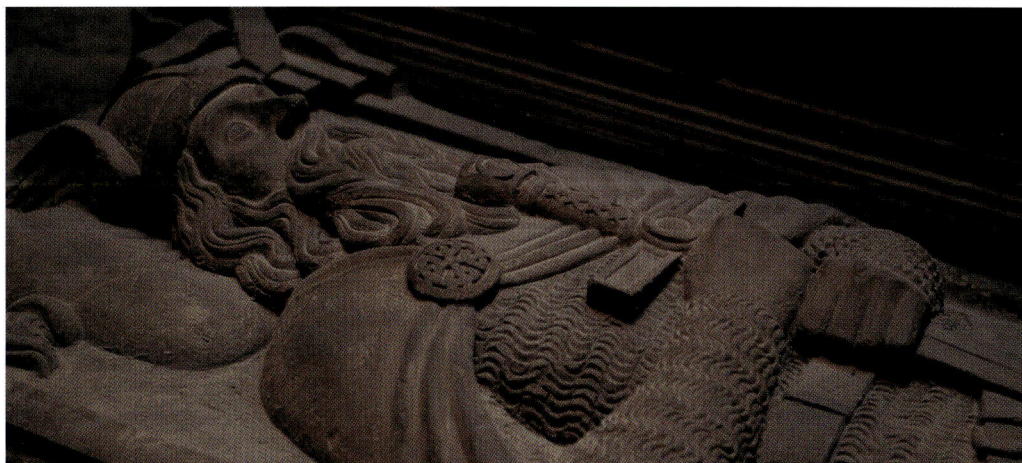
The sarcophagus of a Viking warrior in the church where someone hid the Tesseract on Earth.

The Common Era

The last of the roving Deviants on Earth falls as European invaders attack the Aztec people.

1521 CE | Eradication of the Deviants

The Eternals slay what they believe to be the last remaining Deviants, although some creatures still remain, embedded in ice in arctic regions. The apparent end of the Deviants on Earth occurs during the fall of Tenochtitlan, the heart of the Aztec Empire, to invading conquistadors from Europe. Prohibited from interfering to stop the genocide, the Eternals question their purpose. "Their weapons have become too deadly," Druig tells Phastos. "Maybe it wasn't such a good idea helping them advance." Thena begins to suffer from Mahd Wy'ry, a mental disorder born from the many times her memory of previous doomed worlds has been erased. With their mission seemingly accomplished, Ajak frees the Eternals to live a more passive existence, standing watch in case the Deviants return.

The Eternal Druig defies Ikaris and intervenes to stop the humans from slaughtering each other.

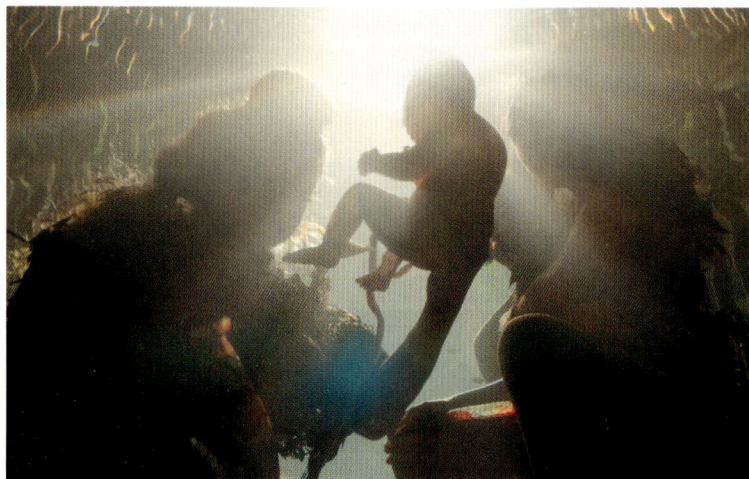

The underwater birth of Kulkulkan, who will lead his people for centuries.

1571 CE | Vibranium in the Water

On the other side of the globe from Wakanda, an undersea deposit of vibranium changes the destiny of a different society. The Talokan tribe from the Yucatan Peninsula discovers they can breathe underwater after consuming an aquatic plant that absorbed the metal's essence—but their lungs lose the ability to function in the open air. The child of a pregnant woman who imbibed the plant is born with wings on his ankles, the ability to survive both above and below the water's surface, and slowed aging. His people name him Kulkulkan (Feathered Serpeant God) and make him their leader for generations to come.

The Common Era | An Uprising From the Sea

By moving their civilization below the waves, the people of Talokan escape the diseases and brutality of the European explorers who ravage their original homeland. Kulkulkan returns to the surface after his mother's death to honor her wishes to be buried where she was raised, but he is disgusted to see the enslavement of their people by the invaders. The young Kulkulkan leads his vibranium-enhanced warriors in a violent revolt and is derided by a Spanish priest who calls him "El Niño sin Amor"—the "child without love." From that day on, Kulkulkan embraces the nom de guerre "Namor" as a warning to his enemies.

Kulkulkan earns the nickname "Namor" after exacting revenge against the conquerors of his historic homeland.

Agatha Harkness faces the accusations while tied to a stake by her coven.

"You stole knowledge above your age and station. You practiced the darkest magic," her mother declares.

1693 CE | The Witch Trial Massacre

A coven of witches living in the Puritan settlement of Salem, Massachusetts, turns against one of their own. Agatha Harkness is accused by her own mother of betraying them by stealing knowledge and practicing "the darkest" magic imaginable. Harkness admits to it all, but when they try to execute her by channeling beams of energy into her body, she merely absorbs the blasts, siphoning away her accusers' lifeforces until only desiccated corpses remain. Agatha escapes, living for many centuries, but is forever in search of more power to consume.

"I did not break your rules," Agatha replies. "They simply bent to my power."

Agatha's persecutors are destroyed in their attempt to annihilate her.

The Common Era | Revolution, War, and Conquest

The close of the second millennium is marked by the rise of democracies on Earth and the beginning of a global movement for peace and equality—but the path ahead is fraught. Global wars await, and many cultures and countries will be caught in the crossfire. The Eastern European nation of Sokovia is a prime example. As the special agent Maria Hill will one day explain: "Sokovia's had a rough history. It's nowhere special but it's on the way to everywhere special." Even those who endeavor to stay out of conflicts cannot avoid them.

The throne that stands in the center of Sokovia has witnessed many rulers—Ultron is just the latest would-be conqueror.

THE 1940S, 50S, AND 60S

The 20th century is marked by impressive strides forward for human beings, who empower themselves through new understandings of physics, chemistry, engineering—and sometimes magic. Inhabitants of Earth become powerful during this time, although not yet on the galactic scale. Their abilities tend to be tethered to their home planet, and their knowledge is honed by conflict with each other (as the Celestials often predict about sentient life). Some seek to protect themselves, while others wish to dominate. These two opposing forces are responsible for most of the change that takes place during this era.

Destiny does not always bow to the physically powerful. Steve Rogers, once deemed too sickly to serve in his country's army, will be one of the first members of humankind to be genetically enhanced in the modern era, but his greatest strengths originate within him: willpower and integrity. Those lead him to make history with the extraordinary physical powers he is granted by science.

Humankind will also find strength by banding together in groups dedicated to uncovering the mysteries of the universe. Some, like S.H.I.E.L.D., will be conceived with altruistic intent, while others, such as Hydra, will be fueled by greed, selfishness, and distrust.

Cosmic intervention was believed to have been minimal during this period, but that begins to change as human technology grants mortals the potential to reach beyond their own world.

1900-1945

In the first half of the 20th century, humanity's advancements in research, industry, and technology increase the presence of beings with remarkable abilities. Science can suddenly generate powers that were previously the domain of the mystical or cosmic. These strengths lead to a rise in heroes who use them to protect the vulnerable or threatened, but instances of altruism are too often matched by others who harness such might for the sake of control, domination, and subjugation. The century to come will be a time of both innovation and danger.

Bucky Barnes and a pre-super soldier Steve Rogers— two friends "until the end of the line."

1920s | The Start of the Line

Two boys grow up in the same neighborhood in Brooklyn. James Buchanan "Bucky" Barnes is the older and stronger of the two friends; Steve Rogers, whose father died in The Great War while his mother was pregnant, is small, frail, and beset by health problems. He learns about strength from his chosen "big brother." Over the decades to come, the love, loyalty, and friendship between these two will repeatedly save them in times of peril. They will also save the world.

1930s | Rising Star

In the early 20th century the Eternal known as Kingo, bored with lying low after the apparent eradication of the Deviants, had become enchanted by the cinematic arts. By the 1930s, Hollywood's moviemaking machine faces a growing rival on the far side of the globe as India's Bollywood flourishes. Kingo steps into the spotlight as a Bollywood star and invents a fictional acting dynasty to disguise the fact that he does not age. At this point, he is billing himself as Raj Kingo Deva, son of the Great Kingo.

Kingo's work in moviemaking ranges from the early days of silent film to the modern blockbuster.

Johann Schmidt examines the fake Tesseract, before locating the real artifact concealed within a wall.

The Tesseract is the key to a new generation of Hydra weaponry, capable of seizing control of the world.

March 1942 | Not For the Eyes of Ordinary Men

As total war rages across Europe, Johann Schmidt assumes command of Hydra, the Nazis' deep-science division. Schmidt becomes known as the Red Skull after being nightmarishly disfigured while experimenting on himself with an incomplete Super Soldier Serum. In March 1942, he leads Hydra forces on an invasion of Tønsberg, Norway, where he seizes "the jewel of Odin's treasure room"—the glowing blue cube known as the Tesseract. It not only contains the Space Stone, but will serve as the power source for the high-tech arsenal being devised by Dr. Arnim Zola.

Aisha's unique bangle clasped to her arm harnesses the light energy of the Noor Dimension.

1942 | The Bangle Uncovered

In British-occupied India, exiles from the Noor Dimension known as the Clandestines explore a destroyed temple that is marked by the symbol of The Ten Rings. Under the rubble, they find a bangle that can harness the light energy within them, potentially opening the barrier back to their homeworld. Before they can use it, British soldiers scatter the group. With the bangle in her possession, Clandestine leader Aisha takes shelter with a rose farmer named Hasan. The two fall in love, get married, and have a daughter named Sana. Now that she has ties to this world, Aisha abandons her quest to leave it.

June 14, 1943 | I Can Do This All Day

Steve Rogers attempts to enlist in the U.S. Army, but a doctor stamps the 90-pound asthmatic young man's recruitment card 4F, meaning "unfit for military service." A dispirited Rogers objects, but the doctor insists, "I'm saving your life." Later that day, he is saved from a back alley fistfight by Bucky, who's shipping overseas with the 107th Infantry Regiment the next day. He urges his old friend to give up and dedicate his efforts stateside. "Don't win the war until I get there," Steve tells him.

"There are men laying down their lives. I've got no right to do any less than them," a repeatedly-rejected Steve Rogers tells Bucky Barnes.

"I don't like bullies, I don't care where they're from," Steve Rogers will later tell Dr. Erskine.

31

1900-1945

Steve and Bucky attend one of Howard Stark's earliest technology showcases.

June 14, 1943 | Future Shock

While Steve and Bucky enjoy a night on the town at the World Exposition of Tomorrow, Howard Stark shows off his prototype for a flying car, which he predicts will be all the rage in a few years. Stark has become world famous as a pilot, engineer, profiteer, and heartthrob, but his Stark Gravitic Reversion Technology makes the candy-apple Cadillac hover only for a moment before crashing to the stage. "I did say 'a few years,' didn't I?" he quips.

"I can offer you a chance. Only a chance." — Dr. Abraham Erskine

June 14, 1943 | The Doctor's Orders

Dr. Abraham Erskine overhears Steve arguing with Bucky that despite his ailments, he has no right to sacrifice less than the countless soldiers laying down their lives fighting the Nazis. Impressed by Steve's resolve, Erskine recruits him to participate in his upcoming Super Soldier Program for the American government, aimed at creating an army of unbeatable fighters. "There are already so many big men fighting this war," Erskine says, explaining he is looking for qualities of strength beyond the physical. "Maybe what we need now is the little guy."

"Don't win the war until I get there," Steve Rogers tells Bucky Barnes.

"Gentlemen, I'm Agent Carter. I supervise all operations for this division."

June 1943 | Agent Carter

During training for the Strategic Scientific Reserve's Super Soldier Program at Camp Lehigh, Steve Rogers meets British agent Peggy Carter, who is supervising recruits on behalf of the program's director, Col. Phillips. She witnesses Rogers' respect, ingenuity, and bravery, particularly when he throws himself on what he believes is a live grenade to protect his fellow recruits—a test from Phillips that Steve passes. She feels a kinship with him, since she also had to fight harder than everyone else to prove her worth.

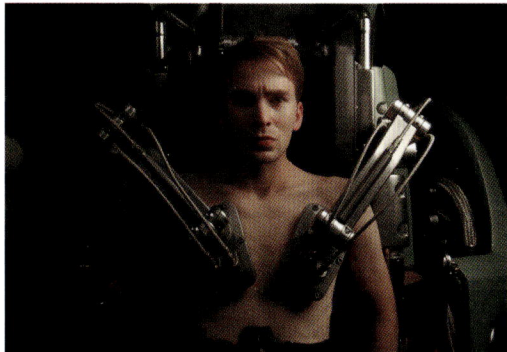

A small and physically frail Steve Rogers prepares to undergo Project Rebirth, knowing there is a real chance the experiment could kill him.

While being fired at by a Hydra saboteur, the newly-enhanced Steve Rogers grabs a rudimentary shield.

June 22, 1943 | The Procedure

Steve Rogers undergoes the super soldier transformation. During the experiment, Erskine is killed by a Hydra agent who has infiltrated the laboratory. The scientist's death takes the secrets of the serum with him, meaning that (for now) no super soldier army will be created despite the success of the test. Rogers pursues Erskine's assailant on foot with his freshly enhanced body, stumbling through a shop window and slamming into cars as he becomes accustomed to his new abilities. Although Steve captures the assassin, the agent takes a cyanide pill before he can be questioned. The next day's newspapers boast about the Nazi-fighting "mystery man." A legend is born.

Peggy Carter: "How do you feel?"
A gasping Steve Rogers: "…Taller."

1900–1945

"You were meant for more than this, you know?" Agent Carter tells Steve Rogers after a USO performance.

November 3, 1943 | The Star-Spangled Man

To Steve's disappointment, the U.S. government uses him as a morale-boosting propaganda tool rather than a fighter. In November of 1943, the so-called "Captain America" performs in Italy with a USO tour 5 miles from the battlefront. After entertaining and raising funds for the war effort for several months, he is only now getting close to the fighting. After one of his performances, he learns that a large group of American soldiers has been captured by Hydra near Azzano. They're from the 107th. Bucky is one of them.

"For the longest time I dreamed about coming overseas and being on the front lines, serving my country. I finally got everything I wanted ... and I'm wearing tights." — Steve Rogers on "Captain America"

Steve Rogers abandons showmanship and uses his enhanced abilities to rescue captured soldiers, including his childhood friend Bucky Barnes.

November 3–10, 1943 | One-Man Army

Agent Carter and Howard Stark fly Rogers into enemy territory, defying the wishes of Col. Phillips. Captain America has a fiery encounter with the Red Skull as he infiltrates the prison camp and liberates Bucky and his fellow soldiers—some of whom will become part of Cap's elite Howling Commandos. The Red Skull flees the battle, and Rogers returns to the U.S. camp leading a column of rescued men just as Col. Phillips is drafting a report labeling him "missing in action." From here on, Captain America will be a warrior, not a performer.

Steve Rogers finds Barnes in a bad way, having suffered unknown torments at Hydra's hands.

Rogers confronts the Red Skull for the first time.

A Hydra train carrying weapons—and scientist Dr. Arnim Zola—is attacked by the Howling Commandos.

⊙ ⭐

Mid-1940s | Bucky Barnes Vanishes

Throughout the rest of the war, Captain America repeatedly confronts the Red Skull's forces, demolishing their facilities and beating back their soldiers, often with Bucky at his side. During a raid on a Hydra train to capture Dr. Zola, Bucky is thrown into the fathomless, icy void of a mountain canyon and presumed killed. A mourning Rogers vows never to rest until he stops the Red Skull and all of Hydra's forces.

After the raid on Hydra's speeding train, Bucky Barnes is declared missing in action.

Steve Rogers shares what may be his final words with Peggy Carter over the *Valkyrie*'s radio.

⭐

March 1945 | A Long Goodbye

Before Rogers vanishes, he exchanges a radio message with Peggy Carter, vowing to meet her again so she can teach him how to dance. Someday, he might fulfill that promise.

Steve Rogers faces the Red Skull aboard the doomed Hydra aircraft.

⊙ | Ⓥ

March 1945 | The *Valkyrie* Showdown

Just before the war ends in Europe, Captain America has his final confrontation with the Red Skull aboard Hydra's flying wing known as the *Valkyrie*, which is loaded with Tesseract-powered energy detonators designed to devastate America's homefront. The Red Skull vanishes in a column of energy after seizing hold of the cube during the battle, and Captain America steers the badly damaged ship into the polar ice cap to prevent its bombs from harming innocent civilians. This time he is throwing himself on a real grenade. Through his sacrifice, millions are saved.

REDLINE ALERT!

Howdy folks! When did Bucky fall from that train? We'd all like to know! The Smithsonian's Captain America exhibit says 1944, but Arnim Zola claims he was captured in 1945. Those Analysts must be gettin' their britches in a stir!. Let me investigate who filed that paperwork.

Phastos surveys the devastation of Hiroshima.

€

August 1945 | An Eternal, Grieving

The Eternal Phastos weeps in the aftermath of the first atomic bomb dropped on human beings. For eons, his ingenuity has helped people develop new technology and thrive. Now, standing in the ruins of Hiroshima, he is overwhelmed with sadness at the path humanity has taken.

THE FIRST AVENGER

Steve Rogers is just a kid from Brooklyn who becomes the "star-spangled man with a plan," and decades later, leader of the Avengers. All he ever wanted to do was fight bullies. By volunteering to take the Super Soldier Serum, Steve becomes Captain America, a symbol for the United States military in World War II. He proves himself to be a hero countless times, on more than one occasion selflessly volunteering to sacrifice himself to save others. He always does the right thing, no matter how hard it may be or if it causes disagreements, and though loyal to his friends, he never hesitates to call them out if they do something wrong. He is a born leader, and guides the Avengers until he passes the mantle.

2014 | A Returning Past
Steve continues working for S.H.I.E.L.D. but soon two monumental aspects of his past emerge into the present day: he learns his best friend Bucky Barnes, presumed dead in WWII, is now the Hydra operative known as the Winter Soldier, and that Hydra has infiltrated S.H.I.E.L.D. Captain America clings to his belief in doing the right thing as he goes on the run, and finds new allies as he vanquishes Hydra once again.

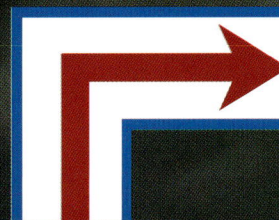

2011-2012 | Back in the Fight
Steve's final mission in World War II is followed by almost 70 years frozen in the Arctic ice. Located and defrosted, Steve emerges with his desire to fight bullies undimmed. S.H.I.E.L.D. Director Nick Fury approaches him with a new mission—one Steve needs to find purpose. Cap's natural leadership returns as he guides the Avengers against Loki's army in the Battle of New York.

1943 | The Little Guy
Steve Rogers longs to fight for his country in World War II. Though his heart is true, the army rejects him because of his health issues. Steve readily accepts Dr. Erskine's offer to join Project Rebirth for a chance to serve. He takes the Super Soldier Serum and his life changes forever. As the world's first super soldier, Captain America, he battles the evil legions of Hydra, defeats the villainous Red Skull, and meets Peggy Carter, the love of his life.

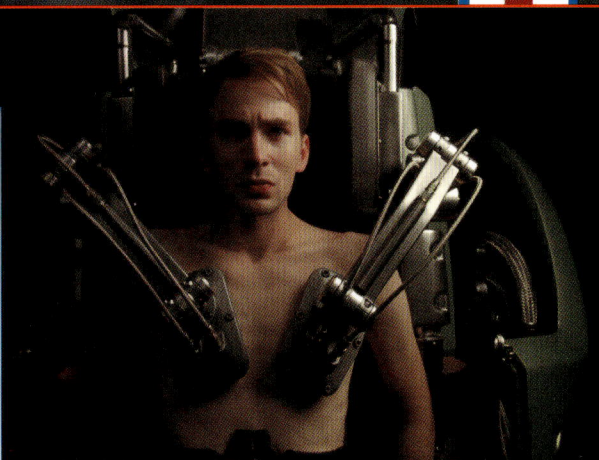

2015 | Meeting Ultron
Steve finally captures Baron Strucker, the last known leader of Hydra, alongside the Avengers. The defeat of Hydra gives Captain America a brief moment of victory before the robot Ultron, created by Tony Stark, decides to wipe out humanity. Ultron's existence causes conflict in the team. Steve, ever the peacekeeper, plans the path forward and takes point on the offensive against Ultron in Sokovia.

2016 | Avenger versus Avenger
The aftermath of the battle in Sokovia causes a rift in the Avengers, with Tony in favor of the Sokovia Accords granting the United Nations power over the Avengers and Steve in opposition. Though it pains Steve to see the group split, he defends the Avengers' right to choose their own actions. The conflict deepens and the two factions battle in Germany. When the dust settles, Steve and Tony are no longer on speaking terms.

2018 | Protecting the Stones
Finding himself again a wanted man, Steve keeps his distance, but returns when he learns of Thanos' plans. Steve puts everything aside to stop Thanos from taking the Infinity Stones. Captain America prepares the Avengers to work alongside the Wakandan army against Thanos' invaders. When Thanos arrives, Rogers resists with all his strength, never flagging even when he is one of the last Avengers standing.

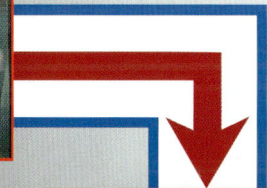

2023 | Saving the Universe
The Snap and loss of his friends has a profound effect upon Steve. He remains with the Avengers and tries to move on. But when he sees a glimmer of hope, Steve can't resist. He champions the Time Heist and eventually assembles the Avengers in the Battle of Earth. After he returns the stones, Steve finally puts himself first, and returns to the past to spend his life beside the woman he loves.

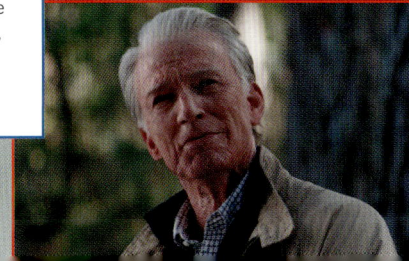

37

1940s-1960s

The post-World War II era is shaped by a newfound wariness about power falling into the wrong hands. Peggy Carter will devote herself to creating a new organization to combat such threats, while remnants of Hydra will masquerade to continue their nefarious activities. Sometimes, even those committed to safety and security will find themselves veering into morally indefensible territory.

Howard Stark in his workshop in the 1940s.

1945-46 | Search and Recovery

Howard Stark continues his work with the U.S. government, maintaining a strong tie with the principal consumer of his defense manufacturing business. He personally scans the last known coordinates of Captain America, but does not find the lost super soldier. However, he does pinpoint the energy signature of the Tesseract, recovering it from the deep to be studied by a new governmental organization he is helping to create.

1946 | Starting Over

The world rebuilds in a time of brief and relative peace. Agent Carter continues her work with the Strategic Scientific Reserve, now as a codebreaker and data analyst in its New York office under the supervision of Agent Flynn, who is dismissive of her ambition to resume duties as a field operative. After she objects to three months of office busywork, he tells her, "Relax. The war is over. We'll handle the rough stuff."

1946 | The Zodiac Mission

Agent Flynn and "the boys" of the SSR office head out for an after-hours drink, leaving Peggy Carter to finalize some field reports. A call comes through with coordinates on a deadly chemical weapon the office has been tracking. Unable to contact the team, Carter decides to venture to the appointed location alone, subduing several well-armed hostiles and securing the vial of rogue material. It is a triumph for Agent Carter, but Flynn regards it as an embarrassment to be bested by "Captain America's old flame."

Agent Carter proves to be formidable in the field, as well as an ace tactician.

Carter tackles the Zodiac mission alone, despite a briefing recommendation that up to five agents will be necessary.

Agent Carter becomes
Director Carter of S.H.I.E.L.D.

1946 | S.H.I.E.L.D. Promotion

Agent Carter is recruited by Col. Chester Phillips and Howard Stark to join them in Washington, D.C. to become the founding director of a new security agency known as the Strategic Homeland Intervention, Enforcement, and Logistics Division. Stark calls Agent Flynn to present the offer personally. "Let her know you are honored to bring her the news," Stark says. Through gritted teeth, Flynn even offers to help her gather her belongings. All she takes from her desk is a snapshot of a scrawny, pre-super soldier Steve Rogers. "Thank you, Agent Flynn," she tells him. "But as has always been the case, I don't require your help."

Late 1940s | The Zola Mole

Dr. Arnim Zola remains in Allied captivity following the war. As part of Operation Paperclip, the U.S. government decides to harness the expertise of former enemies rather than have them face consequences for their crimes. Zola is incorporated into S.H.I.E.L.D.'s research and development team, but his allegiance has never truly wavered: he begins rebuilding Hydra from within, a parasitic terror group operating inside the global security operation.

A dedicated opportunist, Arnim Zola was happy to serve the Red Skull if it meant advancing his research.

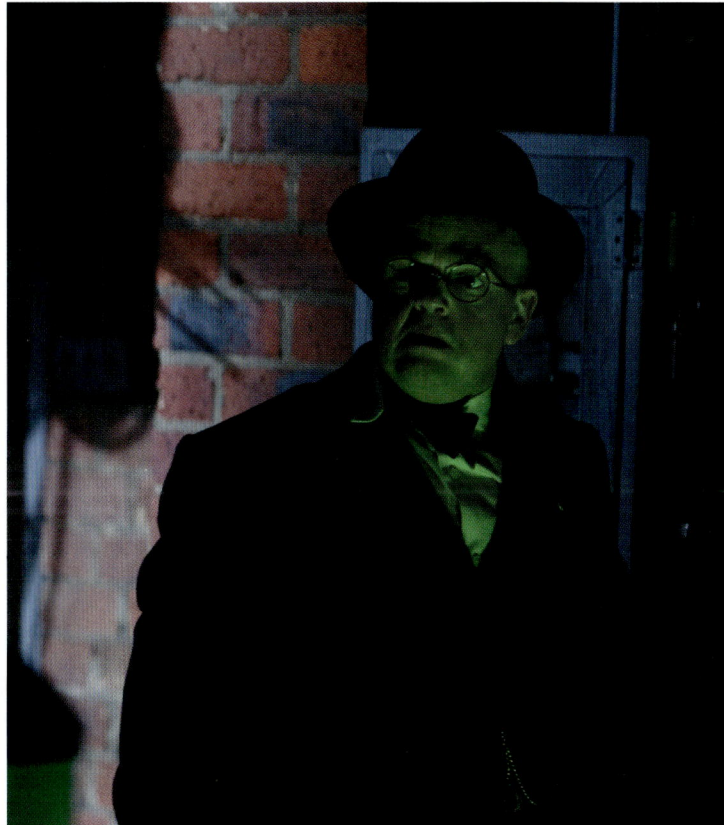

As a captive of the U.S. military, Zola's value as a researcher protected him from facing consequences.

1940s–1960s

Late 1940s | A Mind of Winter

Among the covert projects Hydra undertakes is a shadow assassin program that utilizes the body, if not the mind, of one of its fiercest opponents: Bucky Barnes. After his plunge from the icy train, Barnes' severely damaged body was recovered by Hydra scientists. Zola reconnects with this division, and oversees the rebuilding of Barnes' body, replacing his amputated left arm with a mechanical limb. Hydra uses cryogenic storage to keep this mind-controlled Winter Soldier on ice until his deadly services are required.

After his brainwashing, Bucky Barnes remains under the control of Hydra for decades, serving as the lethal operative known as the Winter Soldier.

Kamala Khan's great-grandparents, with their young daughter Sana.

1947 | Walkway of Stars

During the partition of India and creation of Pakistan in the summer of 1947, the Clandestine Najma finally tracks Aisha down at her family home. Unwilling to relinquish the bangle to Najma, Aisha and Hasan rush to the train station to escape from both Najma and the tension and chaos caused by the partition. However, Najma catches Aisha at the train station and stabs her. As she is dying, Aisha connects with the bangle, which falls off and summons her great-granddaughter Kamala Khan to the past. Kamala's grandmother, Sana, has gotten lost from her father in the crowds, and Kamala finds her, using her own powers to show Sana how to get back to her father.

40

1951 | A fight in Goyang

Hydra unleashes the Winter Soldier during the Korean conflict. Bradley is sent to hunt down this mysterious foe, and the two clash in this city just outside Seoul. "Everyone they sent after him, never came back," Bradley would recall decades later. "So the U.S. military dropped me behind the line to go deal with him. I took half that metal arm in that fight in Goyang." Both men ultimately survive, and one day a penitent Bucky Barnes will be among the few who remembers Bradley's service.

Even in the future, Bucky Barnes, remains haunted by the past, forever reminded of wrongs he did as the Winter Soldier.

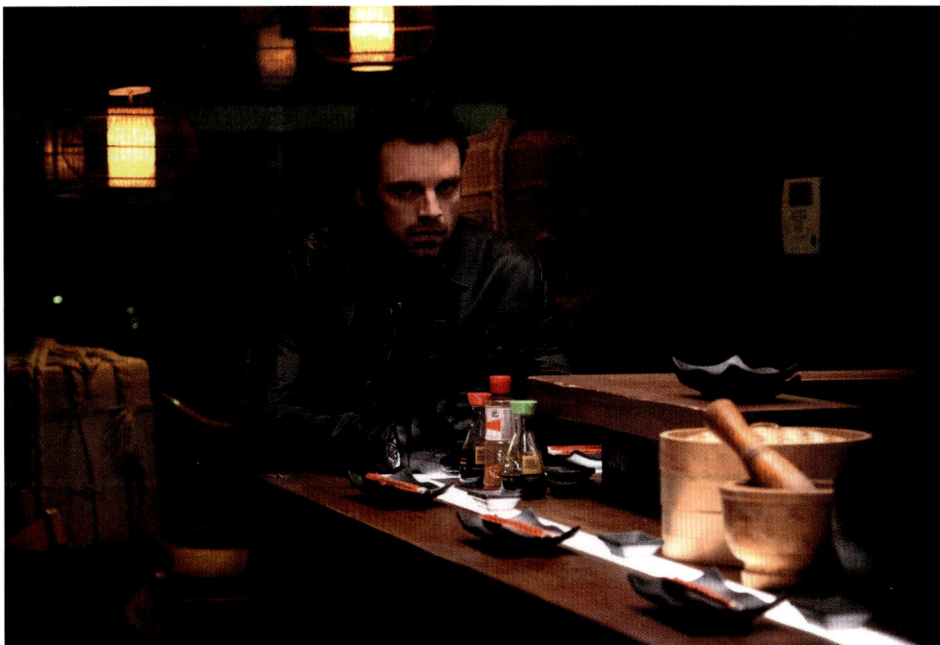

Late 1940s/Early 1950s | A Shameful Experiment

The U.S. government reactivates its Super Soldier Program, again hoping to create an army of unstoppable warriors. Unlike the late Dr. Erskine's WWII experiment, which had the full awareness of volunteer Steve Rogers, this project is undertaken with deceit and disregard for human life. Unable to precisely replicate the original serum, multiple variations are created by researchers and secretly forced upon a group of African-American soldiers against their will or knowledge. Only one, Isaiah Bradley, transforms successfully and with stability. Many other test subjects suffer unspeakable pain and ongoing volatile effects from the procedure.

Early 1950s | The Expendable Men

Despite the instability of the surviving African-American super soldiers, the military continues sending them on covert missions throughout the Korean War. Several are captured alive by enemy forces, and Bradley learns that senior officials are planning to bomb the POW camp and kill their own men to cover up evidence of the Super Soldier Program. "Those were my men, my brothers— not evidence," a still outraged Bradley would recall years later. The super soldier stages a rescue mission, not unlike the one Steve Rogers undertook in 1943, but is imprisoned for his actions instead of being honored.

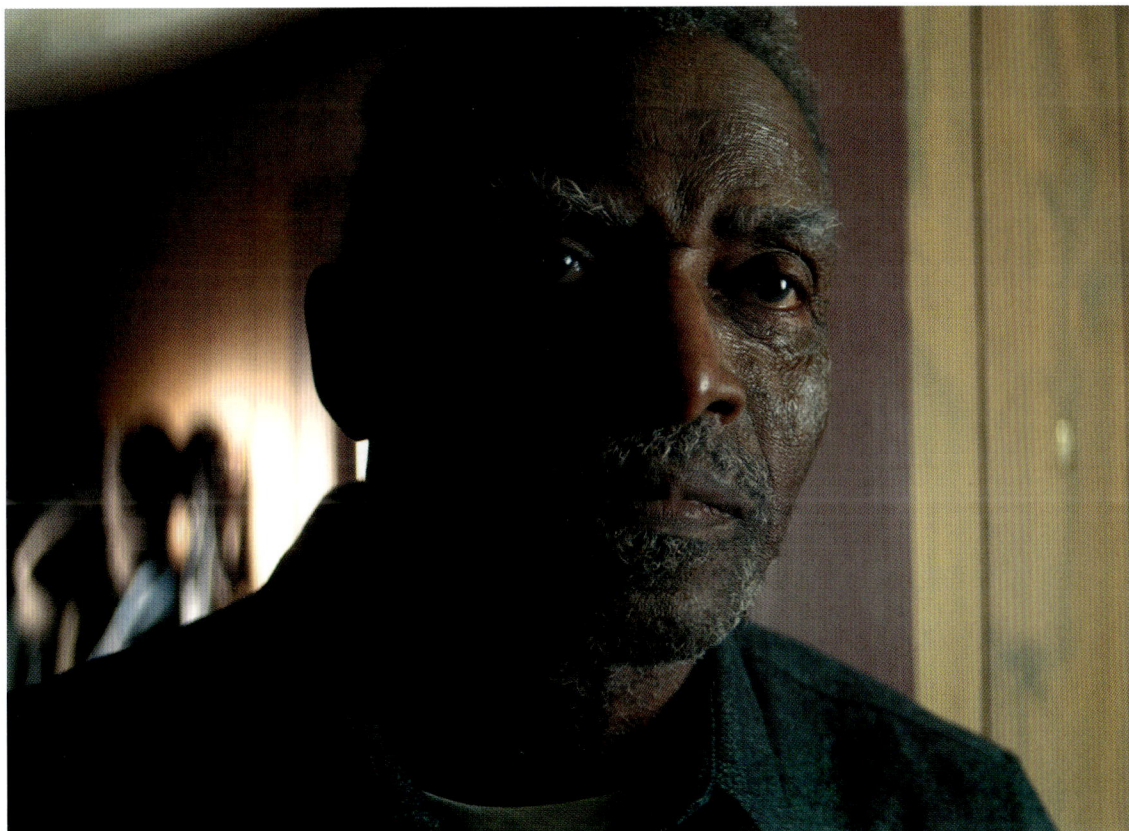

Isaiah Bradley, later in life, confronting the wrongs perpetrated against him.

1940s–1960s

A lifetime later, Isaiah Bradley shares his memories with the new Captain America, Sam Wilson.

1950s | A Wrongful Punishment

Due to the experiment's side effects and the dangerous military operations the subjects are sent on, it's not long before Isaiah is the last living subject of the Super Soldier Program. He is seen by certain unethical government figures as a liability, and is wrongfully imprisoned, in part to cover up the experiment but also to continue batteries of involuntary testing. "For the next 30 years, they experimented on me, trying to figure out why the serum worked," Bradley says years after his eventual release.

1950s | The Cover-Up

Isaiah's wife works tirelessly to communicate with her husband, sending countless letters—all of which are intercepted by the government before reaching him. As years pass, officials decide to end her crusade to prove his innocence by concocting the lie that he died in prison. "They were worried my story might get out. So, they erased me, my history. But they've been doing that for five hundred years," Bradley would one day reveal. Isaiah's brokenhearted wife later passes away, never knowing the truth.

Isaiah Bradley and his grandson Eli watch Sam Wilson tell the world: "The only power I have is that I believe we can do better."

The Winter Soldier, one of Hydra's most lethal and effective weapons for manipulating world events.

1950-60s | Hydra's Growing Reach

Throughout the tumultuous events of the 1950s and 60s, Hydra uses the Winter Soldier and its burgeoning network of adherents to expand its influence and shape global events. The organization believed humanity could not be trusted with its own freedom, but they also found people resisted whenever that freedom was curtailed. A series of political crises, coups, wars, economic unrest, and assassinations were engineered by the group in the years to come, guiding many ordinary citizens to fearfully crave security over liberty.

1963 | An Energy Race Explodes

Soviet physicist Anton Vanko forges an alliance with industrialist Howard Stark after defecting to the United States in 1963. The two combine their expertise to develop prototypes for what will become the Arc Reactor. The project was intended to "make the nuclear reactor look like a triple-A battery," as Nick Fury would later describe it. But the Arc Reactor remains unrefined tech after Vanko falls under suspicion for attempting to sell the information on the criminal market. Howard Stark not only cuts ties with him, but orchestrates his deportation back to the Soviet Union.

A primitive, large-scale version of the Arc Reactor, used to power Stark Industries manufacturing.

THE 1970s, 80s, AND 90s

Humans begin to venture into the broader galaxy. The latter portion of the 20th century will see the birth of several individuals who will go on to change the universe in astonishing ways, but at this point in history travel beyond Terra (also known as Midgard) is relatively rare.

A military test pilot named Carol Danvers will be among the first to journey to other worlds after accidentally absorbing the powers of the Tesseract into her mortal body. A half-human, half-Celestial child named Peter Quill will also be taken from Earth to be raised amongst the stars, fighting for basic survival while his surprising potential remains hidden, even from himself.

Tony Stark, a genius and exceptional inventor, will come of age and use his considerable resources and innate brilliance to build ever more advanced technology, helping to craft the world of tomorrow.

Global events still tend to be shaped by formidable groups like the U.S. government's S.H.I.E.L.D., the Soviet Union's Red Room, and the parasitic remnants of Hydra. Soon, however, individuals with extraordinary abilities will begin tipping the balance of that power.

1970s– 1980s

"Hey man, make love, not war!" The 1970s are a freewheeling time on Earth-616. The Cold War is at its peak, but—for now—threats of global annihilation from beyond are at a minimum. It's a time of experimentation and innovation in which the world—for better or worse—lets its guard down.

1970 | Bustling Camp Lehigh

The New Jersey military base where Steve Rogers once received basic training before undergoing "Project Rebirth" to become Captain America, is once again on the vanguard of global security innovation. S.H.I.E.L.D. Director Peggy Carter focuses on the field work of boundary-pushing operatives. Howard Stark turns up frequently while preparing for the birth of his first child. A young scientist named Dr. Hank Pym experiments with particles that can manipulate size and density, and the Tesseract is stored here for study and safekeeping. Even Arnim Zola, the captured Hydra researcher, now works freely at the base after his crimes were overlooked by the U.S. government due to his value as a technologies developer. Few know he is actually rebuilding the tendrils of Hydra from within S.H.I.E.L.D.

Howard Stark works as part of a S.H.I.E.L.D. that is still in its heyday, before it begins to rot from the inside.

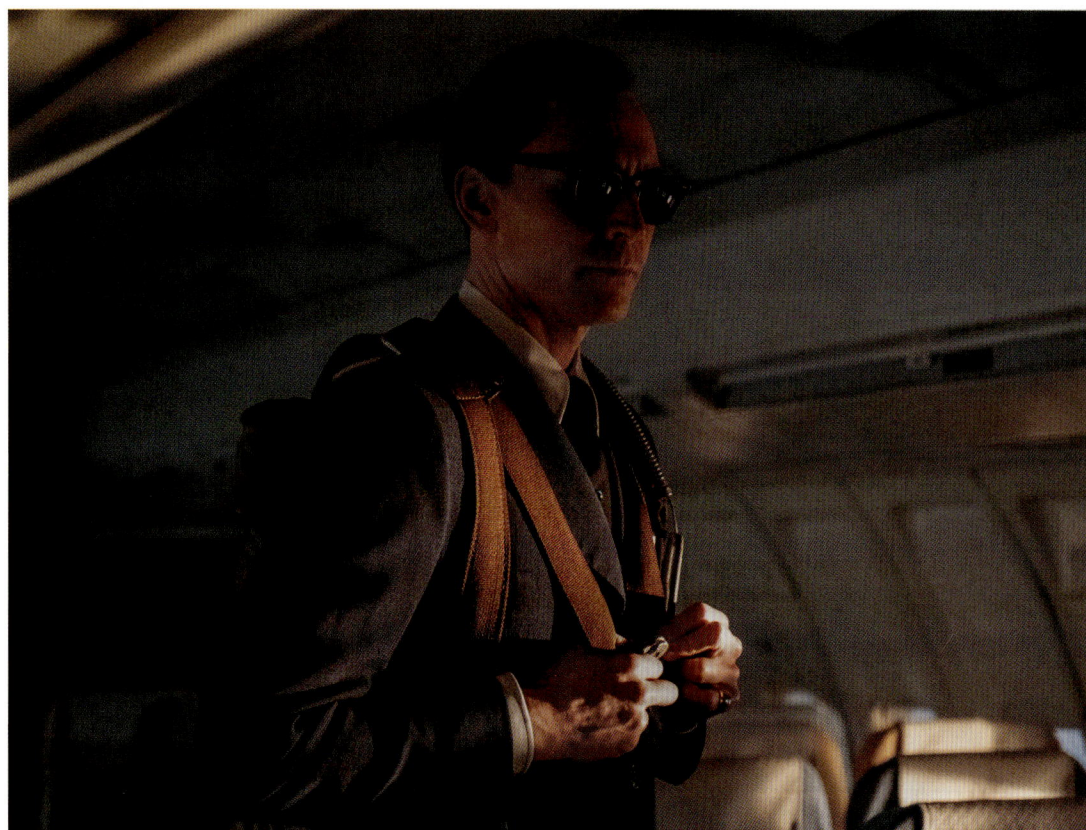

November 24, 1971 | Loki's Dare

Loki, the God of Mischief, undertakes a dare on Earth after losing a bet to his brother Thor. In the guise of "D.B. Cooper," he hijacks a Boeing 727 mid-flight by claiming to have a bomb. After securing a $200,000 ransom, he parachutes away during the escape flight, evading authorities but losing most of the money when Heimdall sends the Bifrost to return him to Asgard. The unsolved hijacking and the bizarre disappearance of the perpetrator creates an enduring mystery for the humans of Midgard.

Loki in the guise of skyjacker "D.B. Cooper."

Hardware upgrade: Arnim Zola uploads his consciousness before his biological brain dies.

September 15, 1973 | Howard Stark's Hidden Element

Howard Stark prepares what will be the last of his World Expos. He uncovers the atomic structure for a new kind of energy-creating element, but is unable to replicate it in real life. He uses the design to create a model of the Expo's fairgrounds, and in a filmstrip recorded for his then 3-year-old son, he hints at the hidden meaning. "This is the key to the future," he says. "One day you'll figure this out. And when you do, you will change the world."

1972 | The Not-Quite Death of Arnim Zola

After living for decades under the protection of the U.S. government, Arnim Zola's human body receives a terminal diagnosis, but the Hydra scientist is once again spared final judgment. Before dying, Zola's consciousness is transferred onto 200,000 feet of databanks, preserving his brain as a form of artificial intelligence. Not only does he continue providing S.H.I.E.L.D. with insight, but he continues overseeing his hidden effort to revive Hydra by identifying agents who might be sympathetic to his amoral views.

Years after his father's death, Tony Stark will discover the message and legacy that Howard Stark had left him.

Mid-1970s | The Ageless Star

A man named Karun Patel becomes the assistant and lifelong sidekick to the Eternal known as Kingo. Their relationship begins when Patel notices that the Bollywood actor never ages. After becoming a movie star during the silent era, Kingo stays in the limelight by rebranding himself every generation as the new descendant in an acting dynasty. Patel believes he knows the truth—Kingo is a vampire! After confronting the actor in the 1970s, Patel learns about the Eternals and goes on to be Kingo's trusted confidant through the time of the Emergence.

The Eternal Kingo and his assistant Karun Patel, after five decades together.

47

1970s-1980s

Isaiah Bradley and his grandson Eli, around 40 years after he gained his freedom.

Mid-to-Late 1970s | Heroes in the Making

Two children demonstrate extraordinary skills that will make them historic in the years to come. Tony Stark constructs a circuit board at age 4, and a V8 engine two years later, landing him on a magazine cover with his industrialist father. While he is propelled forward by encouragement, Carol Danvers dodges obstacles. She enters her teen years at full speed, riding go-carts, racing bikes, and playing her heart out in baseball games—undaunted by discouragement, crashes, or loss. Neither one is yet Iron Man or Captain Marvel, but both are on their way.

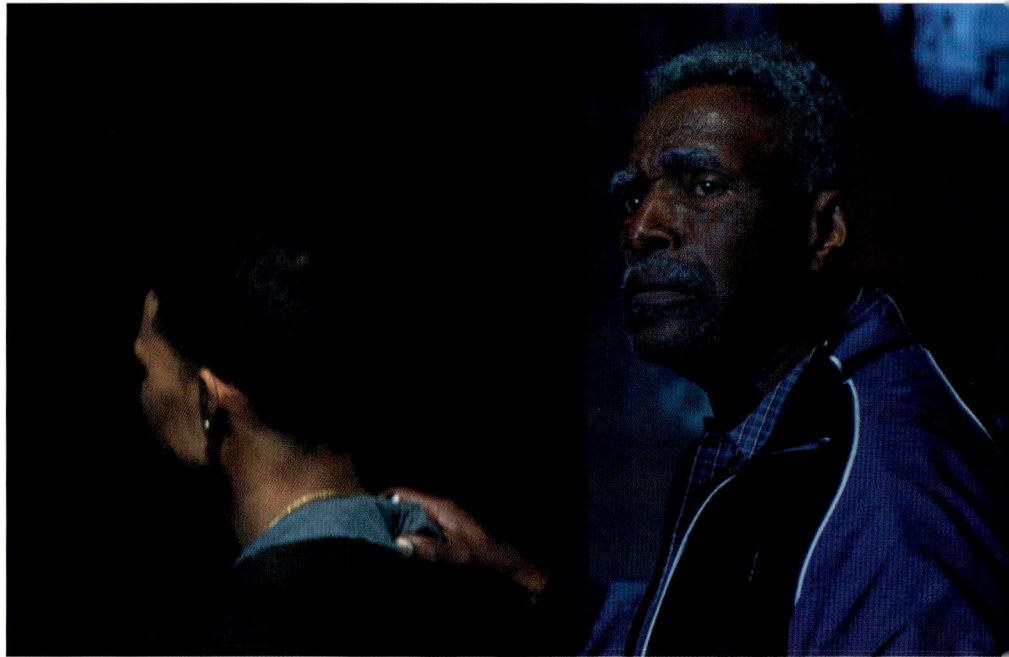

Early 1980s | Isaiah Bradley's Overdue Freedom

After spending decades wrongfully imprisoned, Isaiah Bradley gains his freedom. He was incarcerated because he was shameful proof of the United States' illicit Super Soldier Program, tested on men without their consent. A sympathetic nurse helps Bradley fake his own death, and he quietly escapes, living off the grid in Baltimore to avoid attention that might return him to prison.

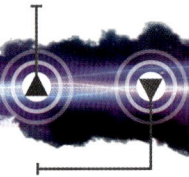

1980 | Ego Expands to Earth

After thousands of years of planting the seeds of his universal Expansion, the Celestial known as Ego sends his avatar to Earth (specifically, Missouri) and falls in love with the human Meredith Quill. She gives birth to a son, Peter, and raises him mostly as a single mother. Ego finds himself inextricably drawn back to Meredith, but he implants a tumor in her head that will eventually kill her—a murderous impulse derived from a wish to avoid entanglements that might distract from his grand plan.

Ego's human avatar, Meredith Quill's lover "from the stars," sings along with her during happier times.

1985-1986 | Trevor Slattery's Almost Breakthrough

Long before Trevor Slattery gains infamy for impersonating "the Mandarin," he has a fleeting moment of actual fame. A Cold War crime series casts Slattery as a Russian cop with anger problems, rampaging through Los Angeles on a quest for revenge. His sidekick is a hard-drinking monkey. Still, the network rejects the pilot episode and the series never airs. Taking the job in Hollywood costs Slattery more than it gives him, especially since he is absent for his beloved mother's death back in England.

The car (with personalized plates) driven by Trevor Slattery's character.

Trevor Slattery's regret about the unused pilot: "I wish I had a copy."

1987 | Lost in the Quantum Realm

Hank Pym's shrinking particles make him an invaluable asset as a top-secret U.S. spy and saboteur—work he frequently performs alongside his wife, Janet Van Dyne. She goes subatomic in order to disarm a Soviet missile hurtling toward the United States, but once the miniaturization begins she is unable to halt or reverse it, becoming lost somewhere in a dimension known as the "Quantum Realm." She leaves behind a young daughter, Hope, who never gives up the search for her missing mother.

Janet Van Dyne's farewell to her daughter: "Jellybean ... Daddy and I have a last-minute business trip." It is the last time they will see each other for more than 30 years.

49

1970s-1980s

A mixtape of classic rock, left by Meredith Quill for her son Peter.

1988 | Meredith Quill's Goodbye

Meredith Quill succumbs to the brain tumor that was intentionally inflicted on her by the Celestial Ego. Before dying, she gives her son mixtapes of her favorite music. They are among the few mementos he takes with him when he is abducted by Ravagers, who were sent by Ego because he needs a powerful descendant who shares his Celestial abilities to help activate his Expansion. Guilt-stricken Ravager chief Yondu Udonta doesn't complete the delivery, choosing instead to keep the human boy as one of their roaming criminal crew.

Late 1980s | Mar-Vell in Hiding

At the height of the Kree-Skrull war, a Kree scientist named Mar-Vell becomes ashamed of the way her own people have subjugated the Skrulls. She helps a group of Skrull refugees escape to Earth, where they live in Mar-Vell's orbiting laboratory while Mar-Vell takes on the identity of human scientist Wendy Lawson. She joins the U.S. government's "Project Pegasus" to access the Tesseract, using it to develop a light-speed engine that she hopes can help the Skrulls find a new home, safe from the Kree.

Mar-Vell comes to Earth to continue research she hopes will find peace for the Skrulls.

Late 1980s | Dangerous Science

Scientists Elihas Starr, Hank Pym, and Bill Foster work together within S.H.I.E.L.D., conducting quantum research. Foster also explores an enlargement process as part of Project Goliath, growing to a record of 21 feet high. A clash between Starr and Pym leads to Starr's ouster, and the desperate scientist continues independent experiments at a lab in Argentina. Starr and his wife will die in an explosion of quantum energy, which also disrupts their daughter Ava's molecular stability, allowing her to pass through solid objects. Only Foster offers the child care and support. Ava is later recruited by S.H.I.E.L.D. to use her abilities for high-level espionage under the codename "Ghost."

Bill Foster helps care for Ava Starr for years after her accident.

Ghost's suit was developed by S.H.I.E.L.D. to help Ava control her body's ability to phase.

Howard Stark urges the Pym Particle's creator to "help us put it to good use."

"As long as I'm alive, nobody will ever get that formula."

S.H.I.E.L.D. Director Peggy Carter advises not going to war against Dr. Pym.

1989 | The Resignation of Hank Pym

Hank Pym storms into one of the conference rooms of the unfinished Triskelion building in Washington after discovering that S.H.I.E.L.D. has been trying to secretly replicate his particles, which would prevent him from supervising their use. He resigns in protest to Peggy Carter and Howard Stark, and breaks the nose of S.H.I.E.L.D. Head of Defense Mitchell Carson for saying Pym should have protected his lost wife as intensely as he does his research.

Carol Danvers is urged by a dying Mar-Vell to prevent their Kree attacker from getting control of the light-speed engine's core.

1989 | Carol Danvers Takes Flight

Air Force test pilot Carol Danvers (Callsign: Avenger) is selected for the first flight of the *Asis*—a jet that utilizes scientist Wendy Lawson's (Mar-Vell's) new Tesseract-powered engine. Yon-Rogg of the Kree's Starforce shoots down the renegade inventor's experimental craft mid-flight. After crash-landing, Danvers destroys the engine's core to prevent the attacker from seizing it, but her body absorbs a column of energy from the explosion that empowers her with superhuman abilities beyond any yet recorded. Yon-Rogg kills Lawson/Mar-Vell, then takes the wounded human pilot with him for study.

1989 | Vers Joins Starforce

Carol Danvers is gone—even to herself. Her memories remain, but they've been detached from her consciousness and buried beneath the currents of Space Stone energy now circulating through her body. The amnesiac pilot is nursed back to health on the Kree world of Hala by Yon-Rogg, then is recruited to the Starforce under the name Vers (the last remaining letters on her damaged dog tags). Unaware that the Kree are the aggressors in the conflict, she joins Yon-Rogg and Starforce in battling the Skrulls that Mar-Vell gave her life to protect.

After losing her memories but gaining the powers of the Tesseract, Carol Danvers trains with Yon-Rogg.

51

1990s

The 1990s are claimed by some to be "the end of history," as America's foes are vanquished, the Cold War ends, and democracy triumphs around the globe. In fact, the decade marks the beginning of a new history, one in which Earth is but a small part of a far larger universe, and subject to powerful new forces. A series of events and tragedies that occur in the final years before the new millennium will have massive repercussions decades into the future.

December 16, 1991 | The Stark Murders

Just before Christmas, Howard and Maria Stark are assassinated by the Winter Soldier (their deaths are disguised as a car accident). The Winter Soldier also acquires five samples of Super Soldier Serum from the vehicle. Hydra uses the packets to create more unstoppable assassins who, like the Winter Soldier himself, are kept in cryogenic storage when not on assignment. Decades from now, after the collapse of the parasitic Hydra operation that grew within S.H.I.E.L.D., the lab in Siberia where these super soldiers are stored will be abandoned and largely forgotten. But deadly potential lives on within.

Howard and Maria Stark are assassinated by the Winter Soldier after Howard spends a lifetime fighting against Hydra.

Early 1990s | Missing Carol Danvers

On Earth, Carol Danvers is presumed dead after the *Asis* crash, although no remains are found among the ruins of the prototype. She is mourned by friend and fellow test pilot Maria Rambeau and her young daughter Monica, the two people Danvers considers her true family. Above them, in the skies where the trio used to stargaze, the Skrull refugees remain trapped aboard Mar-Vell's laboratory, orbiting the planet and awaiting rescue as years go by.

Maria Rambeau and Carol Danvers, in happier days as test pilots for the U.S. military.

Tony Stark takes over Stark Industries, but Obadiah Stane maintains a close watch.

1992 | Tony Stark Takes Over

Despite graduating Summa Cum Laude from MIT at age 17, Tony Stark has been adrift for years, and his lifestyle and partying was a source of constant friction between him and his parents. While visiting their home for the holidays, his final conversation with them before their deaths was a tense argument—a source of regret for the young man, as he missed his last chance to share his true feelings. Obadiah Stane, his father's longtime business associate, becomes interim CEO of Stark Industries immediately after their deaths, but Tony decides to rally and assume control of his inheritance within a few months.

1992 | The Tragedy of N'Jobu

T'Chaka confronts N'Jobu in Oakland, California, after learning his brother helped Ulysses Klaue stage a deadly heist to steal a quarter ton of vibranium from Wakanda. The radicalized N'Jobu says he only wished to supply vibranium weapons to oppressed people around the globe to overthrow those who exploit them, but T'Chaka insists he return home to answer for his "crimes." After realizing his trusted friend "James" is actually the Wakandan spy Zuri, N'Jobu draws his gun, intending to kill him—and is instead killed by his own brother. The king departs, leaving behind N'Jobu's son, Erik, who grows up to continue his father's mission—and becomes one of Wakanda's fiercest adversaries.

Following N'Jobu's death, the items he left behind for his son teach Erik about Wakanda and his birthright, setting him on a path of revenge.

53

1990s

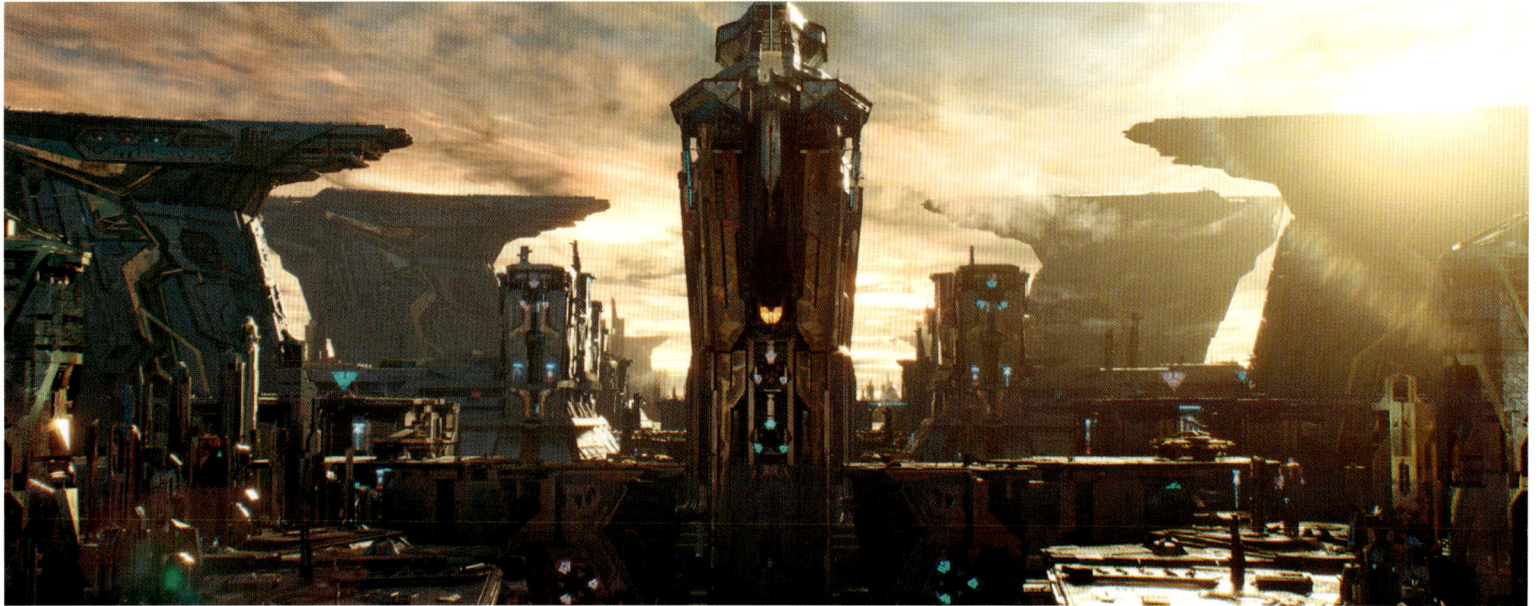

Carol Danvers lives on the Kree capital world of Hala as the Starforce warrior known as "Vers."

Early 1995 | The Kree-Skrull Conflict

The Kree authorities claim the Skrulls have attacked the Kree homeworld of Hala. The truth about the incident may be more complicated than the way the Kree's Supreme Intelligence has positioned it to the people of its Empire.

A young Natasha Romanoff finds herself in Cuba, following the end of her "family's" mission in America.

General Dreykov, leader of the Red Room, in the mid-1990s.

Summer 1995 | The Family That Wasn't

In a small town in Ohio, young Natasha Romanoff lives with her adopted sister Yelena, cared for by Russian super soldier Alexei (a.k.a the Red Guardian) and Red Room researcher Melina. During their three-year mission posing as a family, Alexei has infiltrated S.H.I.E.L.D.'s North Institute. One day, he steals mind-control data from what is actually part of Hydra's Winter Soldier program, which the Red Room plans to use to create its own assassins. Once the data is acquired, the family flees the United States and returns to Russia, with both "daughters" tragically forced into the Widow assassin training program themselves.

"Vers" struggles to find her purpose among the Kree.

(From left): Korath, Att-Lass, "Vers," Bron-Char, and Minn-Erva embarking on a Starforce assignment.

Summer 1995 | Inexplicable Dreams

Six years after her disappearance, Air Force pilot Carol Danvers lives and fights under the name Vers on the Kree Empire world of Hala. She is now an elite agent with the Kree's Starforce division, overseen by her commander Yon-Rogg. She does not remember her past identity, or that Yon-Rogg is responsible for the incident that caused her memory loss, but she is haunted by chaotic dreams of Mar-Vell, the renegade Kree scientist he assassinated. Vers has no idea who this mystery woman is, or how they were once connected.

Summer 1995 | The Torfa Ambush

Vers and her Starforce squad are dispatched to the border planet Torfa, but their mission to rescue a Kree spy goes sideways. Vers is captured by Skrull general Talos, who forcibly reads her memories, seeking information about Mar-Vell's research into light-speed engines. That leads them to Planet C-53 (a.k.a. Earth), where Vers escapes their ship, plummeting through the atmosphere and crash-landing in a video store.

Stranded on Earth, "Vers" channels photon blasts at Skrull adversaries.

Summer 1995 | Suspect Dressed For Laser Tag

S.H.I.E.L.D. agents Nick Fury and Phil Coulson arrive to question Vers, who alerts them to the shape-shifting alien menace threatening their planet. They are unfamiliar with the Skrulls and dubious about the claim, but the photon blasts emanating from her fists do encourage them to listen to her.

S.H.I.E.L.D. agents Nick Fury and Phil Coulson investigate the appearance of a Kree warrior in Southern California.

NICK FURY

Walking a line between light and dark, Nick Fury is a complex man, even to those who know him well. As director of S.H.I.E.L.D., Fury creates the Avengers Initiative, a program bringing together a group of individuals with unique skillsets to defend Earth from global threats. Fury recruits Iron Man, Black Widow, Captain America, Hawkeye, Thor, and the Hulk who prevent an alien invasion led by Thor's brother Loki. When Fury discovers Hydra has infiltrated S.H.I.E.L.D., he makes the difficult decision to dismantle the organization.

2011 | Defrosted Hero

After years of searching for the lost Captain America, S.H.I.E.L.D. finally locates Cap in the Arctic. When Steve Rogers is brought out of his ice-induced hibernation, he escapes S.H.I.E.L.D. headquarters where he's being held and runs out into Times Square. Fury tracks him down and informs Steve that he's been missing for almost 70 years. Fury will help the super soldier adjust to the modern world by offering him a new mission and a place with S.H.I.E.L.D.

2010 | Fury's Big Week

Fury places Natasha Romanoff undercover at Stark Industries to observe Tony Stark and see if he qualifies as an Avengers candidate. Fury meets with Tony after he defeats Ivan Vanko and hands him a file with Natasha's assessment, which concludes that Tony is narcissistic with self-destructive tendencies and is better suited, for now, to serve as a consultant. Meanwhile, Thor's hammer has landed in New Mexico and the Hulk faces Abomination in Harlem. In the space of a week, the foundations for the Avengers are laid.

2008 | Meeting Iron Man

When Tony Stark reveals to the world that he's Iron Man, Fury, now director of S.H.I.E.L.D., pays him a visit and tells him he isn't the only Super Hero in the world. Fury introduces himself and tells Tony about the Avengers Initiative.

1995 | Threats from Above

S.H.I.E.L.D. agent Nick Fury is dispatched to investigate a mysterious woman who has crash-landed into an LA video store. The woman is former Air Force pilot Carol Danvers, now part of the elite Kree Starforce, who has returned to Earth ahead of what appears to be a Skrull invasion. As Danvers and Fury find themselves in the midst of a war between the Skrulls and Kree, Fury comes to realize that humanity is not prepared to face such threats. He is inspired to create the Avengers Initiative.

2012 | The Avengers

Fury activates the Avengers Initiative when Loki steals the Tesseract. In their first battle as a team, Captain America, Black Widow, Thor, the Hulk, Iron Man, and Hawkeye defeat Loki and the Chitauri in the Battle of New York. The battle validates Fury's fears about extraterrestrial threats, but also the value of the Avengers Initiative.

2014 | Faked Demise

Fury is attacked by Hydra agents when he starts to look deeper into Project Insight and finds refuge in Steve Rogers' apartment. Fury shares his suspicions about S.H.I.E.L.D. being compromised before being shot by the Winter Soldier. Fury fakes his death to expose Alexander Pierce and bring down the Hydra-corrupted S.H.I.E.L.D. from inside.

2015 | Pep Talk

Fury meets the Avengers at Clint Barton's farmhouse to get them back on track after they lose a battle to Ultron and the Maximoff twins. Fury then joins the Avengers in the battle in Sokovia, arriving in a requisitioned Helicarrier, transporting civilians to safety, and sending War Machine to join in the fight.

2018 | Dust to Dust

Fury is driving with Maria Hill when he witnesses people disappearing due to the Snap. Fury watches in horror as Hill disappears and grabs an old pager to send an alert to Captain Marvel seconds before he disappears as well.

2023 | Sad Occasion

Fury is brought back when the Avengers are successful in reversing the Snap. He attends Tony Stark's funeral where he remains in the background, but is briefly reunited with Captain Marvel.

2024 | Far from Earth

While he is away in space, Fury asks the Skrull Talos to impersonate him on Earth. Posing as Fury, Talos gives Peter Parker the E.D.I.T.H. glasses that Tony Stark had wanted him to have, unwittingly triggering a battle between Parker and discontented former Stark employee Quentin Beck.

1990s

"Vers" and Nick Fury form an alliance.

Summer 1995 | Danger from on High

Fury realizes Vers was telling the truth when one of the shape-shifting Skrulls is killed while mimicking Coulson. For six years, Fury has been trying to determine where future enemies might emerge. "It never occurred to me they would be coming from above," he tells Vers. She and Fury agree to join forces to investigate the mysterious "Pegasus" program using fragments of her memories that her Skrull interrogation unlocked.

Summer 1995 | The Project Pegasus Papers

A NASA/U.S. Air Force archive shows Project Pegasus was overseen by Dr. Wendy Lawson, who was using the energy of the Tesseract to power a light-speed engine. Vers recognizes her as the woman from her dreams and discovers that Lawson's papers are full of Kree glyphs. She also learns that Lawson died in the 1989 crash of an experimental *Asis* jet, and Vers finds a photo of herself in the documents as the test pilot, along with records of a witness: Maria Rambeau.

"Vers" uncovers evidence of her past in the archives of Project Pegasus.

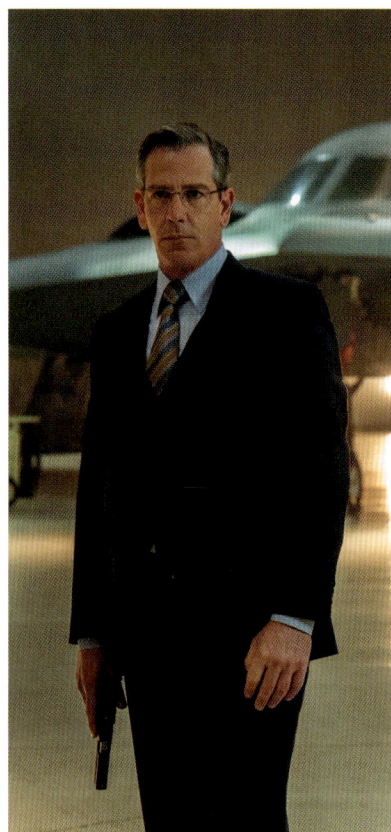

Skrull shape-shifter Talos takes human form, masquerading as a S.H.I.E.L.D. official.

Nick Fury and Carol Danvers escape Project Pegasus in an experimental ship.

Summer 1995 | Taking Flight

Fury's S.H.I.E.L.D. supervisor Agent Keller is being simmed by Skrull general Talos, who pursues Fury and Vers through the Project Pegasus facility. The two escape him in a prototype for a new government airship—the Quadjet.

Maria Rambeau, reunited with her lost friend Carol Danvers, who still struggles to remember their history.

Carol Danvers, during her days as a top test pilot.

Summer 1995 | Memories of Another Life

At the Rambeau home in Louisiana, Vers reunites with her former fellow pilot Maria and her daughter Monica, who reveal her former life as Carol Danvers. The "Vers" of her Starforce identity came from a fragment of her old dog tags. Some of her memories rush back. After the crash, she gained her blue Kree blood from a lifesaving transfusion provided by Yon-Rogg. Danvers' body had become a vessel for the energy of Dr. Lawson's experimental engine when it exploded, imbuing her with cosmic powers limited only by her ability to control them.

Flying jets never felt like work for Carol Danvers.

"I just want to talk..."

Summer 1995 | Yon-Rogg's Betrayal

With her memories restored, Danvers realizes that Yon-Rogg actually murdered Mar-Vell, and spared her own life only because he and the Kree Supreme Intelligence wanted to control the cosmic energy that now courses through her body. It is revealed the Kree Empire has actually been the aggressor in the conflict against the Skrulls.

Summer 1995 | The Truth

Talos and his Skrulls arrive and reveal that despite their earlier menacing behavior they are not actually hostile. They are refugees, trying to track down information about a long-lost ally. Lawson was creating the light-speed tech as a way to help the Skrulls find a new planet, restore their civilization, and defy the brutal subjugation of the Kree. Lawson, whose real identity was the Kree scientist Mar-Vell, felt she had to make amends after spending her life on the "shameful" side of the conflict. Now Vers feels the same.

Yon-Rogg poses as a friend, but his intentions are far from honest.

1990s

Captain Marvel, in a new uniform designed with help from young Monica Rambeau.

Summer 1995 | Captain Marvel Rises

No longer Vers, but also something much more than the pilot she once was, Carol Danvers takes on a new heroic role. Young Monica Rambeau helps her remake her Starforce uniform in colors of blue, red, and gold.

Mar-Vell's laboratory orbiting Earth, aboard an old Kree Imperial cruiser.

The Quadjet ventures outside of the planet's atmosphere.

Captain Marvel holds the Tesseract containing the Space Stone, the origin of her immense power.

Summer 1995 | Mar-Vell's Hidden Lab

Danvers, Fury, and Rambeau forge a tenuous alliance with Talos. They use the Quadjet to help him locate Lawson's laboratory, which is cloaked in invisibility in orbit just outside Earth's atmosphere. Here, they find the Tesseract, the power source of her engine technology. Also hidden aboard the space station is the long-lost family of Talos, along with other Skrull survivors who had been given sanctuary by Mar-Vell, and who were left stranded after she was killed.

The Kree extremist Ronan the Accuser.

Captain Marvel batters through a fleet of Kree starships that attempt to bombard Earth.

As Captain Marvel flies through the vacuum of space, she singlehandedly demolishes the Kree onslaught.

Summer 1995 | The Accuser Flees

Yon-Rogg's team track Danvers and her allies to the lab, where they capture her and link her mind to the Kree Supreme Intelligence. This backfires badly as Captain Marvel realizes the Kree have only been inhibiting her true abilities. She breaks free of the Supreme Intelligence, destroying the inhibitor chip that the Kree placed in her neck, and activates her full powers. She easily wipes out the Starforce team as Fury, Rambeau, and the Skrulls escape back to Earth with the Tesseract. As Yon-Rogg pursues them to the surface, the Kree commander Ronan the Accuser arrives above Earth with plans to eradicate the Skrull "infestation." Danvers, now supercharged with cosmic energy, shreds Ronan's fleet and sends him retreating. Ronan vows one day to claim her as his own new weapon.

Summer 1995 | A Life Spared, a Promise Made

A battered and vastly outmatched Yon-Rogg is returned to Hala with a message for the Supreme Intelligence to stand down. "I'm coming to end it— the war, the lies, all of it," Captain Marvel tells him.

Carol Danvers, unleashing vast cosmic powers that were previously restrained.

The battle between Yon-Rogg and Captain Marvel is over in mere seconds—she blasts him in the chest, knocking him down.

Summer 1995 | Elsewhere

Captain Marvel bids farewell to Maria and her daughter Monica, then leaves with the Skrull refugees in search of a new place to call home. Young Monica watches her go, much like Carol Danvers once looked to the stars herself, longing to be brave, adventurous, and heroic.

Nick Fury carries Goose, a potentially deadly Flerken who is easily mistaken as an Earth cat.

Goose, in cuddly housecat mode.

Summer 1995 | "Mother... Flerken!"

Dr. Lawson's cat, Goose—in reality a temperamental alien creature known as a Flerken—had swallowed the Tesseract to safely transport it back to Earth. Aboard the Quadjet, Nick Fury loses an eye when he gets too friendly with the creature.

61

5000 BCE | Eternals

The arrival of the Eternals marks humanity's first encounter with extraterrestrial life. The Eternals' peaceful invasion has two objectives—to protect the world from the Deviants, and to nurture humanity, encouraging civilization to spread and the world's population to grow. Unbeknown to most of the Eternals, this expansion of life feeds the growing Celestial within the planet's core.

The Eternals kick-start humanity's development, gifting them with technology that allows early civilizations to form.

965 | Frost Giants

The Frost Giants of Jotunheim invade Tønsberg in Norway, using the weapon known as the Casket of Ancient Winters to try and trigger a new ice age. They are beaten back by Odin and the armies of Asgard.

Laufey, king of the Frost Giants, does not forget his defeat at Odin's hands, and waits for centuries for the chance of revenge.

The battle in Greenwich sees the Dark Elves and their leader Malekith defeated by Thor and his allies.

2013 | Dark Elves

The Dark Elves are an ancient species, pre-existent to the creation of the universe. Hailing from The Dark World, when the Nine Realms came into being, the Dark Elves plotted to revert the universe to its former state of primordial darkness. To that end, Malekith, the leader of the Dark Elves, wields the Aether, otherwise known as the Reality Stone. His forces invade London during the Convergence of the Nine Realms, but are soundly beaten.

Under the control of Loki, Dr. Erik Selvig uses the power of the Tesseract to open a portal on top of Stark Tower, allowing the Chitauri to invade New York.

2012 | Chitauri

The Chitauri are cybernetically enhanced beings who operate under a hive mind intelligence and under Thanos' control. When Loki plans to steal the Tesseract on Earth, Thanos provides him with the Chitauri to use as his personal army, and the use of a scepter, which contains the Mind Stone. The Chitauri invasion is the first time modern humans recognize the threat posed by extraterrestrial foes.

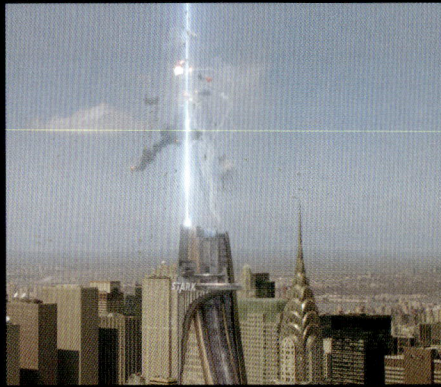

EARTH INVASIONS

Earth has been no stranger to alien invasions, having been visited by beings from other worlds since time immemorial. Nick Fury is first made aware of extraterrestrial beings in 1995, when he encounters Carol Danvers and helps her to prevent a Kree assault led by Yon-Rogg. In 2012, Thanos dispatches Loki and the Chitauri to invade Earth but they are stopped by the Avengers. Thanos attempts two more Earth invasions—in 2018, when he acquires all of the Infinity Stones and wipes out half the universe through the Snap, and again when a Thanos from 2014 time travels through the Quantum Realm to 2023 to battle the Avengers and claim the Infinity Stones.

2018 | Thanos

After a brutal showdown with Thor, Loki, and the Hulk, Thanos overpowers them, and kills Loki after procuring the Space Stone. Heimdall uses the last of his power to summon the Bifrost and send Bruce Banner to Earth to warn them of Thanos' impending arrival. Thanos dispatches his "Children" to New York City to obtain the Time Stone, then follows with a full-scale invasion of Wakanda in pursuit of the Mind Stone.

Doctor Strange, Iron Man, Bruce Banner, and Wong confront Ebony Maw and Cull Obsidian in Greenwich Village to prevent them from taking the Time Stone.

The Avengers travel to Wakanda, seeking Black Panther's help in keeping Vision and the Mind Stone away from Thanos, but Thanos soon locates them, sending an army to invade Wakanda.

1995 | Skrulls and Kree

The Skrulls and the Kree have been engaged in a centuries-old conflict. The Kree hail from the planet Hala, and are human-like in appearance (though some have blue skin). Militaristic by nature, they are also one of the most technologically advanced races in the galaxy. As rulers of the Kree Empire, they have long sought to conquer the shape-shifting Skrulls. The war between the two sides spills over onto Earth in the mid-90s, but this event is concealed from the public.

The Tesseract-empowered Air Force pilot Carol Danvers takes flight, destroying a Kree warship in orbit, and heads to Earth to battle her former mentor, Yon-Rogg.

2010 | Asgardians

The inhabitants of the realm of Asgard are long-lived and mighty warriors, regarded as gods by ancient humans. Asgard is also home to the Bifrost, a bridge made of dimensional energy that connects to eight other realms, including Midgard (Earth). The Asgardians use the Bifrost in order to travel and maintain peace amongst the Nine Realms, but it is also used to banish Thor to Earth, where he is subject to an assassination attempt by his brother, Loki.

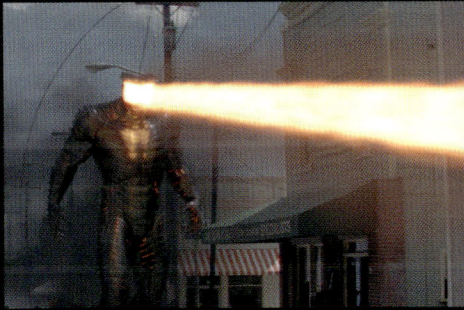

Loki sends the Destroyer, an Asgardian automaton, to New Mexico to destroy Thor. Thor sacrifices himself, and due to this selfless act, regains his powers and mystical hammer, Mjolnir.

2023 | Past Thanos

When James "Rhodey" Rhodes and Nebula time travel to Morag in 2014, they intercept Peter Quill/Star-Lord in order to obtain the Power Stone. Unfortunately Nebula's presence alerts her past self, who kidnaps her and brings her back to 2014 Thanos. The past Nebula uses the Quantum Tunnel to transport this Thanos and his army to 2023, sparking a final showdown against the Avengers.

The massed armies of Thanos swarm over the twisted rubble of the Avengers Compound, but all are reduced to dust with a snap of Tony Stark's fingers.

During the battle against Thanos and his army, Ant-Man turns into a giant and punches a Leviathan.

1990s

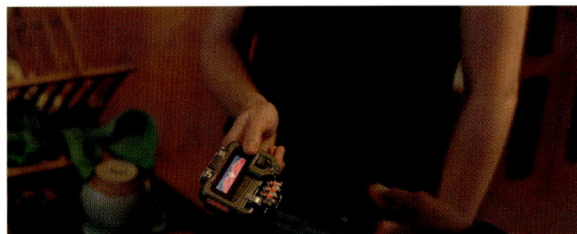

Carol Danvers gives Nick Fury a cosmic pager that will one day help save the universe.

Nick Fury earns Carol Danvers' lifelong trust.

Summer 1995 | The Cosmic Pager

Captain Marvel leaves Nick Fury with a modified pager that has a range of "a couple galaxies." While her responsibilities now lie far beyond Earth, she tells him to call if their homeworld ever has a problem it can't handle on its own. Almost a quarter century will pass before he encounters a threat ominous enough to make him use the device.

Summer 1995 | Some Assembly Required

Fury's experience with Captain Marvel inspires him to begin assembling a team of other powerful beings who might serve as Earth's protectors. He names the initiative after her pilot callsign: Avenger.

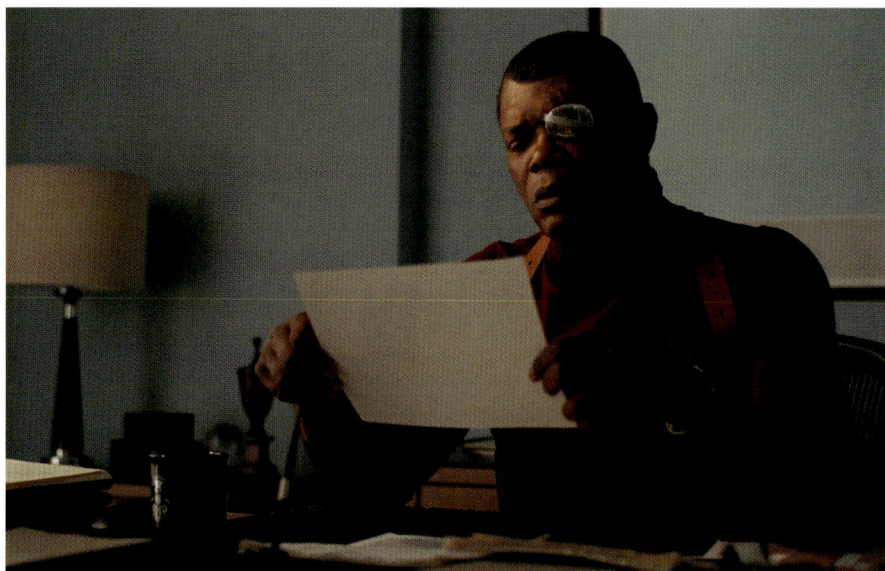

After witnessing an alien attack, Nick Fury begins a long-term plan for protecting Earth.

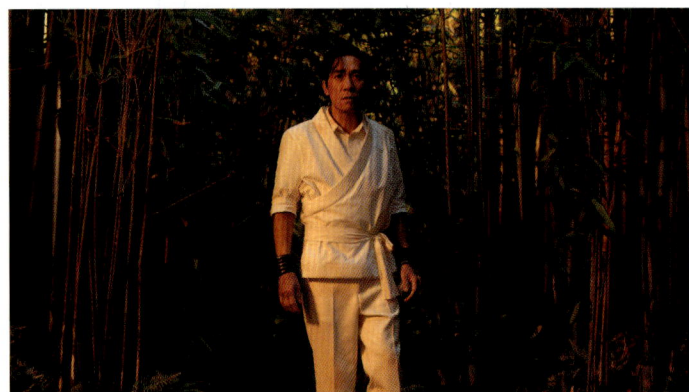

Wenwu in search of the mystical village of Ta Lo.

1996 | The Lost (and Found) Village of Ta Lo

Wenwu, the immortal warlord and leader of The Ten Rings, searches for the mythical village of Ta Lo and finally locates it in 1996. First he battles, and then befriends one of its protectors, Li. The two fall in love, and eventually have two children—Shang-Chi and Xialing. However, Wenwu's warlike past leads the elders of Ta Lo to reject the couple's request for sanctuary in the mystical realm.

1996 | The Lost Brother

Marc Spector, age 9, and his younger brother Randall are both obsessed with the action adventure film *Tomb Buster*. They perpetually look for patches of woods to explore, and one area that has a rocky subterranean cave is a particular obsession. While playing in it one rainy day, a flash flood traps the boys and only Marc escapes. Randall's drowning shatters the family, and Marc becomes the subject of his mother's grief filled torment as she relentlessly punishes him for the accident.

The evenly matched opponents develop a respect and friendship that blossoms into love.

Late 1990s | Gamora Speaks Her Mind

In deep space, Thanos has forged a plan to bring balance to the universe through ruthless population control. He considers this a necessary management of resources; others call it genocide. One of his earliest atrocities was against the Zehoberei people. Thanos left that world devastated, and claimed one courageous young girl, Gamora, as his adopted daughter. Later, that girl begins to voice complaints to her father about both his plans and his "chair" (throne). It is her first small sign of rebellion, and a harbinger of her future opposition.

Gamora as a child, brought into the service of Thanos.

Aldrich Killian waits on a freezing rooftop for a meeting with Tony Stark that will never take place.

December 31, 1999 | Happy New Year

As one millennium gives way to another, an arrogant and careless Tony Stark travels to Bern, Switzerland for a New Year's Eve party. There he meets genetic botanist Maya Hansen, creator of the Extremis virus that speeds bodily repair, and Dr. Ho Yinsen, a scientist he will encounter again one day while imprisoned inside an Afghan cave. Researcher Aldrich Killian, who is living with disabilities, requests funding from Stark for his think tank, but his hope turns to scorn when Stark casually stands him up for a meeting.

Spring 1999 | The Fracturing of Marc Spector

Marc Spector, now 12, remains traumatized by the accidental drowning of his little brother Randall three years earlier. His mother continues to blame him, abusing him physically and mentally, and Marc's psyche eventually dissociates in order to cope. He imagines a different identity for himself, using the name of the *Tomb Buster* character Dr. Steven Grant—a favorite of both the boys. Marc's personality continues to absorb torment, shielding the Steven alter, who grows up blissfully unaware and somewhat naive. The two alters will share one body for many years to come.

The abuse from his mother is too much for young Marc Spector to bear—so he creates an alter to escape the burden.

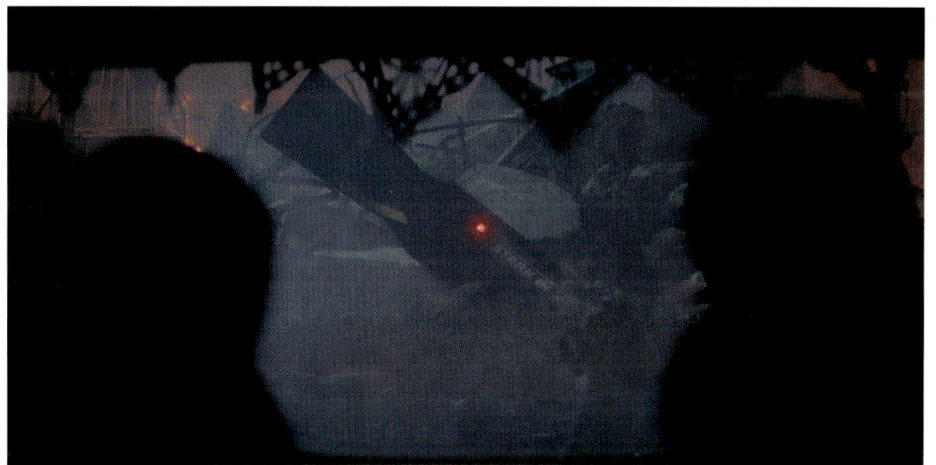

Pietro and Wanda Maximoff, hiding during the bombing of their apartment building.

March 1999 | No Laughing Matter

War again rips through the eastern European territory of Sokovia. The Maximoff family holes up in their apartment, seeking relief from the unrest by bingeing old American sitcoms. A missile strikes the building one night, killing the parents but sparing the children, Wanda and Pietro. The twins remain trapped in the rubble while the unexploded bomb—emblazoned with the Stark Industries logo—continues to flash. The television also continues to play, forever merging Wanda's trauma with a laughtrack.

65

THE 2000S AND 2010S

"I am ..." These two short words come to have profound meaning in the first two decades of Earth's 21st century. From Tony Stark's public declaration of "I am Iron Man" to a distant, tree-like alien's unifying transition from "I am Groot" to "We are Groot," these words often precede revelations of a new and powerful force in the universe: identity.

Mortal beings are no longer constrained by capabilities that come to them naturally. They are free now to become whatever they can create, often giving themselves colorful new names in the process. Through innovation, resilience, and fearlessness, they begin to tap powers that once seemed unthinkable or belonged exclusively to god-like beings. For some, like Bruce Banner, this empowerment will come at a severe cost and lack of control, but for others it is a chance to defend not only themselves but those they love. The truly courageous will even protect those they have never met.

Earth becomes a frequent battleground during this time. The emerging generation of Super Heroes will be matched by equally powerful beings driven by a desire to rule and dominate. Among the most formidable is the Titan known as Thanos, who will seek the Infinity Stones so that he can break the universe in half. The wishes of others will have no meaning to him as he operates by a single guiding principle: "I am ... inevitable."

The 2000s

It's a new millennium, a time of reflection and starting over. Unfortunately, mistakes of the past still hold sway despite the rollover of years. Pressure continues to build to find a way to reliably strengthen ordinary humans into super soldiers, while reluctant assassins are motivated by revenge or redemption. This new age begins with efforts to fix persistent old problems that often only create new ones.

The fateful lab where Bruce Banner subjects himself to his own experiments with gamma radiation.

Mid-2000s | The Creation of the Hulk

Gen. Thaddeus Ross reactivates the U.S. Super Soldier Program. Two of the scientists he brings in at an early phase are his daughter, Betty Ross, and her boyfriend, Bruce Banner, who are both unaware of the research's true purpose. Believing he is working on radiation resistance, Banner heedlessly volunteers as a test subject and absorbs a devastating gamma burst that transforms him into a rampaging giant with impervious green skin during times of severe distress. Fleeing the lab after injuring General Ross and Betty, he remains a fugitive from the government for five years, trying his best to suppress the monster that is forever threatening to erupt within him.

2007 | A Mother's Sacrifice

Wenwu removes his powerful rings and stores them away in an attempt to reform, but the Iron Gang seeks retribution for Wenwu's past actions. In his absence, they attack and kill his wife Li as her young children Shang-Chi and Xialing flee the home. Wenwu brutally retaliates against most of the Iron Gang, and recruits his son to take up martial arts training to become an assassin for The Ten Rings. One day, Shang-Chi will be sent to slay the final gang member responsible for his mother's death ... but the revenge will only push him further away from his father.

Li urges her two young children to escape while she holds off the Iron Gang.

The Danube river in the heart of Budapest.

2000s | Caught in a Web of Spies

S.H.I.E.L.D. sends agent Clint Barton to Budapest to target Natasha Romanoff, a Black Widow agent of General Dreykov and a product of his Red Room training facility. Instead of eliminating Romanoff, Barton chooses to recruit her instead. Presented with the opportunity to redeem her past, Natasha's final step in her defection to S.H.I.E.L.D. is the assassination of her former boss, General Dreykov.

2000s | Black Widow's Budapest Operation

Natasha Romanoff and her recruiter, S.H.I.E.L.D. agent Clint Barton, rig General Dreykov's office with explosives. With no other options to confirm her target, Natasha relies on seeing Dreykov's young daughter, Antonia, at the site to establish her father's presence. The targeted bombing seems to eliminate General Dreykov, but Natasha believes she has also killed Antonia—adding more "red" to her own moral ledger. After imploding a five-story building and shooting it out with Hungarian Special Forces, Natasha and Clint spend 10 days in hiding before they are able to escape Budapest.

After the Dreykov bombing, Natasha and Clint are forced to hide in a Budapest metro ventilation duct, playing tic-tac-toe and hangman to kill time.

Years later, Natasha and her sister Yelena will have to hide in the same duct.

2008

Until now, beings who possess extraordinary powers have tended to remain hidden, subtly shaping world events from the background and at times saving a population that has no idea they exist. Captain America was an exception, inspiring hope and admiration before his disappearance generations ago. Now a new generation of hero is emerging. Tony Stark is the first to surprise the world when he steps forth to declare "I am Iron Man." His candid admission opens the possibility for other heroes to follow and exist out in the open.

At his weapons demonstration, Tony Stark asks Gen. Gabriel in Afghanistan: "Is it better to be feared or respected? I say, is it too much to ask for both?"

Early 2008 | Near-Death Experience

Tony Stark's motorcade is hit by an ambush during a visit to Afghanistan to demonstrate his company's new Jericho carpet bombing missile. He suffers a debilitating heart injury when he is hit by shrapnel from enemy ordnance emblazoned with his own logo: Stark Industries. Stark is taken captive by the terror group known as The Ten Rings, and his life is saved by another imprisoned scientist named Dr. Ho Yinsen, whom he had treated dismissively several years before. Stark doesn't even remember that.

"I'll probably be dead in a week," Stark says. "Then this is a very important week for you," Yinsen replies.

"That could run your heart for 50 lifetimes," Yinsen notes. "Yeah," Stark says. "Or something big for 15 minutes."

Early 2008 | Change of Heart

Dr. Ho Yinsen attaches a crude electromagnet to Stark's chest to draw the metal fragments he could not extract away from any vital organs. He has treated many such injuries from Stark Industries weapons in his war-torn village of Gulmira. Yinsen's innovation inspires Stark. The Ten Rings have given him weapon materials and ordered him to re-create a Jericho missile, but Stark instead constructs an Arc Reactor for his chest, a miniature version of the kind powering his factory. He and Ho Yinsen get to work building something bigger— but it's not what their captors think. It's a suit of armor to wrap around himself and hopefully break them free of this cavernous prison.

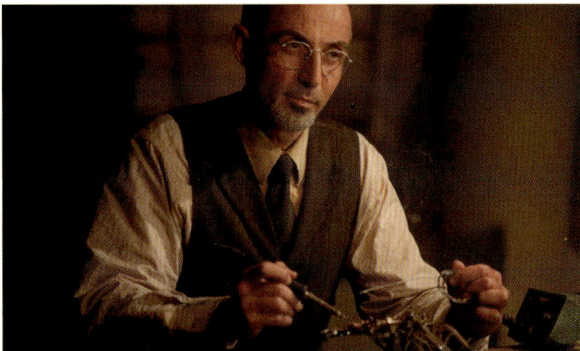

The Ten Rings threaten to torture Yinsen with a scalding ingot, and give Stark only one more day to complete his project.

Yinsen and Stark hide their plans for an armored suit from The Ten Rings by disguising it as pieces of a missile.

"I'm going to buy you some time," Yinsen says, as Stark finalizes his armor.

Spring 2008 | The Mark I Iron Man Suit

Stark and Dr. Ho Yinsen hastily finish the armor and assemble it around Stark's body. It's too clunky for him to see clearly, so he has memorized the number of steps and turns it takes to emerge from the cave. As panicked members of The Ten Rings descend on them, Stark's "Iron Man" suit blasts through doorways and sends them scattering. Yinsen is fatally wounded in the firefight and uses his final words to admonish Stark to change his ways once he escapes. "Don't waste it," he says. "Don't waste your life."

The Mark I emerges from the cave. The hero who will become known as Iron Man takes his first steps.

Spring 2008 | New and Improved

After his three-month imprisonment, Tony Stark returns to the United States a different man. Weapons manufacturing has made him unfathomably rich, but internally he feels bankrupt. Stark calls a press conference to announce that Stark Industries is withdrawing from the arms dealing business. "I came to realize that I have more to offer this world than just making things that blow up," Stark says. Among those caught off guard is Obadiah Stane, his longtime family friend and chief operating officer.

"Tony, we're a weapons manufacturer. That's what we do. We're ironmongers," Obadiah Stane warns.

2008

Spring 2008 | Honing the Iron Man

With help from his A.I. assistant JARVIS, Tony Stark begins refining his Iron Man design to create a personal suit of armor he can use to help save people in need. The Arc Reactor in his chest is still necessary to protect his heart, but he has already proven it can also power an advanced, near-indestructible suit. Now it's just a matter of pushing that to the limit with the most precise engineering possible. It's a long process of trial and error, with some bruises to both his body and ego, along the way. But soon, the design not only works—it soars.

Tony hones the Mark II Iron Man suit.

Iron Man's appearance catches the attention of his old friend Col. James "Rhodey" Rhodes in the Air Force's Weapons Development department.

Spring 2008 | Battle in Gulmira

Tony Stark sees a troubling news report out of Gulmira, Yinsen's home village, where local warlords have been conscripting innocent people as soldiers while driving the farmers and shepherds from their homes. They've somehow acquired Stark Industries weapons to dominate the region. He decides it is time to put his Mark III armor to the test and engages in a supersonic flight to the far-off region. Once there, he quickly liberates a group of refugees with the tactical elimination of the marauding soldiers, and his suit even survives a direct hit from a tank (the tank does not fare as well). The mysterious hero Iron Man becomes an international sensation.

Stark clings to the bottom of an F-22 sent to intercept him—then rescues the pilot of another jet when he falls off and damages its wing.

Agent Phil Coulson of the Strategic Homeland Intervention, Enforcement, and Logistics Division follows developments around Stark very closely.

The Ten Rings retrieve the remnants of the Mark I armor from the desert to trade with Obadiah Stane. Instead, Stane takes the armor and has them all killed.

Spring 2008 | Obadiah Stane's Plot

"If you'd killed him when you were supposed to, you'd still have a face." That's how Obadiah Stane greets the badly burned Raza, commander of this division of The Ten Rings, after his most recent battle with Iron Man. Not only has Stane been trafficking weapons illegally to the terror group, but he orchestrated the mercenaries' kidnapping of Stark to eliminate the only obstacle to his total control of Stark Industries. The Ten Rings have since assembled the remnants of Stark's Mark I armor, and Stane acquires them to begin reverse engineering his own Iron Man suit.

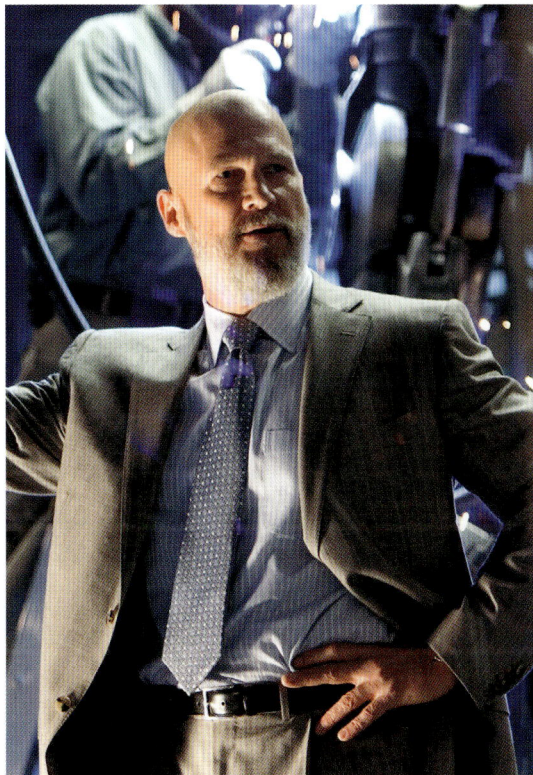

"Recruit our top engineers," Stane orders. "I want a prototype right away."

Spring 2008 | "I am Iron Man"

In the aftermath of Stane's rampage, Tony Stark must answer to the public. S.H.I.E.L.D. provides him with a cover story he can blame for the damage, about a malfunctioning prototype battling his bodyguard in a suit of armor, but Stark chooses to open up before the cameras and microphones. "The truth is... I am Iron Man," he declares. Later, he is visited by S.H.I.E.L.D.'s director, Nick Fury, who wants to recruit him for a new initiative. "Mr. Stark, you've become part of a bigger universe," Fury says. "You just don't know it yet."

"For thirty years, I've been holding you up," Stane tells Stark. "Nothing is going to stand in my way."

Spring 2008 | Fall of the Iron Monger

Back in California, Pepper Potts—Tony Stark's most trusted associate—uncovers Stane's illegal weapons trafficking operation, exposing his betrayal. But his engineers have worked quickly. A rough recreation of the Iron Man suit has already been crafted, and Stane incapacitates Stark to steal the compact Arc Reactor from his chest necessary to power it. Clinging to life, Stark replaces it with an older model, then flies off to confront Stane, who he finds attacking Pepper. Stane's "Iron Monger" suit matches the power of Stark's, but it has the old bugs. It freezes as Stark leads the fight into the upper atmosphere, and Stane plummets to Earth, but this isn't enough to stop him. Stark orders Pepper to overload the Stark factory's giant Arc Reactor, and Stane perishes in the resulting explosion.

73

2008 | Becoming Iron Man

Trapped in a cave with a gun to his head and a box of scraps in his hands, Tony Stark discovers the hero within. Being captured by The Ten Rings causes Tony to reflect on his arrogant playboy lifestyle and the damage Stark Industries inflicts on the world. He realizes he can use his resources to do better. The miniature Arc Reactor and powered armor he builds give him a new heart and purpose.

2010 | A New Ally

Though Tony projects invincibility as he stops threats around the globe, two issues plague him: the U.S. military want to appropriate and use his technology, and his Arc Reactor is slowly poisoning him. He works with Nick Fury to address both problems and becomes a consultant for S.H.I.E.L.D.

2012 | Forming the Team

Tony is the first Super Hero to learn about the Avengers Initiative. Ready with his Mark VI armor, he jumps into the mission to locate the stolen Tesseract and then stop Loki. The gathering of heroes tests Stark's capacity to play well with others, but he rises to the occasion, and together, the Avengers save Earth from the Chitauri invasion.

2016 | Being a Mentor

After bringing Spider-Man into the Avengers' battle at Leipzig-Halle airport, Tony takes an active interest in the young hero's life and becomes his mentor. Tony's tough exterior doesn't hide that he cares about Peter. He guides the teen as Peter fights the villainous Vulture and eventually offers him a place with the Avengers—an offer that Peter declines.

2016 | Friends to Enemies

Guilt lives in the corner of Tony's mind from the beginning of his tenure as Iron Man and when he sees the Avengers becoming as dangerous as Stark Industries' weapons once were, he takes a stand. His support of the Sokovia Accords causes a dramatic split from Steve Rogers, and the collapse of the Avengers.

IRON MAN

Tony Stark's heroic path hinges on two pivotal moments: being kidnapped by The Ten Rings and witnessing the Chitauri come through Loki's portal to invade Earth. The first incident opens Tony's eyes to the harm Stark Industries causes and leads him to build his first suit of armor and embark on a mission to make the world a better place. The latter dramatically broadens Tony's horizons with potential enemies and haunts his thoughts for years to come, making him by turns scared and resolved. As Iron Man, Tony Stark fights for humanity above all else.

2018 | Fighting Thanos

Until Thanos, the Avengers have defeated every enemy they have encountered. Tony has no reason to believe they can't stop this new foe. Using the tried and true combination of his determination, brilliance, and technology, Iron Man makes every effort to stop Thanos, defeating his ally Ebony Maw in space and then confronting Thanos himself on Titan. The failure to prevent the Snap and the ensuing loss of his friends bruises Tony's very core.

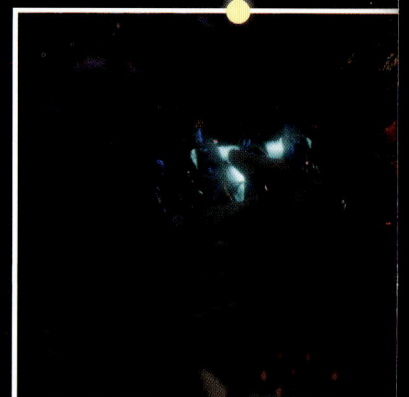

2023 | Ultimate Sacrifice

In the aftermath of the Snap, Tony tries to start afresh, settling down with Pepper Potts and raising their daughter, Morgan. He initially refuses to get involved in the Time Heist, wanting to protect his family from further ordeals, but he can't put aside the possibility of success. In the final conflict with Thanos, Tony sacrifices himself to save the universe.

2013-2015 | Looming Anxiety

In the years following the Battle of New York, the psychological aftermath takes a toll on Tony. Beset by nightmares, he frenetically works on the Iron Legion, making a suit of armor for every possible threat he can imagine. Tony's spiral worsens when he is faced with "the Mandarin"—an enemy created by his own past arrogance. Eventually, the original Iron Legion is replaced by a new one: an army of armored sentries that are deployed into battle alongside the Avengers.

2015 | Creating Artificial Life

Tony remains plagued by fears of extraterrestrial threats. He longs for global peace and thinks, in typical Tony Stark fashion, that he and Bruce have the means to ensure that by creating the artificial intelligence Ultron. The plan backfires when Ultron attempts to destroy the world and build a more peaceful one in its place.

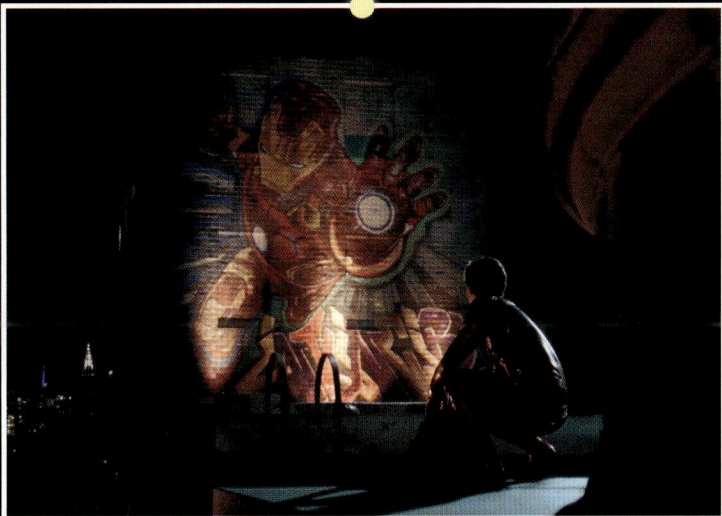

2024 | Tony's Legacy

Tony Stark leaves behind a profound legacy that spans the world. One of the people most affected by the loss is Tony's protégé, Peter Parker. Tony believed in Peter and designated him the recipient of E.D.I.T.H., which gives the teen control over Stark Industries' tech. Peter struggles to live up to Tony's reputation but does the best he can to honor his mentor.

2008–2010

Spring 2008 | Vanko's Rage

Anton Vanko, the researcher who was deported back to Russia in 1967 after helping Howard Stark devise early plans for the Arc Reactor, watches footage from Tony Stark's "I am Iron Man" press conference from the Moscow apartment he shares with his son, Ivan. "That should be you," his father says. Anton dies in obscurity, leaving piles of old schematics. His son Ivan was also once a promising physicist, but is now adrift and impoverished after spending 15 years in a Siberian prison for selling Soviet plutonium to Pakistan. After Anton's death, the embittered Ivan begins building his father's Arc Reactor prototype, driven by hatred of the Starks.

In the wrong hands, Arc Reactor technology has terrifying destructive potential.

Ivan Vanko works tirelessly to build his late father's Arc Reactor designs.

2008–2010 | Engineering Revenge

Ivan Vanko puts together the raw materials, tools, and data necessary to complete his father's Arc Reactor designs. While the results are not as refined as Tony Stark's, they're brutally effective. By focusing the repulsor beams through ionized plasma channels, he weaponizes the tech into a pair of lacerating whips. Once the research and design is complete, Vanko devises a plan to use his deadly weapon against Stark.

June 2009 | The Extremis Deaths

Aldrich Killian and Maya Hansen make a breakthrough in their Extremis research, using the technology that activates bioelectrical potential in the body to heal wounded soldiers, including the regrowth of lost limbs. But Extremis remains extremely volatile, and the Phase I trials cause some of their subjects to spontaneously combust in violent, fiery detonations. To cover up this deadly side effect, Killian will later devise an elaborate false narrative to disguise the explosions as terrorist attacks, creating "the Mandarin" persona as cover for the accidents.

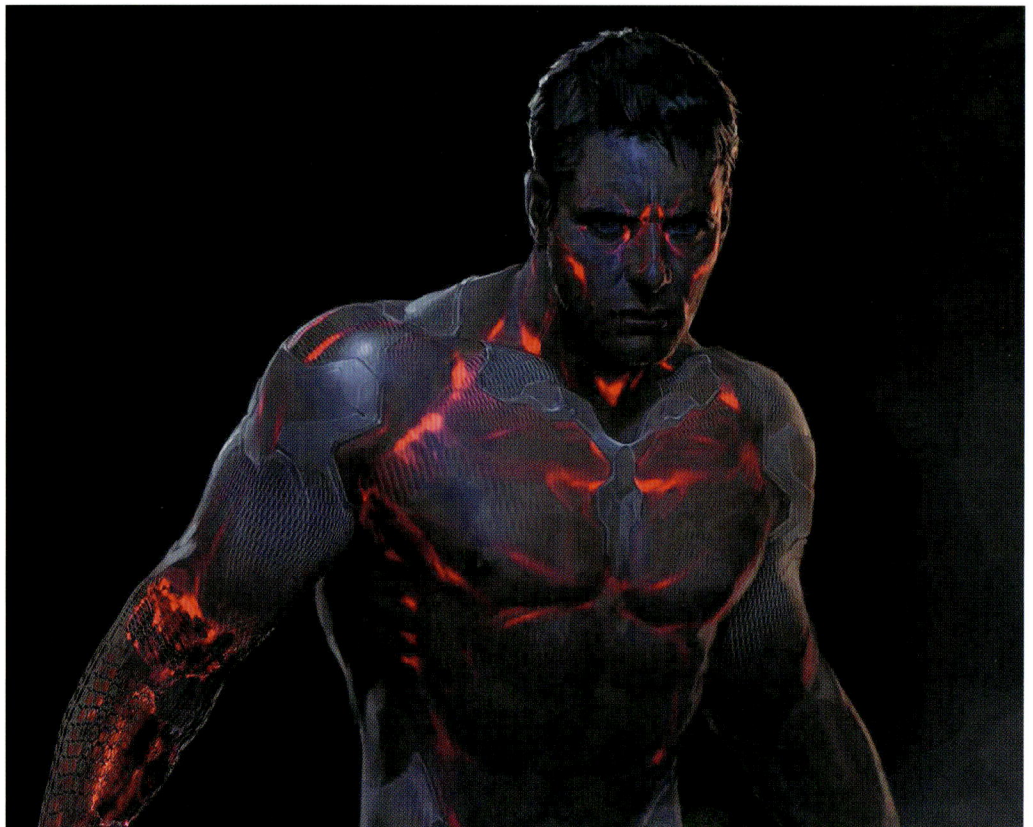

The healing and strengthening powers of Extremis come with deadly and destructive side effects.

76

2010

Living in the public eye means heroes sometimes face scrutiny for their actions. Tony Stark's Iron Man identity leads the U.S. government to question whether he—or any one individual—can be trusted with such power. Others with enhanced abilities, like Bruce Banner, will strain to control their powers, while Thor, the God of Thunder, is exiled to Earth to prove himself worthy. All learn they are now answerable to those they seek to protect.

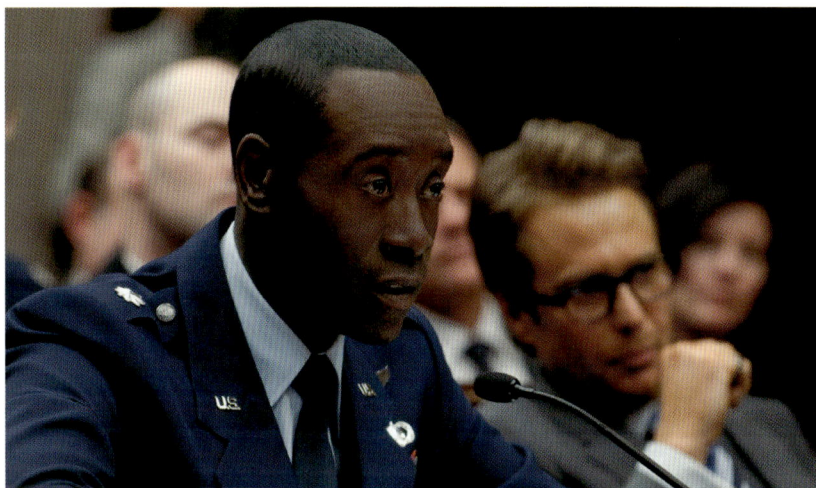

Lt. Col. James Rhodes and military contractor Justin Hammer testify before the U.S. Senate.

Spring 2010 | Bruce Banner in Hiding

It has been 158 days since Bruce Banner has transformed into the Hulk. During those five months, he has lived quietly in the Rocinha favela of Rio de Janeiro, working at a beverage company where he often helps fix breakdowns in the machines. He practices meditation to remain calm, and communicates anonymously with a biologist known as "Mr. Blue" to brainstorm possible cures for his unique disorder. Banner accidentally contaminates a bottle of soda after cutting his finger at work, and the resulting gamma radiation sickness in a consumer leads the U.S. government to his hiding spot.

Spring 2010 | Privatizing World Peace

At an Armed Services Committee hearing, Senator Stern pressures Tony Stark to turn over his Iron Man armor to the U.S. government. "You can forget it," Stark says. "I am Iron Man. The suit and I are one." The hearing puts him in conflict with a longtime rival, military contractor Justin Hammer, who testifies that hostile countries are racing to develop similar tech. Meanwhile, Lt. Col. James Rhodes proposes trying to recruit Stark himself into the Defense Department. Stark is dismissive of the idea. "I'm your new nuclear deterrent," Stark tells the committee. "I did you a big favor! I've successfully privatized world peace."

Tony Stark has ensured his Iron Man armor fits comfortably over a tuxedo.

Spring 2010 | Pepper Potts Promoted

JARVIS informs Tony Stark that using the Iron Man suit rapidly accelerates his palladium poisoning. His blood toxicity reaches 24% just before Pepper Potts urges him to keep his focus on Stark Industries. Instead, Stark has been consumed by his expo, his work as Iron Man, and his private illness. He surprises Potts by stepping back as CEO and appointing her to run the corporation. He tells her he has been considering a successor for some time. "Then I realized it's you," he says. "It's always been you."

Spring 2010 | Stark's Big Show

After around two years as Iron Man, Tony Stark flies onstage to inaugurate the year-long Stark Expo. Adoring fans cheer for him to "blow something up," but Stark prefers to highlight his peacekeeping work as the Super Hero. The Expo, being held for the first time since 1974, will bring researchers and innovators together from around the world. Behind the scenes, Stark grapples with the side effects of the Arc Reactor embedded in his chest that powers his armor and protects his heart from shrapnel. It is also slowly poisoning him with palladium.

CEO Pepper Potts in her office at Stark Industries.

2010

Spring 2010 | Black Widow, Undercover

After being wounded by the Winter Soldier in Odessa, Ukraine, in 2009, while on a mission to extract a high-value nuclear engineer, Natasha Romanoff is dispatched by S.H.I.E.L.D. to an undercover assignment: monitoring Tony Stark under the guise of administrative assistant "Natalie Rushman."

"Natalie Rushman" infiltrates Stark Industries as an effective assistant to Pepper Potts.

As he closes in on Bruce Banner, Emil Blonsky realizes he is hunting something bigger than he expected.

Spring 2010 | Blonsky Targets Banner

General Thaddeus Ross puts together an international raid to capture Bruce Banner, led by the British Royal Marines commando Emil Blonsky. "Your target is a fugitive from the U.S. government who stole military secrets," Ross says, leaving out some important facts. The mission goes sideways when a terrified Banner Hulks out. Tranquilizer darts bounce from his impervious green skin, he smashes through walls, and hurls a forklift "like it was a softball," a stunned Blonsky reports back. The raging Hulk escapes, and when Banner wakes up, he is more than 4,000 miles away in Guatemala.

May 5, 2010 | The Grand Prix Assault

With his blood toxicity now at 53%, Tony Stark is living like there's no tomorrow. He decides to get behind the wheel of his own Formula 1 car in the Monaco Grand Prix, but is attacked during the race by Ivan Vanko, wielding his twin Arc-powered whips that slice the speeding vehicles in half. Happy Hogan (Stark's bodyguard) and Pepper Potts hurry the suitcase-sized portable Iron Man Mark V suit to Stark, but he continues to be overpowered by Vanko. Finally, Stark subdues Vanko by ripping away the Russian's homemade power source.

Tony Stark drives his own car during the Monaco Grand Prix.

Ivan Vanko roughly examines the battle armors devised by Hammer Industries.

Spring 2010 | Hammer Hires Vanko

The jailed Ivan Vanko declares victory over Tony Stark, despite failing to kill him. "If you can make God bleed, then people will cease to believe in him," he tells the self-appointed hero. The existence of non-Stark Arc tech alarms the U.S. government, but it only intrigues Justin Hammer, who fakes Vanko's death and recruits him to improve the subpar brand of armored suits Hammer hopes to sell to the Pentagon.

REDLINE ALERT!
Hi there, folks! When JARVIS tells Tony Stark about Anton Vanko's history, he says the Soviet physicist defected to the United States in 1963, but a yellowed newspaper Stark reads cites Oct. 16, 1966. During the Cold War, sometimes high-level defections were kept classified for several years—or it might just be a misprint!

Spring 2010 | Stark out of Control

With his palladium concentration at 89%, Tony Stark celebrates what might be his last birthday by getting drunk and chaotic at his Malibu estate, shooting bottles and fruit out of the air with his repulsor blasts while guests cheer him on. Fearing for everyone's safety, Lt. Col. James Rhodes puts on the Mark II Iron Man armor and forces his old friend to "shut it down." Their fight wrecks the mansion—and a disgusted Rhodes leaves the premises with the armor.

James Rhodes to a reckless Tony Stark: "You don't deserve to wear one of these."

Spring 2010 | Thor's Canceled Coronation

Far off in the cosmic kingdom of Asgard, Thor raises his mystical hammer Mjolnir to a roar of cheers in the throne room of his father Odin. Boastful and proud, the God of Thunder is set to be crowned as their new king. But Frost Giants from Jotunheim, a cold, dark realm that has long been hostile to Asgard, infiltrate Odin's treasure room seeking their society's long-lost weapon, the Casket of Ancient Winters. They are killed by the Destroyer automaton during the raid, but the attack nonetheless interrupts and postpones Thor's ceremony.

Thor feels confident about his impending coronation, not knowing that Loki's plot is already in motion.

Rhodes questions Justin Hammer's involvement in the project, but complies when given a direct order.

Spring 2010 | The War Machine

Rhodes flies his new armor to Edwards Air Force Base, where the military begins to work on Stark's tech. Justin Hammer is called in to help weaponize the suit, augmenting it with a devastating new array of firepower. The Pentagon doesn't realize that Hammer has also connected the War Machine armor to his own network, which will allow Vanko to hack in and control it at will, while also puppeteering his squadron of Hammer drones.

2010

"I'm gonna have to ask you to exit the donut!"

Spring 2010 | Full Circle

A hung over Tony Stark meets Nick Fury at a Los Angeles-area donut shop, where he learns that his administrative assistant, Natalie Rushman, is really Natasha Romanoff, an agent of S.H.I.E.L.D. nicknamed Black Widow. "You're ... fired," he says. They provide Stark with lithium dioxide, which temporarily relieves his palladium poisoning. But he still needs to devise a new, less toxic power source if he hopes to stay alive and continue his work as Iron Man.

Spring 2010 | Thor's Banishment

Odin is outraged by Thor's actions. "You are a vain, greedy, cruel boy," he declares. Thor shouts back: "And you are an old man and a fool!" Odin issues an edict that Thor is not only unworthy of the throne, but unworthy of his hammer as well. He strips Thor of his powers and banishes him to the realm of Midgard (a.k.a. Earth). After Thor is beamed away, Odin inscribes Mjolnir with a new command: "Whosoever holds this hammer, if he be worthy, shall possess the power of Thor." Odin then casts away the hammer, as well.

An argument between Odin and Thor results in the God of Thunder being stripped of his powers.

Spring 2010 | An Ill-Planned Counterattack

Goaded by his brother Loki, Thor defies his father's wishes and leads Lady Sif and the Warriors Three—Fandral, Hogun, and Volstagg—on an attack against Jotunheim. Heimdall, the all-seeing guardian of the Bifrost gateway between the Nine Realms, allows them to pass, hoping to understand how the Frost Giants entered Asgard without him knowing. The Asgardian fighters end up provoking a new war with Frost Giant ruler Laufey before being rescued by an enraged Odin.

Laufey and Odin face each other after Thor's hot-headed assault on Jotunheim.

Spring 2010 | Jane Foster's Discovery

Thor lands on Earth in the desert outside Puente Antiguo, New Mexico, where astrophysicist Dr. Jane Foster, her mentor Dr. Erik Selvig, and intern Darcy Lewis are studying unusual auroras in the skies overhead. They accidentally strike Thor with their van, then Lewis uses her taser to incapacitate the seemingly disoriented man. Later, when they see his silhouette in imagery of the aurora, they realize he truly might be the otherworldly being he claims.

Dr. Jane Foster, Dr. Erik Selvig, and Darcy Lewis encounter a disoriented Thor, following his banishment from Asgard.

Spring 2010 | Howard's Hidden Message

While looking through old documents relating to his father and the elder Vanko, Stark finds a film reel from Howard in which he speaks directly to his son, lamenting about being "limited by the technology of my time." Later, he discovers that a scale model created for the 1974 Stark Expo is actually a hidden diagram of a theoretical element that could power a clean energy reactor. Stark retrofits his Malibu estate with a sprawling prismatic accelerator, balancing one part of it with a work-in-progress version of Captain America's shield from Howard's collection. Once activated, it successfully generates the safe new element that can replace the core that is poisoning him.

Stark and Rhodes have each other's backs as they face Vanko's Hammer drones.

Tony examines the model of the 1974 Stark Expo after watching a cryptic video message from his father.

Spring 2010 | The Fall of Vanko

Happy Hogan and Natasha Romanoff attempt to stop Vanko at Hammer's offices, but the Russian researcher escapes in his own new flying armor, outfitted with powerful new versions of his electrified whips. Romanoff reboots Rhodes' suit, allowing him to take control again, and Iron Man and War Machine join forces to bring down Vanko's drones. When Vanko entangles the pair in his whips, they defeat him by ricocheting their repulsor blasts against each other, creating a shockwave. A wounded Vanko dies when he self-destructs his suit.

Black Widow pursues Ivan Vanko as he remotely attacks the Expo.

Hammer drones, augmented by Ivan Vanko's Arc Reactors.

Spring 2010 | Stark and Potts Fall Hard

Stark saves Pepper Potts from the remaining drones just before they self-destruct. Potts remains frustrated by Stark's antics, but grateful for the rescue. She and Stark kiss, acknowledging for the first time that they have deeper feelings for each other. Over time, the relationship only grows. Hammer is arrested for his various crimes involving Vanko, while Senator Stern is required to bestow medals on Stark and Rhodes for averting the tragedy caused by the politician's previously favored weapons contractor.

Spring 2010 | The Expo Catastrophe

Justin Hammer prepares a presentation of his new drones at the Stark Expo, with James Rhodes' War Machine armor at the center. Although Hammer intends to show how humans and machines can work in tandem, the armors are hacked and overtaken by Ivan Vanko from afar. A recovered and newly empowered Tony Stark arrives to stop the onslaught and save the crowd of civilians, battling once more against Rhodey, who is trapped in his suit with no control this time.

81

2010

Betty Ross realizes Bruce Banner has returned after years on the run.

Spring 2010 | 17 Days Without Incident

Bruce Banner sneaks back across the border into the United States so he can return to Culver University in Virginia, where he and fellow scientist Betty Ross first did the research that inadvertently transformed him into the Hulk. The data has been purged from the computer system, but the next day he crosses paths with his ex-girlfriend, Ross herself. Bruce flees, but Betty follows him, resurrecting long-buried feelings in both of them. She urges him to turn himself in to her father, but Banner refuses, saying the general wants to dissect him to better understand and harness the Hulk. "He wants to make it a weapon," Banner says.

Spring 2010 | Loki's Power Play

Loki has deliberately created discord in a bid to claim Asgard's throne. First, he allowed the Frost Giants into Odin's treasure room to derail Thor's coronation, then he encouraged Thor to attack Jotunheim for revenge—creating the rift between father and first-born. With his brother gone, Loki confronts his father about his true origin, and Odin confesses that Loki was an abandoned Frost Giant baby he once took in the hope that raising him would bring unity to the two warring civilizations. Loki's rage causes the weakening Odin to collapse, and he then enters the coma-like Odinsleep, clearing the way for the God of Mischief to seize Asgard.

Loki examines the Casket of Ancient Winters, which triggers a reversion to his Frost Giant form.

Thor gains access to the S.H.I.E.L.D. camp surrounding Mjolnir, but his unworthiness prevents him from lifting the hammer.

Spring 2010 | The Discarded Hammer

Mjolnir lands not far from where Thor touched down, and curious locals gather to drink beer and pull on the immovable object with their trucks until S.H.I.E.L.D. arrives to secure the area. Agents Phil Coulson and Clint Barton (Hawkeye) are among the operatives sent to watch over the strange item as its energy signatures are studied. Thor infiltrates the S.H.I.E.L.D. perimeter to reclaim his weapon, but finds he cannot lift the hammer. He remains unworthy.

Spring 2010 | Loki's Lies

Loki travels to Earth to visit a despondent Thor, who remains in S.H.I.E.L.D. custody after his failed effort to retake Mjolnir. Loki deceives his brother into believing their father is dead—and Thor is to blame. "Your banishment, the threat of a new war, it was too much for him to bear," Loki explains. Then Loki travels to Jotunheim to strike a deal: he will return the Casket of Ancient Winters if Laufey will assassinate his slumbering father. Laufey accepts, but when the deed is about to be committed, Loki betrays him, killing the Frost Giant king just as he is poised to slay Odin. To the people of Asgard, the trickster has transformed himself into a savior.

Loki and his mother Frigga stand watch over Odin as he slumbers.

Emil Blonsky goes down an unfortunate path believing he is one of the good guys.

Spring 2010 | Emil Blonsky—Super Soldier

General Ross briefs Emil Blonsky on the experiment that transformed Banner, revealing that it was part of a revitalized effort from World War II to create enhanced human warriors. The notion intrigues Blonsky. "I'm a fighter," he says. "If I could take what I know now and put it in the body I had ten years ago, that would be someone I wouldn't want to fight." Ross informs him: "I could probably arrange something like that." With a willing subject, Ross takes some of the experimental Super Soldier Serum his team was developing and has it injected into the body of the Royal Marine.

Blonsky undergoes an experimental super soldier procedure.

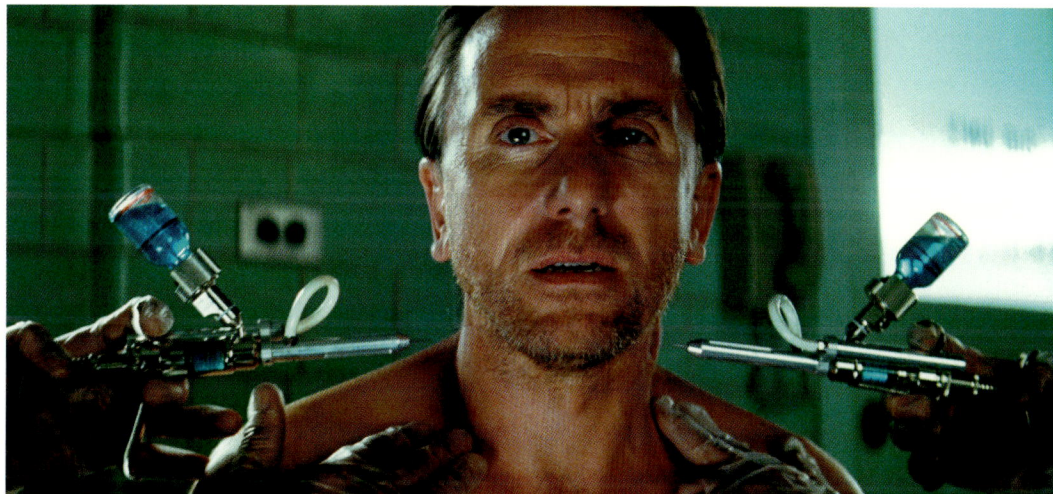

The Destroyer brings fire and destruction to Puente Antiguo, ripping through the town with white-hot blasts from its maw.

Spring 2010 | The Destroyer Arrives

Lady Sif and the Warriors Three come to Earth to warn Thor that Loki has taken over the kingdom. Thor is shocked to learn his brother lied, and that his father still lives. Loki uses the Casket of Ancient Winters to freeze Heimdall and seize control of the Bifrost, dispatching the Destroyer to Earth to eliminate his brother and all his allies.

Spring 2010 | Just a Man

On Earth, the Destroyer obliterates the forces of S.H.I.E.L.D., then begins to wipe out the town of Puente Antiguo in relentless pursuit of Thor. The Warriors Three and Lady Sif try to stop it, but are defeated by the automaton's heat beam. Thor helps evacuate local citizens, but ultimately faces down his attacker. "These people are innocent. Taking their lives will gain you nothing," Thor says. "So take mine. And end this." The furnace within the Destroyer emits a blast that leaves the mortal Thor gravely wounded.

Thor stands before the Destroyer as a mortal man, prepared to sacrifice himself to protect innocent bystanders.

ASGARD

Asgard, one of the Nine Realms, is the home of Thor and Loki. Ruled by Odin, before the event known as Ragnarok the gleaming kingdom stands as a beacon of peace. As Odin tells Thor, Asgard is its people. This proves true as the Asgardians show resilience again and again. It doesn't matter that Hela's short-lived reign leads to the destruction of their home, or that Thanos attacks their escape vessel, or that they must then endure the Blip—despite these tragic setbacks, the Asgardians persist. They adapt and rebuild, taking up residence on the coast of Norway with their new kingdom, smaller but not any less mighty.

2013 | Sacrifice

The Dark Elves invade Asgard in anticipation of the Convergence, a rare cosmic event, in order to retrieve their super weapon, a substance known as the Aether—in actuality the Reality Stone, one of the immeasurably powerful Infinity Stones. An enraged Odin uses his mighty spear to wipe out countless enemies, but cannot stop Malekith from killing Frigga, Thor and Loki's mother.

The Distant Past | A Violent History

Odin inherits the throne of Asgard from his father Bor, and then with his daughter Hela, they conquer realm after realm. But eventually Odin sees another way. He banishes Hela, expunges Asgard's violent history, and makes the realm one of peace.

2010 | Separation

When Odin decides to pass the throne to Thor, Loki stages a coup. In order to prevent Loki from destroying the realm of Jotunheim, Thor destroys the Bifrost, effectively cutting Asgard off from the other realms. With Asgard's peacekeepers bottled up on their homeworld, the Nine Realms fall into chaos.

84

2017 | Destruction of Asgard
Thor, Loki, Valkyrie, and Hulk attempt to stop Hela, but she is too powerful. With no other choice, Loki raises the fire demon Surtur to fight Hela, even though he knows unleashing Surtur will bring about Ragnarok and the destruction of Asgard.

2017 | A New Ruler
When Odin dies, Hela emerges from her prison. She returns to Asgard and swiftly conquers the realm. Thor and Loki are stranded across the universe and unable to help, so those Asgardians not wishing to live under her rule are forced to flee to a hidden stronghold in the mountains.

2018 | Survivors
Many Asgardians escaped aboard the *Statesman*. As they flee to Earth to rebuild, Thanos captures the ship to take the Tesseract from Loki. Thanos destroys the ship, but some Asgardians survive.

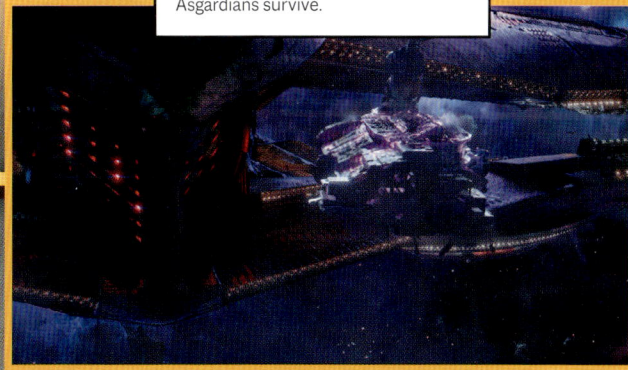

2018 | More Loss
With their population already whittled down after Hela's invasion and Thanos' attack on the *Statesman*, the surviving Asgardians face even more loss when Thanos performs the Snap.

2018-2023 | New Asgard
In the wake of the Snap, the surviving Asgardians and their allies move to Tønsberg in Norway, where Odin once fought the Frost Giants of Jotunheim, and Hydra leader the Red Skull found the Tesseract. Here they build the settlement of New Asgard while Thor grapples with his guilt and sorrow.

2023-2025 | Tourism and Diplomacy
In the wake of Thanos' defeat, Thor passes leadership of New Asgard to Valkyrie. King Valkyrie helps the city thrive, gaining diplomatic recognition, transforming the city into a tourism hub, and guiding New Asgard through attacks from Gorr, the God Butcher, who kidnaps the settlement's children.

2010

Thor gives Jane Foster a goodbye (for now) kiss.

Spring 2010 | Worthy

Thor's sacrifice activates the spell Odin placed on Mjolnir. Through humility, selflessness, and bravery, Thor has again become worthy. Mjolnir flies from its resting place and lands in Thor's hand, energizing and healing him. Thor uses Mjolnir to channel a whirlwind over the town, drawing the Destroyer into the vortex. Battering away the Destroyer's blasts, he forces the hammer into the facial vents of the machine until its energy backs up. The Destroyer ultimately destroys itself. Before returning to Asgard to confront Loki, Thor makes a pledge to Jane Foster: "I give you my word. I will return for you."

Spring 2010 | Destroying the Bifrost

To save Jotunheim, Thor uses Mjolnir to pulverize the bridge that channels the energy of Asgard into the Bifrost. But the bridge is his only pathway back to Earth—and Jane Foster. "If you destroy the bridge you'll never see her again," Loki warns him, but Thor continues shattering it until they both are falling into the void of space. Odin awakens in time to grasp his sons, but Loki lets go, plunging into a collapsing field of energy as it fades away.

Odin reaches for his sons as they dangle off the edge of the shattered Bifrost.

The mischief maker, multiplied.

Spring 2010 | Loki's Desperation

Heimdall breaks free from his icy imprisonment and opens the Bifrost so the Warriors Three, Lady Sif, and Thor can return to Asgard. In a thoughtless act of destruction, Loki reorients the Bifrost to channel all its energy at Jotunheim, which will build in intensity until it destroys that entire world. Loki says he is doing it "to prove to father I am a loyal son. When he awakens, I will be true heir to the throne." In a fight with Thor, Loki appears to hang from the edge of the bridge, but it's a mirage. He clones himself many times over, laughing at Thor's torment.

Spring 2010 | The University Clash

Bruce Banner is cornered by soldiers at Culver University after General Ross becomes aware of the fugitive's return. As he transforms, machine gun fire ricochets off him, and he hurls Humvees and rips out engines on the university grounds. Betty Ross stands before part of the convoy, begging her father to stop the attack. Emil Blonsky, newly energized with his super soldier injections, dashes onto the campus-turned-battlefield—and his bones are shattered when Hulk kicks him against a tree. After causing the fiery crash of a helicopter gunship while shielding Betty from its cannon fire, Hulk carries Betty away and escapes.

Hulk faces down Blonsky, whose super soldier abilities are still no match for the big green guy.

Spring 2010 | Recovery and Rendezvous

A weary Bruce Banner and Betty Ross lay low in the wilderness of the Great Smoky Mountains, then find a motel before journeying to New York City to meet Mr. Blue and bring him the data from their earlier research. His real name is Dr. Samuel Sterns, and he hopes to concoct an antidote that will rid Banner of the Hulk. S.H.I.E.L.D. personnel who are scanning internet traffic for keywords intercept the email, allowing General Ross to track them to the meet-up.

An exhausted Bruce Banner is comforted by Betty Ross in the wilderness.

Spring 2010 | The Hulk Suppressed

When Bruce Banner and Betty Ross finally meet Dr. Sterns in New York, Banner is disturbed to discover the blood sample he sent the researcher has been replicated thousands of times. Sterns hopes to use this gamma-infused DNA to develop cures for diseases, but Banner is troubled. After studying the data they sent, Sterns creates a dialysis treatment for Banner, but it's unclear if the Hulk has been erased completely or just blunted in this one instance. Banner finds himself unable to transform when a U.S. military sniper hits him with a tranquilizer shortly after the procedure, taking him and Betty into custody.

Blonsky's combination of Super Soldier Serum and Banner's blood creates ... Abomination.

Spring 2010 | Birth of a Monster

Although doctors describe the bones in Blonsky's body as "crushed gravel" after the Culver University battle, he makes a rapid recovery thanks to the super soldier treatment General Ross gave him. Craving even more power, Blonsky orders Dr. Sterns to infuse him with Banner's DNA. The doctor balks, warning of terrible side effects. "The mixture could be ... an abomination," says Sterns, who complies with the order. His fears are realized when Blonsky undergoes a metamorphosis into a spiky gargantuan who runs amok in the lab, throwing the scientist against his blood samples. Some of Banner's cloned blood drips into the cut on Sterns' head, causing the doctor's skull to enlarge.

2010-2011

Spring 2010 | The Harlem Brawl

Bruce Banner and Betty Ross are being flown away in a military helicopter with General Ross when they see the Abomination below, trashing the streets of Harlem. Banner leaps from the chopper, unsure if he can still become the Hulk. Only after striking the ground does the big, green guy emerge. The two goliaths rampage through the streets, with Hulk ripping a police cruiser in half and beating Abomination with the pieces. When their fight causes the helicopter carrying General Ross and Betty to crash, Hulk claps a shockwave that extinguishes the flames. Hulk beats the Abomination nearly to death, sparing his life only when Betty cries out for him to stop. Hulk roars at the sky and kicks the defeated Blonsky at the feet of a shamefaced General Ross.

The streets of Harlem are ripped to pieces as the two evenly matched titans grapple each other.

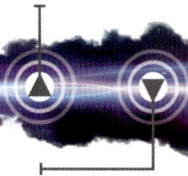

Summer 2010 | Hulk in Hiding

After the Harlem incident, the Hulk flees the United States, and Banner lives for a time in the Bella Coola Valley of British Columbia before eventually ending up half a world away in India. Betty Ross returns to her life at the University, with only one photo of Bruce to remember this time they spent together.

With the Bifrost destroyed, Asgard is cut off from the Nine Realms.

Spring 2010 | Thor at a Distance

At least temporarily, the doorway between the Nine Realms is closed after the destruction of the Bifrost. Thor mourns for his lost brother, despite Loki's betrayals, and tells his mother Frigga that he yearns to reunite with Jane Foster. Meanwhile, he and his father make amends. "You'll be a wise king," Odin says. "I have much to learn," Thor replies. Thor visits Heimdall, the now-gateless gatekeeper who can still turn his gaze to far-off worlds. Thor asks if he can see Foster, and Heimdall confirms he can: "She searches for you."

S.H.I.E.L.D. agents Sitwell and Coulson.

Summer 2010 | The Consultant

General Ross imprisons Blonsky, but the World Security Council wants him to be released, asking Nick Fury to recruit the monstrous being into the Avengers Initiative—they want Bruce Banner alone to be scapegoated for the destruction in Harlem. Unable to directly refuse the order, Fury and S.H.I.E.L.D. agents Jasper Sitwell and Phil Coulson devise an indirect solution. They send the newly minted S.H.I.E.L.D. "consultant" Tony Stark to make the ask of Ross—hoping Stark will irritate him so much that the general will refuse to release Blonsky. Stark fulfills their hopes, beginning the meeting by telling Ross he smells of "stale beer and defeat." The conversation devolves until Ross tries to have Stark thrown out of the bar. Request denied.

TVA ALERT!

Wowee! Y'all ever think about the impact of a single moment in time? The World Security Council wanted to make Emil Blonsky a public hero and Avenger, leaving the sole blame for Harlem's damage on the Hulk. Instead of a beloved Super Hero in the Battle of New York, Emil went to prison for 15 years! Just think... what if?

2011 | General Ross' Heart Attack

Gen. Thaddeus Ross suffers a severe heart attack during a golf outing. After 13 hours of surgery, he awakens from the triple bypass feeling a new sense of "perspective." His long military career may be at an end, but Ross will continue to play a major role in the halls of power, eventually serving as U.S. Secretary of State. In that role, Ross will doggedly apply his belief that individuals with enhanced powers are more of a risk than a reward.

His obsessive pursuit of the Hulk and the ensuing debacle with Abomination take a heavy toll on General Ross.

2011 | Captain America Recovered

Nearly seven decades after it disappeared during World War II, the wreckage of Hydra's *Valkyrie* is uncovered in the Arctic. Steve Rogers is miraculously alive, preserved in stasis by the cold and his super soldier enhancement. He is brought to New York and gradually revived, with S.H.I.E.L.D. creating a hospital room that replicates the 1940s to try and soften the blow. Rogers immediately detects the ruse—the baseball game being broadcast "live" on the radio was one he attended in 1941. He breaks loose and finds himself in present-day Times Square, thinking only of the lifetime that has passed, and the unfulfilled promise he made to return to Peggy Carter. "I had a date ..." Rogers tells Nick Fury.

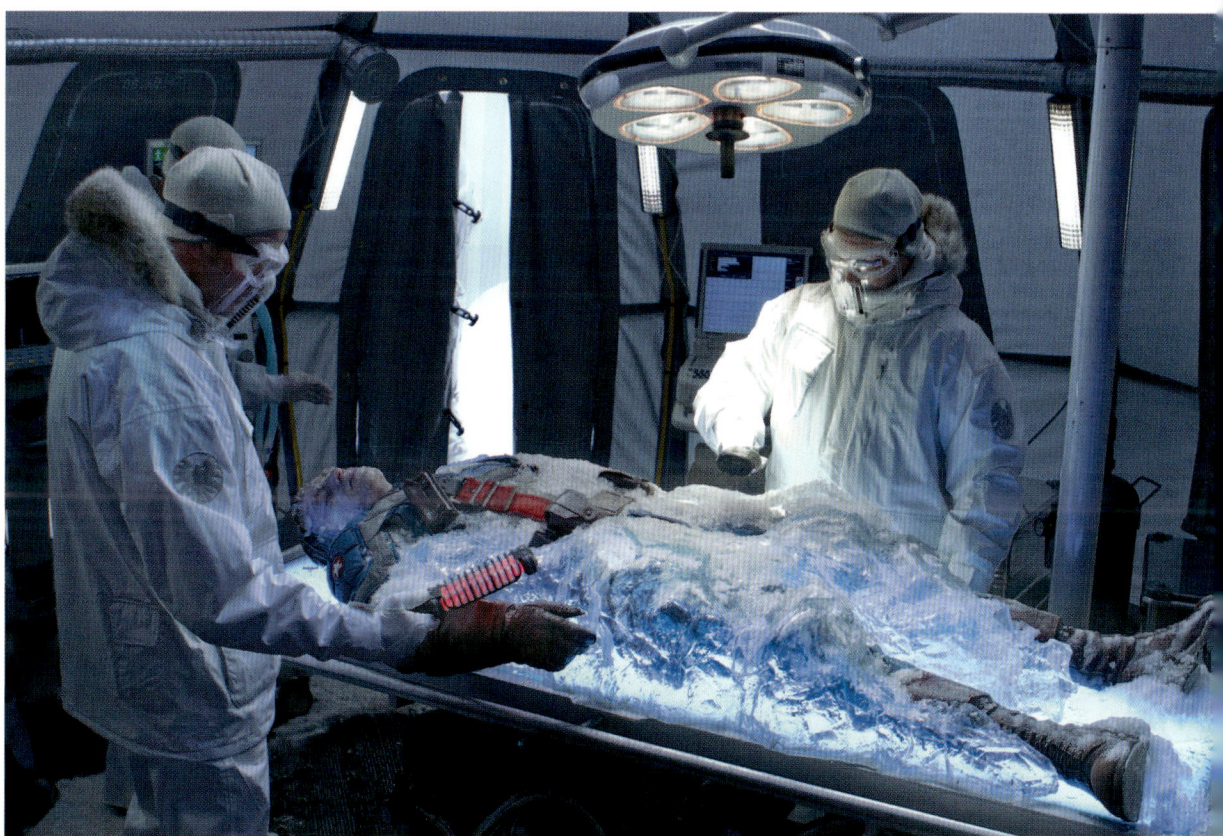

Steve Rogers, recovered from the Arctic ice after almost seven decades in suspended animation.

THE HULK

To be the Hulk is to embrace change. The mild-mannered Bruce Banner has gone on a journey of self-loathing, transformation, and acceptance since his body first absorbed high amounts of gamma radiation, giving him the ability (or curse) to transform into the Hulk. Over the years Bruce uses his exceptional scientific knowledge to bring the Hulk's brute strength together with his intelligence and patience, ultimately reconciling the best aspects of both his personalities to live a shared existence. By accepting the giant green side of himself, Bruce finds the inner peace that eluded him for so long.

Mid-2000s | Birth of the Hulk
Dr. Bruce Banner, a scientist working at Culver University, conducts experiments for U.S. General Thaddeus Ross as part of Project Gamma Pulse. Thinking that he has made a breakthrough in radiation resistance, Banner tests his discovery on himself and is transformed into a gigantic, almost invincible creature with immense strength (and anger issues).

2010 | Facing Abomination
After years on the run, trying to control his alter ego, Bruce begins to believe he can use the green giant's powers to make a difference. He focuses the Hulk's strength on stopping Emil Blonsky, a government operative who has been transformed into a monstrous creature known as Abomination. Hulk does eventually defeat the other giant, nearly killing him in a battle in Harlem, but at the cost of ravaged streets and putting his more monstrous qualities on full public display.

2012 | Becoming an Avenger
Believing the Hulk can be nothing more than a menace, Bruce hides out in India and uses his talents as a scientist to help others until Natasha Romanoff shows up with a missive from Nick Fury. Bruce, who is perpetually trying to make up for his violent other half, agrees to help S.H.I.E.L.D. locate the stolen Tesseract. That leads him to overcome his fear, willingly transform into Hulk, and become one of the Avengers. He plays a vital role in the Battle of New York by incapacitating Loki.

2015 | Hulk Unleashed
The difficulty controlling the Hulk transformation causes Bruce to fear his abilities, and when Wanda Maximoff uses her powers of mind control to force him to become Hulk in Johannesburg, his fears come true. Iron Man uses armor and tech he specially designed together with Bruce to stop the Hulk, but the battle leaves yet another city in ruins. The guilt and humiliation from the event leave a mark on Bruce's psyche, and transformed into Hulk, he leaves the Avengers, ending up on the planet Sakaar in a stolen Quinjet.

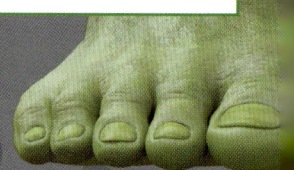

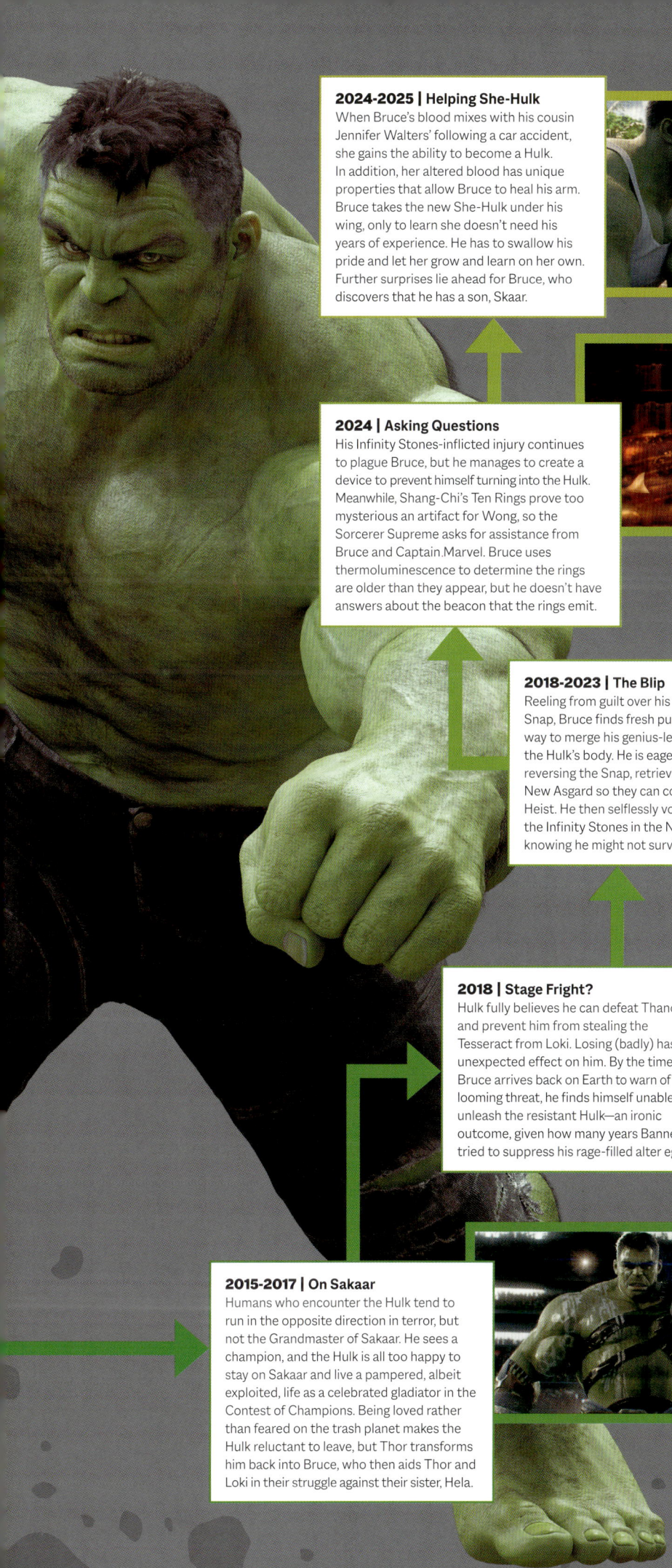

2024-2025 | Helping She-Hulk

When Bruce's blood mixes with his cousin Jennifer Walters' following a car accident, she gains the ability to become a Hulk. In addition, her altered blood has unique properties that allow Bruce to heal his arm. Bruce takes the new She-Hulk under his wing, only to learn she doesn't need his years of experience. He has to swallow his pride and let her grow and learn on her own. Further surprises lie ahead for Bruce, who discovers that he has a son, Skaar.

2024 | Asking Questions

His Infinity Stones-inflicted injury continues to plague Bruce, but he manages to create a device to prevent himself turning into the Hulk. Meanwhile, Shang-Chi's Ten Rings prove too mysterious an artifact for Wong, so the Sorcerer Supreme asks for assistance from Bruce and Captain Marvel. Bruce uses thermoluminescence to determine the rings are older than they appear, but he doesn't have answers about the beacon that the rings emit.

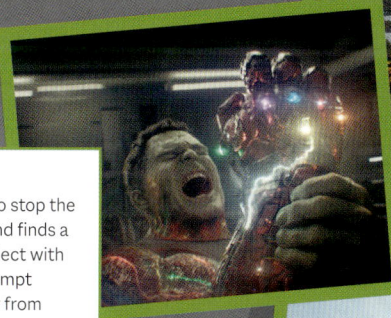

2018-2023 | The Blip

Reeling from guilt over his failure to stop the Snap, Bruce finds fresh purpose and finds a way to merge his genius-level intellect with the Hulk's body. He is eager to attempt reversing the Snap, retrieving Thor from New Asgard so they can conduct the Time Heist. He then selflessly volunteers to wield the Infinity Stones in the Nano Gauntlet, knowing he might not survive the attempt.

2018 | Stage Fright?

Hulk fully believes he can defeat Thanos and prevent him from stealing the Tesseract from Loki. Losing (badly) has an unexpected effect on him. By the time Bruce arrives back on Earth to warn of the looming threat, he finds himself unable to unleash the resistant Hulk—an ironic outcome, given how many years Banner tried to suppress his rage-filled alter ego.

2015-2017 | On Sakaar

Humans who encounter the Hulk tend to run in the opposite direction in terror, but not the Grandmaster of Sakaar. He sees a champion, and the Hulk is all too happy to stay on Sakaar and live a pampered, albeit exploited, life as a celebrated gladiator in the Contest of Champions. Being loved rather than feared on the trash planet makes the Hulk reluctant to leave, but Thor transforms him back into Bruce, who then aids Thor and Loki in their struggle against their sister, Hela.

2012

Power attracts power. The beings with enhanced abilities who now populate the world are naturally drawn to each other, and sometimes are pushed together by outside entities like S.H.I.E.L.D. As destructive forces unify from afar, so too must the defenders of Earth. The ensuing battles shake the world, opening humanity's eyes to a universe far larger than they once thought possible.

2010-2012 | Loki's Revenge

A banished Loki finds refuge with Thanos, who gives him the scepter containing the Mind Stone and sends him on a mission to seize the Tesseract. Loki will use the Tesseract to open a portal that will allow the Titan to invade and conquer Earth. All Thanos needs is for Loki to hook it up to a suitable power source on Earth. Meanwhile, due to his experience with Thor, Dr. Erik Selvig has been recruited by Nick Fury to join Project Pegasus, S.H.I.E.L.D.'s attempt to study the Tesseract. Fury, unaware that Selvig's mind has been infiltrated by Loki, tells him the cube could be a "gateway to another dimension."

Dr. Erik Selvig, working in the service of S.H.I.E.L.D ... and, unbeknownst to himself, the God of Mischief.

Spring 2012 | Opening a Gateway

Nick Fury is summoned to Project Pegasus after the Tesseract's energy starts spiking. Before they can evacuate the facility, the Tesseract triggers and opens a portal, through which Loki appears. Upon Loki's arrival, he immediately steals the cube and uses the scepter to fully possess the minds of both Dr. Selvig and S.H.I.E.L.D. agent Clint Barton. Loki's short-lived portal creates an energy vortex that builds in intensity until it completely destroys the Joint Dark Energy Mission facility.

"I am Loki, of Asgard. And I am burdened with glorious purpose."

Spring 2012 | Black Widow Finds the Hulk

Natasha Romanoff is pulled off a deep-cover mission in Russia in order to help S.H.I.E.L.D. recover the Tesseract and rescue Clint Barton. Her first task: recruiting Bruce Banner, whose knowledge of gamma radiation could help them understand the cube—and what Loki might be planning to do with it. S.H.I.E.L.D. has tracked Banner's movements without alerting General Ross, hoping to use the scientist (or the Hulk) in any global crisis that arises. Romanoff approaches Banner in India, where he is serving people as a doctor, and he reluctantly agrees to help since it's his intellect they need, not the monster he is trying to suppress.

Natasha Romanoff, Bruce Banner, and Nick Fury aboard the S.H.I.E.L.D. Helicarrier.

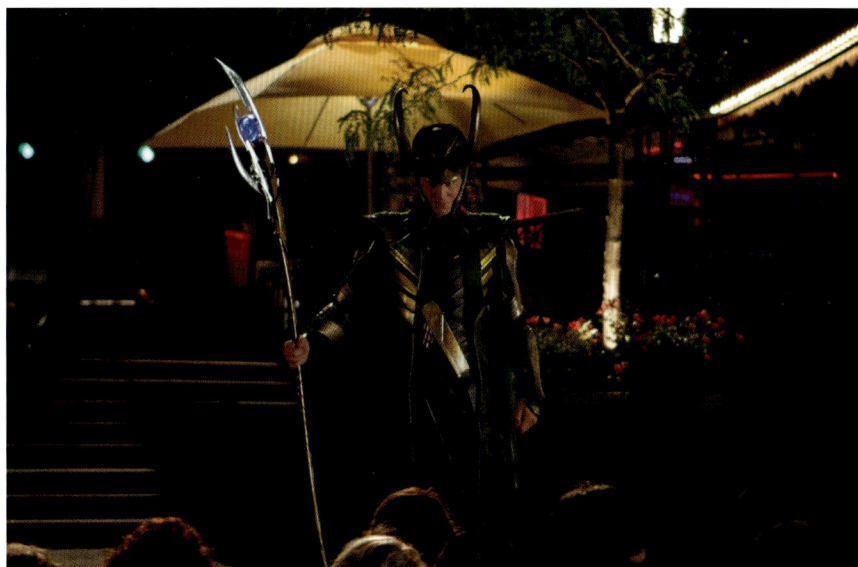

"It's the unspoken truth of humanity, that you crave subjugation."

Spring 2012 | Loki's Stuttgart Spectacle

To stabilize the Tesseract and reopen the portal, Loki needs iridium, one of the rarest minerals on Earth. Hawkeye finds a storage facility containing it, but needs the retinal scan of a particular scientist to gain access. Loki tracks the unlucky researcher to a black-tie event in Stuttgart, Germany, where he uses a device to painfully extract data from the man's eye and transmit it to Barton. Afterward, Loki lords over panicked onlookers, commanding them to kneel. When he attempts to obliterate a single old man who refuses, Captain America and Iron Man intervene to battle the trickster god into submission.

Spring 2012 | Hero Complex

Steve Rogers struggles to find a place and purpose in this new world. Given his history with the Tesseract, Nick Fury asks him to join a new squad he's assembling to recover the cube. Aboard the S.H.I.E.L.D. Helicarrier, Rogers meets Natasha Romanoff and Bruce Banner. It's an uneasy pairing—something that will become increasingly common within the Avengers Initiative. Tony Stark, who was earlier deemed to be a poor fit for the program, is also asked to help. No one is certain these individuals can unite as a functioning team, but times are desperate…

Captain America's first encounter with Thor.

Nick Fury asks Steve Rogers to help recover the Tesseract.

REDLINE ALERT!
Hi folks! Were y'all thrown when Thor said he first came to Earth recently? Just remember, Selvig notes that Thor's mythology dates back centuries and the Eternal Kingo says a young Thor used to follow him around. Thor was simply sayin' it was the first time coming to Earth in his current adventures! Not worth putting Analysts on this one!

Spring 2012 | Thor Returns to Earth

While a captive Loki is being transported in the Quinjet, a lightning storm starts around the aircraft and Thor arrives to forcibly apprehend his troublesome brother. On the ground, Thor is both relieved to find Loki alive, and angry that he has returned to his destructive tendencies. Iron Man and Cap confront the Asgardians in the middle of their family feud, which Stark derisively refers to as "Shakespeare in the park," and Thor battles them to a draw. An unstoppable force (Thor's hammer) collides with an immovable object (Cap's shield) creating a shockwave that shatters a clearing in the forest. Thor agrees to let them keep Loki until the Tesseract can be reclaimed. The God of Thunder has now joined the Avengers.

2012

Loki, detained in a chamber designed to hold the Hulk.

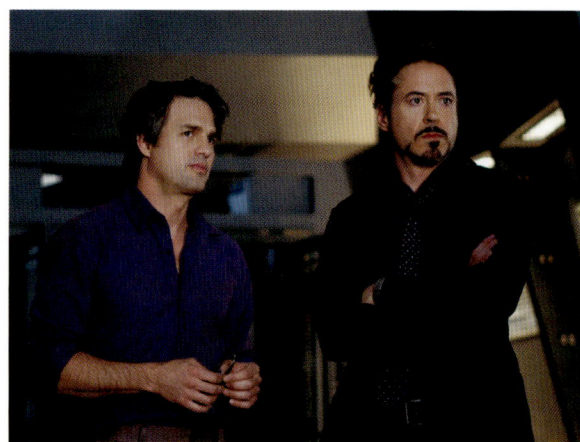

Banner and Stark respect each other's abilities as scientists and engineers.

Spring 2012 | Regrouping

Loki is detained on the S.H.I.E.L.D. Helicarrier in a chamber designed for the Hulk. Tony Stark strikes up a quick friendship with Bruce Banner. "I'm a huge fan of the way you lose control and turn into an enormous green rage-monster," Stark says. Rogers and Stark chafe instantly, however. ("That's the guy my dad never shut up about?" Stark cracks.) Banner and Stark are skeptical of S.H.I.E.L.D.'s motives, but Steve Rogers is a true believer until they learn that S.H.I.E.L.D. intends to use the Tesseract to devise new and deadly weaponry, reverse engineering Hydra's tech from WWII. The weapons program was started in response to the destruction that Thor brought to New Mexico in 2010. The only one happy about the way the team is going is Agent Phil Coulson—who also hopes to get his vintage Captain America cards autographed.

Phil Coulson engages in some hero worship.

Steve Rogers and Tony Stark are far from fast friends.

A rampaging Hulk destroys a jet accompanying the S.H.I.E.L.D. Helicarrier.

Spring 2012 | Loki Sows Discord

Bruce Banner and Tony Stark are studying the scepter while Natasha Romanoff interrogates Loki, discovering he allowed himself to be captured in order to trigger the Hulk and destabilize the team. Tensions between the Avengers have become unbearable, with arguments and mistrust growing between them. The still-mesmerized Hawkeye flies up to the Helicarrier aboard a stolen Quinjet and blows up one of the engines, crippling the massive aircraft. The Hulk erupts from within Banner, causing even greater internal damage as Captain America and Tony Stark try to stabilize the damaged turbine. Hulk leaps from the Helicarrier to attack a jet, and plummets to the ground.

Spring 2012 | The Death of Phil Coulson

Loki escapes from his holding chamber when his minions board the Helicarrier. Natasha Romanoff battles the mind-controlled Clint Barton, hoping to snap her old friend out of his spell, and Agent Coulson confronts Loki with one of S.H.I.E.L.D.'s prototype weapons. Loki distracts him with an illusion and spears him through the chest with his scepter. "You're going to lose," a dying Coulson says. "It's in your nature … You lack conviction." After Loki's escape, Nick Fury uses Coulson's death (and the hero trading cards he doctored with blood) to inspire that sense of conviction in his perpetually clashing Avengers.

Phil Coulson's sacrifice is a defining moment for the Avengers.

Spring 2012 | Selvig Opens a Bigger Gateway

The still-mesmerized Erik Selvig continues his work activating the Tesseract to bring the Chitauri invasion to Earth. In need of a massive power source, he attaches his device to the top of Stark Tower in the heart of New York City, drawing on its newly installed energy reactor. Tony Stark finds Loki in his penthouse, brimming with hubris. "What have I to fear?" Loki says. Stark tells him about the Avengers: "That's what we call ourselves. Earth's mightiest heroes type of thing." Loki hurls him from the skyscraper, and JARVIS deploys the self-assembling Iron Man Mark VII armor that attaches to Stark just before he hits the ground. The Battle of New York begins…

Erik Selvig activates his Tesseract device atop Stark Tower.

The Space Stone opens a doorway for the Chitauri fleet to invade from deep space.

The Avengers assess the alien attackers.

Spring 2012 | Devastation from Above

Chitauri warriors race through the portal above Manhattan's skyline. They rampage through the corridors of buildings as Chitauri Leviathans swim through the sky, dropping more alien fighters to the ground. As the devastation grows, the Avengers gather back-to-back to hold off the invasion. Meanwhile, the World Security Council panics, ordering a nuclear strike on New York to close the gateway and stop the otherworldly onslaught before it spreads.

An armored Leviathan pursues Iron Man.

Chitauri soldiers on the streets of New York.

Chitauri vessels ride over the skyline.

2012

Spring 2012 | The Victims

Despite being outnumbered, the Avengers successfully save countless lives. Only 74 civilian casualties result from the attack on New York, out of hundreds of thousands at risk. One of the deaths is Derek Bishop, who just prior to the attack assures his young daughter, Kate, he will always keep her safe. Soon after, Derek dies when the Chitauri invaders rip through their building. Through the gaping hole in their apartment, little Kate sees Hawkeye fighting valiantly against the attackers. He becomes her new personal hero.

A nuclear missile streaks toward New York to destroy the alien threat—and everything else in the city.

A young Kate Bishop looks out through the ruins of her family's highrise apartment.

Spring 2012 | The Nuclear Strike

Iron Man intercepts the nuclear missile aimed at closing the portal and steers it up into the gateway, even though Captain America warns him over their comms channel that it could be "a one-way trip." All the S.H.I.E.L.D. studies that determined Tony Stark was too narcissistic to be a team player are proven wrong as he guides the missile through the portal and hurls it at the Chitauri mothership, creating a deep-space detonation that fells the remainder of the alien army. An incapacitated Stark tumbles backward through the portal, which closes just as the blast radius reaches it.

Spring 2012 | Loki Pulverized

One of Hawkeye's arrows destroys Loki's own chariot, sending him crashing back into Stark Tower where the Hulk pounces. "I am a god, you dull creature," Loki snarls at him. "And I will not be bullied by—" His words are cut short when Hulk grabs him by the ankles and slams him back and forth against the ground repeatedly. Loki survives, but can make only a mewling sound as the Hulk looms over him, grumbling: "Puny god." Although the portal remains open, the leader of the invasion has been sidelined.

Captain America, in the midst of the battle.

Spring 2012 | The Avengers Vindicated

Hulk grabs Iron Man as he falls, softening the hit, but Tony Stark is still shaken from his near-death encounter. He covers up with his signature wisecracks, encouraging the team to gather at a nearby shawarma restaurant after taking Loki into custody. In the aftermath of the attack, the Tesseract is given back to Thor for safekeeping on Asgard, and Loki is sent to that realm for imprisonment. Bruce Banner and Stark continue their new partnership, while Clint Barton, Steve Rogers, and Natasha Romanoff continue their work with S.H.I.E.L.D. Fury's plan to unite them was proven wise, and he rejects the World Security Council's concerns about the Avengers, and about the return of Loki and the Tesseract to Asgard.

Spring 2012 | Item 47

Desperate for cash, the hard-luck couple Benny Pollack and Claire Weiss hack into a Chitauri weapon left behind during the invasion and use it to go on a cross-country bank robbing spree. This attracts the attention of S.H.I.E.L.D. Agent Sitwell who is assigned to retrieve the weapon and "neutralize" the outlaws. After detaining them, he reveals that there were 47 pieces of alien tech recovered by the government, but all of the rest fell dormant. He chooses to bring the would-be Bonnie and Clyde into S.H.I.E.L.D. to help reverse engineer their discovery.

Ann Marie Hoag delivers bad news to contractor Adrian Toomes.

Spring 2012 | A Scavenger Rebuked

Back in New York, the salvage contractor Adrian Toomes leads his crew in removing the wreckage and rubble from the Chitauri invasion. He is abruptly forced aside by Ann Marie Hoag, the director of the new U.S. Department of Damage Control. Toomes decides to illegally keep some of the scrap he has collected, harvesting the alien tech and devising new weapons for sale. Once a legitimate businessman, Toomes becomes embittered. With a wife and daughter to support, he feels he has no choice but to bend the law, eventually becoming an arms dealer for the criminal underworld.

Spring 2012 | Thanos Changes Course

The Thanos minion known as the Other delivers news of Loki's failure. Not only was the invasion stymied, but the Tesseract and scepter are now lost—removing two Infinity Stones from the Titan's grasp. "Humans are not the cowering wretches we were promised," the Other says. "They are unruly, and therefore cannot be ruled. To challenge them is to court death." Thanos just smiles.

The Chitauri weapon at the center of the crime spree.

Odin scolds his wayward son.

2012 | Consequences of Power

Loki is sentenced to spend the remainder of his long life in Asgard's dungeon for his various crimes and conspiracies. He is spared from execution only by the intercession of his mother, Frigga, but he remains defiant. "Do you not truly feel the gravity of your crimes?" Odin asks. "Wherever you go, there is war, ruin, and death." Loki points out that he is not so different from all who wield great strength. "I went to Midgard to rule the people of Earth as a benevolent god," he tells his father. "Just like you."

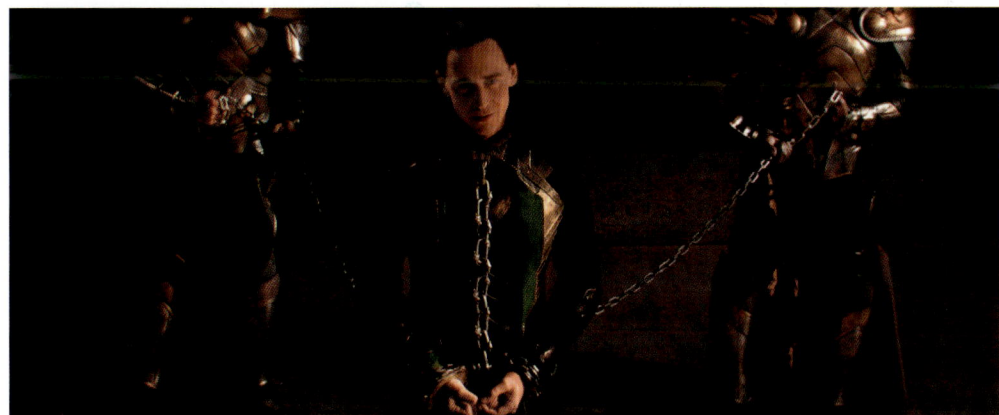

Loki to Odin: "It's not that I don't love our little talks, it's just … I don't love them."

Opening the Portal

Under the control of Loki's scepter and the Mind Stone within it, Dr. Erik Selvig crafts a Tesseract-powered device that will open and sustain a large portal to space, admitting the Chitauri army. The device is protected by a seemingly impenetrable shield, and Iron Man's attempts to destroy it are unfruitful.

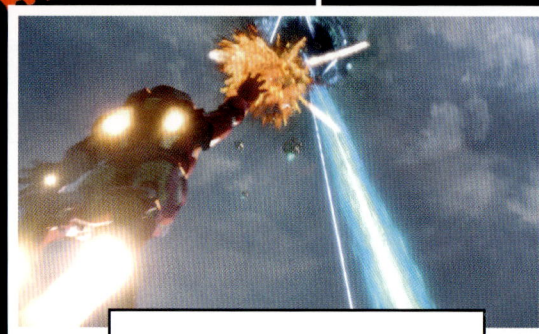

Arrival of the Chitauri

After trying to threaten Loki and failing, Tony Stark dons a new Iron Man armor just in time to watch the first Chitauri vessels come through the portal to Earth. He lands the first shots against the enemy but quickly becomes overwhelmed by their numbers.

THE BATTLE OF NEW YORK

The pivotal event that brings the Avengers together for the first time devastates New York City and leaves lingering marks on all those involved in the battle. It also marks the dawn of a new era for humanity, who are now aware that they are not alone in the universe. Empowered by Thanos and believing Earth deserves a new ruler, Loki attacks the city using Chitauri warriors from Thanos' army. While he seemingly plans the attack carefully, he does not anticipate that the Avengers will stand united, despite his attempts to divide them. The talented individuals selected by S.H.I.E.L.D. Director Nick Fury in hopes that they would one day defend the Earth from an alien threat, prove themselves up to the task.

Inspiring Future Generations

The battle inspires one witness to become a Super Hero. When an exploding arrow stops a Chitauri craft from crashing into her home, a young Kate Bishop sees it was Hawkeye who saved her and watches him loosing arrows from a nearby rooftop and fighting the enemy. Sadly, her father is among the victims of the Chitauri. A moment of tragedy becomes the inspiration that sets her life on a new path.

A Nuclear Ejection

As the Battle of New York unfolds, the panicking World Security Council decide to drop a nuclear device on Manhattan to stop the Chitauri. Iron Man intercepts the missile and asks Black Widow to hold the portal open long enough for him to fly the weapon into space, where the bomb destroys the Chitauri flagship. Cut off from their hive mind, the Chitauri in New York instantly fall dead. Iron Man escapes back through the portal with seconds to spare, but is left mentally scarred by the experience.

Closing the Portal

Knowing they need to close the portal, Natasha goes to the device atop Stark Tower and learns how to shut it down from Dr. Selvig, who has been freed from Loki's control. She uses Loki's scepter to penetrate the shield and break the device's connection to the Tesseract.

Reinforcements Arrive

After commandeering a Quinjet, Black Widow, Hawkeye, and Captain America enter the fray. Just as Iron Man drives the Chitauri towards the Quinjet, Loki targets the ship and eliminates one of its engines. The craft crash-lands and the trio of heroes then continue the battle from the ground.

Soldiers from Space

As the first alien creatures to attack Earth en masse, the Chitauri have an immediate advantage simply by shocking the planet with their existence. The vast army's vicious troops turn their advanced energy particle weapons on New York City's innocent civilians.

Leviathans Over New York

When the first Chitauri Leviathan comes through the portal, the heroes stare at the enormous beast in awe as it flies over New York. Chitauri soldiers leap from the creature onto surrounding buildings. But it is not invincible. When Bruce Banner transforms into the Hulk, he stops the Leviathan with a single punch.

Becoming the Avengers

Standing together for the first time as the Avengers, the heroes brace for the reinforcements Loki summons through the portal. Captain America takes the lead and formulates a defense plan that leverages every hero's unique abilities, culminating in telling Hulk to "smash."

Hulk Smashes

Unleashed by Bruce Banner's ever-present rage, the Hulk crushes the Chitauri soldiers. He barrels into buildings and enemy vessels with angry, imprecise abandon. Hulk then teams up with Thor before stopping Loki in his tracks by giving the "puny god" a clobbering for the ages.

Calling the Shots

From his perch above the streets, Hawkeye calls out the enemy's positions to the group, noting weaknesses and places where civilians are in imminent danger. All the while Hawkeye continually fires at the Chitauri, picking them off with his trick arrows.

2013

The past intrudes on the present. Old wars, old enemies, and old grudges resurface to confront the powerful. From Asgard as well as Earth, unsettled conflicts and long-remembered slights re-emerge to create new crises.

Thor and Lady Sif battle marauders on Vanaheim.

Fall 2013 | Peace for the Nine Realms

After the destruction of the Bifrost, Asgard was largely cut off from the rest of the Nine Realms of Yggdrasil, leading to outbreaks of anarchy. Now that the connection has been restored, peace must be as well. Thor joins Lady Sif and the Warriors Three in leading the forces of Asgard against the warlords and marauders. The conflict culminates in a final battle on Vanaheim that ends the uprisings just as the 5,000-year Convergence of the Nine Realms is about to begin.

Thor faces a mighty Kronan warrior, but easily smashes him into gravel with Mjolnir.

Fall 2013 | Jane Foster Infected

The gravitational anomalies that precede the Convergence begin to appear on Earth. Dr. Jane Foster and her research assistant Darcy Lewis discover a London warehouse full of invisible portals and areas of "lightness" that allow shipping containers and cement mixers to be easily lifted and stacked like blocks. Foster is drawn into one wormhole that deposits her at the obelisk where Odin's father, Bor, concealed the Aether—the Reality Stone, which the Dark Elves once harnessed as a weapon. The Aether escapes by seeping into Foster's body, but its immense power causes havoc within her mortal form.

Dr. Jane Foster stumbles into the ancient hiding place of the Aether.

100

Thor returns to Dr. Jane Foster of Midgard.

Fall 2013 | Treatment on Asgard

Thor travels to Earth when Heimdall tells him he has lost sight of Jane Foster. The God of Thunder finds her bursting with energy from the Aether and transports her to Asgard in the hope of saving her life. Although she remains conscious, her prognosis is dire: Unless the Aether is removed, it will kill her—and it is violently defending itself from all efforts to extract it.

Fall 2013 | The Death of Frigga

During the jailbreak, an embittered Loki advises Kurse about how to escape to Asgard's upper levels. This inadvertently sends the attackers toward his mother Frigga, who protects Jane Foster as the Dark Elves attempt to reclaim the Aether contained within her. Frigga puts up a formidable defense, but is seized by Kurse and murdered when she refuses to turn over Foster. Thor arrives just as Malekith escapes. All of Asgard mourns the fallen queen, including the imprisoned son whose thoughtless act contributed to her death.

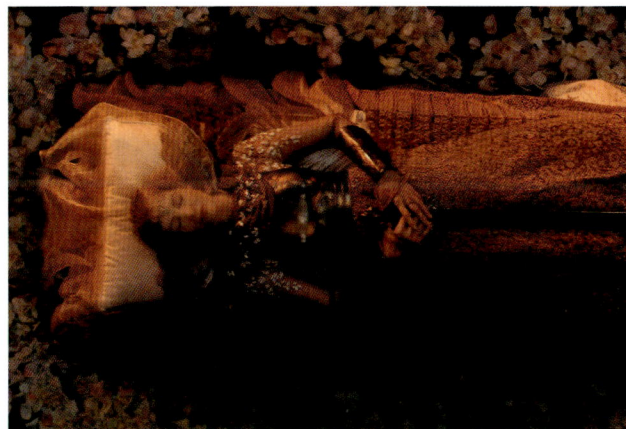

The funeral of Asgard's queen. Frigga's funeral boat sails off the edge of Asgard and vanishes into star dust.

Fall 2013 | Malekith's Return

The Aether awakens Malekith and his Dark Elves from their millennia of hibernation. The coming Convergence presents another chance to restore darkness to the realms of Yggdrasil, so Malekith devises a new plan. He dispatches his loyal servant Algrim to be arrested by the Asgardian forces. Once inside their dungeon, Algrim activates one of the Dark Elves' Kurse Stones, which causes him to metamorphose into an unstoppable behemoth. While the reborn Kurse frees prisoners to ransack the kingdom from within, Malekith's reaper-like starships converge in a sneak attack overhead.

Malekith, ruler of the Dark Elves.

Heimdall sees the Dark Elf invasion too late.

101

2013

Fall 2013 | Escape from Asgard

A widowed Odin tightens his grip on the Nine Realms, imprisoning the ailing Jane Foster to safeguard the Aether, even though it is killing her. Determined to save her life, Thor turns to an unlikely ally—his brother, Loki, who knows secret routes out of Asgard. With his help, Thor and Jane flee Odin's forces and escape through a portal hidden deep within one of the realm's mountains. It deposits them on The Dark World, the homeworld of the Dark Elves, where they are surrounded by Malekith's forces.

"You still don't trust me, brother?"

Thor steals Loki from the dungeon to help find a path out of Asgard.

Fall 2013 | Another Ruse

As Kurse pulverizes Thor in the dunes of The Dark World, Loki attacks and kills the monstrous Dark Elf, but appears to be stabbed through the chest during the fight. Thor promises to tell their father of his sacrifice, but with what seem to be his dying words, Loki insists he didn't do it for Odin's approval. Jane and Thor leave him behind, finding another portal leading from The Dark World to Earth. Later, Loki returns to Asgard, where he enchants his father, hiding him away in a home for the elderly back on Earth. Disguised as Odin, Loki once again takes the throne of Asgard.

Fall 2013 | The Scheme to Save Jane Foster

The Dark Elves watch as Loki turns against his brother, stabbing him in the stomach and slicing off his hand as he summons Mjolnir. Loki offers Jane Foster to Malekith as a "gift," saying he shares the Dark Elf's desire to see Asgard destroyed. But it's all a manipulation. Malekith possesses the unique ability to extract the Aether from Foster, and once he draws it from her body into his, her wellbeing is assured. That's when Thor reveals his amputation was an illusion projected by Loki. He uses his hammer to electrify the Aether, but it cannot be destroyed. Foster's life was saved, but the reality-bending Aether is now in the possession of the enemy.

Malekith uses his powers to remove the Aether from Jane Foster's body.

Fall 2013 | The Greenwich Conflict

Thor and Jane Foster track the nine open wormholes to an area above the Old Royal Naval College in Greenwich, southeast London, where Malekith attempts to use the Aether to return the Nine Realms (and beyond) to a state of eternal darkness. The God of Thunder confronts the Dark Elf ruler, and they clash with each other while tumbling through the aligned worlds.

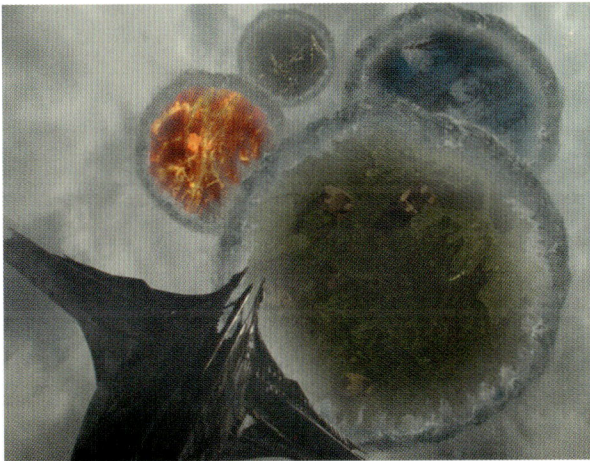
The Convergence aligns portals to the Nine Realms.

Malekith's Ark rips into Greenwich, London.

Fall 2013 | Thor's Choices

After saving the Nine Realms, Thor realizes he can better serve these worlds as a defender than as a ruler. Though Odin offers him the throne of Asgard, Thor tells his father that he wants him to remain ruler (unaware that he is actually talking to a disguised Loki). The decision allows Thor to return regularly to Earth, where he and Jane Foster rekindle their relationship.

"You needn't have come so far, Asgardian. Death would've come to you soon enough."

Fall 2013 | Malekith's Defeat

Thor ends Malekith's onslaught by spearing him with one of Dr. Erik Selvig's gravimetric spikes, allowing Jane Foster to teleport the Dark Elf back to The Dark World, where he is crushed by his own falling battleship. The Aether is then offered to the Collector, Taneleer Tivan, a wealthy curator from the mining world of Knowhere, who maintains one of the most secure vaults in the galaxy. Keeping the Aether on Asgard was not an option, since Odin's trophy room already contains the Tesseract, and having Infinity Stones in proximity to each other is considered too dangerous.

Thor tells "Odin" that he would rather be a good man than a great king.

2010 | Arrival on Earth
The arrival of Frost Giants on Asgard disrupts Thor's plans for the future and his beliefs about the universe. Headstrong and quick-tempered, Thor chooses decisive retribution, his fatal flaw, resulting in banishment to Earth and the temporary loss of his powers. Aided by Dr. Jane Foster, Thor learns humility and regains his hammer and his abilities.

The Distant Past | Destined to Rule
Odin and Frigga raised Thor as a warrior, just like his father. He never questioned that he would follow in his father's footsteps, which meant he was confident, perhaps overly so, all his life.

2013 | Rejecting Ruling
The Avengers and Jane Foster connect Thor to Earth, while his family and history tie him to Asgard. Thor tries to keep a foot in each world but he can no longer do so after stopping Malekith's invasion of the Nine Realms. A changed man, he chooses Earth.

2012 | Brother Knows Best
Thor returns to Earth to help stop Loki's planned invasion. No one knows his brother and his many tricks better than Thor. Feeling responsible for Loki turning his attention to Earth, Thor stands with the Avengers in the Battle of New York.

2015 | Power of Creation
Thor respects humans and lives among them, but the God of Thunder does not appreciate when they meddle with alien technology they don't understand. He scolds Tony Stark for creating Ultron, while later using his lightning to help make Vision.

THOR AND LOKI

Brothers and Asgardian princes, Thor and Loki grow up together with their parents, Odin and Frigga. While Thor pursues honor and glory for Asgard, Loki favors mischief and magic. They are as likely to support one another as they are to tear each other down, but when a moment truly matters, the brothers often find a way to unite—especially over matters involving the protection of their home, Asgard. Even with their extreme differences, neither Thor or Loki could accomplish their goals and growth without each other.

2012 | Claiming Midgard
Loki believed himself to be the rightful king of Asgard. Fresh from being defeated by Thor, Loki channeled his anger into a pact with Thanos. If he can't have Asgard, he will make Midgard bend the knee.

The Distant Past | In Thor's Shadow
Odin found Loki as a Frost Giant infant abandoned on Jotunheim and raised him alongside Thor. He grew up envious that Thor would be king one day and did everything possible to impress his father.

2013 | Shape-shifter Supreme
Bitterness festers within Loki during his imprisonment on Asgard after the Battle of New York. When Malekith the Dark Elf invades Asgard, Loki's actions inadvertently lead to the death of Frigga. Though crushed by guilt, he elevates his craftiness to new heights with layers of deceit, faking his death and replacing Odin as ruler.

2010 | Frost Giant Lineage
A supreme holder of grudges, Loki concocts an elaborate plan to keep Thor off the throne of Asgard. That leads to the discovery of his heritage as a son of the Frost Giant Laufey. It makes him question everything, and after a failed attempt at usurping the throne, he abandons Asgard.

2015-2017 | The Legend of Thor and Jane

For a time, Thor and Jane Foster have a happy relationship, and in the aftermath of a particularly joyful costume party, Thor fatefully asks Mjolnir to always protect her. Though Thor and Jane finally break up in 2017, years later the hammer will keep its promise.

2017 | The Fall of Asgard

Losing his father, discovering the existence of a hell-bent sister, losing Mjolnir, being forced to fight Hulk on Sakaar, then watching Asgard fall—it is a lot for Thor to process. Ragnarok, the long-prophesied destruction of his home, makes Thor question whether he is worthy of Asgard.

2018 | Grieving Loki

Saying goodbye to Loki breaks Thor's heart. After a brush with death, vengeance drives the God of Thunder to forge a weapon to replace Mjolnir. With Stormbreaker, he unleashes his fury against Thanos' army in the battle in Wakanda.

2018-2023 | A Third Chance

Like many Avengers, guilt burdens Thor after the Snap. He exacts revenge on Thanos, but it does not fix his inner turmoil. Thor sinks into a deep depression but rallies to stop Thanos once and for all in the Battle of Earth.

2023-2025 | Renewed Purpose

Thor leaves New Asgard and spends years soul-searching in the cosmos alongside the Guardians of the Galaxy. He devotes himself to building both his mind and body.

2025 | Endings and Beginnings

Thor continues to grapple with his place in the universe as he defends New Asgard against Gorr the God Butcher, alongside Valkyrie and Jane Foster's Mjolnir-empowered Mighty Thor. He finally says goodbye to Jane as her essence departs the mortal realm, but finds new hope with Gorr's young daughter, whom he adopts.

2017 | Survival Instincts

Odin's death and Hela's rage land Loki on Sakaar. Ever the charismatic force, he befriends the planet's ruler, the Grandmaster. He is content to stay on the planet in order not to face Hela's wrath again. With great reluctance and after multiple betrayals, he helps Thor fight Hela on Asgard.

2018 | Defiant End

Wielding his talents for false flattery and trickery, Loki tries to gain the upper hand when fighting Thanos aboard the *Statesman*. He shows his true heart by saving Thor from harm and risking himself to stop the Titan, a move that costs Loki his life. He remains defiant until the end.

2012 BRANCH | A New (Old) Loki

The variant Loki of 2012 doesn't know anything of his future, so when the Time Heist gives him the chance to reclaim the Tesseract, he takes advantage of it and uses a portal to escape. He is immediately captured by the Time Variance Authority, who then prune the branched reality his time hijinks have created. It marks a return to a more selfish, power-hungry Loki.

END OF TIME | TVA Discoveries

While in TVA captivity, Loki reviews his own past and future, making the God of Mischief reflect on his choices and their consequences. Thanks to the TVA and his many variants, Loki learns more about himself than ever before. In the Citadel at the End of Time, Loki faces "He Who Remains," and then witnesses the Multiverse collapse into chaos.

2013

"The Mandarin," a fake warlord devised by Aldrich Killian and modeled on the legend of Wenwu—as played by Trevor Slattery.

Winter 2013 | The Mandarin Steps Forth

An explosion at a church on the United States' Ali Al Salem Air Base in Kuwait kills the spouses and children of military personnel out on maneuvers. It was an accident, caused by the volatility of another of Aldrich Killian's Extremis test subjects, but to hide his project from scrutiny, he has a fictitious terrorist persona—the Mandarin—claim credit for the attack. Actor Trevor Slattery, plied with drugs and luxuries, plays the role with oblivious dedication. The world comes to fear the ominous and mysterious figure, and the U.S. government responds by rebranding Lt. Col. James Rhodes as the Iron Patriot.

Winter 2013 | Tony Stark in Crisis

Traumatized by his near-death experience during the Battle of New York, Tony Stark has spent the past year obsessively building variations on his Iron Man armors. He is currently on Mark XLII—a new suit that can fly to him from a great distance, assembling around his body one segment at a time. He has never been so well-armored—or so personally vulnerable.

Tony Stark stores his earlier armor designs beneath his Malibu mansion.

December 22, 2013 | The Chinese Theatre Explosion

Aldrich Killian, still harboring a grudge over Stark's dismissal of him 13 years ago, tries unsuccessfully to convince Pepper Potts to align Stark Industries with his Extremis project. A suspicious Happy Hogan follows Killian's right-hand man, Savin, to the Chinese Theatre in Hollywood. There, Savin meets with one of the ailing Extremis test subjects, who loses control of the fiery substance within him and detonates. Among the injured is Hogan, who falls into a coma, unable to share what he witnessed, but before he passes out he leaves a clue for Stark: he points at the dead test subject's charred dog tags.

Happy Hogan confronts Eric Savin, an Extremis test subject and mercenary for Aldrich Killian.

The Mandarin bombings become personal for Stark after Happy Hogan is injured in an explosion.

December 23, 2013 | Stark's Dare

Infuriated by the bombing that nearly killed his friend, Stark publicly taunts the Mandarin to come after him. JARVIS helps Stark uncover a 3,000-degree heat signature from a suspected suicide bombing in Rose Hill, Tennessee, a year ago that predates the Mandarin's emergence. Still, it matches the intense temperature of the Chinese Theatre attack. Stark programs his Mark XLII armor to fly him to the location and is preparing for the trip when a visitor arrives: Maya Hansen, DNA coder overseeing the Extremis project for Killian's Advanced Idea Mechanics think tank. She intends to inform Stark and Pepper Potts that her boss, Aldrich Killian, may be working with the Mandarin.

Aldrich Killian orders a missile strike on Tony Stark's Malibu home.

Pepper Potts—and the rest of the world—fears Tony Stark was lost in the attack.

December 23, 2013 | Home Invasion

During Maya Hansen's visit to Stark's home, helicopters sent by Killian launch a missile strike on the Malibu estate, sending the cliffside structure tumbling into the Pacific. Pepper Potts and Hansen escape, but Stark is caught in the rubble and knocked out within his Mark XLII suit, disappearing below the waves. JARVIS takes control of the armor and activates the last available flight plan, which sends the unconscious Stark hurtling across the country to Rose Hill, Tennessee. In his absence, news reports speculate that Stark was killed in the attack and that the Mandarin was responsible.

December 23-24, 2013 | The Mechanic

With his Mark XLII suit damaged and drained of power, Stark takes shelter in the garage of an innovative local boy named Harley Keener, who shows him the site of the previous year's bombing. Stark notes that six people died, including the soldier suspected of setting off the explosion, but the blast imprinted only five shadows on the wall. He reasons the bomber's own body must have been the source of the explosion, and receives a file from the late soldier's mother that confirms his suspicion. It also connects the incident to Killian's Extremis program. Leaving his suit with Harley to recharge, Stark builds a collection of makeshift weapons to confront the Mandarin in Florida, where he has pinpointed the terrorist's most recent broadcast.

Harley Keener shows Tony Stark the memorial at the site of the Rose Hill bombing.

2013-2014

December 24, 2013 | Iron Patriot Compromised

Now working under his more patriotic-sounding title of Iron Patriot, Lt. Col. James Rhodes is ambushed by Killian agents who leaked false Mandarin coordinates to the government in order to seize Rhodey's armor. Killian uses his own Extremis heat-generating abilities to force Rhodes from the suit, allowing Savin to use it for a mission to capture President Ellis. The President had placed a ban on "immoral biotech research" like Extremis, and Vice President Rodriguez, whose disabled young daughter could benefit from such treatment, is part of the conspiracy to seize power and reverse the ban.

Lt. Col. James Rhodes, rebranded as Iron Patriot.

Aldrich Killian uses his Extremis heat-generating powers to force Rhodes from his armor.

December 24, 2013 | Curtain Calls

In Florida, Tony Stark discovers that the Mandarin is not a terrorist mastermind at all, but merely the befuddled actor Trevor Slattery. Killian's involvement becomes clear when Stark is captured, and Maya Hansen reveals she has been trying to manipulate Stark Industries into supporting their research. She helped take Pepper Potts hostage to force Stark's cooperation, but she is overcome with regret when she learns that Killian infected Potts with Extremis against her will. Killian murders Hansen when she turns against him.

Maya Hansen comes to regret her affiliation with Killian.

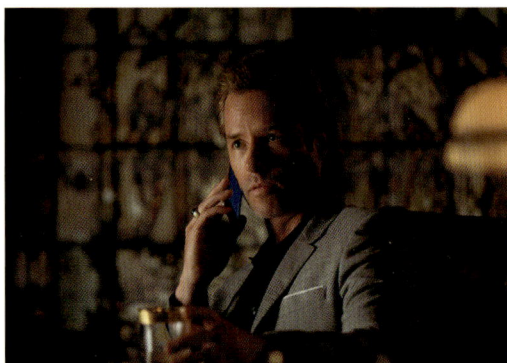

Killian is prepared to eradicate anyone who gets in the way of his rise to power.

Iron Man's remote-controlled Mark XLII armor leaves Air Force One to rescue falling passengers.

December 24, 2013 | Air Force One Assault

Disguised in the Iron Patriot armor, Savin boards Air Force One and takes President Ellis hostage by placing him in the suit and sending it remotely back to Killian. Stark escapes from Killian's custody by remotely summoning his Mark XLII armor from Rose Hill, then frees the imprisoned Rhodes. Controlling the armor remotely, Stark kills Savin and rescues 13 people who fall from the damaged plane.

108

A fleet of Iron Man armors—the Iron Legion—arrives as an A.I.-powered air force.

December 24-25, 2013 | A Sky Full of Iron Men

Tony Stark and James Rhodes track Killian to a shipyard where Pepper Potts and President Ellis are both being detained. As the rubble of Stark's Malibu estate is cleared, he activates the "House Party protocol," summoning dozens of Iron Man suits from his now-exposed basement. The Iron Legion help them defeat Killian's forces and rescue the President, but Potts is feared lost when she falls into the fiery ruins. The Extremis in her system saves her, however, and she overpowers Killian, saving Stark by taking one of his Iron Man gauntlets onto her own arm and annihilating the renegade researcher.

An Extremis-energized Pepper Potts uses an Iron Man gauntlet to blast Aldrich Killian.

2014

On Earth, the limits of long-standing institutions like S.H.I.E.L.D. are exposed, and what lies beneath is both disturbing and challenging. Off in deep space, a disparate group of outcasts find each other, forming an alliance that seems absurd—but also absurdly effective at guarding the galaxy.

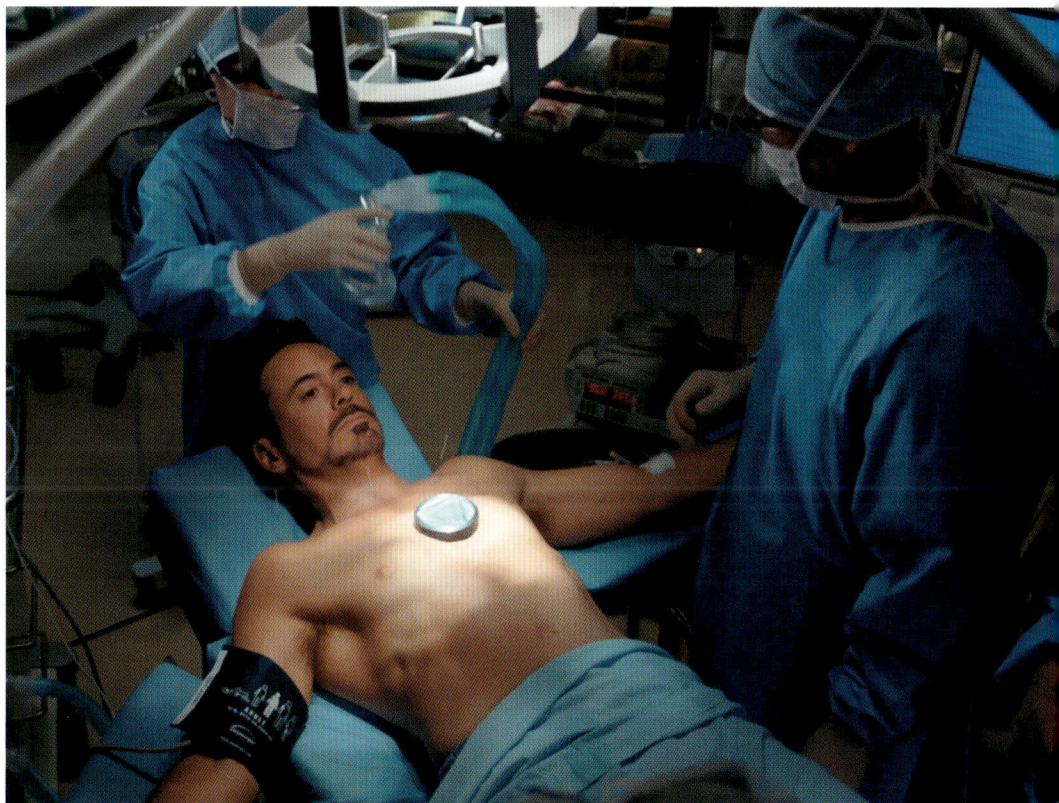

Early 2014 | Disarming Decisions

Stark successfully researches a way to purge Extremis from Pepper Potts' body, then turns that ingenuity on his own persistent malady. He finally extracts the shrapnel in his heart, making the Arc Reactor in his chest unnecessary. Having already destroyed his collection of armors, he now seeks to further decouple himself from Iron Man, if possible. Remote control made an Iron Legion of sentinels possible, and he will begin exploring whether artificial intelligence might be a better—and less personally harrowing—way of protecting the world.

Tony Stark finally has the shrapnel near his heart removed, along with the Arc Reactor.

IRON MAN ARMORS

Once Tony Stark completes his first suit of Iron Man armor in an Afghan cave, he becomes obsessed. Tony is not someone who settles—he tinkers, always looking for opportunities for improvements and iterating upon his first design over and over. In total, he designs and constructs at least eighty-five suits of Iron Man armor in his life. Over the years, Tony adjusts the suits to accommodate new technology and face new adversaries. He finesses every component, from the Arc Reactor to deployment methods, and remote-control functions to nanotech. A drive to protect those he cares about and the Earth fuels him to pursue the perfect Iron Man armor.

2008 | Mark III
With the Mark III armor, Tony adds color to the plain silver suit for the first time, using a gold-titanium alloy to address the previous armor's icing issues. The new red-and-gold color scheme will become Tony's iconic Iron Man look. Though the suit is powerful, deployment is slow, and requires an extensive system of robotic arms to attach it to Tony's body.

2010 | Mark IV
Tony's battle with his nemesis Obadiah Stane badly damages the Mark III suit. With the Mark IV armor, Tony retains much of the previous armor's capabilities while making slight adjustments to fit and mobility.

2008 | Mark I
To escape The Ten Rings, Tony works alongside Dr. Ho Yinsen to create the first Iron Man armor and a miniature Arc Reactor, using only basic tools, a box of spare parts, and palladium from repurposed Stark munitions. The technology becomes the basis for all future designs. The suit itself is captured by The Ten Rings and acquired by Obadiah Stane, who uses it as the blueprint for his own armor.

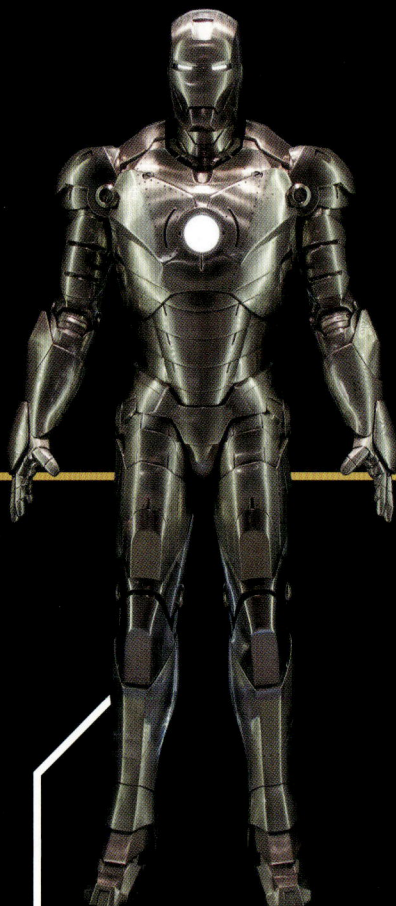

2008 | Mark II
Once Tony escapes, he comes up with a more aerodynamic design for the Iron Man armor. He finesses the repulsors to allow for sustained flight and integrates JARVIS, his A.I. assistant. A high-altitude icing flaw sends him back to the drawing board for further refining. The Mark II armor later becomes Lt. Col. James "Rhodey" Rhodes' first War Machine armor.

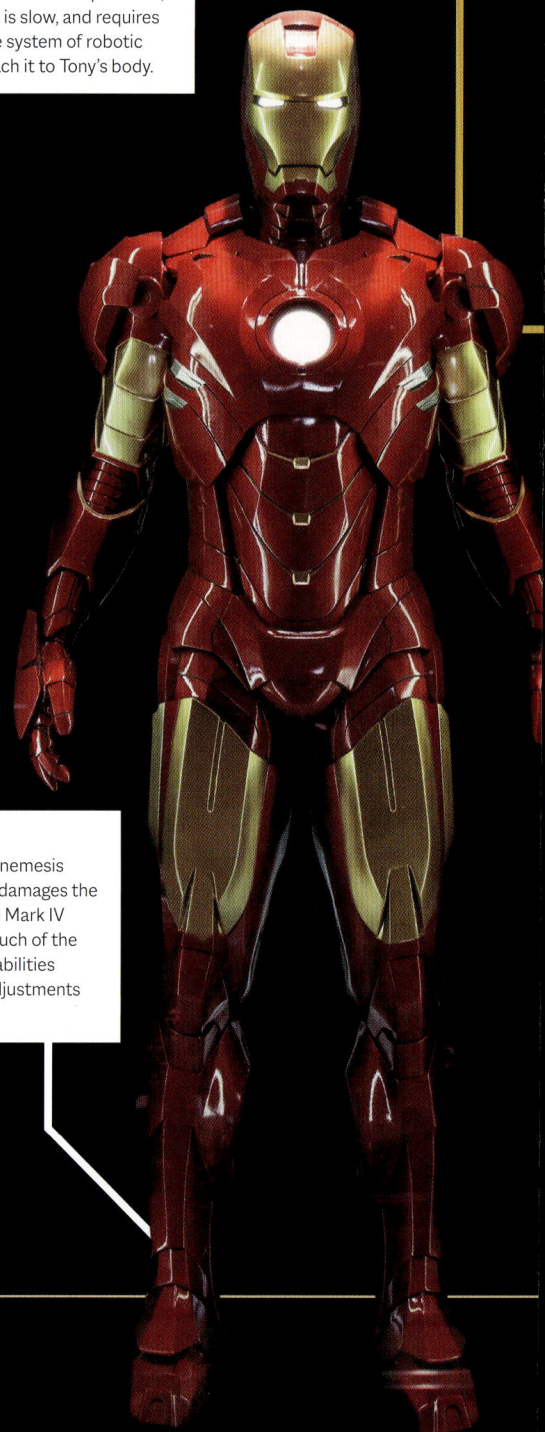

2010 | Mark V
Tony sees the value of having a more portable and mobile suit and so crafts the Mark V. The armor emerges from a briefcase that can be discreetly carried; when needed, it opens out and Tony can step into the suit, which then snaps around his body.

2013 | Mark XLII
The Mark XLII isn't fully ready when Killian's henchmen attack Tony's mansion. The suit can be controlled remotely and its components are independently propelled—Tony uses them to encase and save Pepper from the collapsing mansion, then later uses the suit to escape Killian's captivity and rescue the passengers of hijacked Air Force One.

2010 | Mark VI
By replacing the original Arc Reactor's palladium core with a new element, Tony makes it more powerful. He designs this armor to harness the reactor's increased energy output. In 2010 he uses it to defeat the villain Ivan Vanko, but in 2012 the armor takes damage when Tony uses it to restart S.H.I.E.L.D.'s Helicarrier turbine and it gets chewed up in the spinning propeller blades.

2012-2013 | Mark VIII-Mark XLI
The Battle of New York causes Tony to worry about the Earth's defenses. The anxiety drives him to create the Iron Legion—sets of specialized, automated armor that Tony can control remotely. The suits aid him in his final battle against new foe Aldrich Killian—however Tony later destroys the Iron Legion using the "Clean Slate" protocol.

2012 | Mark VII
Needing a new suit to face Loki and the Chitauri invasion, Tony calls the Mark VII into action despite it not being fully ready. This armor features an upgraded delivery system, made for automatic deployment by responding to metal bracelets worn on Tony's wrists.

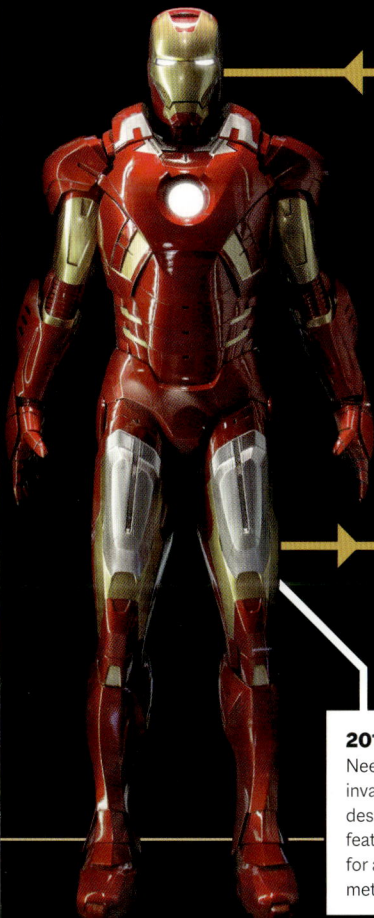

2016 | Mark XLVI
The Mark XLVI armor sees action against Tony's fellow Avengers, when he uses it to fight the Accord-refusing members of the group in the battle at Leipzig-Halle Airport. It features a fully retractable helmet, rather than just a retractable face mask.

2015 | Mark XLIV
Bruce Banner helps Tony design the Hulkbuster armor in order to restrain the Hulk should it become necessary. The giant modular suit overlays Tony's other armors and can rapidly deploy worldwide from a Stark Satellite, accompanied by an independently propelled system called Veronica, which stands by with a selection of additional armaments and tech available by request, as well as a self-assembling, electrified cage. The robust armor stands up well, considering the Hulk's immense strength.

2015 | Mark XLV
With Hulk and Ultron damaging Tony's previous suits, he takes the Mark XLV into battle in Sokovia. This is the first armor to use the A.I. known as FRIDAY, replacing JARVIS as Tony's guiding voice after JARVIS becomes an element of the new being known as Vision.

2015 | Mark XLIII
Tony dons the Mark XLIII armor during the Avengers' attack on Hydra's Sokovian research base. While nearly identical to the Mark XLII, this design brings red back as the predominant color, and features powerful arm-mounted missiles.

2016 | Mark XLVII
Initially, Tony sends the Mark XLVII armor via remote control to save Spider-Man and lecture him for his recklessness in fighting Adrian Toomes. Later he occupies the armor and uses its mini-thrusters to help Spider-Man save the sinking Staten Island Ferry.

2018 | Mark L

The Mark L's design represents a leap forward in armor technology by utilizing nanotech. Tony activates the suit merely by pressing on a unit that houses the nanites, which then spread across his body. They can adjust on the fly to cover damaged areas and to shape a variety of on-demand weapons including energy cannons, blades, jackhammers, immobilizing traps, and repulsor-enhanced appendages.

2018 | Mark XLVIII

Instead of it restraining Hulk, Bruce himself uses the Hulkbuster 2.0 armor. Left unable to transform into Hulk after an attack by Thanos, Bruce wears the hefty armor so he can more safely participate in the battle in Wakanda, where he uses it to defeat Cull Obsidian.

2023 | Mark XLIX

After years of building armor for himself, Tony begins designing suits for Pepper Potts, who had herself shown an aptitude for armored combat during the battle against Aldrich Killian. She wears the armor while fighting alongside Tony and the Avengers during the Battle of Earth.

2023 | Mark LXXXV

Having crafted numerous suits during the years of the Blip, Tony's eighty-fifth suit would be his final creation. He wears the powerful armor in the final battle against Thanos, where he uses its nanite technology to create his own gauntlet, allowing him to briefly withstand wielding all six Infinity Stones.

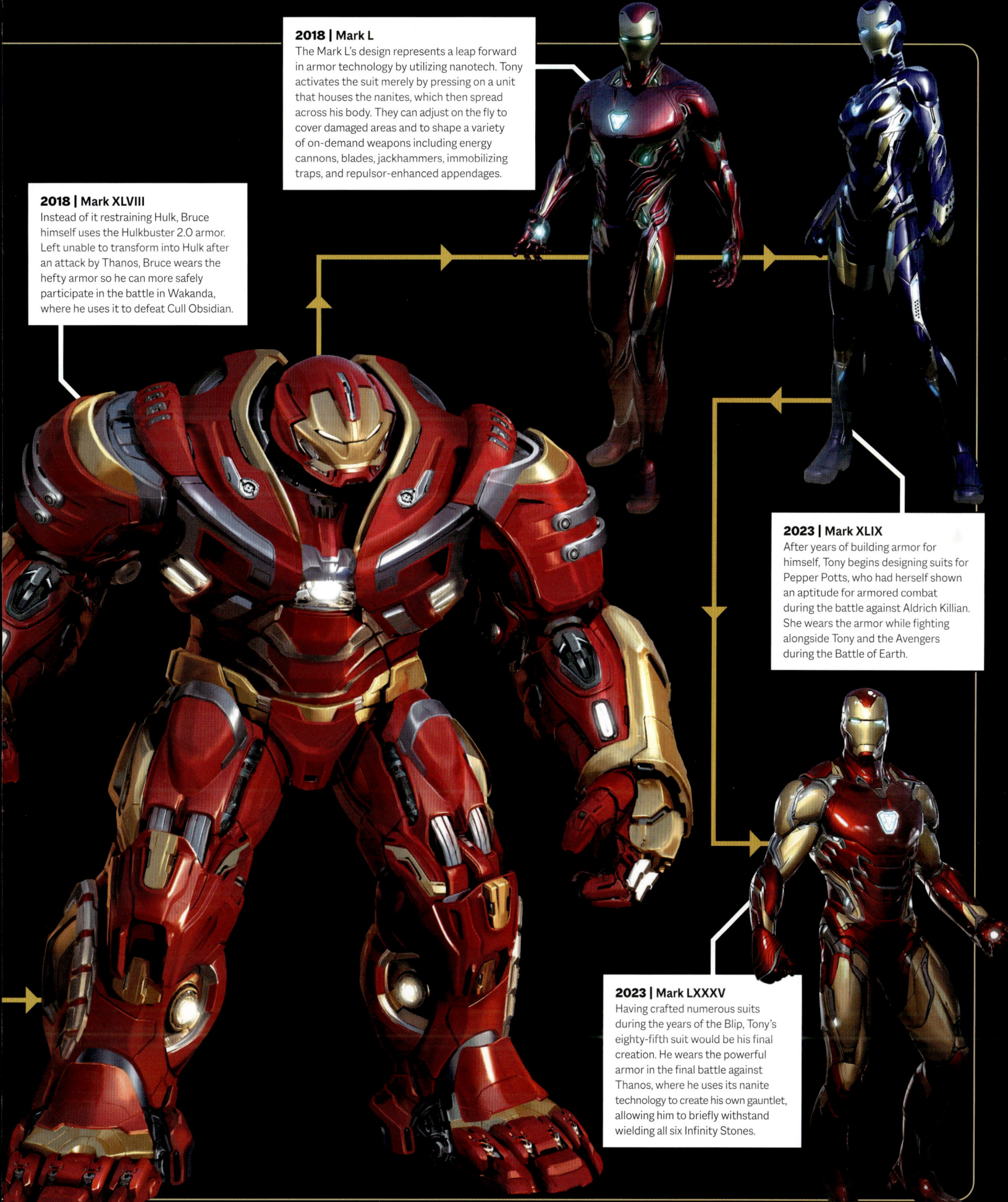

2014

Early 2014 | Wenwu vs. Trevor Slattery

The Ten Rings leader Wenwu sends an operative disguised as a documentary filmmaker to interview Trevor Slattery in Seagate penitentiary. At first, Wenwu intends to punish the actor who disgracefully impersonated him as "the Mandarin," abducting him from prison in order to execute him. But just before the sentence is carried out, Slattery breaks into a Shakespeare performance that Wenwu so enjoys, he decides to keep Slattery as a kind of court jester rather than kill him.

Trevor Slattery will learn his interviewer is not who he claims to be.

Sam Wilson and Steve Rogers strike up a friendship.

Spring 2014 | "On Your Left"

Steve Rogers, now working as one of S.H.I.E.L.D.'s top agents, befriends fellow soldier Sam Wilson after meeting him while jogging around the reflecting pool at the Lincoln Memorial. After repeatedly lapping Wilson, who is impressed by the super soldier's stamina, they bond over shared combat experience—and difficulty returning to civilian life. Wilson, who once flew a prototype EXO-7 Falcon wing pack with the 58th Pararescue Unit in the Air Force, now works for the Department of Veterans Affairs. Soon, he'll become an invaluable ally.

Death Dealer, the brutal trainer who turns Shang-Chi into an assassin.

2014 | The Ten Rings' Lost Son

Wenwu has bigger problems elsewhere—the cabal leader's 14-year-old son, Shang-Chi, successfully undertakes his first targeted killing on behalf of his father, slaying the last Iron Gang leader responsible for his mother's murder. But the act leaves the boy ashamed and disgusted. He refuses to return to The Ten Rings and sets up a new identity in San Francisco, where he befriends classmate Katy Chen and attempts to live as an ordinary American teenager.

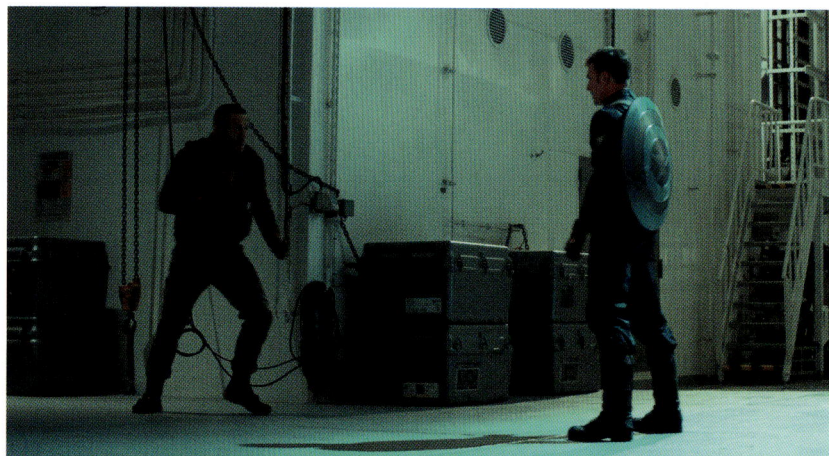

The Algerian mercenary Batroc battles Steve Rogers during the *Lemurian Star* rescue.

Spring 2014 | The *Lemurian Star* Incident

Steve Rogers, Natasha Romanoff, and S.H.I.E.L.D.'s elite S.T.R.I.K.E. team led by agent Brock Rumlow conduct a mission to rescue hostages aboard a satellite launch ship that has been hijacked in the Indian Ocean. Among the hostages is Agent Jasper Sitwell, whose high rank within S.H.I.E.L.D. makes his presence on the ship unusual. The mercenary Georges Batroc has demanded the steep ransom of $1.5 billion. Captain America subdues him and his soldiers of fortune, but Batroc escapes while Romanoff is fulfilling a secret assignment from Nick Fury: to retrieve the data that S.H.I.E.L.D. was about to send into orbit.

Captain America learns about Project Insight from Nick Fury, and voices his unease about its potential implications.

Spring 2014 | Fury's Suspicion

Nick Fury actually shares Captain America's concerns about Project Insight, which is why he secretly hired Batroc to hijack the *Lemurian Star*, giving Black Widow cover to find out exactly what program S.H.I.E.L.D. was loading into its targeting satellites. When he discovers he is locked out of the file she collected, a suspicious Fury approaches his longtime friend and member of the World Security Council, Secretary Alexander Pierce, and asks him to postpone the launch of the new Helicarriers. Pierce agrees to let Fury investigate his concerns—but it's a lie, with potentially fatal consequences to come.

Nick Fury harbors doubts about S.H.I.E.L.D.'s Project Insight program, which will target individuals before they engage in wrongdoing.

Spring 2014 | Need-to-Know Basis

Back at The Triskelion, S.H.I.E.L.D.'s headquarters in Washington, D.C., Steve Rogers confronts Nick Fury over the data he collected during the *Lemurian Star* hostage crisis. Fury reveals that the ship was launching a satellite as part of a top-secret program known as "Project Insight." He shows Rogers a massive hangar built beneath the Potomac River, where three next-generation S.H.I.E.L.D. Helicarriers will be launched, using the satellites to identify terrorists, criminals, and other assorted menaces from afar. "We're going to neutralize a lot of threats before they even happen," Fury explains. But Rogers is disturbed. "I thought the punishment usually came after the crime," he says.

Spring 2014 | The Carter Legacy

Steve Rogers has reunited with his long-lost love Peggy Carter. She is now bedridden and grappling with memory issues, so although she recognizes and remembers him from the past, she repeatedly loses track of the present. He confides in her that he is no longer sure that following the orders of S.H.I.E.L.D. is the same as doing what's right. Neither of them is aware that Peggy's niece, Sharon Carter, who has also joined S.H.I.E.L.D., is currently serving undercover as Rogers' neighbor, keeping track of his activities for Nick Fury.

Sharon Carter, a.k.a. Agent 13, who was assigned to monitor Steve Rogers as his neighbor.

Struggling with her memory, Peggy Carter is astonished time and again by the return of Steve Rogers.

2014

The Winter Soldier attempts to kill Nick Fury on the streets of Washington, D.C.

Spring 2014 | The Winter Soldier Strikes

After his meeting with Pierce, Nick Fury is attacked by undercover Hydra agents and the notorious Winter Soldier, who overturns his SUV with an explosion and moves in to assassinate the S.H.I.E.L.D. director. Fury escapes from his wrecked vehicle, and takes shelter in Steve Rogers' apartment, revealing his belief that S.H.I.E.L.D. has been compromised. He gives Rogers the flash drive with the inaccessible *Lemurian Star* files on it, but is shot through the window by the Winter Soldier. The gunfire draws the attention of Rogers' neighbor, Sharon Carter, who reveals she was sent by Fury to monitor him. Together they hurry Fury to the hospital, but during emergency surgery he appears to succumb to his wounds.

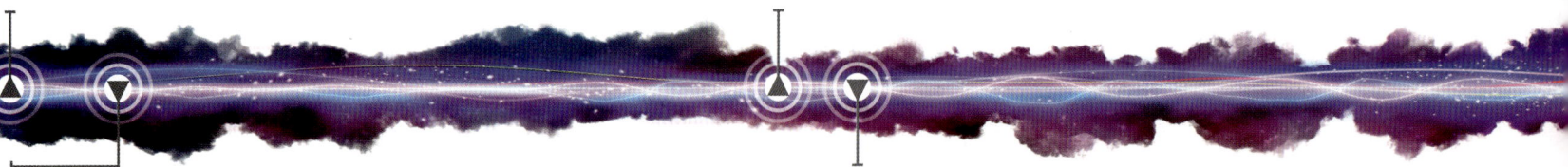

Spring 2014 | Alexander Pierce's Explanation

After Fury's demise, Steve Rogers meets with Secretary Pierce and learns that Georges Batroc has been taken into custody and is currently being interrogated. Pierce reveals that anonymous payments to Batroc for the *Lemurian Star* hijacking were traced back to Nick Fury himself. Although Fury was trying to gain further understanding of Project Insight, Pierce says some believe Fury was trying to steal and sell classified intelligence. Rogers refuses to believe this. Never one to "just follow orders," Captain America undertakes his own investigation.

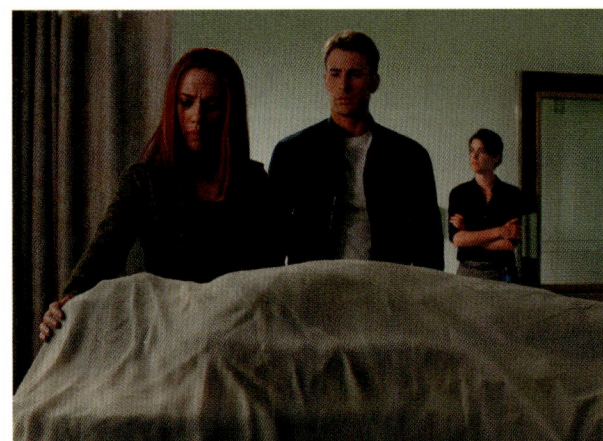

Natasha Romanoff and Steve Rogers grieve over Nick Fury's body. Only Maria Hill knows that he is still alive.

Spring 2014 | Captain America Breaks Protocol

After his meeting with Pierce, Captain America is surrounded inside a Triskelion elevator by S.H.I.E.L.D. agent Brock Rumlow, his S.T.R.I.K.E. team, and others who try—and fail spectacularly—to capture him. Rogers goes on the run with Natasha Romanoff, who shares Fury's concerns about S.H.I.E.L.D. and is also reluctant to follow orders without question. Although they can't access the targeting file from the *Lemurian Star*, they are able to uncover a geo-tag indicating where that file was created. This leads them to a familiar location in Wheaton, New Jersey...

Steve Rogers: "Before we get started, does anyone want to get out?"

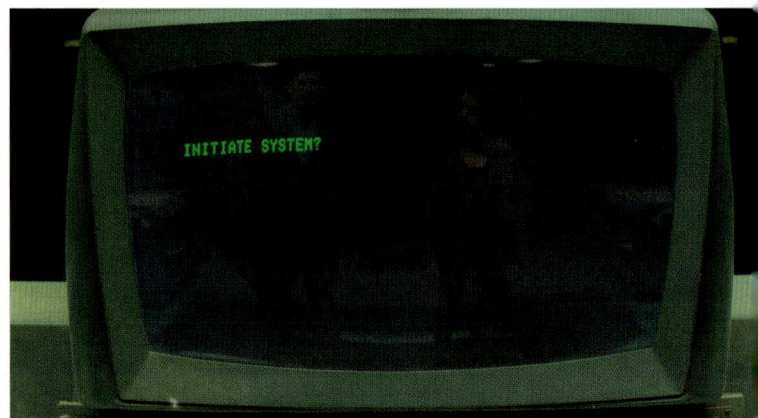

The Arnim Zola A.I. boots up in a bunker beneath Camp Lehigh.

Spring 2014 | The Immortal Arnim Zola

Rogers and Romanoff pinpoint the origin of the targeting file to Camp Lehigh, the now-abandoned former S.H.I.E.L.D. headquarters where Captain America first trained during World War II. In a subterranean computer lab, they discover an artificial intelligence program built from the consciousness of Rogers' long-ago nemesis Arnim Zola. Although Zola died, his mind lives on in this program, and he confesses that over the remainder of his life he helped rebuild Hydra from within S.H.I.E.L.D. The locked Project Insight file is an algorithm he devised to identify targets. Zola then reveals he has been stalling them, as a missile launched by S.H.I.E.L.D. demolishes the building.

Alexander Pierce meets with remote members of the World Security Council.

Spring 2014 | The Hydra Parasite

When he is not manipulating the World Security Council, Alexander Pierce meets with less savory figures. One such face-to-mask encounter is with the Winter Soldier himself, to personally assign him to take out Captain America and Black Widow after their meddling led to the destruction of Zola. Pierce was among those in the U.S. government corrupted by the resurgent Hydra, and while the Winter Soldier operates against his own will, Pierce is fully aware of his actions. When his housekeeper, Renata, accidentally sees him with the assassin, Pierce murders her in cold blood. He is prepared to take far more lives than that to achieve his goal of authoritarian global order.

Spring 2014 | Falcon Recruited

In need of allies, Steve Rogers and Natasha Romanoff turn to Sam Wilson, helping him secure one of the EXO-7 wing suits so he can join their mission to expose and stop Project Insight. The trio capture Agent Jasper Sitwell, who reveals that Zola's algorithm will use data mining to identify not just criminals and terrorists, but countless others who have the potential to disrupt or resist Hydra. "Your bank records, medical histories, voting patterns, emails, phone calls, your damn SAT scores... Zola's algorithm evaluates people's past to predict their future," Sitwell reveals. "Then the Insight Helicarriers scratch people off the list—a few million at a time."

Sam Wilson in flight as the Falcon.

117

2014

Old friends, new enemies—Steve and Bucky come to blows.

Spring 2014 | The Face of Bucky Barnes

The Winter Soldier attacks—ripping Agent Sitwell out through a car window and throwing him into oncoming traffic. In the ensuing fight with Steve Rogers, Natasha Romanoff, and Sam Wilson, the legendary assassin loses his mask and Captain America recognizes the face of his childhood friend Bucky Barnes. "Who the hell is Bucky?" the killer says when Rogers calls to him. The fight against the reborn Hydra movement becomes personal as Rogers realizes his best friend is among those who have been forcibly corrupted by it.

The Winter Soldier doesn't know the name Bucky Barnes.

Spring 2014 | Nick Fury Lives

Maria Hill helps Rogers, Romanoff, and Wilson escape S.H.I.E.L.D. and brings them to a bunker where they discover Nick Fury faked his death using Tetrodotoxin B, a drug once developed by Bruce Banner to slow heart rate to a near stop. Hill and Fury devise a plan to infiltrate the Project Insight Helicarriers and replace their targeting chips, while simultaneously exposing S.H.I.E.L.D.'s secret Hydra network to the world. If they fail, Alexander Pierce will use Zola's predictive algorithm to kill nearly 20 million people.

Natasha Romanoff, reunited with Nick Fury.

Falcon evades fire from the Project Insight Helicarriers' cannons.

Spring 2014 | The Fall of S.H.I.E.L.D.

As the Helicarriers of Project Insight rise over Washington, D.C., Captain America and Falcon fly from ship to ship, replacing their targeting chips with a new directive: turn their arsenal of cannons against each other. Natasha Romanoff hacks into the organization's database, transferring its classified documents online so the public can see its widespread corruption. Alexander Pierce is shot by Nick Fury. Pierce's final words—"Hail Hydra"—are spoken as the collapse of Project Insight literally reduces S.H.I.E.L.D. to rubble around him.

Reprogramming the massive gunships turns their fire on each other.

118

The Winter Soldier batters Captain America aboard one of the Project Insight Helicarriers.

Spring 2014 | A New Insight

The Winter Soldier confronts Steve Rogers aboard the final Helicarrier, gravely wounding him with gunfire, but failing to stop him. When Rogers refuses to fight back against his old friend, it awakens remnants of the old Bucky Barnes that survived Hydra's brainwashing. As the ship crashes into the Triskelion, the Winter Soldier saves Captain America's life rather than killing him, dragging him from the waters of the Potomac and leaving him—and his shield—safely on the shore.

Spring 2014 | The Twin Test Subjects

Wanda and Pietro Maximoff, who became radicalized after a Stark Industries bomb blew apart their home and killed their parents in the 1990s, volunteer themselves for Baron Strucker's secret Hydra experiments. These involve being exposed to Loki's scepter and the Mind Stone that powers it. Wanda's exposure amplifies her yet-to-be-revealed Chaos Magic abilities, while Pietro gains the ability of hyper-speed. Wanda also encounters a haunting and prophetic vision of The Scarlet Witch that she will one day become.

Natasha Romanoff experiences a vision of The Scarlet Witch during experiments with the Mind Stone scepter.

Spring 2014 | Hydra Cleanup

As well as the millions of deaths that are averted when the Project Insight Helicarriers crash to the ground, the leaking of S.H.I.E.L.D.'s files allows countless covert Hydra loyalists to be exposed and arrested, including Sen. Stern, who had previously used his position to undermine Tony Stark. Some Hydra agents escape justice, among them Brock Rumlow, who goes underground as the mercenary Crossbones after being scarred in the battle.

The ruins of Project Insight and the Triskelion in Washington, D.C.

1940s | The Rise of Hydra

Hydra is the Nazi regime's deep science division, bent on world domination. During WWII, the organization is led by Johann Schmidt, who injects himself with the Super Soldier Serum created by Abraham Erskine, turning himself into the fearsome Red Skull. Their plans are halted by Captain America and the Allied Forces.

1940s-1950s | Creation of the Winter Soldier

After the war, Dr. Arnim Zola and other Hydra scientists create their own Super Soldier Program. Bucky Barnes, who had survived a train explosion during a mission with Captain America but was captured by Hydra, is taken to a Hydra facility where he is brainwashed and given a new cybernetic arm. Barnes becomes the Winter Soldier, one of Hydra's most efficient and lethal assassins.

1970s | S.H.I.E.L.D. Infiltration Worsens

Having been recruited by the U.S. government in the late 1940s as part of Operation Paperclip, Hydra scientist Arnim Zola was brought into S.H.I.E.L.D. He spends years corrupting S.H.I.E.L.D. from within and secretly building an advanced computer, into which he uploads his consciousness before he dies. This allows Zola to continue his work from beyond the grave, bringing in more sleeper agents to infiltrate S.H.I.E.L.D.

1980s | Pym Particles

Mitchell Carson, S.H.I.E.L.D.'s Head of Defense, works with Howard Stark to replicate Hank Pym's size altering particles. Pym interrupts a meeting between Carson, Stark, and Peggy Carter, furious they were trying to steal his designs, and resigns from S.H.I.E.L.D. Although it is unknown if Carson is already sympathetic to Hydra, decades from now, he will offer to help them obtain Pym Particles.

HYDRA AND S.H.I.E.L.D.

Two sides of the same coin, Hydra and S.H.I.E.L.D. have a complicated and entangled history. Hydra, a powerful and secretive terrorist organization, rises to power during World War II, bent on world domination. S.H.I.E.L.D. is created by the U.S. government to counter threats to Earth and maintain national and global security. As a result of Operation Paperclip, S.H.I.E.L.D. recruits a former Hydra scientist, which allows Hydra to infiltrate the peacekeeping organization. They orchestrate countless global crises and assassinations, including that of S.H.I.E.L.D. co-founder Howard Stark. However, Hydra's operations take a massive hit after S.H.I.E.L.D. Director Nick Fury realizes his organization is compromised and has to be shut down.

1995 | First Contact

Agents Nick Fury and Phil Coulson are sent to investigate a woman who mysteriously crashes to Earth. The woman is Carol Danvers, a U.S. Air Force pilot who had been abducted by the Kree. Fury and Danvers team up to prevent a Kree attack.

1940s | Proto-S.H.I.E.L.D.

S.H.I.E.L.D.'s predecessor, the Strategic Scientific Reserve (S.S.R.) instigates Project Rebirth, a plan to use Dr. Abraham Erskine's serum to turn Allied soldiers into super soldiers. Erskine selects Steve Rogers to be the first American super soldier. The experiment is successful, transforming Steve into Captain America.

1940-1950s | Infiltrated by Hydra

S.H.I.E.L.D. is founded in the aftermath of World War II by industrialist Howard Stark, S.S.R. agent Peggy Carter, and S.S.R. chief Colonel Chester Phillips, all of whom had battled against Hydra. In a fatal error, S.H.I.E.L.D. recruits Hydra scientists like Arnim Zola into their organization.

1995-2008 | New Focus

S.H.I.E.L.D. continues to grow in strength as Nick Fury becomes director. Under Fury's direction, S.H.I.E.L.D. takes an increased interest in individuals showing enhanced abilities, both as potential threats and potential members of Fury's so-called Avengers Initiative. Among them is Tony Stark, a.k.a. Iron Man.

2010 | In the Desert

Agent Coulson and his team head to New Mexico, where they find a crater with a hammer at its center. They set up a base of operations around the crater to study the immovable alien object. Later that night, Thor breaks into the facility to retrieve his hammer, Mjolnir, but when he can't lift it, he is captured by S.H.I.E.L.D. agents. After Thor's victory over Loki, S.H.I.E.L.D. comes into possession of some Asgardian technology.

1990s | The Stark Assassination
Hydra takes the Winter Soldier out of cryo-sleep for a mission to retrieve recreated Super Soldier Serum from Howard Stark. The Winter Soldier tracks down Stark and his wife Maria while they are driving. He murders both, stealing the serum, and Hydra uses it to create five more Winter Soldiers.

2015 | War in Sokovia
Hydra establishes an underground facility in Sokovia, conducting human experiments on its residents. The Avengers discover the location of the Hydra research base, and have their first encounter with the Maximoff twins, Wanda and Pietro. The Avengers successfully destroy the base and retrieve Loki's scepter, which holds the Mind Stone. The remaining known Hydra leader is subsequently killed by the rogue A.I. Ultron.

2015 | The Yellowjacket Suit
Darren Cross offers to sell Pym Particle technology to Mitchell Carson, who is now working with a remnant Hydra. Cross creates the Yellowjacket suit, which would give Hydra the upper hand in world domination. Their efforts are shut down by Scott Lang, who was given the Ant-Man suit by Hank Pym. Carson manages to escape with a vial of Cross' modified Pym Particles.

2014 | Project Insight
Hydra's infiltration of S.H.I.E.L.D. is uncovered by Steve Rogers and Natasha Romanoff. World Security Council member Alexander Pierce tries to activate Project Insight—a plan to use advanced Helicarriers to wipe out all of Hydra's potential foes. Pierce is exposed as a Hydra agent and is killed by Nick Fury.

2011 | Finding Captain America
S.H.I.E.L.D. agents discover the remains of the *Valkyrie*, buried under ice in Greenland. Steve Rogers is found inside and is sent to their headquarters in New York City after they defrost him. When Rogers awakes, he escapes the facility and is shocked to find out he's been asleep for nearly 70 years.

2014 | The Fall of S.H.I.E.L.D.
The full scale of Hydra's corruption is revealed when numerous S.H.I.E.L.D. agents turn on their colleagues. S.H.I.E.L.D.'s Triskelion headquarters is badly damaged, and Romanoff releases its classified files onto the internet. The U.S. government shuts S.H.I.E.L.D. down permanently.

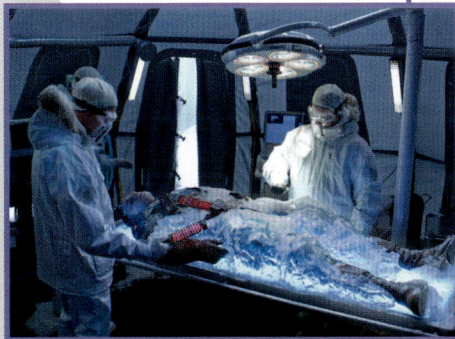

2015 | Back in Action
When the Avengers go into hiding after losing a battle against Ultron and the Maximoff twins in Johannesburg, Nick Fury arrives to formulate a plan to stop Ultron. The Avengers travel to Sokovia for a final battle, and Nick Fury and other former S.H.I.E.L.D. personnel join them, using a reactivated Helicarrier to transport civilians to safety.

2012 | The Avengers
When Loki steals the Tesseract, Nick Fury activates the Avengers Initiative to counter the threat of the impending Chitauri Invasion. The Avengers are given equipment and a base of operations by S.H.I.E.L.D., allowing Captain America, Black Widow, Iron Man, Thor, Hawkeye, and the Hulk to come together in New York City and bring down Loki and thwart his plans to take over the world.

WASHINGTON, D.C.

As the United States capital, it's no surprise Washington, D.C. hosts numerous important moments connected to the Avengers. The U.S. government and military is often affiliated with the actions of super powered humans, sometimes supporting them and sometimes trying to exert control over their powers or associated technology for political gain. Government organizations such as S.H.I.E.L.D. and S.W.O.R.D. answer to U.S. intelligence agencies, meaning Congress committees have input on strategies and funding. These factors make Washington, D.C. a hub of power that can make or break the Avengers' efforts to help Earth.

1989 | Resignation
The Triskelion in Washington, D.C. is one of S.H.I.E.L.D.'s official headquarters, home to offices, labs, and training facilities. When Hank Pym discovers the organization is secretly attempting to recreate his Pym Particles, he goes to the Triskelion to demand they leave his technology alone. There he is confronted by S.H.I.E.L.D. co-founders Howard Stark and Peggy Carter, as well as head of defense, Mitchell Carson. Hank tenders his resignation despite Howard's protests.

2010 | Iron Man Tech
The government summons Tony Stark to a Senate committee hearing in Washington to press their case for acquiring the Iron Man technology for the U.S. military. Senator Stern, a secret Hydra operative, employs manipulation and guilt, even trying to turn Tony's friend Lt. Colonel James "Rhodey" Rhodes against him. The senator fails to convince Tony to cede control of the armor, with Tony proclaiming he and the suit are one.

2013 | Iron Patriot
Concerned for the nation's safety following the Chitauri invasion and the Mandarin's terrorist attacks, President Matthew Ellis appoints Rhodes to be the government's face of opposition. Research and development agency AIM re-designs Rhodes' War Machine armor and rebrands him as Iron Patriot. Unbeknownst to Rhodey, the Mandarin is Aldrich Killian, founder of AIM, and the Iron Patriot armor will be used to kidnap President Ellis.

2014 | "On Your Left"
Sam Wilson's life changes forever when he meets Steve Rogers while jogging laps around the Lincoln Memorial Reflecting Pool in Washington, D.C. Steve passes Sam, a veteran, multiple times before they pause for introductions and end up bonding over their shared struggles of getting back into the routines of day-to-day life after serving in combat.

2014 | Project Insight
Beneath S.H.I.E.L.D.'s Triskelion headquarters, Director Nick Fury shares with Steve the existence of Project Insight, intended to neutralize threats to Earth before they happen. The advanced Helicarriers will remain in perpetual sub-orbital flight. Steve says it amounts to "holding a gun to everyone on Earth and calling it protection."

2016 | Sightseeing

Washington, D.C. hosts Peter Parker and his school's academic decathlon team. Peter uses the trip as cover to track his nemesis Adrian Toomes' crew as they steal from Department of Damage Control trucks loaded with alien technology. Spider-Man only partially succeeds, reaching the Washington Monument just before the Chitauri engine core he'd used to track Toomes explodes, threatening his schoolmates inside.

The top of the Washington Monument is blasted apart, but thankfully no lives are lost.

2014 | Battle in D.C.

A significant number of S.H.I.E.L.D. agents are actually loyal to Hydra and they attempt to kill Fury and Steve. With Alexander Pierce allied with Hydra, bringing them down is a daunting task. Steve brings in Natasha Romanoff and Sam Wilson to help, and though the presence of Bucky, or the Winter Soldier, compromises Steve, the heroes still infiltrate the Triskelion. They unmask Hydra, with the Triskelion being destroyed in the process.

2024 | Exhibit for a Legacy

When Steve Rogers retires, he passes on the mantle of Captain America to Sam Wilson by giving him the iconic shield. Sam decides he's not the right person to carry the legacy forward, though, and donates the vibranium shield, a symbol of hope and doing the right thing, to the Smithsonian Institution. It goes on display alongside other mementos from Captain America's life.

2024 | Captain No More

The U.S. Department of Defense removes Cap's shield from the exhibit and grants it to John Walker, appointing him the new Captain America. John gives the government good publicity in Washington, D.C., but while he believes he embodies the principles of Captain America, he shows otherwise with his selfish and lethal actions. The government renounces him, discharging him from the Army and taking away the mantle of Captain America.

2014 | Hydra Rises Again

Fury secretly has his own suspicions that the project housed inside the Triskelion is a cover up for something sinister. He voices them to Alexander Pierce, a member of the World Security Council, who is secretly a Hydra loyalist. Hydra operatives immediately try to assassinate Fury, pursuing him in a dangerous car chase through the streets of Washington and unleashing the Winter Soldier on the S.H.I.E.L.D. director.

2014

Baron Strucker and Dr. List in Hydra's research base in Sokovia.

Spring 2014 | Unintended Consequences

Some branches of Hydra continue undeterred. Baron Strucker's operation in Sokovia, which had already secured Loki's mind-control scepter from S.H.I.E.L.D., continues its experiments despite the collapse of the broader organization. Others who operated under S.H.I.E.L.D.'s auspices, like the phase-shifter Ava Starr, find themselves adrift. She served as a loyal saboteur and spy on countless black-ops missions, but the fall of S.H.I.E.L.D. leaves her with no one to help manage her body's struggle to maintain a physical form. For help, she turns to her father's old researcher friend, Bill Foster.

Spring 2014 | Missing Persons Case

Steve Rogers and Sam Wilson begin a manhunt for the Winter Soldier, who is also hunting his own past. The former Hydra assassin visits the Captain America exhibit at the Smithsonian in Washington, D.C. and discovers he is really Bucky Barnes, which helps him begin the painful process of deprogramming.

Xandar's leader, Nova Prime, speaks with Corpsman Dey.

Summer 2014 | Ronan's Power Grab

Out in deep space, the Kree-Nova conflict ends in a peace treaty after a millennium of war, but renegade Kree zealot Ronan the Accuser refuses to honor the deal. He begins a guerrilla effort to demolish the Nova Empire by aligning with Thanos, agreeing to secure an artifact known as the Orb for the Titan; in return, Thanos will help Ronan destroy the Nova capital, Xandar. Thanos orders his adopted daughters, Gamora and Nebula, to aid Ronan.

"They call me terrorist, radical, zealot. Because I obey the ancient laws of my people, the Kree, and punish those who do not."

Peter Quill attempts to make a name for himself.

A perplexed Korath has never heard of Quill.

Summer 2014 | ...Who?

Peter Quill betrays the clan of Ravager bandits who raised him as a foundling. He steals their map to the mysterious Orb—and the Power Stone within—before they can retrieve it from the ruins of Morag, intending to keep the bounty for himself. Korath arrives seeking the stone for Ronan the Accuser, but he is outmaneuvered by Quill, who reveals his identity as the supposedly legendary outlaw Star-Lord. (Korath is unimpressed—he's never heard of him.)

Summer 2014 | Xandar Street Fight

Gamora is dispatched by Ronan to steal the Orb from Quill while Star-Lord tries to pawn it on Xandar. Meanwhile, a different caper is underway as a cranky creature named Rocket and the humanoid tree known as Groot scheme to claim the bounty that the Ravagers have placed on Quill's head. After a knock-down, drag-out fight on the streets of Xandar, all four scoundrels are apprehended and imprisoned at the Kyln, a facility populated by countless prisoners "who lost their families to Ronan and his goons," as Rocket explains.

Groot prepares to capture Peter Quill in a sack.

Summer 2014 | Rise of the Guardians

In the Kyln, fellow prisoner Drax recognizes Gamora as an agent of Thanos and Ronan, and tries to exact revenge for his wife and daughter, killed during Ronan's campaign of terror. He is prevented from doing so by Quill, and Gamora reveals she had already decided to turn against her former masters. She will no longer help the pair inflict suffering on other worlds as Thanos once did hers. Quill, Gamora, Groot, Rocket, and Drax form a new alliance—one that will eventually lead to them being known across the stars as the "Guardians of the Galaxy."

Peter Quill, Groot, Rocket, Drax, and Gamora stage a jailbreak from the Kyln.

2014

Knowhere, the remains of a Celestial, now being mined for rare materials.

Summer 2014 | Journey to Knowhere

The Guardians stage a jailbreak from the Kyln and venture to the mining colony of Knowhere, the moon-sized severed head of an ancient Celestial where the Collector, Taneleer Tivan, mines rare materials from the Celestial's skull. He uses his immense wealth to gather "fauna, relics, and species of all manner" from around the galaxy, according to his neon-pink Krylorian servant Carina. Gamora knows he will pay 4 billion units for the Orb.

Peter Quill meets with the Collector.

Summer 2014 | "I Will No Longer Be Your Slave!"

The Collector shows the group the extraordinary Power Stone contained within the Orb, but Carina decides to seize it to escape from Tivan's control. The energy within it overwhelms her, triggering a blast that rips through the Collector's gallery. Carina is obliterated, but her impulsive action does free many others from her master's cruel imprisonment.

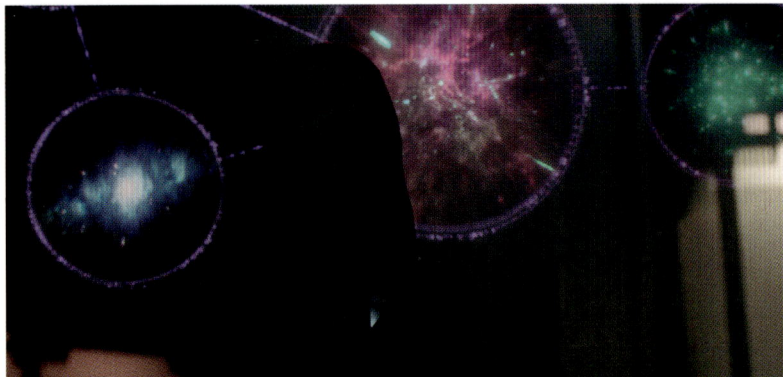

The Orb is revealed as a relic that contains the Power Stone.

The five other Infinity Stones are revealed to the Guardians of the Galaxy.

Drax prepares to exact revenge on the forces of Ronan and Thanos, but the fight doesn't go as he expects.

Summer 2014 | The Showdown

Ronan and his forces arrive on Knowhere, summoned by a signal from Drax, who was impatient for his showdown with the Kree warlord. But Drax is overconfident and underprepared. Ronan easily batters the warrior into submission and leaves him for dead.

Summer 2014 | Mining Pod Chase

Nebula pursues and destroys her sister Gamora's getaway capsule, and retrieves the Orb for Ronan. Peter Quill risks his own life to save Gamora from the vacuum of space, and both are scooped up by the Ravagers, who are keen to make an example out of their traitorous former member. Gamora and Quill convince Ravager leader Yondu Udonta to let them live if they help him steal the Power Stone back from Ronan. Rocket is not convinced they can do it: "We're gonna rob the guys who just beat us senseless?"

Peter Quill rescues Gamora from the void of space after her ship is destroyed by Nebula.

2014

Nova Corps Starblasters align to form a barrier to hold back Ronan the Accuser's *Dark Aster*.

Ronan faces down the Guardians of the Galaxy.

Summer 2014 | Siege of Xandar

The Guardians of the Galaxy successfully unite the Ravagers and the Nova Corps in an elaborate assault on Ronan's battleship, the *Dark Aster*, as it approaches Xandar. But they are still outmatched. Ronan embeds the Power Stone in his Universal Weapon and uses it to eradicate the Nova Corps, which had formed a blockade barrier around his ship.

Groot grows a protective barrier around his friends.

Summer 2014 | Groot's Sacrifice

The Guardians find themselves united by a newfound sense of purpose, and a shared desire to cause chaos in the name of good. Drax kills Korath in single combat, and the team knocks out the control center of the *Dark Aster*, bringing it plummeting to the ground. Groot uses his body to grow a protective cocoon of vines around his friends. He is killed as the ship collides with the ground, but the other Guardians survive thanks to his selfless act.

Summer 2014 | Dumbstruck

Ronan also survives the crash, but before he can use the Power Stone to unleash his rage on Xandar, Quill distracts him by using his own secret weapon: he challenges Ronan to a dance-off. Quill does the wave, a shuffle kick, and a rudimentary Running Man while Drax sneaks up on Ronan with Rocket's Hadron Enforcer. The missile shatters the Universal Weapon as Quill grasps the falling Power Stone.

Peter Quill and Ronan the Accuser each lunge for the Power Stone.

The Guardians link hands to disperse the destructive energy of the Power Stone in Peter Quill's hand.

Summer 2014 | Holding Together

Before the Power Stone can annihilate Quill, the Guardians unite to share its energy. "Take my hand, Peter," were the last words of his dying mother in 1988. Quill ran away from her then, but this memory surges through his mind as his friends channel the Power Stone into a beam that vaporizes Ronan in a purple haze.

Summer 2014 | Baby Steps

The sapling version of Groot grows ever bigger, tended by attentive robots. However, after a crack develops in his pot, the robots replace him with a galactic bonsai tree. Overcome with jealousy, Groot battles his new foe, tearing off one of its branches before finally breaking free of his pot and using his legs for the first time.

"I may be as pretty as an angel, but I sure as hell ain't one."

Summer 2014 | Xandar Aftermath

The Ravagers take their reward (a decoy Orb), while the real Power Stone is left with the Nova Corps for protection. Rocket salvages a twig from Groot's remains and nurtures it in a pot of soil. Baby Groot soon sprouts and makes his first movements, gyrating to the restorative power of the *Awesome Mix Vol. 2*. As the Guardians leave Xandar together after being cleared of their crimes, a despondent Collector sits amidst his shattered museum, comforted by the Soviet space dog Cosmo and having cocktails with Howard the Duck, who is celebrating being released from his display case.

Groot in his pot, feasting on one of his favorite treats: cheese puffs.

129

The Ravagers
Swayed by Star-Lord's promise that they will receive the Orb in exchange for their aid, Yondu leads his Ravager mercenaries and their M-Ships into battle. The Ravagers blast Ronan's ship with energy, providing cover for the M-Ships to attack.

Into Battle
The Guardians join the Ravagers and sneak underneath the *Dark Aster*. Rocket and the Ravager Kraglin use their ships to specifically target the enemy vessel's engines. If the ship reaches the surface and Ronan touches the Power Stone to the ground, Xandar will be devastated.

The Blockade
Nova Prime instructs the Nova Corps to interlock their ships and form a blockade to stop Ronan's ship from landing. The Starblasters link around the ship and form a dynamic energy barrier around the vessel, temporarily halting its descent.

Xandar Besieged
As Ronan's colossal warship, the *Dark Aster*, flies towards Xandar, Corpsman Dey of the Nova Corps shares intel about the impending attack with Nova Prime. The intel comes from the wanted criminal Star-Lord, and the Nova Corps must decide if they believe his claims.

Darkness Descends
Nebula warns Ronan that the Ravagers' forces are under the ship, and the warlord launches his fleet of Sakaaran mercenaries in defense while the *Dark Aster* continues to descend. Rocket's ship blasts a hole in the mighty vessel's exterior and the other Guardians fly inside and board it.

Enter the Nova Corps
Having decided to believe Star-Lord's warning, Nova Prime orders the Nova Corps in their Starblaster ships to help the Ravagers counter Ronan's fleet. The reinforcements arrive just in time.

ATTACK ON XANDAR

A thousand years of war doesn't simply fade from memory when a peace treaty is signed. For Ronan the Accuser, peace isn't an acceptable outcome of the Kree-Nova conflict. Nothing less than the destruction of the Nova Empire will satisfy the warlord and avenge his slain ancestors. To exact his ultimate revenge, Ronan negotiates a deal with Thanos to retrieve the Orb in exchange for Thanos destroying the capital of the Nova Empire, Xandar. But when Ronan discovers the Orb conceals an Infinity Stone, he betrays Thanos and launches an assault on Xandar himself. A desperate defense is mounted, as the fate of the galaxy hangs in the balance.

Yondu Down
After Yondu is shot down, Sakaaran soldiers surround him and his crashed ship; they believe they have an easy win. Yondu, however, has his arrow. At his whistle, the arrow eliminates all of the soldiers and one of their ships.

Dance Off
The Guardians and Ronan emerge from the wreckage. Before Ronan can destroy Xandar with the Power Stone mounted in his Universal Weapon, Peter begins to sing and challenges the warlord to a dance off. The successful distraction confuses Ronan long enough for the Guardians to attack.

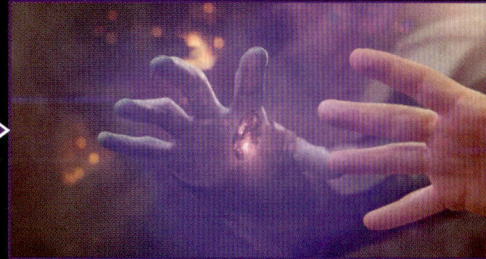

Taking the Stone
Drax and Rocket fire the Hadron Enforcer at the flummoxed Ronan. The blast destroys the Universal Weapon and sends the Power Stone flying into the air. Star-Lord grabs it with his bare hand.

Protecting the City
Ronan orders his Necrocraft pilots to enact the immolation initiative; they dive-bomb their ships into the city, hoping to distract the Nova Corps. Rocket takes the lead and orders the Ravagers to shoot the ships down before they hit the ground.

We Are Groot
With the ship's impact on the surface imminent, Groot protects his friends. He grows branches from his body to cover the Guardians in a protective cocoon, even though Rocket pleads with him not to sacrifice himself.

Take my Hand
The Power Stone's energy is killing Peter, surrounding the group in swirling black and purple flames. In a surprising display of trust, Gamora takes Peter's hand and the energy is shared, lessening the Power Stone's effects.

Gamora Versus Nebula
Nebula intercepts the Guardians aboard the *Dark Aster*. Though Drax shoots her with a blast strong enough to wipe her out, she snaps her robotic body back into place and attacks Gamora with her electroshock batons. Evenly matched, they fight while the battle rages on.

The *Dark Aster* Falls
Rocket crashes his ship into the *Dark Aster*'s bridge and collides with Ronan, which stops the warlord from killing Drax, but triggers catastrophic damage across the ship. Explosions rock the *Dark Aster* as it crashes to the surface.

Guardians of the Galaxy
Drax grabs Peter's arm, Rocket takes Drax's hand, and together, they make wielding the stone bearable. With the group at his back, Peter unleashes the Power Stone on Ronan and it blasts him apart.

Nebula Escapes
The Nova blockade fails as Ronan blasts it with the Power Stone. Gamora nearly knocks Nebula off the ship, but reaches out asking Nebula to help them fight Ronan. Instead, Nebula refuses and escapes on a stolen ship.

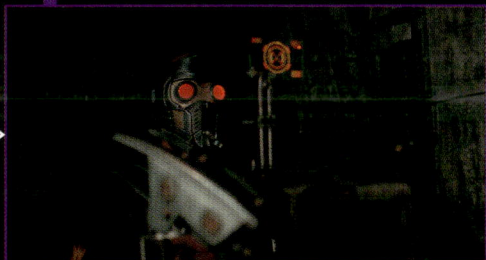

False Dawn
Gamora rejoins Star-Lord, Drax, and Groot as they face Ronan on the *Dark Aster*'s bridge. Star-Lord fires the Hadron Enforcer—a powerful weapon designed by Rocket—at the warlord. But as the dust clears, Ronan still stands, unaffected.

Aftermath
The Guardians save Xandar, and safely conceal the Power Stone just before Yondu demands it as payment. As Peter gives the Ravager a fake, Drax comforts Rocket over the loss of Groot. For their selfless actions their criminal records are wiped.

2014

Gamora uses her blade to save her friends from the Abilisk.

Fall 2014 | Word of Mouth

The legend of the Guardians of the Galaxy soon spreads to other worlds. The group is hired by Ayesha, the golden High Priestess of the Sovereign people to vanquish the aurora-breathing, multi-tentacled inter-dimensional Abilisk beast that feasts upon their main power source, Anulax batteries. In exchange for their services, Ayesha releases the captive Nebula into their custody.

Fall 2014 | A Ship Destroyed

The Guardians fly into an asteroid field, but the attacking Sovereign drones go around the cloud of boulders and fire a barrage at the Guardians on the other side. Suddenly, a mysterious "guy" riding on top of his own egg-like ship annihilates the Sovereign fleet, and the Guardians' badly damaged ship reaches its jump point—only to crash-land in the woodlands of a planet known as Berhert. The ship Peter Quill has been flying since he was 10 years old is "totaled" (as they say on Earth).

Gamora holds on for dear life as the Guardians' ship crashes, saving Drax from being thrown to his death.

Fall 2014 | The Sovereign Fleet

Rocket helps himself to some of the Sovereign's precious (and dangerous) Anulax battery cells, hoping no one will notice. But they do—immediately. The High Priestess sends her remote-controlled fleet to attack.

Ayesha, High Priestess of the Sovereign.

Rocket can't resist stealing some of the valuable power source they were hired to protect.

Ego's arrival gives the Guardians a boost.

Fall 2014 | Me, Myself, and I

Shortly after crashing, the Guardians are greeted by the Deus ex Machina who saved them: Ego, who identifies himself as: 1) a Celestial—basically a god ("With a small G," he adds), 2) Peter Quill's long-lost father, who has been searching the cosmos for him, and 3) the human manifestation of a sentient planet.

Fall 2014 | Events on Berhert

Ego invites Quill, Drax, and Gamora to return to his world for a tour, while Rocket and Baby Groot remain in the forests of Berhert trying to repair the damaged ship. They are beset by bounty hunting Ravagers, dispatched by the Sovereign. Rocket brutalizes them with a series of ambushes and booby traps, but Yondu eventually gains the upper hand. Nebula gets free and wounds Yondu by blasting off the head-fin that controls his deadly arrow, creating a leadership crisis among the Ravagers.

Baby Groot tries to bring an imprisoned Rocket and Yondu what they need to escape.

Rocket is finally captured after terrorizing the Ravagers.

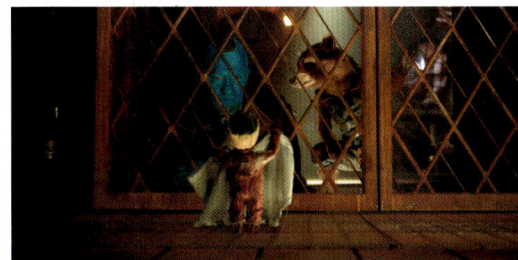

Kraglin, distorted by rapid travel through space.

Fall 2014 | The Scenic Route

The conscience-stricken Ravager Kraglin helps Baby Groot recover a head-fin for Yondu that allows him and Rocket to escape their cell, using Yondu's whistle-controlled arrow to obliterate their mutinous crewmates. The quartet head to Ego's planet, but the fastest route sees them pinballing through 700 jumps, far more than the 50 that mammalian bodies can healthily withstand.

The idyllic, artisanal world of Ego conceals a sinister truth.

Fall 2014 | Ravager Mutiny

The Ravager known as Taserface stages a mutiny against the wounded Yondu, killing all who still support him, and Nebula takes a Ravager starship and ventures off to seek revenge against her sister. A captive Yondu reflects on a life of bad choices, including rounding up Ego's children from around the galaxy—an act that made him an exile among the wider community of Ravagers. He wonders if it is still possible to make it all right...

Fall 2014 | The Worldbuilder

Ego's world, about the size of Earth's moon, contains his history of seeking connection in the universe, including his experiences with Quill's mother. He claims to have found his empathic assistant, Mantis, in a larva stage on her homeworld, but in fact she is also one of his children. Ego says he sought Quill for years. "When I heard of a man from Earth who held an Infinity Stone in his hand without dying, I knew you must be the son of the woman I loved," Ego explains.

Taserface claims his name is "metaphorical." Regardless of its origins, it inspires mirth rather than fear in those he threatens.

2014

Fall 2014 | Sibling Rivalry

On Ego's world, Nebula attempts to kill Gamora, finally ending their lifelong conflict. Instead they both become stranded deep beneath the surface of the planet, and bond again as sisters who were unfairly pitted against each other. In a forgotten cavern, they find the skeletal remains of Ego's other "children." Their confrontation with Thanos will come another day, but now they have a chance to stop a different kind of horrible father.

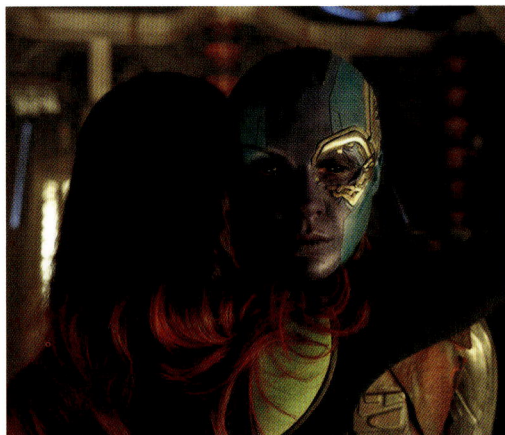

Two lifelong enemies finally become true sisters.

Ego's humanoid avatar restructures after being blasted apart by his son.

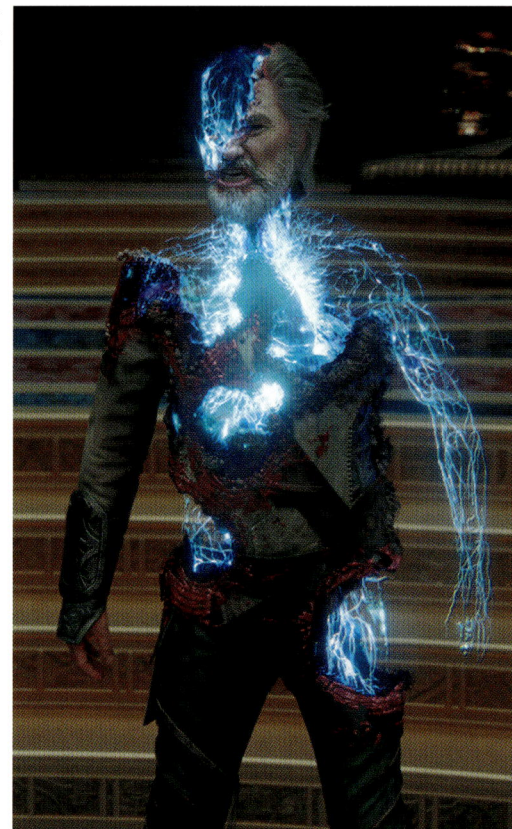

Fall 2014 | Malignant

Ego tries to quash his son's sentimental impulses by explaining that he too once felt love holding him back. In that case, it was Peter's mother, Meredith, who made Ego feel like ending his Expansion plans. Instead he ended her. "It broke my heart to put that tumor in her head." This revelation snaps Quill out of his trance—he draws his blaster and shoots apart Ego's human body, moments before his friends crash-land on the planet.

Fall 2014 | Father of Lies

Ego explains to Quill that Quill is the only one of his countless children who actually shares the Celestial genes, which Ego needs to power the Expansion—his parasitic takeover of thousands of other worlds. Ego uses his Celestial powers to enchant Quill, and invites him to join him and rule the galaxy. But Quill begins to fight through the enchantment as he considers what this would do to his friends... and Gamora. And the rest of life as he knows it.

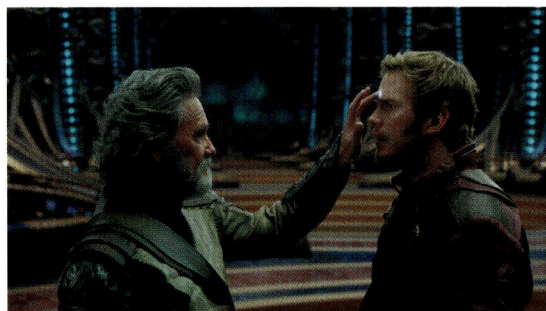

Ego reveals the Expansion to Peter Quill, and asks for his help taking over the universe.

Fall 2014 | Heart of the Matter

As the Guardians rescue Quill and take off, Yondu reveals that he kept Star-Lord around as a Ravager and never delivered him to Ego because he learned that Ego was destroying the other children Yondu had harvested for him. Quill tells them that they must venture deep into the center of Ego to stop him, or all the planets that the Celestial has implanted with his spores are in danger of being overtaken, including Earth. Meanwhile, a fleet of Sovereign drones arrives above the planet, still seeking revenge for the Guardians' theft.

Peter Quill and Gamora share a dance.

Fall 2014 | Ego Blow

Joined by Mantis, the reunited Guardians launch an attack to end Ego's galactic conquest. Rocket makes a bomb using the stolen Anulax batteries, which Groot plants (so to speak) at Ego's center. As the attacking Sovereign ships are wiped out by the other Guardians, Quill uses his Celestial abilities to battle his father's avatar. Finally the bomb explodes, reducing Ego to nothingness.

Mantis helps subdue Ego by putting his consciousness to sleep, allowing the Guardians to infiltrate his core.

The birthing pod for Adam, described by Ayesha as the next step in their evolution: "More powerful, more beautiful, more capable of destroying the Guardians of the Galaxy."

Fall 2014 | Eve of Adam

The embittered leader of the Sovereign, High Priestess Ayesha, creates a genetically engineered warrior whom she calls "Adam," planning to one day punish the Guardians of the Galaxy for their insolence.

Fall 2014 | Yondu's Redemption

Clutching his ascending arrow, Yondu helps a drained Quill escape the cataclysm. However, Yondu only has one portable force-field suit, using it to protect Quill as they reach the deadly void of space. As his last act, Yondu Udonta sacrifices his own life to save the man he treated like a delinquent, but secretly loved as a son.

Yondu's final words to Quill: "He may have been your father, but he wasn't your daddy ... I'm damn lucky you were my boy."

Groot decides to take a bath on an alien world, but discovers the warm mud has a strange effect on him.

Fall 2014 | Groot's Family Portrait

Groot's adventures continue. He is worshiped as a food-providing god by tiny alien creatures when he drops a leaf on their civilization, confronts a dancing liquid monster that copies his every move, and grows luxurious foliage after a mud bath. The recent family-themed conflicts that have embroiled the Guardians of the Galaxy also make toddler Groot appreciative of the ragtag group of space misfits he considers his own relations. He decides a family portrait is in order, and assembles materials for his collage from one of Peter Quill's old comic books, a chunk of Rocket's tail, Drax's pink soap, and green glitter from a detonated microchip. The effort blows a hole in their ship, reinforcing the idea that family relationships can sometimes be chaotic.

GAMORA AND NEBULA

Adopted by Thanos, Gamora and Nebula grow up as sisters. Thanos constantly pits them against each other, fostering a lifelong rivalry and bitterness between the two. They both become fierce and cruel assassins working for their father. Gamora breaks free from Thanos' grip first, and Nebula follows in her footsteps. They pursue their own paths away from their father; eventually, both find their way to the Guardians of the Galaxy, making choices for the good of others as part of the group, and reconciling.

2014 | Gamora betrays Ronan
Both sisters are ordered by Thanos to serve the Kree warlord Ronan. Gamora convinces Ronan to send her to Xandar to retrieve the Orb (which actually contains the Power Stone) instead of Nebula, claiming she knows the planet better. In reality, Gamora has turned against both Ronan and Thanos and plans to take the Orb for herself.

2014 | Battle on the *Dark Aster*
After Star-Lord saves her, Gamora tries to persuade Nebula to side with her against Ronan. Instead, Nebula continues their rivalry and they face off over Xandar, before Nebula escapes.

2014 | Knowhere Showdown
Nebula remains loyal to her father, even when he tells Ronan that Gamora was his "favorite daughter." Battling for opposing sides on Knowhere, Nebula doesn't hesitate to blast Gamora's space pod apart, leaving her for dead and taking the Orb.

2014 | Collecting a Bounty
Gamora continues to keep her sister at arm's length. When the Sovereign give custody of the imprisoned Nebula to Gamora, the latter calls her nothing more than a bounty.

2014 | Sisters at War
Free from captivity, Nebula finds her sister on Ego and unleashes her grudges upon Gamora. The sisters talk through past grievances while trying to kill each other, but join forces against Ego after resolving their issues in a heart-to-heart.

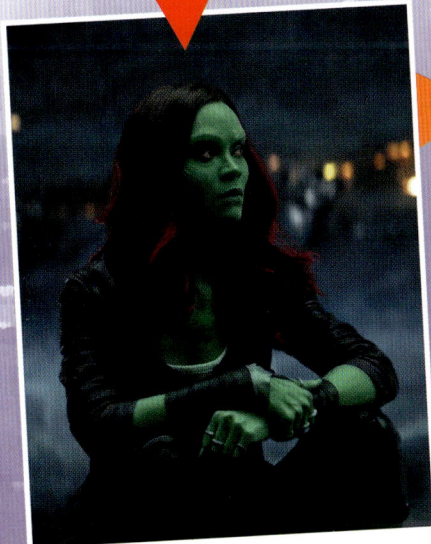

2014 | An Uneasy Alliance
With a new understanding of how Thanos manipulated them both, Nebula and Gamora reconcile. Gamora even asks Nebula to join the Guardians, but she sets off alone to kill Thanos.

2018 | Thanos' Sacrifice
Keeping Gamora close, Thanos travels to Vormir. Upon being told that he must sacrifice that which he loves to receive the Soul Stone, Thanos realizes he truly loves Gamora and must sacrifice her. Gamora is in disbelief and fights to the end, but Thanos throws her to her death.

2018 | Gamora's Capture
Long estranged from Thanos, Gamora wants to prevent him from gaining the Infinity Stones. She knows where the Soul Stone is, and would rather die than pass the information to Thanos, but Thanos kidnaps her.

2018 | Protecting her Sister
Thanos previously captured Nebula when she made an attempt on his life. With Gamora now also in hand, he further torments the sisters by forcing Gamora to watch him torture Nebula, demanding the location of the Soul Stone. Feeling compassion for Nebula, Gamora reveals the stone's location.

2018 | Nebula Fights Back
On Titan, Nebula confronts her father about Gamora, showing her love for her sister. When Nebula realizes Thanos sacrificed her, she tells the rest of the group, causing their plan to unravel as Star-Lord lashes out.

2024 | Past Meets Present
Nebulas from different eras confront each other in the aftermath of the Time Heist, with 2014 Nebula still loyal to Thanos and angry at the universe. She is slain by her present-day self.

2024 | Together Again
The Gamora of 2014 helps the present-day Nebula, and the latter offers honesty, explaining how the two have grown, despite their differences, to become actual sisters. Together they face their father and aid in his final destruction.

2015

Super Heroes have rescued the world from repeated threats in recent years, but the sudden collapse of S.H.I.E.L.D. and the revelation of its hidden corruption has also shaken the public's confidence in those who wield the greatest power. Could those who vow to protect the world also inadvertently cause catastrophic harm? Even the heroes themselves begin to question their roles, and whether they can be fully trusted with the strengths and abilities they control. In the age of Super Heroes, this is a most uncertain hour...

Steve Rogers' present echoes his past as he fights Hydra forces in a European forest.

Spring 2015 | The Avengers' Sokovia Incursion

The Avengers zero in on Strucker's redoubt in the Sokovian mountains as one of Hydra's last remnants, and unite for a full-scale attack on the facility. Thor, Captain America, Hulk, Black Widow, Iron Man, and Hawkeye, accompanied by robots of Stark's Iron Legion, easily defeat Hydra's tanks, infantry, and fortifications, but the battle takes a turn when the Maximoff twins are unleashed. Moving faster than the eye can see, Pietro snatches Hawkeye's arrows out of midair, causing the distracted sharpshooter to be seriously wounded by an energy cannon blast.

The Avengers align outside Hydra's research station in Sokovia.

Spring 2015 | Triggering Stark's Nightmare

While Strucker quickly surrenders to Captain America, Tony Stark emerges from his Iron Man armor to explore the laboratories of the Hydra lair. He becomes overwhelmed by an ominous vision of his fellow Avengers' deaths when Wanda Maximoff uses her powers to enchant his mind. He pictures an unstoppable army of alien invaders entering a portal over Earth's atmosphere. Stark retrieves the scepter and Wanda and Pietro withdraw, knowing she has nourished a fear that will only grow and consume him.

Pietro and Wanda Maximoff study the intruders to Hydra's facility.

Tony Stark examines the robotics research Hydra was performing.

Spring 2015 | A Suit of Armor Around the World

Back at Avengers Tower in New York, Tony Stark and Bruce Banner perform a scan of Loki's scepter that reveals an energy core that resembles the firing of neurons. They theorize that this could be the key to a project Stark has codenamed "Ultron," which would merge his Iron Legion robotics tech with sentient artificial intelligence, creating an army of Iron Man sentries. He believes this could also free the Avengers from their overwhelming responsibilities. "What if you were sipping margaritas on a sun-drenched beach, turning brown instead of green?" Stark tells Banner.

Tony Stark shows Bruce Banner a visualization of JARVIS, compared to the advanced algorithm emanating from the Mind Stone scepter.

"I had strings ... but now I'm free."

Spring 2015 | Ultron Awakens

During the party, Stark's A.I. assistant JARVIS successfully interfaces with the power in Loki's scepter, leading to a spark of electric life. Ultron immediately questions his existence and purpose, lashing out at JARVIS for trying to contain him, and uploading into Stark's nearby Iron Legion. A legionnaire robot, badly scarred by acid during the Sokovia mission, lurches into the afterparty to declare that Ultron has assessed the Avengers themselves—and humanity in general—to be Earth's preeminent dangers. One legionnaire flies off with Loki's scepter, but the others are destroyed. Ultron is not restricted to a physical form, and his consciousness escapes into the global computer network.

Spring 2015 | Recovery and "Revels"

Genetics pioneer Dr. Helen Cho helps to repair Clint Barton's battle wounds, noting that instead of taking hours, her Regeneration Cradle back in Seoul could restore him in minutes. Meanwhile, the latest defeat of Hydra leads to a celebration in Stark's penthouse. "Victory should conclude with revels!" Thor declares. Later that night, the Avengers play a party game: Is it true no one but Thor can lift his hammer? The God of Thunder is amused by their various efforts to pry Mjolnir from its resting place. But ... did Steve Rogers budge it slightly?

Thor is confident that he is the only one worthy. Until Steve Rogers budges Mjolnir.

2015

Spring 2015 | A Time to Build

Ultron's consciousness returns to Strucker's abandoned robotics lab in Sokovia, where he begins assembling more powerful physical forms that venture out to kill Strucker while he is in custody, and raid weapons manufacturers and engineering facilities around the world. At the church in the center of Sokovia's capital, Ultron's latest prime avatar makes contact with the Maximoff twins and enlists them to his cause.

Ulysses Klaue makes the mistake of comparing Ultron to Tony Stark.

Ultron in the heart of Sokovia, recruiting Pietro and Wanda Maximoff.

Spring 2015 | The Vibranium Merchant

Ultron and the Maximoff twins meet with the criminal arms dealer Ulysses Klaue on his ship off the African coast. They are seeking the cylinders of vibranium Klaue once stole from the kingdom of Wakanda, intending to use it to create indestructible new forms for Ultron. Billions of dollars are uploaded to Klaue's shell accounts as payment, but when the mercenary notes that Ultron shares some personality traits with his creator, Tony Stark, Ultron indulges a moment of rage and severs Klaue's arm.

Spring 2015 | Avengers Tension

Back at the Avengers Tower, Tony Stark's fellow heroes are incensed by his creation, but he remains adamant that they need a larger protective force to save Earth from galactic threats. "We can bust arms dealers all day, but that up there...? That's the endgame," Stark insists.

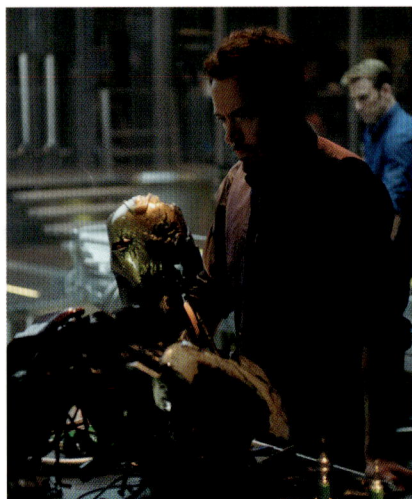

Spring 2015 | Hulk vs. Hulkbuster

The Avengers track Ultron to Klaue's ship, but they are mesmerized and confounded by Wanda Maximoff, who conjures unnerving illusions while her brother dashes through the vessel launching sneak attacks. When she influences the mind of Bruce Banner, the Hulk emerges and rampages viciously through the city of Johannesburg. Tony Stark summons his Hulkbuster armor and Veronica system from his Stark Industries satellite, and finally subdues the disoriented Hulk—but not before widespread destruction and injuries are inflicted. When Banner returns to normal, he is horrified by what he has done.

Tony Stark realizes his miscalculation.

The Stark Industries satellite dispatches Veronica and the Hulkbuster armor from orbit.

Hulkbuster vs. Hulk in South Africa.

Pietro Maximoff turns against Ultron in South Korea.

Spring 2015 | Hawkeye's Hideway

The Avengers regroup at a location so secret not even S.H.I.E.L.D. knew it existed—Clint Barton's family farm. There they meet his pregnant wife, Laura, and his two children, all of them kept hidden to protect them from vengeance-seeking enemies. It is a place of calm to form a new plan for containing the rapidly evolving Ultron menace, but long-simmering disagreements between Tony Stark and Steve Rogers also surface. Nick Fury, one of the few who knew of the farm's existence, joins them and gives the team a much-needed morale boost.

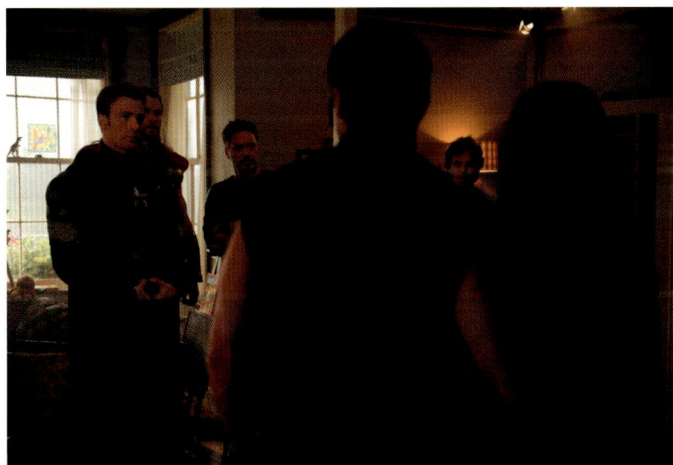

The Avengers lay low at the Barton family farm.

Spring 2015 | A Race Through Seoul

Ultron is forced to halt his uplink when Captain America, Black Widow, and Hawkeye track him down at Dr. Cho's facility. As the Regeneration Cradle containing Ultron's new form is evacuated by truck through the city, the trio do everything in their power to stop it. They are only successful when Wanda and Pietro Maximoff join the fight, this time on the side of the Avengers. When the cradle is secured aboard the Quinjet, Hawkeye flies it back to New York for analysis.

Spring 2015 | The Cradle of Life

Ultron and the Maximoffs escape with Klaue's vibranium cache and take a portion of it to Dr. Helen Cho's clinic in Seoul. With Loki's scepter, they compel her to use her Regeneration Cradle to weave the powerful metal into an organic form, creating a synthezoid body for Ultron to possess. "The most versatile substance on the planet, and they used it to make a Frisbee," Ultron scoffs. He then embeds the Mind Stone from the scepter in the new being's forehead. As Ultron gradually uploads his consciousness into the body, Wanda Maximoff realizes she can now read his thoughts. She is appalled to discover Ultron's plan to annihilate humanity, and she and Pietro immediately turn against him.

Wanda Maximoff picks up on Ultron's extinction plans for humanity.

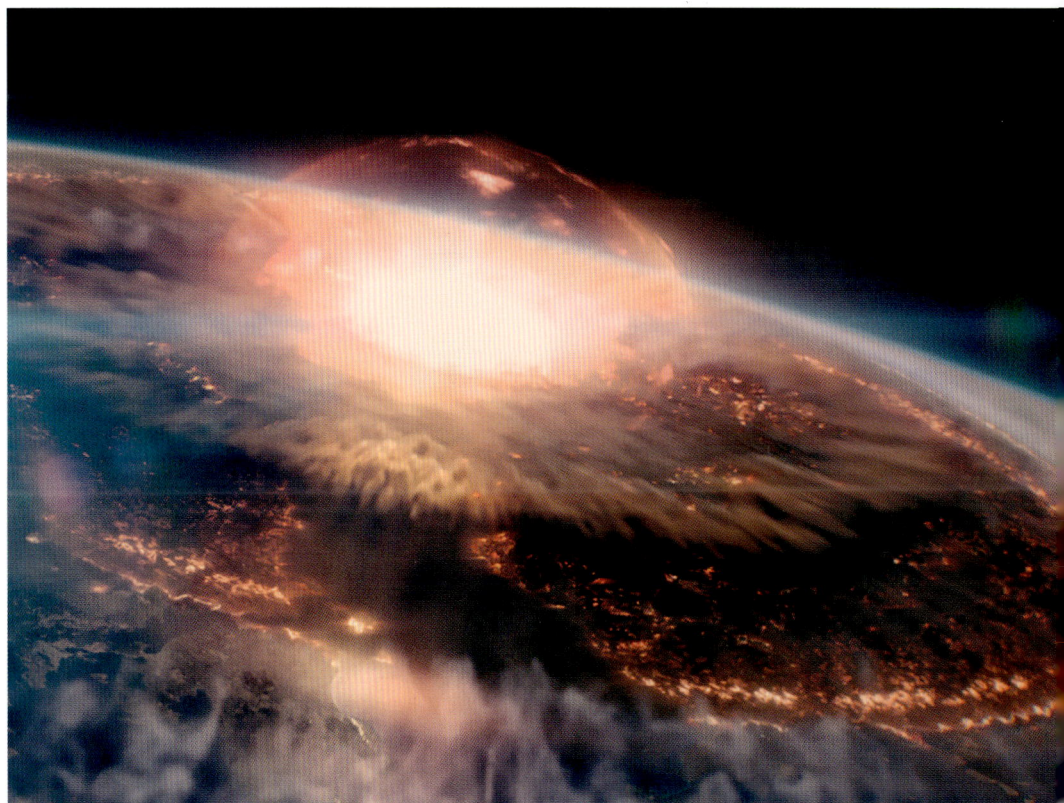

A vision of Ultron's genocidal ambitions.

141

2015

Supercharged by Mjolnir's lightning, Vision emerges as a new form of synthetic life.

Spring 2015 | Birth of the Vision

Tony Stark and Bruce Banner decide to upload JARVIS into the synthezoid body as a controlling consciousness. This further fractures the Avengers alliance, with Steve Rogers insisting it's wrong to continue the experiment, especially after the initial Ultron program backfired so horrifically. Thor uses Mjolnir to cast a bolt of lightning at the cradle, supercharging it at a critical moment to finish the process. A being emerges. It is not Ultron. It is not JARVIS. It is a vision of something new—and that term becomes the name by which he is known: Vision.

Spring 2015 | Ultron's Extinction Plan

Ultron has used the remainder of Klaue's vibranium to construct an engine beneath Sokovia's capital, which will force the metropolis to rise into the atmosphere. When it falls back, it will become an extinction-level meteor that will cleanse the earth. "When the dust settles," Ultron declares, "the only thing living in this world will be metal." As the ground fractures and rises into the sky, the Avengers and the Maximoff twins race to evacuate as many people as possible while destroying Ultron's battalion of sentries.

Ultron's giant vibranium engines rip Sokovia apart.

Vision and Thor assess the threat.

Spring 2015 | A Worthy Ally

The Avengers question whether this powerful new being is on their side. "I am on the side of life. Ultron isn't. He will end it all," Vision says, urging them to act quickly to eradicate every physical form Ultron has built, and erase every trace of him lurking online. The Avengers remain fearful of trusting something that Ultron had a hand in making. "There may be no way to make you trust me, but we need to go," Vision says, lifting Mjolnir to hand it to Thor—thereby proving his integrity.

Spring 2015 | Death Toll

Nick Fury and Maria Hill pilot a former S.H.I.E.L.D. Helicarrier into the airspace beside the city to rescue as many citizens of Sokovia as possible. The death toll is reduced from potentially thousands to only 177 civilians. Among those who die is the family of Sokovian paramilitary leader Helmut Zemo, who vows revenge on the "heroes" he blames for the tragedy, and American citizen Charlie Spencer, whose mother will later confront Tony Stark over his death. Pietro Maximoff is also killed—shot by Ultron while using his superspeed to save Hawkeye and an innocent child from the deadly fusillade. His sister Wanda senses his death, and her surge of grief sends out waves of mystical energy that wipe out all the surrounding Ultron sentries.

The rescue of Sokovian citizens by former members of S.H.I.E.L.D.

Wanda Maximoff feels her brother's death.

Spring 2015 | Sokovia Vaporized

With most of Sokovia's citizens safe, Thor and Iron Man destroy the engine's core before it can smash into the ground, reducing the city to rubble and greatly lowering the damage as it falls to Earth. Sokovia is in ruins, but the planet is saved. The consequences of this destruction will be seen not as a victory, but as a needless calamity that could have been avoided if Tony Stark and the Avengers had been more thoughtful, diligent, and careful. In the aftermath, many around the world will support tighter restrictions on individuals who possess such extraordinary powers.

The Helicarrier backs away as the Sokovian capital starts to plunge back to Earth.

The new additions to the Avengers roster gather at their new headquarters: Avengers Compound.

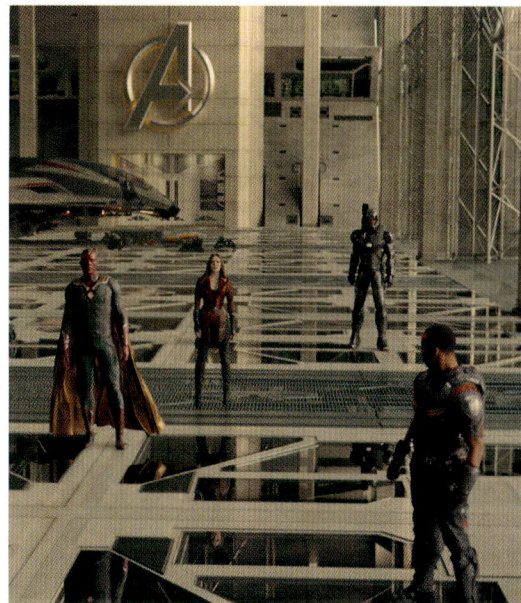

Spring 2015 | A New Line-Up

The Hulk ignores Natasha's pleas to return to the Avengers and leaves Earth in the Quinjet. Thor also ventures into the galaxy, seeking the Infinity Stones that now seem to pose such a threat. A chastened Stark steps back from Iron Man while Captain America and Black Widow bring together a new team of Avengers, including Vision, Wanda Maximoff, James "Rhodey" Rhodes' War Machine, and Sam Wilson's Falcon.

Spring 2015 | Ultron's Last Words

Vision, who had merged with Ultron early in the battle to block his ability to upload and escape, tracks down the last remaining sentry where Ultron's consciousness resides. Ultron is resigned to his defeat, but assures Vision that humanity is also doomed. "Yes," Vision agrees. "But a thing isn't beautiful because it lasts." Ultron calls him "unbearably naive." Vision replies, "Well… I was born yesterday," before eradicating Ultron with a beam from the Mind Stone.

Vision erases the last remnant of Ultron.

Wanda Maximoff and Vision share the bond of being empowered by the Mind Stone.

2015-2016 | Vision and Wanda

For all his great powers, Vision remains wistful to learn more about feelings and emotions that defy easy explanation. At the new Avengers Compound in upstate New York, he and Wanda Maximoff forge an intense friendship, drawn together by their shared feeling of being outsiders. They experience happy times, as Vision comes to share her enthusiasm for retro sitcoms, as well as sadness, when Wanda struggles with heartbreak over the death of her brother. "I've never experienced loss because I've never had a loved one to lose," Vision tells her. "But what is grief if not love persevering?"

143

SOKOVIA

Sokovia is a war-torn country in Europe, whose people live at the mercy of those who do not have their best interests at heart. Hydra operatives run a secret base that experiments on Sokovians, preying upon their desire to help their country. Later, Ultron targets Sokovia's capital city to begin his mission of "world peace"; he plots to use a doomsday device on the city that will kill billions around the world. The ensuing battle ravages the country, and the incident leads to the creation of the Sokovia Accords, intended to regulate those with enhanced powers.

1990s | History of War
Long before Hydra's base is established, or Ultron attacks, Sokovia is a nation in turmoil. Due to the regional unrest, parts of the country are bombed with Stark Industries explosives, leaving the young Wanda and Pietro Maximoff orphaned.

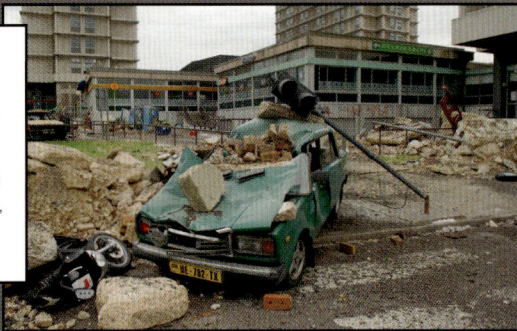

2015 | Hydra Defeated
Following the collapse of S.H.I.E.L.D., the Avengers subdue the remnants of Hydra across the world. Hydra's final redoubt is Baron Strucker's fortress in Sokovia, which the Avengers assault and put out of action while battling the enhanced Maximoff twins.

The Battle in Sokovia (2015)

Evacuation
Pursuing the rogue A.I. Ultron to Sokovia, the Avengers send Pietro and Wanda to evacuate as many citizens as possible. The twins use their powers to get civilians to safety, while Thor and Banner infiltrate Ultron's underground base. Banner rescues the captive Black Widow while Thor hunts for Ultron's weapon.

Never Ending Enemies
The robotic enemies seem to come in endless waves. The Avengers focus on eliminating as many sentries as possible and keeping Sokovians safe, even as the city climbs ever higher. Just when it seems hopeless, Nick Fury brings a former S.H.I.E.L.D. Helicarrier alongside and the civilians begin to evacuate to it.

Hawkeye and Wanda
Surrounded by Ultron's sentries and under heavy fire, Wanda buckles. She feels she and Pietro are responsible for Ultron targeting Sokovia, but Clint provides guidance and tells her that if she chooses to fight back against Ultron, then that makes her an Avenger.

The City Rises
With an ominous rumble, cracks spread across the surface of the city. As the Avengers watch, a section of the city breaks loose and begins to rise into the sky. Ultron broadcasts his intentions: when the city crashes back to Earth as a meteor, it will wipe out all life on the planet.

Vibranium Foes
Vision confronts Ultron at the old church that lies at the center of the city, where Ultron has sited the doomsday trigger. Vision invades Ultron's mind, cutting him off from the internet and trapping him in physical form. In response, Ultron activates the trigger.

Stopping Doomsday

Sensing his victory slipping away from him, Ultron directs his sentries to activate the doomsday trigger early, which will still wipe out billions of people. The Avengers create a human barrier around the device and stop every sentry that tries to turn the key.

Ultron's Assault

Ultron joins his sentries swarming his weapon, but Vision blasts the rogue A.I. with his Mind Stone. Thor joins in with Mjolnir, so does Iron Man with his repulsors. Their combined blasts knock Ultron down. He flees to an unguarded Quinjet and takes off.

The Death of Pietro

Ultron starts strafing the escaping Sokovians in his Quinjet, forcing the Avengers to take cover. Pietro is killed while trying to shield Hawkeye, a tragedy which Wanda instantly senses. After Ultron is thrown from the Quinjet by a raging Hulk, Wanda approaches and rips out his mechanical heart.

Sokovia Falls

Despite the Avengers' best efforts, a sentry activates the doomsday trigger and the raised part of Sokovia falls. Even as the city plunges, Tony is able to supercharge the device from below while Thor strikes the trigger with Mjolnir from above. The city is blasted into fragments that fall into the ocean.

2025 | Honoring the Past

Nearly two hundred Sokovian civilians were killed in the battle. The Sokovian memorial honors them and their families and stands as the only remaining landmark of Sokovia after neighboring countries partition the former nation. Bucky Barnes, Ayo, and other Dora Milaje visit the memorial years after the tragedy to take Zemo back into custody.

2016 | Sokovian Revenge

The Avengers fracture in disagreement over the accords. Baron Zemo, a Sokovian who seeks revenge on the heroes, whom he blames for his family's death, leverages the schism, further dividing them by using the Winter Soldier as a flashpoint between Iron Man and Captain America.

2016 | Control and Power

While the Avengers' battles have caused damage before, the destruction of an entire city is unprecedented. In the aftermath, the United Nations drafts the Sokovia Accords, granting them authority over unsanctioned, enhanced actions. U.S. Secretary of State Thaddeus Ross informs the Avengers about the change in procedure.

Out of the City

A single Ultron sentry survives the battle, and crawls from the wreckage into the forest. There Ultron is confronted again by Vision. The two artificial beings debate humanity's flaws, and while Vision agrees humanity is doomed, he counters that "a thing isn't beautiful because it lasts." He then uses the Mind Stone to put Ultron down for good.

2015

Scott Lang seeks to rebuild his life after his release from prison.

Summer 2015 | I Fought the Law

Scott Lang is released from San Quentin prison after his three year sentence for stealing and redistributing millions of dollars that were improperly taken by VistaCorp from its customers. He reunites with his former cellmate Luis, a not-so-hardened criminal who had been jailed for stealing smoothie machines. Luis has heard tell about a millionaire mark with a vulnerable safe and hopes Lang will join him in the heist. Lang just wants to stay on the right side of the law, make peace with his ex, Maggie, and be a good father to his young daughter, Cassie.

Darren Cross speaks to potential buyers.

Summer 2015 | A Tall Tale

Dr. Hank Pym is invited to Pym Technologies for the first time since he was voted out as CEO. His former protégé, Darren Cross, announces they are close to developing a formula that will mimic the shrinking properties of Pym Particles, which their inventor has withheld from the company since he was ousted. Cross intends to combine the new tech with his Yellowjacket combat suit, which will create an army of miniature warriors conducting surveillance, sabotage, and even assassinations.

Summer 2015 | 20% Over Asking Price

Mitchell Carson, the former Head of Defense at S.H.I.E.L.D., is enthusiastic about Yellowjacket's mercenary applications, and makes an offer for the technology on behalf of Hydra. Dr. Pym and his estranged daughter Hope, chair of the company, are determined to stop the plan. If they can't do it officially, they're willing to disrupt it by nefarious means.

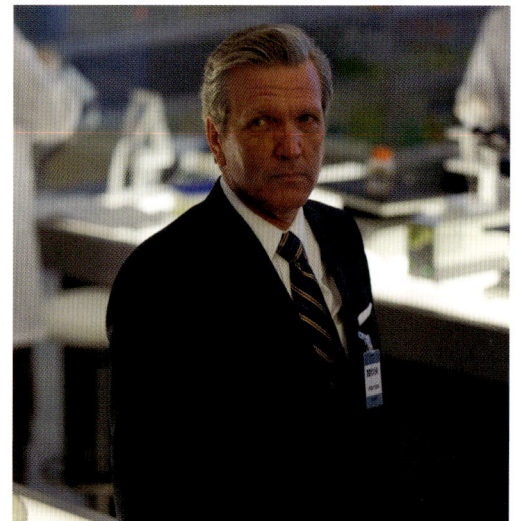

Mitchell Carson: "You sell to me first."

Summer 2015 | Flushed Away

Frustrated by his inability to shrink a living subject with his knockoff Pym Particles, Darren Cross begins to lash out. He confronts an executive who raised alarm about the Yellowjacket suit falling into dangerous hands. When the executive remains unconvinced, Cross "miniaturizes" him—reducing the man to a droplet of red goop that is easily disposed of down a toilet.

Darren's behavior becomes increasingly erratic as he fails to replicate Pym's research.

Having broken into the safe, Scott Lang wonders why he was sent to retrieve this strange old suit.

Summer 2015 | Breaking and Entering

Desperate for child support after losing his job, Scott Lang agrees to Luis' heist. But Luis' mark turns out to be Hank Pym, and inside his safe there is no fortune—just what Lang assumes is "an old motorcycle suit." It's actually the Ant-Man suit the doctor once used to shrink himself for U.S.-sanctioned special missions in the Soviet Union in the '80s. Pym is monitoring the heist on miniature bug-mounted cameras. It was all a ruse to test Lang's skills.

Summer 2015 | Let's Get Small

Lang tries on the Ant-Man suit and has a near-death experience escaping from a bathtub that has suddenly become as vast as the Grand Canyon. After falling through cracks, facing down insects that tower over him, and even getting sucked into the whirlwind of a vacuum cleaner, Lang decides to return the suit, but is arrested in the process. Pym visits him in jail and reveals his ploy, then breaks Scott out. It's obvious Scott will need more training if he is going to help Pym steal the Yellowjacket suit from under Cross' watch and erase the data behind the new shrinking tech.

Scott Lang tests out the incredible shrinking suit.

A bathtub faucet becomes a flash flood when you're miniaturized.

2015

A bug in a jar: Darren Cross captures Ant-Man.

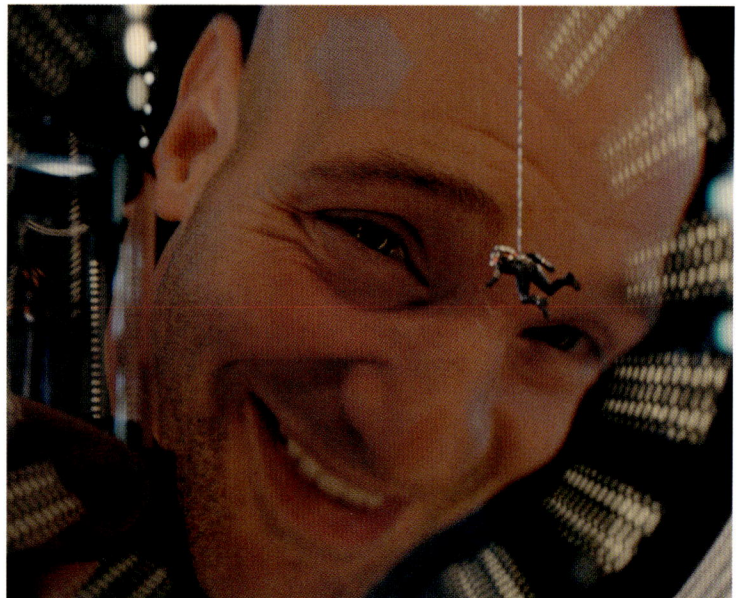

Summer 2015 | Love Tap

Hank Pym dreads losing his daughter Hope Van Dyne the way he lost her mother Janet when she went subatomic in 1987 while disarming a rogue Soviet missile. While he won't consent to Hope wearing the Ant-Man suit, he does ask her to help train Lang: "When you're small, your energy's compressed. You have the force of a 200-pound man behind a fist 1/100th of an inch wide," she explains. "You're like a bullet. Punch too hard, you kill someone. Too soft, and it's a love tap." Meanwhile, Cross finally works out the bugs in his own Pym Particle formula. Time is running out if he is to be stopped.

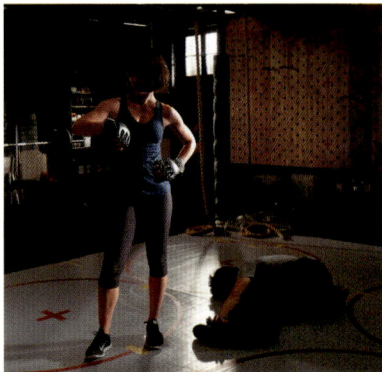

Hope Van Dyne trains Scott Lang.

Hank Pym discusses how to be Ant-Man.

Summer 2015 | Danger Looms Large

Dr. Pym tells Lang to be careful with the Ant-Man suit's regulator, explaining that if it malfunctions "you would enter a reality where all concepts of time and space become irrelevant as you shrink for all eternity. Everything that you know and love, gone forever." An even larger threat is Darren Cross himself. When Lang infiltrates Pym Technologies, Cross puts on the Yellowjacket suit himself to battle the tiny thief for possession of the new shrinking particles.

Scott Lang ventures to the Avengers Compound in tiny form.

Falcon detects something amiss.

Summer 2015 | Falcon vs. Insect

One of Lang's first test-runs is to infiltrate one of Howard Stark's old storage facilities to steal a signal decoy that will aid in the raid on Pym Technologies. That location turns out to be the new Avengers Compound. Sam Wilson detects a sensor trip and does battle with the microscopic trespasser. "I was hoping I could grab a piece of technology for a few days," Lang explains. "I need it to save the world. You know how that is." Faced with this new and unexpected challenger, Falcon can't prevent Lang from escaping with the device.

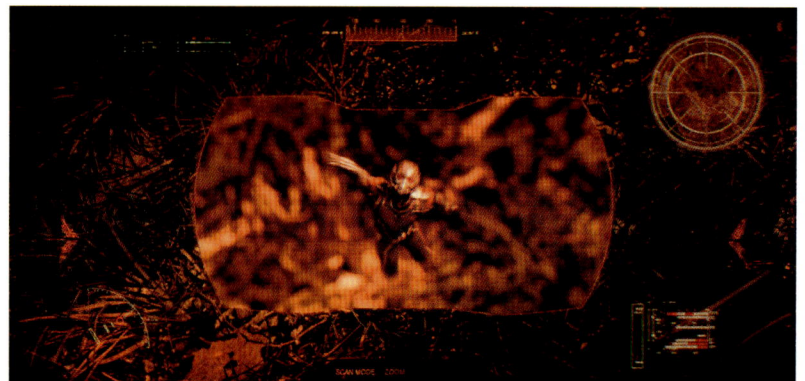

Falcon's goggles analyze the miniature intruder.

Ant-Man battles Yellowjacket. The fight causes mayhem in Cassie Lang's bedroom.

Summer 2015 | Toot! Toot!

The battle between Cross and Lang spills over to Lang's ex-wife's home, where the two miniature combatants clash atop a toy train in Cassie's bedroom. Lang finally defeats Cross by ignoring Dr. Pym's warning and using his regulator to go subatomic, bypassing the Yellowjacket suit's titanium shell and sabotaging it from within. Darren Cross and his suit collapse in on themselves, vanishing to parts unknown. But then Scott keeps on going, sinking further and further into the Quantum Realm. Scott modifies his regulator to escape, but before doing so, he unknowingly encounters Janet Van Dyne.

Darren Cross in the Yellowjacket suit.

Summer 2015 | The Wasp Factory

After Scott Lang successfully emerges from the surreal Quantum Realm, Dr. Pym ponders whether it might be possible to find and rescue his long-lost wife, Janet. Hope's father presents her with the prototype Wasp suit he was working on when her mother vanished. "Maybe it's time we finished it?" he suggests.

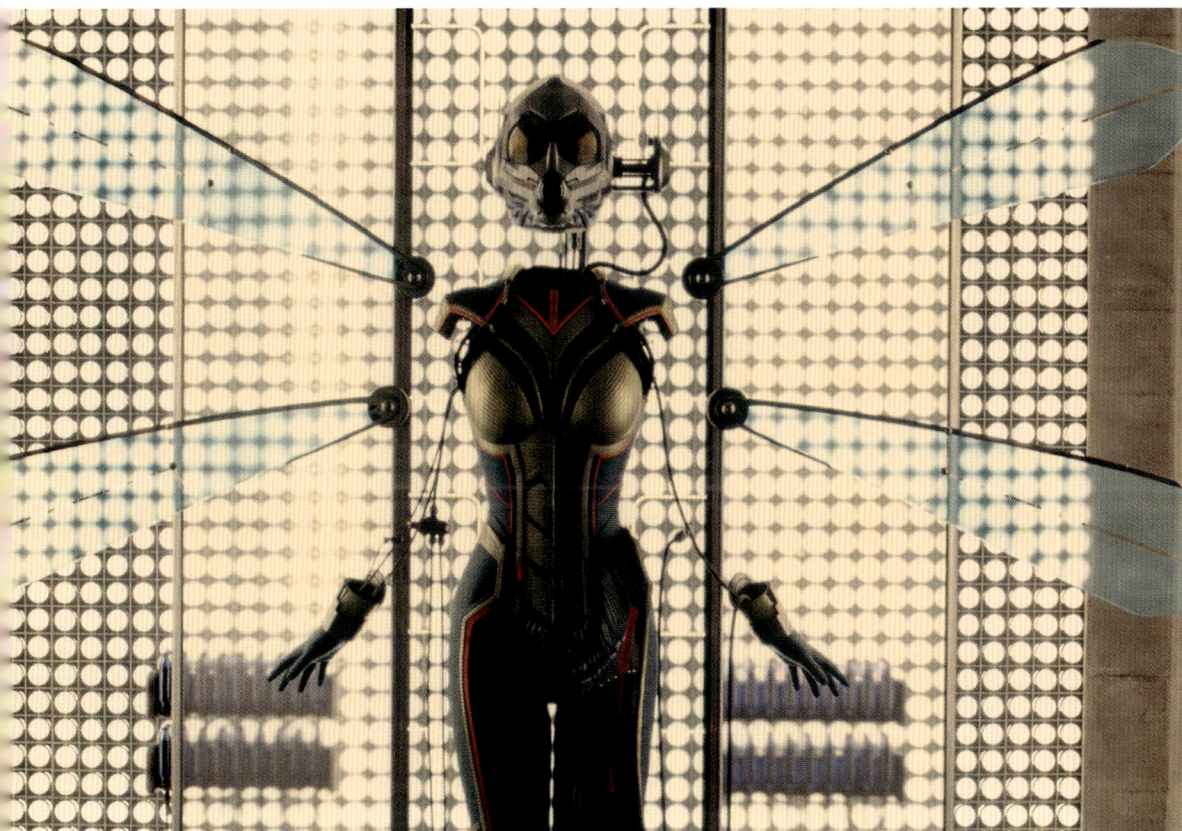

The prototype for a new Wasp suit.

2016

The world turns against its heroes. The emergence of beings with incredible powers has been followed by a rise in global threats that make ordinary people question whether their supposed protectors might actually be endangering them. In this hostile environment, fissures in alliances soon form and friends become enemies.

Kaecilius takes forbidden knowledge for his breakaway sect of Zealots.

Early 2016 | Forbidden Rituals

A power struggle erupts among the Masters of the Mystic Arts as Kaecilius turns against the Ancient One. He and his Zealots violently attack the Kamar-Taj compound, stealing *The Book of Cagliostro* from the Ancient One's private library for the purposes of conducting a banned ritual. They plan to unleash the power of the Dark Dimension and summon its god-like ruler Dormammu to Earth.

Stephen Strange races toward destiny.

February 2, 2016 | Doctor Strange's Devastating Crash

While driving at night to a Neurological Society dinner, Doctor Stephen Strange takes a call about prospective new patients while speeding in his sports car around treacherous curves. A moment of distraction sends him hurtling over a cliff in a crash that shatters his hands, making him incapable of the delicate surgical work that made him famous. The psychological scars of that loss run even deeper than his physical wounds.

Spring 2016 | The Lagos Tragedy

Captain America, Falcon, Wanda Maximoff, and Black Widow are tracking Brock Rumlow, who now operates as the mercenary Crossbones. He attempts to steal a bio-weapon from the Institute for Infectious Diseases in Lagos, Nigeria, but is captured after a ferocious battle. He taunts Captain America by revealing that the Winter Soldier sometimes showed flashes of his former self while in Hydra's captivity. "Bucky remembered you," he says. "He got all weepy about it, until they put his brain back in a blender." When Crossbones attempts to trigger a suicide bomb, Wanda uses her powers to throw the blast away from Captain America—but it instead rips through a nearby building, killing innocent civilians.

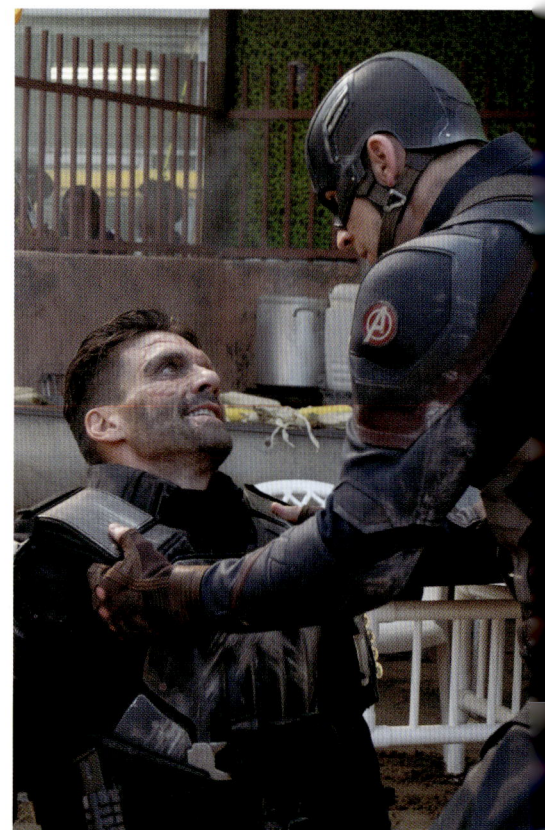

Rumlow: "You know, he knew you? Your pal, your buddy ... Your Bucky."

150

Spring 2016 | Charlie Spencer's Mother

During a speech at MIT, Tony Stark shows off the Binarily Augmented Retro-Framing program devised by his employee Quentin Beck. It transforms a neural memory into a 3-D hologram, and Stark uses it to revisit the last time he saw his father and mother alive, calling "B.A.R.F." a "$611 million therapeutic experiment." After the presentation, Stark encounters someone else who is still grieving a loved one—Miriam, a state department employee who says her son died in Sokovia. "Who's going to avenge my son, Stark. He's dead. And I blame you." The encounter leaves Iron Man stricken.

Stark on Miriam's son, Charlie Spencer: "He decided to spend his summer building sustainable housing for the poor. Guess where? Sokovia. We dropped a building on him."

"If we can't accept limitations, if we're boundary-less, we're no better than the bad guys."

Spring 2016 | For and Against

Stark sides with the accords—as do Natasha Romanoff, James "Rhodey" Rhodes, and Vision. Wanda Maximoff remains unsure. Steve Rogers and Sam Wilson are opposed to the restrictions. The Avengers have always had divisions, but this threatens to pry them ever further apart.

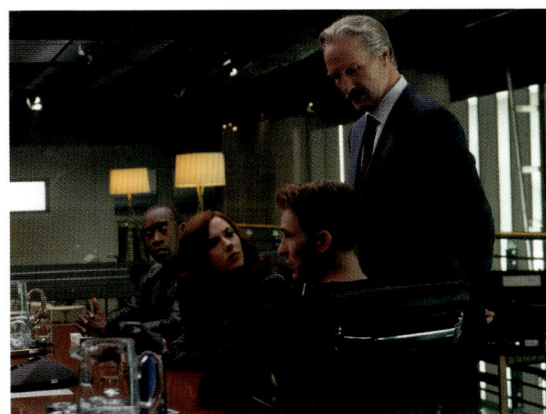

Sec. Ross admonishes the Avengers for perceived recklessness.

Spring 2016 | The Sokovia Accords

The innocent deaths in Lagos inflame a world that's still reeling from the destruction of Sokovia. Although the Avengers prevented a far worse outcome, public opinion has shifted against them. Thaddeus Ross, now the U.S. Secretary of State, visits the Avengers to urge them to support a treaty signed by 117 countries that bans "enhanced" individuals from continuing to operate independently, and instead mandates that their actions be supervised and directed only by the United Nations.

Steve Rogers attends the funeral for Peggy Carter in London, joined by Natasha Romanoff.

Sharon Carter delivers a eulogy for her aunt.

Spring 2016 | The Death of Agent Carter

Peggy Carter dies peacefully in her sleep. Steve Rogers is one of her pallbearers at the funeral in London, and Natasha Romanoff attends so he won't be alone. Sharon Carter delivers an emotional eulogy about her Aunt Peggy. "She said compromise where you can. But where you can't, don't—even if everyone is telling you that something wrong is something right." The words weigh heavily on Rogers, who decides he must resist the Sokovia Accords and follow his own judgment about how his powers should be used.

2016

Spring 2016 | A King Falls

Eleven Wakandans were among those killed in Lagos, so King T'Chaka has been one of the most vociferous supporters of the Sokovia Accords. He is also outraged that stolen vibranium from his nation was utilized by Ultron in the machinery that destroyed Sokovia. At a ceremony in Vienna to ratify the accords, he is joined by his son, Prince T'Challa, to announce his country will end its self-isolation and work more closely with other nations to protect the world they share. His words are cut short by a car bomb outside that tears through the building, ending his life.

Captain America chases the Black Panther, who is determined to kill Bucky Barnes.

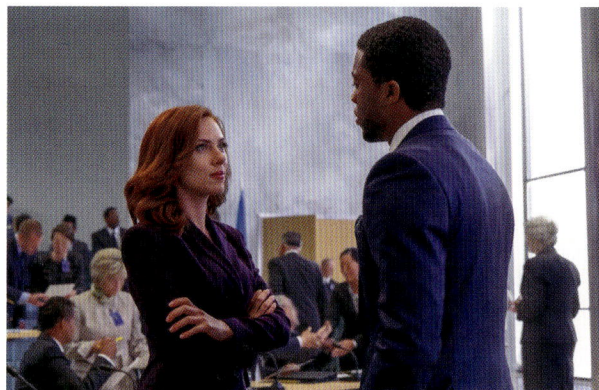

Natasha Romanoff meets T'Challa at the Accords ceremony, moments before the bombing.

Spring 2016 | The Bucharest Pursuit

Special forces storm Barnes' apartment. A firefight erupts with Captain America caught in the middle. The mysterious figure of the Black Panther, unknown outside of Wakanda, enters the chase and grapples with Barnes on a rooftop before their foot chase enters a tunnel full of speeding traffic. Sam Wilson flies in to help contain the Winter Soldier, but amid the wreckage of their pursuit all are taken into custody by government agents. "Congratulations, Cap," Rhodey says. "You're a criminal."

Steve Rogers is arrested after the destructive chase.

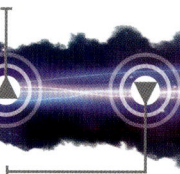

Spring 2016 | Public Enemy

Security footage shows a man matching the description of the notorious Winter Soldier planted the bomb. T'Challa swears vengeance on Bucky Barnes while Steve Rogers and Sam Wilson receive a tip from Sharon Carter about the alleged suspect's whereabouts. They journey to Bucharest to reach him first, hoping to bring him in peacefully. Meanwhile, the C.I.A. has plans to shoot him on sight, and the Romanian authorities are already on their way. Bucky recognizes Steve, but doesn't fully remember their friendship. He is certain, however, he didn't commit the bombing: "I wasn't in Vienna. I don't do that anymore."

While the Winter Soldier protocols still linger inside him, Bucky Barnes has struggled to return to his true self.

Stark to Rogers: "Sometimes I want to punch you in your perfect teeth. But I don't want to see you gone."

Spring 2016 | Deepening Divisions

Following the confrontation in Bucharest, the Winter Soldier, as well as Steve Rogers, Sam Wilson, and T'Challa, are brought to the Joint Terrorism Taskforce Headquarters in Berlin. The authorities seize Cap's shield and Falcon's wings. Tony Stark tries to reason with Steve Rogers. "We need you, Cap," he says. "So far, nothing's happened that can't be undone, if you sign." But Rogers isn't willing to compromise. "If I see a situation pointed south, I can't ignore it," he explains. The growing conflict between the two Avengers only becomes more entrenched.

Spring 2016 | The Infiltrator

As a captive Bucky Barnes is evaluated by a psychiatrist, Steve begins to have doubts about the situation. Could it be that the bombing, the manhunt—all of it, was orchestrated just so that this outsider could gain access to Bucky? Meanwhile, down in the evaluation room something strange occurs. The doctor begins reading a series of seemingly unconnected words, which triggers a violent response in Barnes, awakening the Winter Soldier protocols embedded within his mind. The psychiatrist is actually a former Sokovian death squad commander named Helmut Zemo, whose family died in the Ultron/Avenger conflict that wrecked his homeland. He has since devoted his life—and his considerable ruthless talents—to punishing the Avengers.

Bucky Barnes, perhaps the most dangerous man in the world, detained for evaluation.

2016

On a Berlin rooftop, Steve Rogers grabs a helicopter's landing gear to prevent Bucky Barnes' escape.

Spring 2016 | Baron Zemo's Vengeance

After extracting information about the Winter Soldier program from Barnes, Zemo unleashes the volatile super soldier on the Joint Terrorism Taskforce Headquarters. Battles ensue with Steve Rogers, Sam Wilson, Tony Stark, Natasha Romanoff, and T'Challa. Rogers finally stops his old friend from escaping by causing his helicopter to crash, then flees with the unconscious Barnes rather than see him returned to custody. More of the real Bucky is returning every day. He now remembers Steve's mother's name—Sarah—and that Steve was once a little guy who used to wear newspapers in his shoes to make himself look taller.

Tony Stark recruits a powerful new ally.

Spring 2016 | Enter Spider-Man

With Captain America now a fugitive, Tony Stark decides to shore up support for his side of the dispute. A certain New York streetfighting hero has come to the public's attention, and Stark decides to visit him. Peter Parker is starstruck by the billionaire philanthropist and agrees to help any way he can. Stark offers him funding for new gadgets, and a sleek new costume to replace his shabby sweats.

Spring 2016 | The Others

"Everything Hydra put inside me is still there," Bucky Barnes laments. While he has made progress returning to his true self, he knows he's still a danger to those around him and the world at large. He reveals to Steve Rogers and Sam Wilson that Zemo took control of him to answer questions about Hydra's Siberian facility where he was once kept in storage. "He wanted to know exactly where," Barnes says, "because I'm not the only Winter Soldier."

Part of Barnes' redemption is preventing the legacy of the Winter Soldier from continuing.

Hawkeye and Wanda share a bond after fighting beside one another in Sokovia.

Of the Avengers on Cap's team, only Falcon has seen what Ant-Man is capable of—when Ant-Man defeated him while breaking into the Avengers Compound.

Spring 2016 | Going Rogue

Tony Stark isn't the only one lining up supporters. Falcon tracks down his former rooftop sparring partner Ant-Man and seeks his assistance, while Hawkeye steps out of retirement to help free Wanda Maximoff from the Avengers Compound, where she is being gently watched over by Vision. Vision and Wanda have developed a strong attraction to each other, partly through their mutual connection to the Mind Stone that enhanced their powers. But they are on opposite sides of the Sokovia Accords. Wanda escapes the Avengers Compound by subduing Vision with her magic, and she and Hawkeye hurry to Europe to stand with Cap and Falcon.

The supporters of the Sokovia Accords stand shoulder to shoulder.

Spring 2016 | Weird How You Run into People at the Airport

At the Leipzig-Halle airport, Cap and Falcon attempt to board a chopper to follow Zemo's trail to Siberia. But before they can take off, Iron Man and his allies show up—demanding Bucky Barnes be turned over to them. A knock-down, drag-out battle occurs between the hero factions with Captain America, Falcon, Wanda Maximoff, Ant-Man, Hawkeye, and the Winter Soldier on one side, and Iron Man, War Machine, Vision, Spider-Man, Black Widow, and Black Panther on the other. While both sides pull their punches, Rhodey is left paralyzed after an errant blast from Vision.

Captain America leads his own independence movement out onto the tarmac.

155

THE BATTLE AT LEIPZIG-HALLE AIRPORT

A house divided cannot stand. It is the beginning of the end for Earth's mightiest heroes, after a tragic accident during a mission in Lagos causes world leaders to draft the Sokovia Accords. The accords are intended to rein in the Avengers— whom some view as a team of vigilantes that operate free from government oversight, and with no respect for international borders. Tony Stark, guilt-ridden by the deaths of civilians in Sokovia, agrees they need to be held in check, while Steve Rogers believes the team should operate independently from governments that could become corrupt. When Steve goes rogue, Tony tracks him down to persuade him to turn himself in.

Cap looks up in surprise as his shield is grabbed by Stark's new ally.

No Turning Back
Steve assembles his team of fellow accord renegades (Wanda Maximoff, Hawkeye, and Falcon, plus Bucky Barnes and new ally, Ant-Man) at the airport. They plan to take a helicopter and then track down Helmut Zemo, whom Steve now knows has been orchestrating events. As Cap makes his way to the aircraft, he is intercepted by Tony Stark's team. Tony asks Steve to turn himself in to the authorities and give up Barnes, who is believed to have murdered King T'Chaka of Wakanda at the signing of the accords. Steve refuses, arguing that Bucky is innocent and that the real killer is still at large. Impatient, Tony gives a signal and reveals Spider-Man, who uses his webbing to snatch Steve's shield. Steve's team now have a new objective—get to the Quinjet that Stark's crew arrived in and use it to escape.

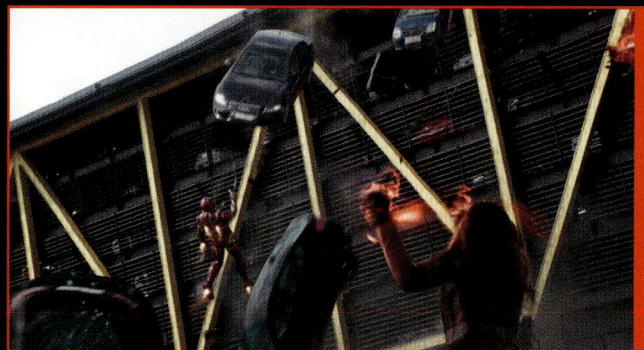
Wanda pulls no punches in trying to take Iron Man out of the battle.

Battle is Joined
Ant-Man intervenes, knocking Spider-Man aside and returning Cap's shield, then the two teams split: Tony goes after Wanda and Hawkeye at the airport parking deck, Spider-Man swings over to the terminal to intercept Bucky and Falcon, Cap trades blows with War Machine and Black Panther, while Ant-Man tackles Black Widow. Stark tries to reason with Wanda, telling her he kept her under guard at the Avengers Compound for her own protection. Clint shoots an arrow at Tony, which appears to miss, but in fact serves as a distraction for Wanda to use her powers to drop the cars from the parking deck on top of Tony, leaving him temporarily immobilized.

T'Challa barely dodges an exploding fuel truck.

Things Turn Nasty
Spider-Man shoots down Falcon, and webs him and Bucky to the floor, but is then thrown through a window by Falcon's drone, Redwing. Black Panther and War Machine continue their attacks on Captain America, but fail to subdue him. Ant-Man then joins in the fight and hands Cap a miniature fuel truck—he tells Cap to throw it at one of his Pym Particle disks. Ant-Man throws the disk into the air and Cap throws the truck as instructed, causing the vehicle to return to its normal size. As it explodes in a huge fireball on impact, a mortified Ant-Man claims that he thought it was a water truck.

Stark's team assemble on the airport's flight line.

Battle Lines
Having briefly gained the upper hand, Captain America, Ant-Man, Hawkeye, Wanda, Bucky, and Falcon sprint toward the Quinjet, but are intercepted by Vision. He asks Cap to think of the greater good and to surrender himself, while Iron Man and his team regroup. Faced with the possibility of battling (and potentially injuring) their comrades, Falcon asks Cap what they should do, and Cap responds, "We fight." Cap and his team charge towards Tony and his team, as they battle their way to escape.

The power of the Heart-Shaped Herb is pitted against the power of the Super Soldier Serum.

Close and Personal

Black Panther and Bucky face off, and Bucky tries to convince T'Challa he wasn't responsible for the explosion that killed King T'Chaka in Vienna. Unconvinced, Black Panther asks Bucky why he went on the run if he was innocent. The two continue to fight; Black Panther kicks Bucky and is about to use his vibranium claws to attack, when Wanda intervenes, using her powers to throw Black Panther away from Bucky.

Spider-Man's technology and agility are matched by Captain America's strength and tactical skills.

Spidey and Cap

In a brief lull in the battle, Spider-Man and Cap pause for breath. Cap tries to explain to Peter Parker that the situation is more complicated than he has been led to believe, but Spider-Man is unconvinced, and strikes Cap with his webbing. Although Spider-Man seems to have the edge, Cap's strength and training pay off as he uses Peter's own web lines to hurl him through the air, then finally traps him under an air bridge. "You've got heart, kid," Cap tells the young hero.

War Machine and Iron Man join forces to take down the gargantuan Scott Lang.

A Giant... Man?

Falcon realizes their team will need a distraction in order for Cap and Bucky to make it to the Quinjet. Ant-Man jumps on War Machine's back and with a press of a button, becomes gigantic. Iron Man, War Machine, and Spider-Man team up to bring the colossus down. Spider-Man comes up with the idea to wrap Lang's legs together with his webbing, and when Lang loses his balance, Iron Man and War Machine knock him on the head, making him fall.

Even though they are on opposite sides of the battle, Wanda and Vision's feelings for each other are only temporarily put aside.

War Machine Falls

As Wanda helps Cap and Bucky make it to the Quinjet, War Machine uses his sonic cannon on her, knocking her down. Black Widow changes sides, and takes down Black Panther, allowing Cap and Bucky to board the aircraft. As they take off, Vision rushes over to Wanda's aid and they both apologize for their part in the battle. War Machine and Iron Man pursue the Quinjet, with Falcon right behind them. War Machine asks Vision to disable Falcon's thrusters, and Vision shoots a beam, but Falcon dodges it and the beam hits War Machine instead, disabling his suit. War Machine crashes to Earth and suffers life-changing injuries. Though Cap and Bucky escape, the other members of their team are captured.

Spider-Man engages in his first battle with (and against) the Avengers.

2016

Spring 2016 | Imprisoned Heroes

Sam Wilson, Wanda Maximoff, Clint Barton, and Scott Lang—all of Captain America's backers—are captured and sent to the Raft, an underwater prison designed to hold beings with enhanced powers. Meanwhile, the authorities find the body of the real psychiatrist that Helmut Zemo murdered and impersonated—along with the facial prosthetics and wig Zemo used to disguise himself as Barnes while planting the bomb that killed T'Chaka and others at the UN. Iron Man follows Cap's trail to Siberia—and is followed in turn by Black Panther piloting a Wakandan stealth jet.

The Raft—a deep sea prison for the most dangerous offenders on Earth.

Iron Man learns the Winter Soldier killed his mother and father.

Spring 2016 | The 1991 Murders

A tentative truce between Steve Rogers, Bucky Barnes, and Tony Stark is shattered when Zemo plays security camera footage of Howard and Maria Stark's death, which clearly shows the Winter Soldier killing them and taking the Super Soldier Serum Howard was transporting. "Do you even remember them?" a shaken Stark asks. "I remember all of them," Bucky answers mournfully.

Spring 2016 | Revenge Served Cold

In Siberia, Cap and Bucky discover that Zemo was not seeking this facility to acquire his own super soldiers. Instead, he came to destroy them. Zemo's grief over the destruction of Sokovia has made him despise enhanced human beings. The true purpose of the bombing and the framing of Bucky was to turn the Avengers against each other. "I knew I couldn't kill them," he says. "More powerful men than me have tried. But if I could get them to kill each other ..." After losing everything, he wanted the Avengers to destroy themselves.

Iron Man, Captain America, and Bucky Barnes infiltrate the Siberian Hydra facility.

Years of frustration explode in a battle between Captain America and Iron Man.

Spring 2016 | Friends No More

A brawl erupts between Cap, Bucky, and Iron Man. Bucky tries to rip out Stark's Arc Reactor, which emits a beam that melts away Bucky's robotic arm. Iron Man is disgusted that Cap knew about the murder of his parents and said nothing. "He was my friend," Cap tries to explain. "So was I," Iron Man shoots back. After a bruising battle, Captain America drives his shield into the Arc Reactor in Iron Man's chest, rendering his armor inert. As Cap and Bucky escape, the iconic shield remains behind. "You don't deserve it," Tony Stark cries out. "My father made that shield."

Bucky Barnes fights for his life against Tony Stark.

T'Challa chooses the path of mercy—years from now, his sister Shuri will make the same choice.

Spring 2016 | Mercy, at Last

Outside the Siberian facility, Black Panther finds Zemo listening to a voicemail left by his wife, which is all he has left of her. Zemo apologizes for causing T'Chaka's death and waits for T'Challa to take his life in turn. "Vengeance has consumed you," T'Challa says. "I am done letting it consume me. Justice will come soon enough." He then prevents Zemo from shooting himself—saving the life of the man who callously took his father's. "The living are not done with you yet," T'Challa says. Steve Rogers and Bucky Barnes are offered sanctuary in Wakanda, where biotechnicians, including T'Challa's brilliant sister Shuri, begin a deprogramming course they hope will erase the last of Bucky's Hydra imprint.

Spring-Summer 2016 | Black Widow's Retreat

Natasha Romanoff becomes a fugitive after switching sides to temporarily paralyze Black Panther and allow Cap and Bucky to escape. She evades Secretary Ross and his arresting agents and retreats to a remote safe house in Norway.

Natasha Romanoff hides among the Norwegian Fjords.

After a mission in Morocco, Yelena goes from Red Room hunter to liberator of her fellow conscripted sisters.

Spring-Summer 2016 | Yelena's Awakening

Red Room agent Yelena hunts down and fatally wounds an operative who defected from their organization. Before dying, the young woman unleashes a cloud of crimson gas that frees Yelena from the chemical mind control that General Dreykov uses to manipulate his team of killers. Now overcome with regret, Yelena seizes the remaining vials of antidote and goes into hiding, unsure if she has anyone left to trust.

159

2016

Spring-Summer 2016 | Deadly Delivery

Natasha's supplier, Rick Mason, stocks her trailer with essential items—and even delivers some mail and personal items that were left behind in her Budapest safe house. One large package is from her estranged "sister" Yelena.

"People who have friends don't call me."

Black Widow faces herself, through the eerily replicated moves of the Taskmaster.

Spring-Summer 2016 | The Taskmaster

While driving into town, Black Widow's car is struck by a vehicle driven by a masked warrior who studies and replicates all of her combat techniques. This mysterious individual has a chance to kill her, but instead focuses on retrieving the unopened package from Yelena. The assailant hurls Natasha into a churning river, then finds Yelena's box empty. Natasha had quickly removed the contents—the vials of synthetic gas that sever the Red Room's psychological control.

Spring-Summer 2016 | Wait ... Dreykov?

Black Widow is stunned to learn Dreykov is still alive. She is still haunted by her Budapest operation with Hawkeye, in which she detonated a bomb in Dreykov's office, believing she had also killed his young daughter. The loss of an innocent was already devastating to her, but the notion that it was for nothing is too much to bear. "No one is even looking for him thanks to you," Yelena says, making it all hurt even worse.

Natasha discovers not only that Dreykov is alive, but that the Red Room is still active.

Yelena and Natasha, reunited.

Spring-Summer 2016 | Sisters Again

After surviving the Taskmaster attack, Natasha Romanoff seeks out her sister Yelena in a Budapest safehouse. First they fight each other, then they fight for their lives against a squad of Red Room operatives sent to track down the mind-control antidote Yelena acquired. "It's a synthetic gas, the counteragent to chemical subjugation," Yelena explains. "The gas immunizes the brain's neuropathways from external manipulation." General Dreykov knows that if he doesn't eradicate it, this substance could cost him all of the unwilling assassins he puppeteers.

Natasha and Yelena race through the streets of Budapest.

Spring-Summer 2016 | Family Reunion

Natasha and Yelena make a pact to track down the Red Room and end Dreykov's reign of terror forever. To do that, they must reconnect with the only two leads they have—their former "parents" Alexei, the Red Guardian super soldier, and Melina, the Red Room scientist whose research led to the mind-control process in the first place. Their entire fake family operation in Ohio was aimed at securing classified mind-control technology. The "daughters" now vow to set these wrongs right.

Natasha tends Yelena's wounds as they discuss the past and their next steps.

An avalanche aids the jailbreak.

Natasha Romanoff lands on a catwalk. "Such a poser," her sister says.

Spring-Summer 2016 | Prison Break

The Red Guardian is locked away at a maximum-security gulag in the frozen wastes of Russia—Alexei claims he was incarcerated for annoying Dreykov. Natasha and Yelena fly a helicopter to the prison and stage a daring rescue of their blowhard father-figure, airlifting him to freedom as gunfire explodes and an avalanche from nearby mountains swallows the entire facility in a shroud of freezing death. "This would be a cool way to die," Yelena says. But they make it—barely.

Yelena fires a rocket at a prison gun tower.

Alexei scrambles to evade the prison riot.

161

CLINT BARTON

An expert marksman, Clint Barton is one of S.H.I.E.L.D.'s most valuable agents. His accuracy and near-perfect eyesight earn him the code name "Hawkeye." Fate intervenes when Hawkeye is sent to assassinate Natasha Romanoff, a deadly KGB operative. In an act of mercy, Hawkeye decides against killing her and aids in her defection to S.H.I.E.L.D. Clint and Natasha's relationship evolves from that of teammates to a deep and abiding friendship. During the Chitauri invasion of New York City, Clint and Natasha become founding members of the Avengers.

2012 | Mind Control
After being mind-controlled by Loki, Hawkeye helps him steal the Tesseract from a S.H.I.E.L.D. compound and then leads an attack on S.H.I.E.L.D.'s Helicarrier. In a battle against Natasha, Hawkeye is knocked unconscious, loosening Loki's hold over him. Hawkeye then teams up with the Avengers to fight the Chitauri when they invade New York.

2015 | Taking a Hit
Hawkeye teams up with the Avengers again, when they travel to Sokovia to take down a Hydra base run by Baron Strucker, who is now in possession of Loki's scepter. Just as Hawkeye is about to blow up one of the compound's bunkers, Pietro Maximoff intercepts the explosive. Hawkeye is distracted by his enemy's speed and is gravely injured when he is shot by a Hydra cannon. After the Maximoffs change sides to help defeat Ultron, Pietro sacrifices himself to save Hawkeye's life.

2000s | Budapest
When S.H.I.E.L.D. tracks down KGB agent Natasha Romanoff a.k.a. Black Widow, Hawkeye is sent to eliminate her. Hawkeye confronts Natasha at her safehouse in Budapest, but decides to spare Natasha's life and the two of them join forces to take down the Red Room assassin program and its leader, General Dreykov.

2010 | Thor
Nick Fury dispatches Hawkeye to New Mexico to assist Agent Coulson, who has found an alien artifact in the desert. The artifact is actually Thor's hammer Mjolnir, which had crashed on Earth. When Thor breaks into the compound to retrieve his hammer, Coulson orders Hawkeye not to attack the intruder, because he wants to observe Thor.

1995 | Young Natasha
Taken from her birth mother as an infant, Natasha is raised and indoctrinated in the Red Room, a Russian organization that trains young girls to be spies and assassins. As a child, Natasha is sent on an assignment to America alongside another young operative, Yelena, both posing as daughters of spies Melina and Alexei. Alexei steals data from the North Institute, a research base secretly run by Hydra. With the mission over, Natasha and Yelena are returned to Russia and sent to the Red Room for further training.

2000s | Budapest
Natasha grapples with guilt following the assumed death of General Dreykov's young daughter in the bombing that targeted her father. She and Hawkeye escape the city after ten days on the run.

2010 | "Natalie Rushman"
Now an agent of S.H.I.E.L.D., Natasha is sent undercover by Nick Fury, posing as Natalie Rushman, a notary at Stark Industries. Natasha's real motive is to spy on Tony Stark, to assess if he'd be an ideal candidate for Fury's Avengers Initiative. Natasha eventually reveals her true identity to Tony and helps him take down Ivan Vanko.

2014 | Uncovering Hydra
Natasha and Steve join the S.T.R.I.K.E. team to rescue hostages aboard the *Lumerian Star*. Unbeknownst to Steve, Natasha's other secret mission is to download confidential information about Project Insight. When Nick Fury is shot by the elusive assassin, the Winter Soldier, Natasha and Steve go on the run, and discover Hydra has been embedded within S.H.I.E.L.D. for decades. In the ensuing battle, Natasha uploads all of S.H.I.E.L.D. and Hydra's secrets onto the internet.

2015 | Natasha and Bruce
Amid the Avengers' battles with the rogue A.I. Ultron, Natasha and Bruce Banner grow closer, and she reveals that she's unable to have children, having been medically sterilized by the Red Room. She faces Ultron in Seoul, where she is instrumental in stealing Ultron's new vibranium-infused body (the future Vision), but is then captured.

NATASHA ROMANOFF

From childhood, Natasha Romanoff is trained in the art of combat and espionage, becoming the Black Widow, one of the deadliest assassins in the world. It isn't until she meets Clint Barton, who sees the good in her, that Natasha starts to see the good in herself. After defecting, Natasha joins S.H.I.E.L.D. and partners with Clint on countless missions. Natasha finds a higher calling through her friendship with Clint and her found family, the Avengers. Her bravery and love for others cause her to make the ultimate sacrifice.

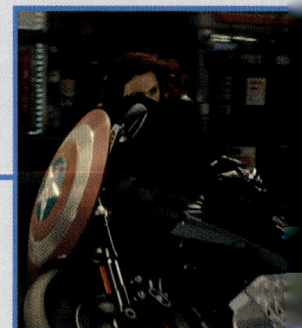

2012 | Joining the Avengers
Natasha is in the middle of a mission to stop Georgi Luchkov, an arms dealer, when she gets a call from Agent Coulson informing her that Clint Barton has been compromised as a result of Loki's mind control. Natasha is sent to India to bring in Bruce Banner, needed for his expertise on gamma rays to locate the Tesseract, then teams up with Captain America, Iron Man, Thor, Banner and Clint to battle Loki and the Chitauri.

2024 | Kate Bishop

Clint takes his children to New York City during the holidays to see *Rogers: The Musical*. Afterward, while watching the news, Clint sees a clip of someone wearing his old Ronin costume rescuing a dog. Clint tracks them down and discovers it's Kate Bishop, who idolizes Hawkeye and is also a skilled archer. Clint and Bishop team up to take down the Tracksuit Mafia, and in their investigation, find out Kate's mother, Eleanor Bishop, is secretly working with the mob boss Kingpin. Hawkeye is confronted by Yelena, seeking vengeance for Natasha's death, but he is able to convince her of the truth.

2016 | Breaking the Law

Hawkeye comes to the aid of Steve Rogers, who is now a fugitive for defying the Sokovia Accords. Barton is sent to rescue Wanda Maximoff, who is being held at the Avengers Compound due to Tony Stark's belief that she should be kept confined until the accords are signed. Wanda and Hawkeye take down Vision, then meet up with the rest of Steve's team for a showdown with Iron Man's group at Leipzig-Halle Airport. In the aftermath, Clint is confined at the Raft prison, but then takes a plea deal.

2018-2023 | Fight to the Finish

Hawkeye goes rogue when his wife and children disappear in the Snap. Overwhelmed with grief, he becomes the costumed vigilante Ronin, taking down criminal organizations around the world. Natasha convinces Clint to return to the Avengers for a mission to time travel and retrieve the Infinity Stones. In 2014, on the planet Vormir, Clint and Natasha each try to sacrifice themselves to save the other. Black Widow "wins," leaving Clint devastated.

2016 | Avenger against Avenger

After a failed mission in Lagos, where Wanda Maximoff fails to contain a blast that kills innocent civilians, Natasha and the Avengers are summoned by Secretary Thaddeus Ross and Tony Stark to sign the Sokovia Accords. Natasha sides with Tony, Vision, and Rhodey in signing the agreement. This leads to a showdown with the Avengers who refused to sign the accords—including Hawkeye.

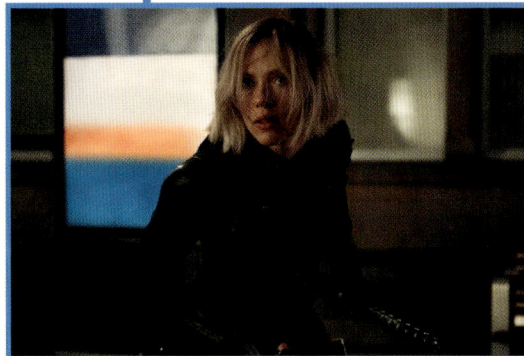

2018 | Facing Thanos

Natasha joins her former Avengers teammates Steve Rogers and Sam Wilson to rescue Wanda and Vision from an attack by the Children of Thanos in Scotland. To prevent Thanos from taking the Mind Stone from Vision, the team heads to Wakanda, in hopes that Shuri can safely extract the stone. After an epic battle with Thanos' army, Thanos himself appears and retrieves the Mind Stone, completing the Infinity Gauntlet and initiating the Snap.

2016 | Family Ties

After helping Steve and Bucky escape in the battle at Leipzig-Halle Airport, Natasha is on the run from Secretary Ross. She is reunited with her adoptive sister, Yelena, who tells her that Dreykov is still alive and that the Red Room program is still active. Natasha and Yelena join their former undercover "parents" Alexei and Melina in bringing down Dreykov and the Red Room for good.

2023 | Ultimate Sacrifice

Five years after being defeated by Thanos, Natasha and Steve find hope when Scott Lang shows up at the Avengers Compound. Scott tells them about the Quantum Realm and after bringing Tony Stark back into the fold, they plan a daring mission to visit the past and retrieve the Infinity Stones to reverse the Snap. Natasha and Clint travel to Vormir to retrieve the Soul Stone, and Natasha sacrifices herself so Clint can claim the stone.

2016

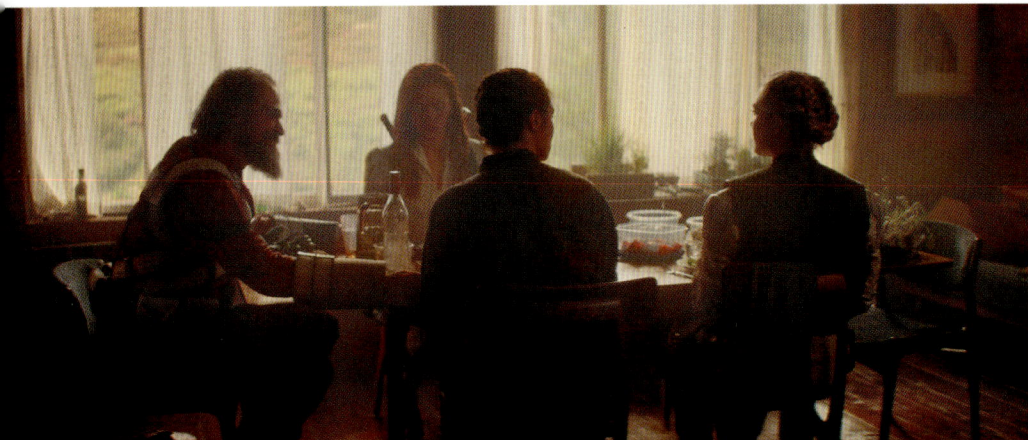

A room full of trained killers sits down for an estranged family dinner.

Spring-Summer 2016 | "You Weren't Abandoned"

Natasha, Yelena, and Alexei pilot their damaged chopper toward Saint Petersburg, falling just short. They locate the fourth member of their conscripted family, Melina, living on a farm where she now tests her remote mind control research on livestock. While being pressed on the whereabouts of the Red Room, Melina reveals that Natasha was not given to the Black Widow program—she was taken. "Your mother never stopped looking for you. She was like you in that way. She was relentless," Melina says. Dreykov ultimately killed the woman to stop her.

Spring-Summer 2016 | Castle in the Air

Aboard the Red Room's hovering base, the full scale of Dreykov's operation becomes clear. He has remained out of sight by floating high above the world, controlling an ever-growing army of stolen young women who are trained to be lethal weapons of war but have no control over how their lethal skills are deployed. Dreykov manipulates them from a single tablet. "One command and oil and stock markets crumble. One command and a quarter of the planet will starve. My Widows can start and end wars. They can make and break kings," he explains. He intends to assert domination over the world "using the only natural resource that the world has too much of—girls."

Dreykov's Red Room facility, hovering in the low atmosphere.

The Red Guardian, festooned with tranquilizer darts.

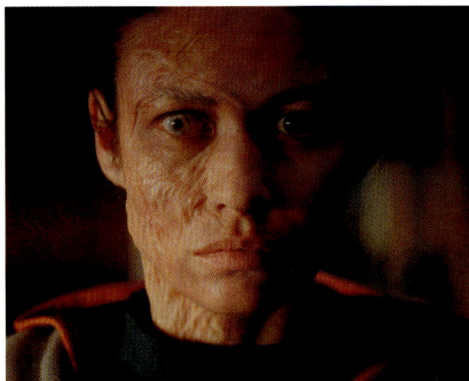

Spring-Summer 2016 | Double Cross

Melina is overcome by remorse. Not only did her mind control work lead to Yelena becoming one of the Red Room's chemically subjugated agents, but she sees what that work has done to harm countless other innocent girls. Sadly she has already alerted Dreykov to Natasha and Yelena's plans. As operatives descend on the farm to capture them, Melina devises a makeshift plan with Natasha to break free after they are all taken to the Red Room and liberate the young women who are still being trained there. Red Guardian attempts to put up a fight, but is subdued with a bouquet of tranquilizers to the chest.

The burned face and intense gaze of Antonia Dreykov, a.k.a. Taskmaster.

Natasha Romanoff learns that she did not kill Dreykov's daughter.

Spring-Summer 2016 | My Antonia...

Natasha finally comes face to face with the tyrant she thought she assassinated long ago. Dreykov laughs off her efforts to kill him, noting that she has only made him stronger. "You gave me my greatest weapon," he says, bringing forth his Taskmaster operative. As the assailant's mask comes off, Natasha realizes it is Antonia, Dreykov's daughter, who is horrifically scarred from the bomb Natasha detonated years before. Dreykov implanted cybernetic material in her neck to keep her alive, which transformed her into a perfect mimic. "She fights just like all of your friends," Dreykov says.

Black Widow hangs
on as the Red Room
falls apart.

🕷️ | Ⓥ

Spring-Summer 2016 | Bringing Down the Red Room

Melina destroys an engine that sends the Red Room's hoverbase
into a controlled crash, then escapes with Alexei. Yelena and
Natasha free a group of Widow trainees by exposing them to the
mind-control antidote, and a panicked Dreykov attempts to flee
with his loyalist soldiers. Yelena finally kills him by plunging her
staff into the turbine of his jet, consuming Dreykov in a fireball.
Natasha leaps to her rescue with a parachute, battling
Taskmaster as they plummet. All three survive their descent
as the ruins of the Red Room litter the landscape.

Yelena ends Dreykov
once and for all.

The end of the
Red Room.

🕷️

Spring-Summer 2016 | Taskmaster Stands Down

On the ground, Natasha exposes Antonia to the
antidote and apologizes for the pain she caused,
expressing deep sorrow that she suffered so
much for her father's wrongs. The fear and
anger in Antonia's eyes turns to relief when she
asks in a whisper: "Is he gone?"

Black Widow and the Taskmaster spar amid the twisted ruins
of the Red Room.

"Enough," Black Widow says, dropping her blade to focus on hitting
Antonia with the antidote to her mind control.

165

2016

"If it can work out with the four of us, there may be some hope for the Avengers."

Spring-Summer 2016 | Recovering the Widows

Natasha decides to return to her old life, joining Steve Rogers to try and free her friends who remain imprisoned after the civil war that ripped apart the Avengers. She parts with Yelena, Melina, and Alexei not as fellow soldiers, but as a strange kind of family—dysfunctional for sure, but dedicated to each other. Now they will join with the women who were saved from the fall of the Red Room to begin the arduous task of decommissioning other Widows around the world.

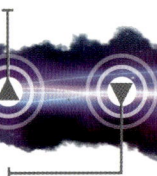

T'Challa with Nakia.

Summer 2016 | Nakia's Extraction

In the Sambisa Forest of Nigeria, T'Challa and Okoye, head of the Dora Milaje warriors, track the Wakandan War Dog spy Nakia as she travels undercover in a convoy of human traffickers. T'Challa takes down most of the militants himself, but the final hostage must be saved by General Okoye after T'Challa lays eyes on Nakia—and chokes. Nakia is initially annoyed to have her mission disrupted, then is heartbroken to learn of King T'Chaka's untimely death. T'Challa asks his former love to return home for his coronation, knowing he needs her support and counsel.

Summer 2016 | Lying In Wait

The death of T'Chaka has awakened two longtime enemies of Wakanda—one well-known, the other a painful secret. Ulysses Klaue, who decades before had killed innocent Wakandans while stealing a quarter ton of vibranium from the country, has joined forces with a man who calls himself "Killmonger," a U.S. black-ops soldier who has a history of destabilizing nations through violence. They test their alliance by stealing a vibranium artifact from the Museum of Great Britain in London. Killmonger is actually Erik Stevens, also known as N'Jadaka, who was orphaned and abandoned in Oakland, California, in 1992. His father, N'Jobu, a Wakandan War Dog operative and brother to King T'Chaka, was killed after being exposed as an ally of Klaue's.

Erik Killmonger and an enemy of Wakanda find common cause.

166

T'Challa prepares for the ceremony at Warrior Falls.

T'Challa engages in ritual combat with Jabari leader M'Baku.

Summer 2016 | Warrior Falls Coronation

During a jubilant celebration, the Merchant, Border, River, and Mining Tribes of Wakanda choose not to challenge T'Challa for the position of king, but M'Baku, the leader of the separatist Mountain Tribe also known as the Jabari, refuses to allow T'Challa to take the crown without a fight. He invokes his right to ceremonial combat and proves to be a formidable opponent, although he is ultimately defeated by T'Challa. Out of respect for M'Baku, the new king of Wakanda spares his life.

Princess Shuri and Queen Ramonda look on.

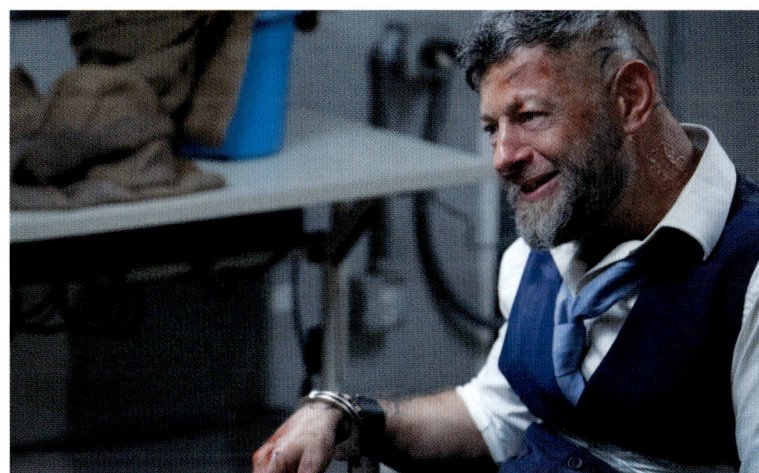

A captive Ulysses Klaue tells Agent Ross about Wakanda's true power.

Summer 2016 | Judgment Calls

W'Kabi, who protects Wakanda on behalf of the Border Tribe, is among those doubtful about T'Challa's priorities and abilities after his failure to capture Klaue. T'Challa's brilliant sister Shuri, head of the Wakandan Design Group, agrees to heal Everett K. Ross, but after working to try and deprogram the Winter Soldier protocols in Bucky Barnes, she questions why her brother has brought "another broken white boy for us to fix." Okoye frets that Ross will reveal the true nature of Wakanda's advancement to the United States. Is the king of Wakanda going soft?

Summer 2016 | The Busan Mission

T'Challa, Nakia, and Okoye unite for a mission to South Korea after learning that Klaue has resurfaced with intentions to sell stolen vibranium on the black market. The buyer turns out to be C.I.A. agent Everett K. Ross, who takes Klaue into custody after the Wakandan emissaries capture the mercenary during a car chase through the port city of Busan. Klaue's interrogation ends abruptly when Killmonger attacks the safehouse and helps his criminal partner escape. Ross is gravely wounded in the firefight when he steps in front of a bullet meant for Nakia. T'Challa risks their country's safety by bringing the outsider to Wakanda for lifesaving treatment.

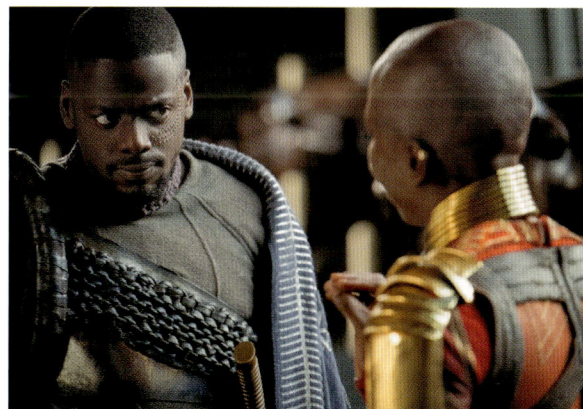

W'Kabi and Okoye, in a marital disagreement.

2016

Killmonger reveals himself as N'Jadaka: "I found my daddy with Panther claws in his chest. You ain't the son of a king. You're the son of a murderer."

Summer 2016 | The Prodigal Prince

Killmonger gains admittance to Wakanda by bringing a rare trophy—the body of his partner Klaue. He declares it, "Justice your king couldn't deliver." By killing one of Wakanda's greatest enemies, he becomes a hero of sorts and uses his audience with Wakanda's tribal leaders to reveal he is the son of N'Jobu, brother of the fallen King T'Chaka. That makes Killmonger a prince of Wakanda—one who has the right to challenge T'Challa for control of the throne.

Killmonger prepares to dispatch vibranium weapons around the world.

Summer 2016 | Upending the World

As Killmonger seizes the throne, he reveals his plans to fulfill his father's dream of using Wakanda's might and resources to empower revolutions led by the marginalized, impoverished, and subjugated. His noble goals come with a disturbing mercilessness. "We're gonna send vibranium weapons out to our War Dogs," Killmonger informs the elders. "They'll arm oppressed people all over the world so they can finally rise up and kill those in power, and their children and anyone else who takes their side." Plans to begin exporting weapons begin immediately.

"I am the cause of your father's death. Not him."

Summer 2016 | The Death of Zuri

During ceremonial combat at Warrior Falls, Killmonger gains the upper hand on T'Challa. The Wakandan spiritual leader Zuri tries to save T'Challa's life by offering his own. He reveals that he was the spy who exposed N'Jobu's treachery, and it was his life T'Chaka was saving when he killed his own brother. Killmonger is unmoved. "I'll take you both," he says, stabbing Zuri through the chest, and hurling T'Challa from the precipice into the river below.

M'Baku in the mountain realm of the Jabari.

Summer 2016 | Sanctuary in the Mountains

The Queen Mother Ramonda flees into the mountains with Shuri, Nakia, and Everett K. Ross, seeking protection with the previously hostile Jabari Tribe. The imperious M'Baku not only grants their request, but reveals that he has recovered T'Challa's body from the river. The fallen king still clings to life. Nakia heals him with extract from the vibranium-infused Heart-Shaped Herb, which restores T'Challa's Black Panther abilities. He awakens not only physically stronger, but with new wisdom: Killmonger's methods may be cruel, but he is a monster created by Wakanda's indifference to the outside world.

T'Challa fights Killmonger for the right to rule Wakanda.

Killmonger makes one more stand against the Black Panther.

T'Challa upends attackers from the Border Tribe loyal to Killmonger.

Summer 2016 | Dueling Sons of Wakanda

Having ordered the gardens of the Heart-Shaped Herb to be burned, Killmonger believes his rule is secure. T'Challa confronts him at the entrance to Wakanda's great vibranium mine in Mount Bashenga, hoping to stop the Wakandan craft that have begun exporting vibranium weapons to the outside world. Killmonger has equipped himself with one of Shuri's other Black Panther suits, matching the powers of the one that adorns T'Challa. W'Kabi sides with Killmonger and leads his Border Tribe against Okoye's Dora Milaje, who are overwhelmed—until M'Baku's Jabari join the fray.

"I never yielded! And as you can see, I am not dead!"

Killmonger in his own Black Panther armor.

Summer 2016 | Killmonger's End

As the brothers and sisters of Wakanda clash, T'Challa and Killmonger plunge into the mine, continuing their battle on the railway within. Just as T'Chaka reluctantly took the life of his brother N'Jobu, so too does T'Challa defeat his cousin, born into the world as N'Jadaka, but shaped by that world into Killmonger. T'Challa offers him medical care, but is refused: "Just bury me in the ocean with my ancestors, who jumped from the ships because they knew death was better than bondage."

T'Challa in the gardens of the Heart-Shaped Herb.

Killmonger and Black Panther fight inside the vibranium mines.

2016 | Death in Vienna
Following his father's death, a vengeful T'Challa wants to kill the Winter Soldier, a.k.a. Bucky Barnes, who has been framed as the assassin. After realizing the truth and ensuring the actual killer is imprisoned, T'Challa offers the innocent Bucky sanctuary in Wakanda.

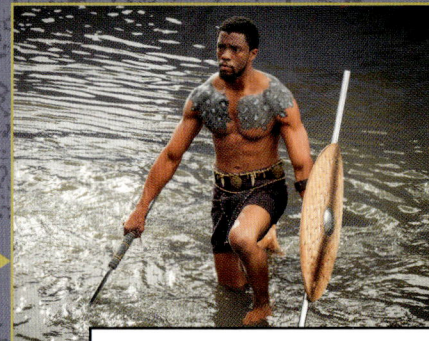

2016 | A New King
Now the king and Black Panther, T'Challa faces challengers to his titles. The gravest threat is from his cousin Erik Killmonger, who deposes him and advocates for Wakanda to take a more active role in global affairs. T'Challa has to kill Erik, yet he takes his cousin's ethos, setting up outreach centers across the world.

2018 | Desperate Defense
T'Challa welcomes the Avengers to Wakanda, combining their forces against Thanos. He leads his army into battle to protect Wakanda, but to no avail. Thanos completes the Infinity Gauntlet and snaps his fingers, eliminating half of all life in the universe, including T'Challa and Shuri.

2023 | Reinforcements Arrive
After the Avengers successfully reverse the Snap, T'Challa leads a contingent of Wakandan forces to fight during the Battle of Earth, allowing the heroes to emerge victorious. He attends Tony Stark's funeral alongside Okoye and Shuri.

WAKANDA'S ROYAL FAMILY

Few have given so much for their country as Wakanda's Royal Family. A former Black Panther, King T'Chaka ruled Wakanda for decades, maintaining the country's isolationist policy and making tough decisions, including killing his younger brother N'Jobu while defending another. However, when Wakandan vibranium is used by the villainous Ultron to craft a doomsday weapon, it causes T'Chaka to question his country's stance, and he starts forging greater connections with the rest of the world. As both Black Panther and Wakandan monarch, T'Chaka is succeeded by his son T'Challa, a charismatic leader, adept military strategist, and powerful Super Hero. T'Challa is supported by his sister Princess Shuri, a technological and scientific genius with a capacity to find innovative solutions to crises. Wise and unwavering, their mother Queen Ramonda is a skilled political tactician and fierce defender of her people. In spite of the many tragedies this family faces, its members remain completely dedicated to serving and protecting their people.

2024 | T'Challa's End
Having been diagnosed with an incurable illness, T'Challa connects with Nakia and their son Toussaint in Haiti and prepares them for his passing. Shuri attempts to find a cure for his illness, but cannot save her brother in time.

QUEEN RAMONDA

2016 | On the Run
Ramonda is proud of her son T'Challa when he becomes the king. After Erik Killmonger claims the throne, Ramonda works with Nakia and Shuri to defeat him, fearful for Wakanda's future under Killmonger. She is relieved to learn T'Challa is alive and joins him as he later reclaims the throne.

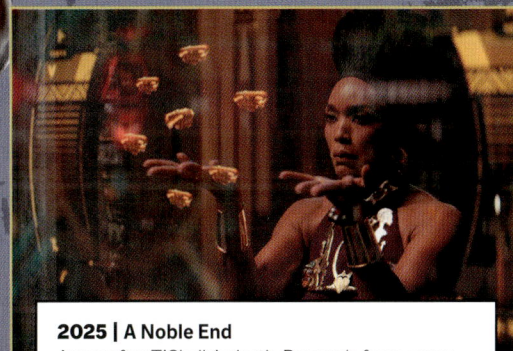

2025 | A Noble End
A year after T'Challa's death, Ramonda faces a new threat. Namor and the people of Talokan, who also have vibranium technology, demand Wakanda join them to take on the world. When Ramonda refuses their request, they attack the Golden City. Ramonda perishes in the assault, saving Riri Williams' life.

2018-2023 | Queen Ramonda
Ramonda loses both her children to the Snap and becomes the ruler of Wakanda. She is reunited with T'Challa and Shuri when the Snap is reversed, and after the defeat of Thanos, all three watch as Wakandans celebrate in the Golden City.

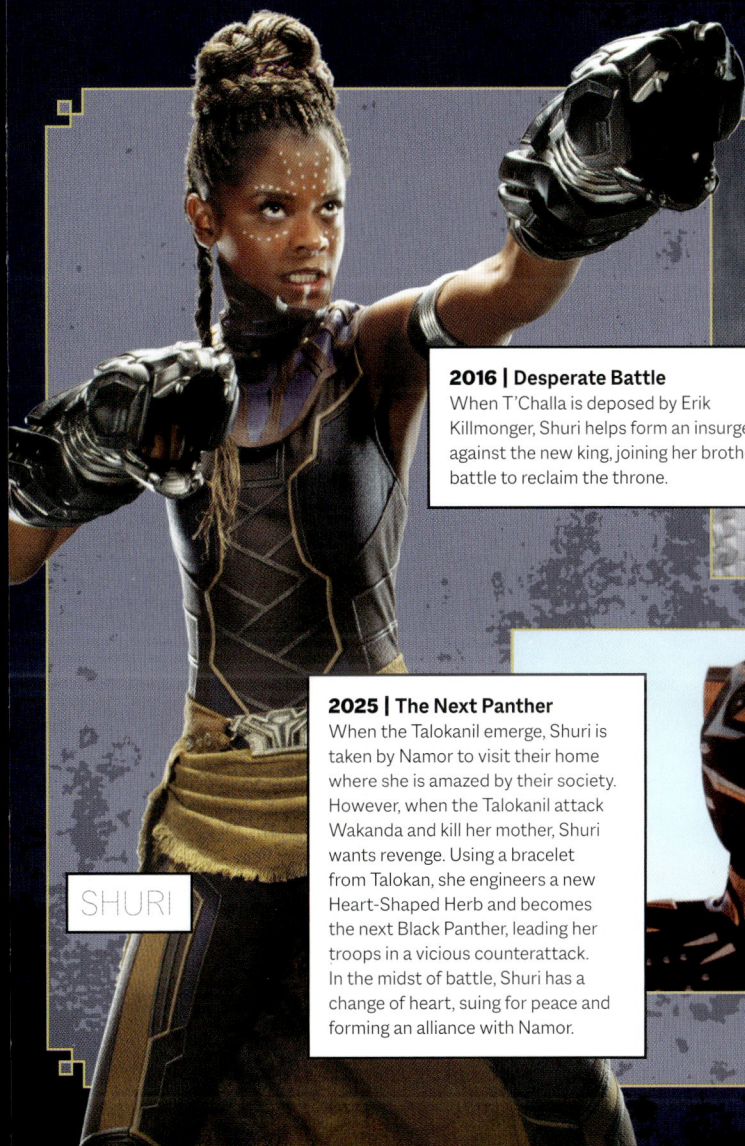

SHURI

2016 | Desperate Battle
When T'Challa is deposed by Erik Killmonger, Shuri helps form an insurgency against the new king, joining her brother in battle to reclaim the throne.

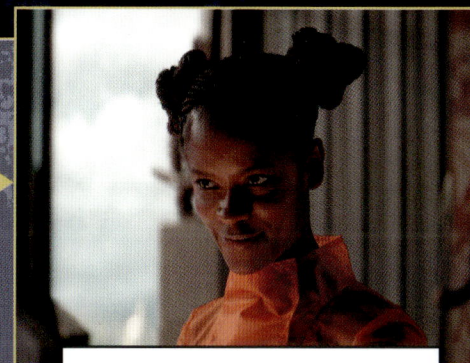

2018 | Expert Aid
Shuri begins to separate the Mind Stone from Vision to prevent Thanos from gaining it. She is nearly successful, but her work is interrupted by Thanos' minion Corvus Glaive, and shortly afterward Shuri is one of those lost in the Snap.

2025 | The Next Panther
When the Talokanil emerge, Shuri is taken by Namor to visit their home where she is amazed by their society. However, when the Talokanil attack Wakanda and kill her mother, Shuri wants revenge. Using a bracelet from Talokan, she engineers a new Heart-Shaped Herb and becomes the next Black Panther, leading her troops in a vicious counterattack. In the midst of battle, Shuri has a change of heart, suing for peace and forming an alliance with Namor.

2023 | Back to Life
Shuri is returned when the Avengers reverse the Snap by recreating the Infinity Gauntlet. She and T'Challa help the Avengers during the Battle of Earth.

2016

T'Challa announces plans for Wakanda to become more open with the world.

Fall 2016 | Poor Peter Parker

Spider-Man is languishing. Months after being summoned by Tony Stark to fight alongside him in enforcement of the Sokovia Accords, Peter Parker struggles with the ordinariness of high school life back home in Queens. His secret Super Hero identity earned him some fleeting YouTube fame, but now he feels like a good Samaritan in a fancy costume. He thwarts a bicycle theft, and is rewarded with a churro for helping a lost old woman find her way, but his crimefighting skills need work.

Peter Parker practices his moves.

Summer 2016 | Wakanda Opens to the World

Killmonger's methods may have been extreme, but his notion that Wakanda should do more to help struggling people in the world continues to resonate within T'Challa. In the months that follow, the new king begins plans for a Wakandan International Outreach Center in the building where N'Jobu lived and raised his son. At a United Nations meeting in Vienna, T'Challa formally announces Wakanda's plans to share its knowledge and resources with the world, stunning those who had no idea of its advancements.

There is little that is broken that can't be fixed again.

Summer 2016 | Civil War Aftermath

Back in the states, James Rhodes begins to recover from his paralysis, taking his first steps again thanks to mechanical Stark braces. Despite his injuries, Rhodey tells Tony Stark that he still believes signing the accords was the right thing to do. Tony then receives a letter and burner phone—an offer from Steve Rogers to stand together if the world ever needs them—and a call from Secretary Ross warning that the Raft prison has been compromised.

Fall 2016 | The "Avengers" ATM Debacle

One night during his usual neighborhood patrol, Spider-Man discovers an actual heist in progress! He descends on a quartet of thugs disguised in Thor, Iron Man, Hulk, and Captain America masks who are using surprisingly advanced tech to perpetrate a smash-and-grab on some cash machines. After thrashing the would-be robbers, one of their weapons triggers, slicing through Mr. Delmar's bodega across the street. Spidey is despondent, having caused more problems than he solved.

Spider-Man thwarts a robbery in progress.

Fall 2016 | Scavengers Exposed

Peter Parker's best friend, Ned Leeds, discovers his high school pal is actually the famous webslinger. They hatch a scheme for Peter to arrive in costume as Spider-Man at their friend Liz's house party to help boost their social standing. While Peter prepares for his entrance that night, he spots Jackson Brice, a.k.a. Shocker, demonstrating a blaster crafted from a reclaimed sub-Ultron arm. He's also peddling black hole grenades, anti-gravity climbers, and Chitauri guns. The buyer, Aaron Davis, gets away when Spider-Man interrupts the deal, but Brice summons his boss, Adrian Toomes, to help deal with Spider-Man.

Spider-Man takes a hit from Shocker.

Adrian Toomes in his weaponry workshop.

TVA ALERT!
Howdy! Maybe y'all noticed a poster for the Academic Decathlon hanging in Midtown High School that says the Washington, D.C. event is set for October, while another poster in Peter Parker's bedroom says it's in September. I'm gonna ask someone about this, but everyone's on their pie break at the moment!

Fall 2016 | A Literal "Firing"

Toomes is furious at Brice for recklessly exposing their operation. When Brice makes a not-so-veiled threat to expose their illicit trade, Toomes seizes a rifle from the Tinkerer's work table and impulsively reduces the "Shocker" to a heap of ash. Toomes winces: "I thought this was the anti-gravity gun."

Adrian Toomes and his flying armor.

Toomes is not a fan of meddling kids.

Fall 2016 | The Vulture Swoops in

When Toomes attacks in his armored exo-suit, Spidey realizes it's no coincidence that so many hoodlums are being armed with hybrid alien weaponry. A network of highly skilled and deeply amoral arms traffickers have been salvaging materials from various Super Hero conflicts and illegally selling them. When the flying assailant overpowers Spider-Man and drops him into a watery abyss, Peter is only saved by the arrival of an Iron Man drone that has been tracking him.

REDLINE ALERT!
Hi again! Adrian Toomes says the Battle of New York was 8 years ago, but that event was only 4 years prior. This one's a real head scratcher for us—I reckon an Analyst misplaced the case file.

173

2016

Liz, Mr. Harrington, and Ned are trapped in the elevator.

Spider-Man ascends the Washington Monument.

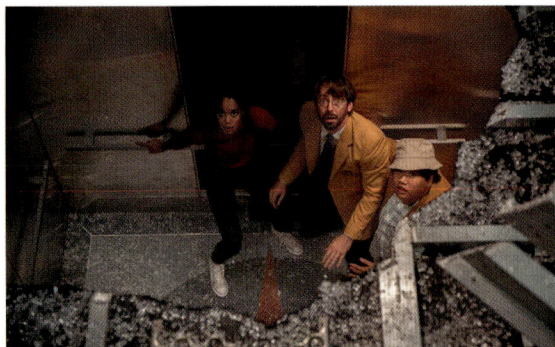

The Chitauri core explodes, damaging a historic site.

Fall 2016 | Washington Monument Rescue

Trouble follows Peter to Washington, D.C., where he is due to take part in the Academic Decathlon. His determination to investigate the Vulture the night before the Decathlon causes him to miss it entirely. Meanwhile, the Chitauri core Peter picked up during his clash with Shocker is unstable, and it emits a blast that damages the Washington Monument, trapping Peter's fellow students in an increasingly shaky elevator. Spider-Man climbs to the top and vaults over a helicopter to propel himself through the four-inch ballistic glass windows in the very peak of the obelisk. Peter manages to save his friends—but only barely.

Spider-Man webs Aaron Davis to his vehicle.

Fall 2016 | That Sinking Feeling

The ferry interception is a fiasco. One of Toomes' hybrid devices goes off, bisecting the ship, and the bad guys get away while Peter desperately tries to web the two sinking halves of the vessel back together. Disaster is only averted by the arrival of Tony Stark, who uses his Iron Man suit and assorted drones to push the ship back together and weld it closed so it can be towed back to port. Everyone is okay… "No thanks to you," Stark adds, asking a devastated Peter to hand over his Spider-Man suit. Peter then spends some time rebuilding his relationship with his aunt, focusing on his friends and studies, and returning to life as a normal high school kid.

Peter tries to web together the split halves of the ferry.

Fall 2016 | The Informant

Spidey tracks down Aaron Davis, who agrees to share information about the hybrid arms dealers because he's worried about the firepower they're putting on the street. "I don't want those weapons in this neighborhood," he says. "I've got a nephew who lives here." He tells Spidey about an imminent trade happening on the Staten Island Ferry, then is left webbed to the back of his car to think about his life choices.

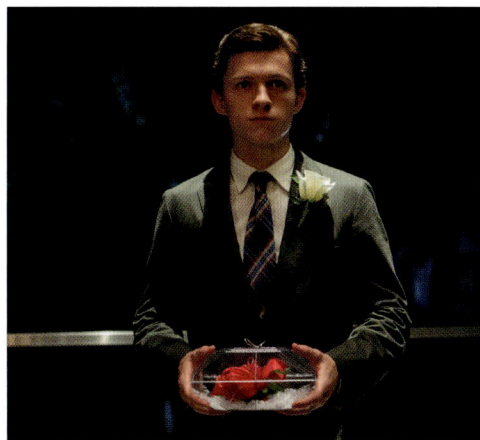

Peter discovers Liz's father is his new foe.

Peter Parker in a panic.

"What did he say to you?" Peter and Liz after getting a ride to the dance from her father.

Fall 2016 | Meet the Parents

After mustering the courage to ask Liz to the homecoming dance, Peter is aghast to discover that her father is the same man he has clashed with in the flying exo-suit. Adrian Toomes gradually picks up the fact that his daughter's date is not just nervous about the dance. Since the boy rescued his daughter at the Washington Monument, he gives him one more chance—but threatens to kill him if he interferes in his business again. But Peter can't let it go. He abandons Liz at the dance and goes after Toomes equipped with nothing but his homemade webshooters and his old Spidey sweatsuit.

Fall 2016 | The Air Raid

Spider-Man confronts Toomes while the arms scavenger is breaking into a jet carrying Avengers gear from Stark Tower to the new Avengers Compound in upstate New York. Their fight damages several engines and the plane crashes along the beach at Coney Island. As Toomes attempts to escape with a crate of Arc Reactors, his exo-suit malfunctions, but Peter saves him from the explosion, leaving him webbed up for the authorities with a handwritten note: "FOUND—Flying Vulture Guy. PS—Sorry about your plane."

REDLINE ALERT!
Hiya! Was that Tony Stark's Mark XLII suit on the cargo plane headed for the Avengers Compound? That's mighty strange, considering Tony blew it up while fighting Aldrich Killian! If he rebuilt it, that plane crash just means he'll have to build it again... golly!

The Vulture in flight.

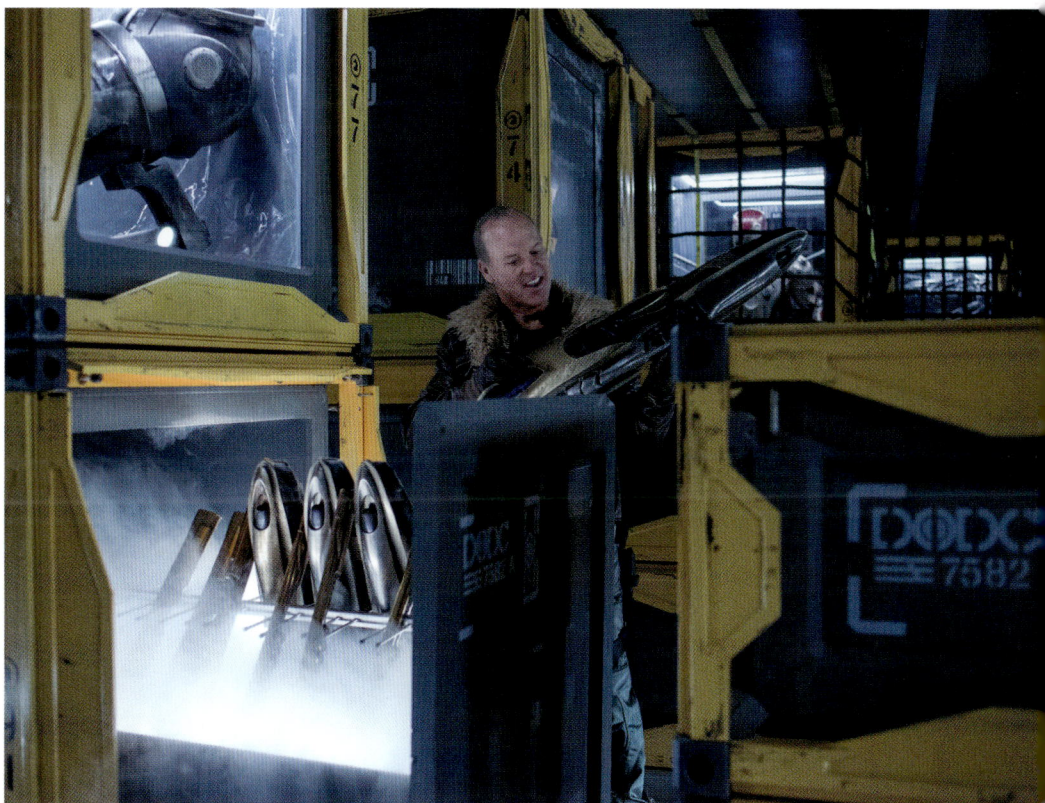

"Hot dog!" Adrian Toomes examines some alien tech aboard the jet.

2016

Liz says goodbye.

🕷 Fall 2016 | Heartbreak High

After the arrest of Adrian Toomes, his daughter Liz leaves school and moves with her mother to Oregon to avoid the spectacle of his trial. "Bye, Peter. Whatever's going on with you, I hope you figure it out," she says, still unaware that Parker is Spider-Man. For reasons known only to himself, her father has chosen to keep the boy's secret, even from other prisoners. Meanwhile, MJ is appointed the new captain of their Academic Decathlon. She is intrigued by Peter Parker, but also finds him somewhat suspicious.

🕷 🔴 Fall 2016 | Stark's Proposal

Tony Stark reconciles with Peter Parker at the new Avengers Compound and apologizes—sort of—for taking back the high-tech suit he once gave him. "Actually it turns out it was the perfect tough-love moment that you needed," Stark says. He offers to introduce Spider-Man to a group of reporters as the latest member of the Avengers, but Parker turns him down, saying he prefers to stay in school and remain "a friendly, neighborhood Spider-Man." Stark accepts his decision and instead uses the press event to resolve other long-unfinished business: asking Pepper Potts to marry him.

Peter Parker has a heart-to-heart with Tony Stark and Happy Hogan.

Stephen Strange regards his ruined hands.

✴ Fall 2016 | The Desperation of Doctor Strange

After seven surgeries, Dr. Stephen Strange still struggles to restore his wounded hands. His bitterness isolates him from friends and colleagues, including former love Dr. Christine Palmer, who tries to convince him there are other things besides returning to his career that can fulfill him. "Like what," he snaps. "You?" He learns about the inexplicable recovery of a man named Jonathan Pangborn, who was paralyzed after breaking his back but has healed completely. Pangborn directs Strange to Nepal, and a place called Kamar-Taj, where he says miracles can be found.

Strange walks the streets of Kathmandu, fruitlessly seeking Kamar-Taj.

The Ancient One gives Stephen Strange a taste of the Mystic Arts.

Fall 2016 | The Miracle Workers

In the city of Kathmandu, a Master of the Mystic Arts named Karl Mordo shows mercy to Stephen Strange and invites him to meet with the Ancient One at Kamar-Taj. Strange is dismissive when she says her method of healing Pangborn involved "reorienting the spirit to better heal the body." "There's no such thing as the spirit," Strange insists. "We are made of matter and nothing more. Momentary specks within an indifferent universe." The Ancient One responds by touching his chest, momentarily knocking his soul out of his body.

Fall 2016 | The Astral Plane

"Open your eye," the Ancient One says, placing her thumb on Strange's forehead. She propels him through tunnels of color, wonder, and radiance. "You think this material universe is all there is. What is real? What mysteries lie beyond the reach of your senses?" she asks. "This universe is one of an infinite number. Worlds without end." After making her point and returning Strange to the temporal world, the Ancient One casts him out, but Mordo persuades her to train him, arguing they need strong allies to face Kaecilius and his rebelling Zealots.

Strange experiences the Astral Plane.

2017

Magic rises to stand alongside the powers of science and the cosmos. Such supernatural abilities have always existed, but typically remained hidden from view. As Dr. Stephen Strange studies the Mystic Arts as a means of healing his hands, he helps introduce a new, magical aspect to the pantheon of heroes who have publicly stepped forth to protect Earth.

Stephen Strange trains among the students of Kamar-Taj.

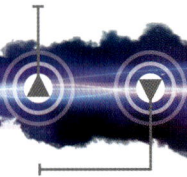

Fall 2016-2017 | Into the Unknown

Stephen Strange's obsessive personality serves him well as a student of the Mystic Arts. He works diligently to understand the order's history, traditions, and practices. He befriends the stoic librarian Wong, and immerses himself in the ancient texts available to him (although he remains most curious about those that are off-limits to novices). He learns that the Ancient One is the most recent of the Sorcerers Supreme, and has lived for hundreds of years. Three Sanctums around the world—in New York, London, and Hong Kong—form a barrier to supernatural threats to Earth.

Strange experiments with the manipulation of time.

2017 | Forbidden Practices

As his skills improve, Strange fixates on *The Book of Cagliostro*, trying to decipher what was on the pages that Kaecilius stole. Strange uses the Eye of Agamotto (a glowing green relic containing the Time Stone) to rewind the book's place in space-time, restoring the missing pages. He discovers the pages contain a ritual for summoning Dormammu, the ruler of the Dark Dimension. Wong and Mordo warn Strange that temporal manipulation can create branches in time, dimensional openings, spatial paradoxes, and time loops. "Do you want to get stuck reliving the same moment over and over forever?" Mordo asks.

2017 | Sanctum Under Siege

Kaecilius and his Zealots begin preparing a path for Dormammu by destroying the Sanctums, starting with London. Doctor Strange helps defend the one in New York, and during the battle a relic known as the Cloak of Levitation bonds itself to him. Strange fends off the insurgent sorcerers and restrains Kaecilius, who reveals why he lost faith in the Ancient One. He calls her a hypocrite for tapping the power of the Dark Dimension to give herself immortality while denying such privileges to others. "Time is what enslaves us. Time is an insult," Kaecilius says.

Kaecilius confronts Doctor Strange.

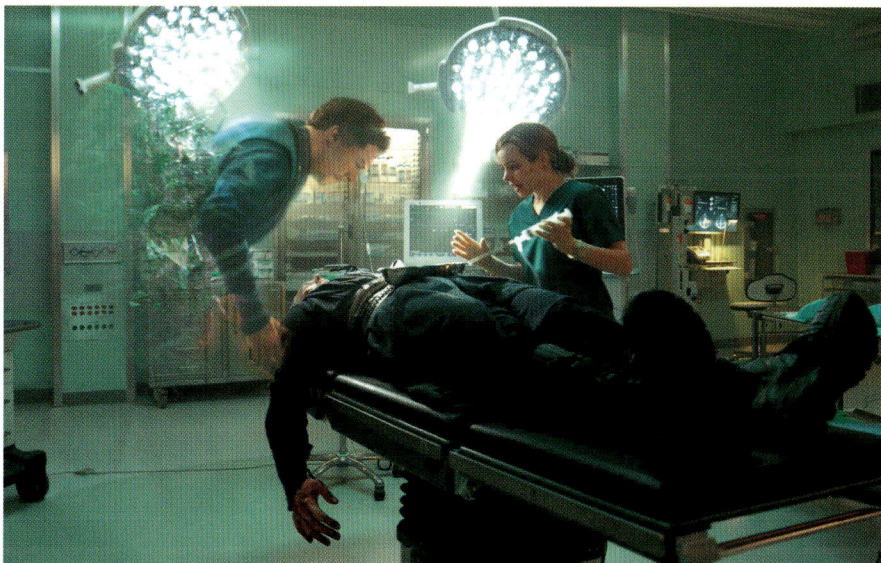

An astral Strange advises Dr. Palmer on his own surgery.

2017 | Mortal Wounds

Kaecilius stabs Doctor Strange during his escape. Strange staggers into the emergency room of his old hospital, pleading with Dr. Palmer to perform emergency surgery to save his life. As she works, his spirit battles the phantom of one of Kaecilius' followers. The two souls clash in the Astral Plane, causing poltergeist-like disturbances around the hospital. Dr. Palmer finally supercharges Strange's body with defibrillator paddles, allowing him to grasp the spirit of his attacker and channel that energy through him, frying his enemy's spiritual and physical forms.

The Ancient One battles Kaecilius and his Zealots.

2017 | The Ancient One Falls

A recovering Doctor Strange confronts the Ancient One about Kaecilius' accusation. "You feed off Dormammu. I know how you did it. I've seen the missing pages from *The Book of Cagliostro*," Strange says. Mordo refuses to believe, but the Ancient One does not deny it. When the Zealots attack again, Strange plunges them into the Mirror Dimension, which replicates the skyscrapers of New York as an endlessly spiraling kaleidoscope. During the fight, Kaecilius spears the Ancient One, sending her falling back to reality, where her body crashes against the street.

2017 | A Final Lesson

Doctor Strange rushes the Ancient One to the hospital, but there is no saving her. Her long life is finally at an end, and even the energy of the Dark Dimension cannot restore her. In their astral forms, she draws out her last seconds to warn Strange that he will only become a source of good in the world if he masters the power of humility and sacrifice. "Arrogance and fear still keep you from learning the simplest and most significant lesson of all," she says. "It's not about you."

The Ancient One extends her final moments of mortal life.

2017 | Backward and Forward

The Hong Kong Sanctum falls. Before Doctor Strange and Mordo even arrive through a portal, Kaecilius and his Zealots have already succeeded. The streets are in ruins, countless innocent bystanders are dead, Wong has been slain, and the globular forms of the Dark Dimension flood the sky overhead. In defiance of natural law, Doctor Strange opens the Eye of Agamotto and uses the Time Stone within to rewind the fight. Destruction is propelled backward. Entropy reverses. Buildings rise from the rubble, and stolen lives are reclaimed.

Doctor Strange prepares to rewind the destruction of Hong Kong.

2017

Doctor Strange temporarily fends off a blast from Dormammu.

2017 | Time to Die

Doctor Strange vaults into the Dark Dimension to stand before the glowing violet eyes of Dormammu himself. "Dormammu, I've come to bargain," he declares. The mystical entity is amused. "You've come to die. Your world is now my ... what is this?" a confused Dormammu says. "Illusion?" Doctor Strange informs him: "No, this is real." An annoyed Dormammu impales the insolent sorcerer.

Strange dies over and over, in increasingly gruesome ways.

2017 | Time to Die

The reversal spell won't hold. Doctor Strange vaults into the Dark Dimension to stand before the glowing violet eyes of Dormammu himself. "Dormammu, I've come to bargain," he declares. The mystical entity is amused. "You've come to die. Your world is now my world," Dormammu says, blasting him with a column of energy that obliterates the insolent sorcerer.

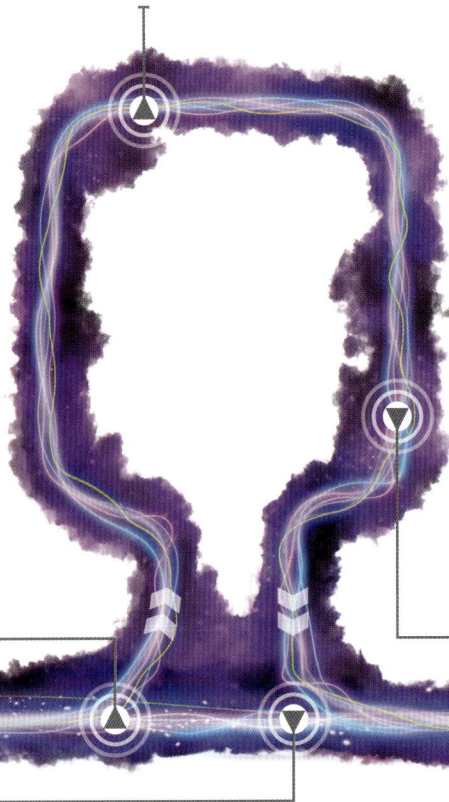

2017 | Time to Die

Doctor Strange vaults into the Dark Dimension to stand before the glowing violet eyes of Dormammu himself. "Dormammu, I've come to bargain," he declares. The mystical entity is ... no longer amused. "What is happening?" Dormammu says, and Doctor Strange explains that he has used the Eye of Agamotto to create a time loop that only he can end. An enraged Dormammu kills him. Then kills him again, and again, and again.

The ruler of the Dark Dimension becomes trapped in a loop.

2017 | Bargaining Power

"You will never win," Dormammu rages as the loop persists into infinity. "No, but I can lose again and again, forever. And that makes you my prisoner," Strange explains. Doctor Strange dies and returns endlessly, until the Dark Dimension's ruler finally relents. "Make this stop! Set me free!" Strange promises he will, but Dormammu must remove the Zealots, end his encroachment on Earth, and vow to never return.

The streets of Hong Kong are returned to their former state, none the wiser of the calamity they suffered.

After looping for an unknown period and suffering countless horrific deaths, Strange makes a deal with Dormammu.

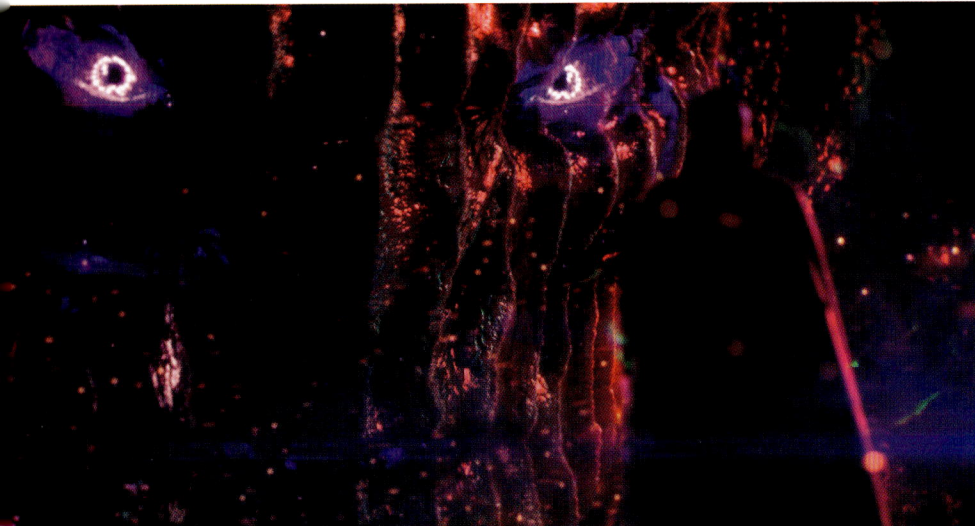

2017 | The Loop Breaks

Doctor Strange returns to the moment he left. For him, an unfathomable stretch of time has passed. For everyone else, it has been only seconds. As Dormammu betrays his adherents, Kaecilius and the Zealots ascend into the Dark Dimension. Their physical bodies begin to blister and scorch. "It's everything you ever wanted," Strange says. Kaecilius desired immortality, and now he has it, but it will be an endless torment. Mordo sees Strange's method as an unforgivable shortcut. "Yes, we did it—by violating the natural law," he says. "I will follow this path no longer."

Fall 2017 | The Boasts of Surtur

While scouring the universe for the remaining Infinity Stones, Thor ends up imprisoned by the fire demon Surtur, who promises he will soon rise to the size of a mountain and bury his sword in Asgard. An end-time prophecy known as Ragnarok foretells that Surtur will destroy the kingdom when a relic known as the Eternal Flame, which is locked in Odin's treasure room, is united with the fire demon's horned crown. "That's a crown? I thought it was a big eyebrow," Thor says, summoning Mjolnir to knock it from Surtur's head, defeating the demon.

REDLINE ALERT!
Hello there! Thor tells Surtur, "I thought my father killed you half a million years ago." Now, we know Asgardians live a long time, but do they live that long? It's hard to say how long Odin has been around, 'cause sometimes he falls into the Odinsleep.

Two brothers witness their father's end.

Thor is dangled by Surtur.

Fall 2017 | Odin's Goodbye

"My sons. I've been waiting for you. Your mother, she calls me. Do you hear it?" Odin says. He warns them that a new danger will arise upon his death. "She's coming. My life was all that held her back. I cannot keep her away any longer." Thor and Loki have no idea who he's talking about. "The Goddess of Death," Odin explains. "Hela—my first born. Your sister." He tells them of her uncontrollable "violent appetites" and urges his sons to unite to stop her. Then he dissipates into windblown tendrils of gold. Odin, the king of Asgard and protector of the Nine Realms, is no more.

Fall 2017 | Loki's Ruse

Upon returning to Asgard with Surtur's skull, Thor exposes "Odin" as his brother Loki in disguise, noting his recent behavioral inconsistencies like lazing about, watching self-congratulatory plays, and banishing the all-seeing Heimdall. Loki admits to stashing their spellbound father in a nursing home on Midgard, but they find the building being demolished when they visit New York. With assistance from Doctor Strange, who has begun maintaining a watchlist of beings from other realms, the brothers locate Odin on an oceanside cliff in Norway, clinging to his final moments of life.

Loki yields after being exposed.

Hela emerges from her long captivity.

Fall 2017 | Sister Breaks her Brother's Toy

Thunder crackles as Odin fades. The sky darkens, and an inky green doorway opens as a woman emerges from centuries of captivity. "So he's gone?" Hela says. "That's a shame. I would've liked to have seen that." She tells Loki and Thor to kneel before her, and when Thor hurls Mjolnir at her, she catches it and crushes it between her fingers. The fragments fall to the grassy field. The brothers retreat into the Bifrost, but Hela follows them, knocking them out into deep space before she arrives alone on Asgard, eager to claim her throne.

2010 | Companion for a King
Having previously been gifted Mjolnir by his father, Thor wields it in what is intended to be his coronation as king of Asgard. But when Thor's arrogance gets the better of him, Odin banishes his son and Mjolnir to Earth, enchanting Mjolnir so that only one who is worthy can lift it. Thor has to prove himself worthy of the hammer again.

2013 | An Old Friend
Thor and Rocket travel back to 2013 to obtain the Aether as part of the Time Heist. While there, Thor is delighted when Mjolnir answers his summons, showing that he is still worthy. Thor takes the hammer back to the present.

2013 | Power of Lightning
Mjolnir is invaluable in the defense of Asgard against the Dark Elves. Thor successfully uses the hammer against the Dark Elf leader Malekith, stopping Malekith and his powers gained from the Aether (the Reality Stone), in a battle in Greenwich, England.

2012 | Return to Earth
Successfully reconciling with Odin, Thor returns to Asgard. However, Loki's plots pull him to Earth once more. Thor makes an entrance, surprising Iron Man and Captain America with the power of Mjolnir before joining the Avengers and using the weapon to fight Loki's forces.

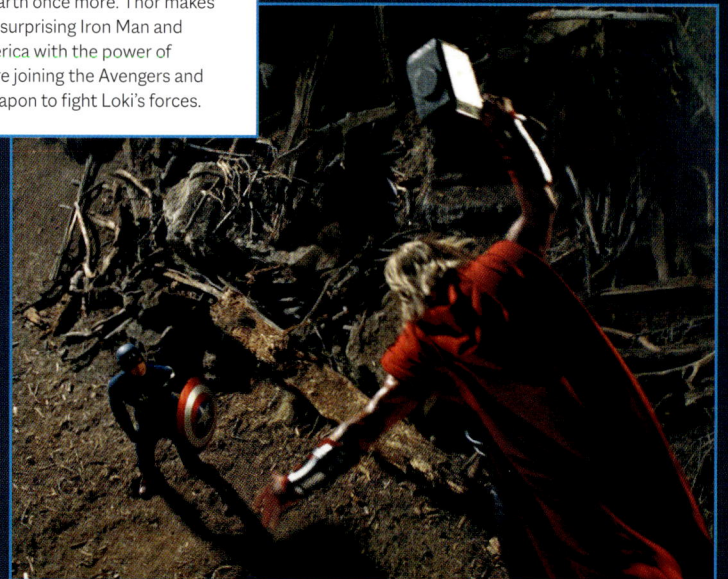

MJOLNIR

The powerful hammer Mjolnir is as much a companion and protector as it is a weapon. Forged by Dwarves in the heart of a dying star in Nidavellir at the behest of Odin, the legendary hammer carries a long legacy. Odin's daughter, Hela, once used Mjolnir for conquest, whereas Thor wields Mjolnir for good as an Avenger. The hammer judges those who try to lift it, only granting the power of Thor to those few that it deems worthy.

2023 | Sharing the Hammer
The intact Mjolnir that Thor retrieves from the past plays a crucial role in the Battle of Earth. Thor fights with the hammer and his new ax Stormbreaker, but when Thor is knocked down by Thanos, Mjolnir judges Captain America worthy—he picks up the hammer and intervenes, smashing Thanos aside and blasting him with lightning.

2015 | Party Trick
During a party at Avengers Tower, the Avengers play the ultimate party game to see if anyone can lift Mjolnir. No one is worthy, although to Thor's shock, Cap nudges it a little. Later, after Vision is created using lightning summoned by the hammer, the synthezoid casually picks up Mjolnir, demonstrating to Thor he is an ally.

2023 | Returned
After Thanos' defeat, Cap returns the unshattered Mjolnir to the past.

2017 | Shattered
Mjolnir helps Thor against many foes, but his sister Hela, who once possessed the hammer, proves to be too much. She blocks the hammer and then shatters it with her bare hand. The destruction of Mjolnir takes a psychological toll on Thor.

2013-2017 | Power of Love
Mjolnir goes on many adventures with Jane Foster and Thor as they renew their relationship. When Thor asks Mjolnir to always protect Jane, his words place an enchantment upon the hammer. Though the couple eventually break up, Thor's request will have huge repercussions for Jane, Thor, and Mjolnir in the years to come.

2025 | The Mighty Thor
After being diagnosed with Stage 4 cancer, Dr. Jane Foster, now Thor's ex, hears Mjolnir call to her. She visits the shattered hammer in New Asgard, and it restores itself and chooses Foster as its wielder. She becomes The Mighty Thor. Thor is shocked to see his former weapon in the hands of another, but after Jane's passing, Thor wields Mjolnir once again.

2017

A bemused Hela welcomes Skurge as her first new follower.

Fall 2017 | Hela's Reign

Two of the Warriors Three—Volstagg and Fandral—try to stop Hela when she arrives in Asgard, but both perish beneath her blades. Skurge, a foolhardy warrior who helped maintain the gateway in Heimdall's absence, surrenders to her immediately. "You look like a smart boy with good survival instincts," she says, naming him her royal executioner. Hela easily wipes out the entire Asgardian military, including Hogun, the last of the Warriors Three, and takes the throne.

Thor in the realm of the Grandmaster's pure imagination.

Fall 2017 | The Grandmaster and the Valkyrie

Thor plummets onto a junkyard planet known as Sakaar, a dumping ground surrounded by cosmic gateways, ruled over by a bon vivant known as the Grandmaster. A disaffected scavenger known as Scrapper 142, who ages ago was the last of Odin's Valkyrie warriors, places an inhibitor chip in Thor's neck and collects him as a potential new combatant in the Grandmaster's gladiatorial competition. As the Grandmaster listens with amusement, Thor explains that he is the God of Thunder—but he struggles to generate any power. "Wow, I didn't hear any thunder," the Grandmaster says. "But out of your fingers, was that, like, sparkles?" Thor spots Loki in the crowd but is helpless as he is taken to the arena.

Topaz, the Grandmaster, and Scrapper 142 assess their new find.

The champion of Sakaar roars his approval.

Fall 2017 | The Champion

In the gladiator pen, Thor befriends a Kronan rock warrior named Korg, and Miek, a bug-like alien riding in a mechanical exoskeleton. Thor braces himself to face the Grandmaster's reigning champion, but when he sees the combatant emerge in the arena, he recognizes him as the long-lost Hulk. "Yes!!" Thor shouts jubilantly. "We know each other. He's a friend from work!" But something has changed...

Fall 2017 | Escape From Sakaar

Thor persuades Hulk to revert back to Bruce Banner for the first time in two years by showing him a recording in the crashed Quinjet of Natasha Romanoff pleading with him to come home. Thor also convinces Scrapper 142 to return to Asgard by explaining that Hela, who long ago exterminated her fellow Valkyrie fighters, is now back on the throne. "If I'm going to die, it may as well be driving my sword through the heart of that murderous hag," the reborn Valkyrie says. While the trio flee through one of Sakaar's largest portals, Korg and Miek stage a gladiator uprising against the Grandmaster. Loki provides some help getting to a starship, but true to form attempts to betray Thor for a hefty reward. This time, the God of Thunder anticipates his brother's treachery, which teaches Loki a lesson (for once).

Having reverted into his human form, Bruce Banner agrees to join Thor's "Revengers" Team.

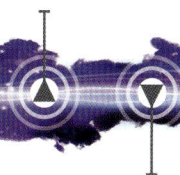

Thor and Hulk clash in the arena.

Fall 2017 | "No Banner. Only Hulk."

"Everybody thought you were dead. So much has happened since I last saw you," Thor says, but the green brute who pulverizes him has no concern for his fellow Avenger. Thor tries Natasha Romanoff's "the sun's getting real low" soothing technique, but Hulk grabs him by the arm and smashes him back and forth. Loki, who has been hiding out in the court of the Grandmaster, cries out: "Yes! That's how it feels!", remembering his own clobbering at Hulk's hands during the Battle of New York. Thor overpowers Hulk by finally summoning a lightning strike. His God of Thunder powers begin to manifest themselves, but the Grandmaster activates the inhibitor in Thor's neck, ending the fight.

Thor and Hela battle in the royal palace in Asgard.

Fall 2017 | Brother vs. Sister

Back on Asgard, Heimdall leads an evacuation of civilians trying to flee Hela's tyranny. As they gather to escape, Thor confronts Hela in Odin's throne room, and she slashes him across the face, cutting out the God of Thunder's eye. Now, she says, he truly reminds her of their father. Without his hammer, Thor wonders if he can defeat her, but a vision of Odin says, "Are you Thor, God of Hammers?" Thor unleashes a lightning storm on Hela, while Valkyrie and Hulk fight the undead Asgardian warriors she resurrected as her soldiers. A powered-up Thor then joins them, blasting through Hela's entire army.

2017

Fall 2017 | Deus Ex Machina

Hela once again overpowers Thor, but hope is on the horizon. Korg, Miek, and a penitent Loki arrive at Asgard with the massive transport ship *Statesman*, which is ferrying Sakaaran refugees and has plenty of room for the fleeing Asgardians. But Hela cannot be stopped. Even Skurge turns against her, giving his own life to hold back her forces while the civilians board the ark.

The *Statesman* descends on Asgard for a mission of mercy.

The Grandmaster declares the rebellion against him a draw.

Fall 2017 | Sakaaran Shakeout

The Grandmaster is surrounded by an army of revolutionaries. The cheerful despot decides to follow the old maxim: if you can't beat them, join them. "I've just gotta say I'm proud of you all. This revolution has been a huge success. Yay us!" he declares. "You can't have a revolution without somebody to overthrow, so ... you're welcome. And, uh ... it's a tie."

Fall 2017 | Ragnarok Fulfilled

With Hela drawing her immense power from Asgard itself, Thor realizes he can only save his people by sacrificing their homeland. He sends Loki to the treasure room to unite two prophetic objects—the crown of Surtur and the Eternal Flame. "You want Asgard," Thor tells Hela. "It's yours." The fire demon, now the size of a mountain, bursts from the royal palace and lays waste to the realm. Valkyrie fulfills her dream of driving her sword into Hela before their escape, but the Goddess of Death is only fully defeated when Surtur reduces the cosmic kingdom to a nebula of gravel. But as Odin told Thor: "Asgard is not a place. Never was ... Asgard is where our people stand."

Surtur fulfills the prophecy by demolishing Asgard—and stopping Hela.

2018

The grand scheme of Thanos, decades in the making, comes to a head as the Titan finally seizes the opportunity to take personal possession of the Infinity Stones. As he prepares to erase half the universe, a discovery made by Scott Lang about the Quantum Realm will also prove to be a critical turn in a cascade of interlocked events.

Scott Lang and Hope Van Dyne on the go.

Spring 2018 | Scott Lang's Smaller Problems

Scott Lang has been cooped up under house arrest ever since taking Captain America's side against the enforcement of the Sokovia Accords. Just days away from freedom, he experiences a vision that emanates from Janet Van Dyne, who vanished when she went subatomic decades ago. Lang calls Hank Pym and Hope Van Dyne to share what happened, and they decide to break him out three days early—sensing this as their chance to rescue her.

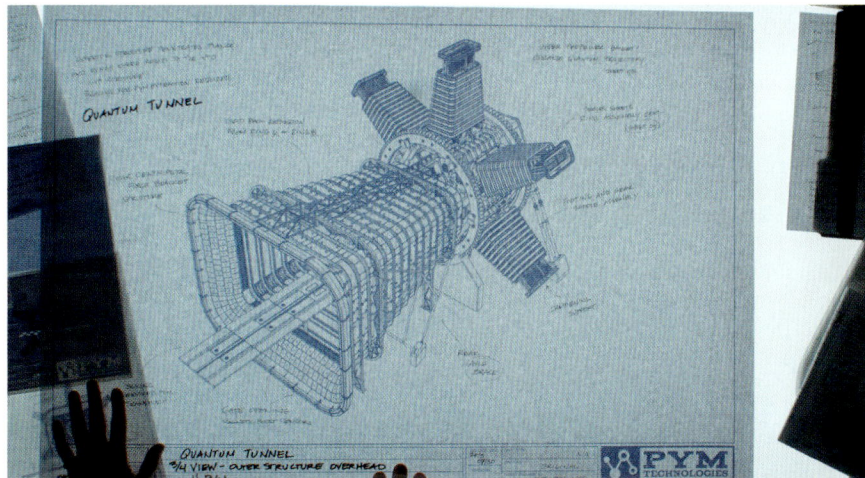

Schematics for the large-scale Quantum Tunnel.

Spring 2018 | The Quantum Tunnel

The long-ago implanted message from Janet was triggered when Pym and his daughter activated their new invention, a tunnel designed as a safe gateway to and from the microcosmic dimension known as the Quantum Realm. When Scott Lang passed through there in his early adventures as Ant-Man, Janet tagged him with an antenna to communicate with her husband and daughter. If they can get the tunnel working again, Janet can use Lang to guide them to her.

Spring 2018 | Working out the Bugs

Unfortunately, the Quantum Tunnel requires a component that only the underworld tech merchant Sonny Burch can provide. Burch wants to know more about their project than they are willing to share, and he is prepared to take their innovation by force.

Sonny Burch extorts Hope Van Dyne.

187

2015 | Quantum Trip
With Hank and Hope's guidance, Scott, the new Ant-Man, takes action against Darren. He's unable to steal the Yellowjacket suit as planned, so Scott must battle his new nemesis. However, Darren's suit is made of titanium—the material that caused Janet to go subatomic in order to penetrate the missile. Scott makes the same decision and uses the Pym Particles to shrink into the Quantum Realm; there, he unknowingly encounters Janet, who sends a hidden message back with him. Cross vanishes when his suit implodes.

1987 | Losing The Wasp
Hank pairs his Pym Particles with the Ant-Man suit and performs missions around the world for S.H.I.E.L.D. Later, he meets Janet Van Dyne and the duo work as government operatives, going into the field as Ant-Man and The Wasp. In 1987, S.H.I.E.L.D. sends them to intercept a rogue Soviet nuclear missile. As the missile hurtles towards its target, Janet shrinks to subatomic size to enter its casing and disarm it, but then disappears into the Quantum Realm.

1970s | Experimentation
Pym works as a scientist and consultant for S.H.I.E.L.D. at the Camp Lehigh research base, where he perfects the size-altering particles that he names after himself.

1989 | Resignation
The loss of Janet crushes Hank. When he discovers S.H.I.E.L.D. is trying to secretly recreate his work, he resigns. Hank takes his Pym Particle formula with him, saying he will never allow S.H.I.E.L.D. to use it. He goes one step further and locks his Ant-Man suit in a safe, believing it too dangerous to use.

2015 | Ant-Man Returns
With Pym Particles and S.H.I.E.L.D. behind him, Hank creates Pym Technologies. But years later, his protégé in the business, Darren Cross, betrays him by trying to recreate the particles. A robbery turns into mentorship after Hank decides he needs assistance to stop Darren. Ex-con Scott Lang piques Pym's curiosity and he decides to test him by tricking him into stealing the Ant-Man suit. Despite his daughter Hope disagreeing, Hank then trains Scott how to use the Ant-Man suit and the Pym Particles.

2015 | Deal with Hydra
Darren goes too far with his study of Pym Particles and makes a new form of the particles to work with a powerful combat suit he dubs the Yellowjacket. He then agrees to sell the suit to Hydra. Darren puts others in mortal danger after he fails to adequately shield his brain from the particles, causing him to descend further into madness and paranoia.

2018 | Saving Janet

Scott's successful return from the Quantum Realm in 2015 prompts Hank and Hope to construct a portal to find and rescue Janet. However, Scott's actions at Leipzig-Halle complicate matters because the use of the Ant-Man suit was a violation of the Sokovia Accords. Facing opposition the entire time, the trio successfully work on the Quantum Tunnel and are able to bring Janet back, but later Thanos' Snap turns Hank, Hope, and Janet to dust, leaving Scott trapped in the Quantum Realm.

2016 | Impressing Captain America

Scott could not be more thrilled when Steve Rogers recruits him, even if it is to fight other Avengers. In the battle at Leipzig-Halle Airport, Scott surprises the opposing Avengers with his ability to shrink and grow at will. He uses Pym Particles to become small enough to crawl inside Iron Man's suit and cause damage, before he grows into a giant and distracts the opposing team while Steve escapes.

2023 | An Idea

Scott returns from the Quantum Realm and learns about the Snap. He shows up at the Avengers Compound with an idea: since he jumped ahead five years in only moments, the Avengers could use Pym Particles to travel back in time, utilizing the Quantum Realm as a bridge. Tony Stark finds a way to target particular places and moments in time to acquire the Infinity Stones. The group plans the Time Heist.

2023 | Time Travel

With a limited supply of Pym Particles, the crucial component to the success of the Time Heist, the Avengers can only briefly test whether the plan works. They have sufficient particles for one round trip each. The Avengers split into teams and activate the particles to shrink and enter the Quantum Realm, then journey to different points in the past. Tony and Steve take a side mission to Camp Lehigh in 1970 to retrieve the Tesseract and extra Pym Particles from Hank Pym's lab, allowing them to complete the Heist and undo the Snap.

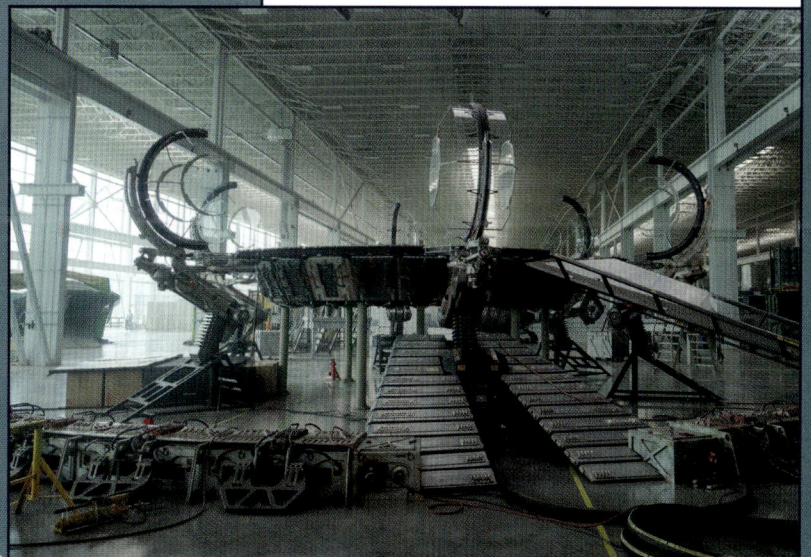

PYM PARTICLES

Decades ago, Hank Pym developed a formula with a unique group of subatomic particles that can affect the density and size of living beings and objects. They become known as Pym Particles. By incorporating the particles into a specially designed suit and changing the distance between atoms, Hank realizes they can shrink a human down to the size of an ant while increasing their density and strength. He uses the Pym Particles as the S.H.I.E.L.D. agent Ant-Man, usually in service to the U.S. government. Many people over the years try to steal or replicate the Pym Particles technology, often for nefarious purposes, and they later become the crucial element to defeating Thanos and saving the universe.

2018

Spring 2018 | Here ... and Gone

Hank Pym and Hope Van Dyne are also being stalked by a mysterious, masked figure they call Ghost, who can phase shift through different states of matter to become solid or ephemeral at will. This being also wants access to their Quantum Tunnel, and Van Dyne must repeatedly fend off the entity in her Wasp suit. When Pym shrinks his entire lab building down to the size of carry-on luggage, the tech becomes especially prone to theft, and Ghost promptly steals it.

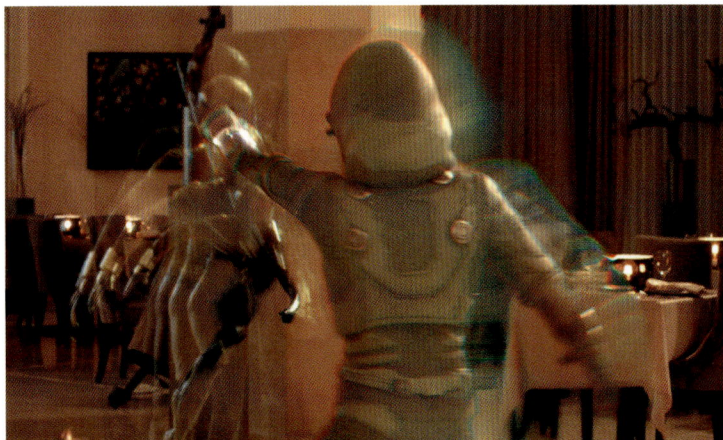

The Wasp vs. Ghost.

Spring 2018 | Antagonized

Ava's phase shifting is a side effect from the lab accident that killed her parents. The Ghost suit temporarily regulates her matter density, but she will soon "fade away to nothing" without healing particles from the Quantum Realm. She plans to steal Janet's quantum energy to stabilize her phasing—even if it kills Janet in the process. Hank, Hope, and Scott are tied up, but manage to escape after Foster unwittingly releases Hank's trained ants. They take the lab with them and set it up again in the woods, and Janet Van Dyne broadcasts through Scott Lang to help them fine-tune the apparatus. Scott rushes home for a check-in with the F.B.I., but Hope and Hank are tracked to the lab's location and arrested. In the confusion, the lab is stolen once again by Ghost.

Spring 2018 | The Ghost Revealed

The group seek help from Bill Foster, a scientist who worked alongside Pym over three decades ago when both were part of S.H.I.E.L.D. The two men still bear grudges against each other from their work on Project Goliath, but Foster tells them that they can locate the missing lab by modifying a regulator on the Ant-Man suit to detect its emissions. Although Pym and the others find the lab, they also discover Foster is harboring Ghost. Her name is Ava Starr, and she is the daughter of another S.H.I.E.L.D. researcher who died conducting rogue experiments, after a feud with Pym forced him out of the agency.

Microscopic tardigrades surround Hank Pym's rescue pod.

Ava Starr struggles to maintain her physical form.

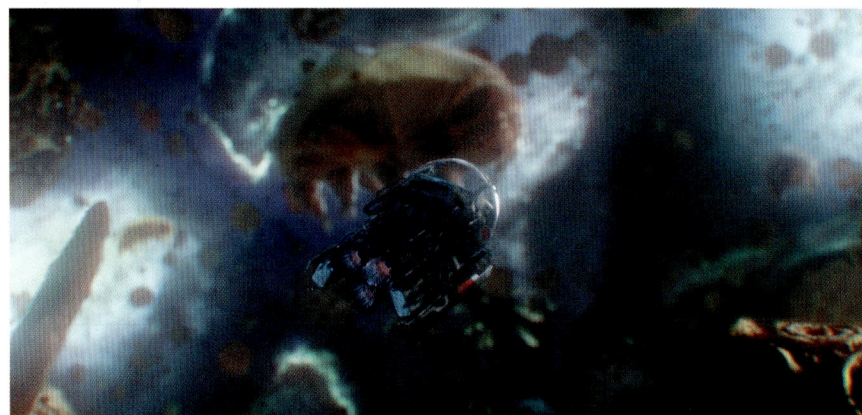

Spring 2018 | Pym Gets Small

Scott manages to break Hope and Hank out, but the clock is ticking on the coordinates Janet provided. They track the lab down and Foster is subdued by Pym's ants while Scott distracts Ghost. Pym vows to help Starr, before venturing into the subatomic realm to rendezvous with his long-lost wife. During his journey, the lab building is again shrunk for easy transportation. Unfortunately, Sonny Burch seizes this opportunity to steal it.

Sonny Burch makes off with the shrunken lab.

Out in San Francisco Bay, a giant Scott Lang looks for Sonny and the miniaturized lab.

Spring 2018 | San Francisco Chase

Scott Lang enlarges himself, and races after Burch using a flatbed truck as a scooter. Burch boards a whale-watching cruise in Fisherman's Wharf, and Lang makes himself gigantic to pursue him through the bay—even bigger than he grew during the clash over the Sokovia Accords. He pinches the lab between his fingers and pries it from Burch's grasp, but Lang's enormous body drains his energy and he sinks below the waves. Hope Van Dyne flies down in her Wasp suit to return him to normal size and bring him back to the surface.

Spring 2018 | Sweet Freedom

Scott Lang hurries home, replacing the giant ant who has been wearing his ankle transmitter just as the F.B.I. arrives. Agent Jimmy Woo expects to find Lang violating his house arrest, but instead he is obligated to make Lang's release official. "I'll be seeing you again," Woo says. "Where?" Lang asks. A bewildered Woo replies: "Like, in general. The next time you do something bad." Lang says he thought Woo wanted to hang out. Stranger things have happened.

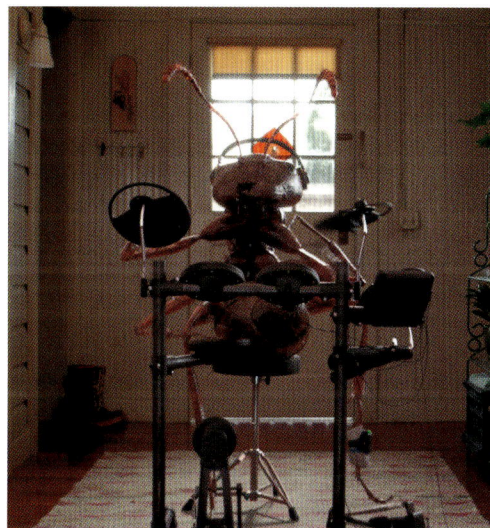

A giant ant finds the beat.

Spring 2018 | Mother and Child Reunion

With the lab restored to its original proportions, Hank Pym emerges from the subatomic dimension with Janet, who is supercharged with energy that can temporarily stabilize Ava Starr. Then Janet embraces Hope, who was only a child the last time they saw each other. "I'm here now," she tells her daughter. "We have time." For a longtime inhabitant of the Quantum Realm, the significance of time looms large.

Hope sees her mother again for the first time in decades.

2018

Thanos aboard the Asgardian rescue vessel.

2018 | The White Wolf

After undergoing intensive deprogramming in Wakanda, Bucky Barnes is finally liberated from the mind control protocols that transformed him into the Winter Soldier. Dora Milaje security chief Ayo, who has been helping him through the process, tests the success by reciting the ten code words that once weaponized him. When the tearful man's consciousness remains unaltered, she whispers: "You are free." Barnes continues his recovery in Wakanda, where he is known under the nickname "White Wolf."

Bucky Barnes undergoing rehabilitation in Wakanda.

Spring 2018 | Chasing the Time Stone

While tracking the Tesseract, Thanos' battleship *Sanctuary II* intercepts the Asgardian refugee vessel the *Statesman*. Some of the Asgardian passengers escape, Valkyrie among them. She leads the survivors to safety while Thor, Heimdall, Bruce Banner, and Loki remain to fight. Still reeling from the destruction of Asgard, they are soon laid to waste by Thanos and his forces. "I know what it's like to lose," Thanos tells them. "To feel so desperately that you're right. Yet to fail, nonetheless."

Spring 2018 | The Hulk Subdued

Bruce Banner attacks Thanos, but even the Hulk is no match for the Titan wielding the Power Stone. A wounded Heimdall summons the Bifrost to send the Hulk spiraling through space toward Earth.

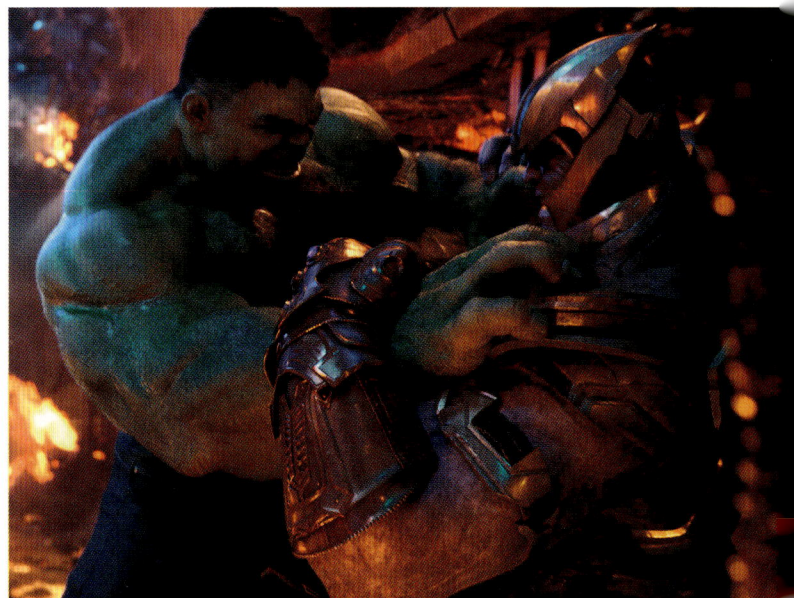

Xandar in more peaceful times.

Spring 2018 | The Power Stone Seized

Xandar falls, as Thanos and his forces overpower the defenses of the Nova Empire's capital world. Their target is the Power Stone, which the Guardians of the Galaxy had entrusted to Nova Prime and the elite Nova Corps. His proxy Ronan was defeated here, but Thanos departs Xandar with the purple stone, leaving the world decimated.

Hulk in a losing fight against Thanos.

192

Loki makes an offering while Thanos clutches Thor by the skull.

Spring 2018 | Heimdall and Loki's End

Thanos spears Heimdall through the chest for casting away the Hulk, and the all-seeing gatekeeper's watch is ended. Thor insists the Tesseract was destroyed back on Asgard, but Loki reveals he has been hiding it since their departure. "You really are the worst, brother," Thor says. These will be his last words to Loki. After Thanos shatters the Tesseract and places the Space Stone into his gauntlet, Loki strikes at his throat—but the blue stone halts his blade inches away. Thanos snaps the trickster's neck, and leaves his body beside Thor as he departs, incinerating the *Statesman* in his wake. "No resurrections this time," Thanos says.

Spring 2018 | Hulk's Warning

Banner crashes through the roof of the New York Sanctum, where Masters of the Mystic Arts, Doctor Strange and Wong, maintain their watch over the Eye of Agamotto and the Time Stone within. "Thanos is coming…" Banner gasps. But Strange can only ask: "Who?"

Bruce Banner crashes into Doctor Strange's New York Sanctum.

The Q-Ship descends on New York.

Spider-Man hangs on as the Q-Ship departs Earth.

Spring 2018 | The Q-Ship Attack

Thanos sends Ebony Maw and Cull Obsidian, two lieutenants from his conscripted "Children of Thanos," to New York to acquire the Time Stone. Doctor Strange, Wong, and Bruce Banner alert Tony Stark to the looming danger just as the massive Q-Ship appears over Greenwich Village. After a destructive street battle, Obsidian is mystically banished to a polar landscape and loses his left hand as the portal closes. Maw cannot break the protective spell around the Eye of Agamotto, so he kidnaps Strange in his entirety and flees back to Titan to rendezvous with Thanos. The starship has two stowaways—Iron Man and Spider-Man—who hastily plot a rescue.

193

2018

Spring 2018 | We Don't Have a Hulk

After living as the Hulk for two years, Bruce Banner discovers his angry alter-ego now refuses to emerge even in times of extreme danger. The two sides of his personality are increasingly estranged, and Banner feels more disoriented and powerless than ever after learning of the feud that fractured the Avengers during his absence. With Tony Stark gone into deep space, Banner calls the flip phone number that was Stark's emergency line to Steve Rogers, bringing Captain America into the fight against Thanos.

Vision unleashes a blast from the Mind Stone.

Bruce Banner struggles to make Hulk emerge.

Corvus Glaive deflects the hit.

Spring 2018 | The Mind Stone Ambush

Wanda Maximoff, still in hiding after running afoul of the Sokovia Accords, is lying low with Vision in Scotland when a second Q-Ship, this one carrying Thanos' agents Proxima Midnight and Corvus Glaive, descends on Edinburgh. As they seek to rip the Mind Stone from Vision, Steve Rogers, Sam Wilson, and Natasha Romanoff join the fight, successfully driving away the Children of Thanos, who vow that they will return.

Spring 2018 | The Guardians Salvage Thor

The Guardians of the Galaxy respond to the *Statesman*'s distress call but find only a field of debris. The only survivor is Thor, whom Drax describes with wonder: "It's like a pirate had a baby with an angel." Thor awakens and tells them what Thanos has done, but Gamora is well aware of his plans to erase half of all living things. "If he gets all six Infinity Stones, he can do it with a snap of his fingers," she explains.

REDLINE ALERT!
Why, hello! Thor says he's 1500 years old, but wasn't he just a baby around 695 CE? I'd have an answer for y'all now, but Casey just spilled coffee all over the mainframe, bless his heart.

Thor stuck to the windshield of the Guardians' ship.

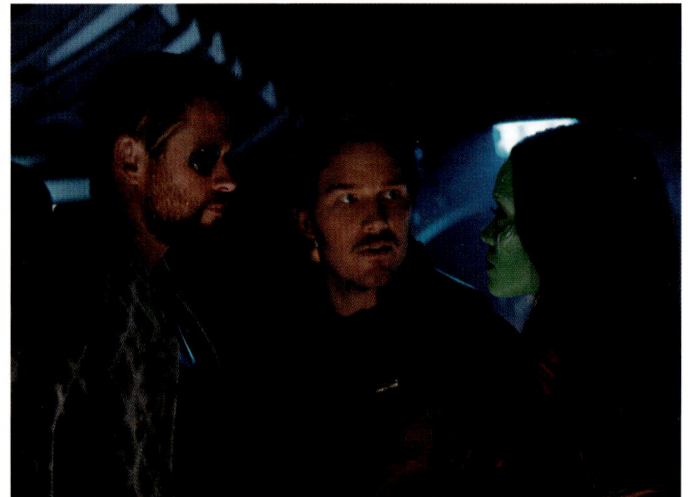

Thor, Peter Quill, and Gamora discuss the threat of Thanos.

Spring 2018 | An Ax to Grind

Thor persuades Rocket and Groot to accompany him to the neutron star forge of Nidavellir to create "a Thanos-killing" weapon. This was the birthplace of Mjolnir, and is famous for its powerful creations. But the trio find it to be a wasteland after Thanos forced the giant Dwarves there to create his gauntlet, then slaughtered them. The lone survivor, Eitri, crafts the Bifrost-summoning battle ax Stormbreaker after Thor reignites the forge and Groot donates one of his own limbs for the handle.

Eitri needs help creating a new weapon worthy of a god.

Thor risks his life to power the forge of Nidavellir.

Spring 2018 | The Reality Stone Hoax

Peter Quill, Mantis, Drax, and Gamora venture to Knowhere, where the Reality Stone has been safeguarded for years with the Collector. They find Thanos brutalizing the charismatic curator, and Gamora stabs Thanos with the "perfectly balanced" twin-bladed knife he gave her as a child. "Why ...?" the dying Titan says. Gamora weeps, proving she still cares for her adoptive father. But it's a cruel trick. Thanos has already acquired the Reality Stone and used it to create this illusion, to test Gamora. He takes her hostage before fleeing through a Space Stone portal.

Ebony Maw tortures Doctor Strange.

Thanos uses the Reality Stone to fool Gamora and Peter Quill.

Spring 2018 | Ebony Maw, Silenced

Aboard the Q-Ship, Ebony Maw uses his telekinetic powers to try to torture Doctor Strange into relinquishing the Time Stone. Tony Stark and Peter Parker secretly devise a plan of attack based on something the teenager once saw in a sci-fi film. "Your powers are inconsequential compared to mine," Maw scoffs when they confront him. "Yeah, but the kid's seen more movies," Stark replies before blasting a hole in the hull of the starship. The vacuum pulls Maw into the void of space where he freezes to death instantly. The ship remains on auto-pilot, destined for Titan.

2018

The civil war between the Avengers ends.

Spring 2018 | Bygones

Despite being fugitives, Steve Rogers, Natasha Romanoff, Sam Wilson and Wanda Maximoff return to the United States to make amends with old allies to help keep Vision—and the stone—safe from Thanos. "The world's on fire, and you think all's forgiven?" Secretary of State Thaddeus Ross says, as he demands to have them arrested. But James "Rhodey" Rhodes welcomes their return on behalf of the Avengers. Earth's mightiest heroes are working together again.

Late Spring 2018 | Sanctuary in Wakanda

King T'Challa welcomes the Avengers to his homeland while his sister Shuri, the nation's lead researcher, gets busy separating Vision's synapses from the Mind Stone. If it can be safely destroyed, Thanos will be unable to complete his genocidal plan, but the surgery is meticulous and precarious, requiring a lot of time and care. Meanwhile, Steve Rogers is reunited with the newly deprogrammed Bucky Barnes, now sporting a Wakandan-made vibranium arm. "How've you been, Buck?" Rogers says, embracing his old friend. "Not bad," Barnes replies. "For the end of the world."

Bucky Barnes and Steve Rogers reunite.

Steve Rogers, T'Challa, Natasha Romanoff, and Okoye prepare for Thanos' arrival.

Spring 2018 | Protecting Vision

To prevent Thanos from acquiring the Mind Stone, Vision offers to sacrifice himself. Since Wanda Maximoff derived her powers in part from the Mind Stone, he suggests her energy could create a feedback loop that destroys the gem's molecular integrity. But it would also end his life. "That's too high a price," Maximoff insists. "We don't trade lives, Vision," Steve Rogers tells him. Cap proposes they regroup in the most heavily fortified and technologically advanced place on Earth.

Vision and Wanda Maximoff share a moment.

The Stonekeeper welcomes Thanos to Vormir.

Thanos acquires the Soul Stone, at great cost.

Spring 2018 | The Soul Stone Sacrifice

Thanos forces Gamora to reveal the location of the Soul Stone not by hurting her, but by torturing her sister Nebula. Unable to bear her suffering any longer, Gamora tells him: "Vormir." On that desolate world, the pair approach the mountaintop where the Stonekeeper, the man once known as Johann Schmidt, was transported decades ago by the Tesseract. "In order to take the stone you must lose that which you love," Schmidt explains. "A soul for a soul." Gamora laughs ruefully, believing Thanos truly cares for nothing and no one. Then the Titan takes her hand—and, despite her resistance, casts her over the edge.

Peter Parker and Tony Stark plan with Drax, Mantis, and Peter Quill.

Spring 2018 | The Ruins of Titan

Iron Man, Doctor Strange, and Spider-Man crash-land on the remains of what was once Thanos' home planet. Overpopulation and overconsumption led to its downfall, inspiring Thanos' destructive, misguided quest. All that stands there now is the lifeless, decaying husk of a once-great civilization. Hiding there are Drax, Star-Lord, and Mantis, who attack the Earthlings after mistaking them for more of Thanos' minions. After a brief and confusing fight, they realize they are all on the same side.

Spring 2018 | The Odds of Strange

While awaiting Thanos' arrival, Doctor Strange meditates and uses the Eye of Agamotto to peer forward in time at 14,000,605 alternate outcomes of the battle. "How many did we win?" Tony Stark asks. Strange fixes him with a sorrowful look and answers: "One."

Doctor Strange examines the possible futures.

A dropship collides with Wakanda's energy shield.

The Outriders surge forward through the gap in the barrier.

Spring 2018 | Wakanda Under Siege

Dropships carrying Thanos' ferocious army of Outriders plunge into Earth's atmosphere over the African nation. An energy shield over the capital city protects most of the population, as well as Vision and the Mind Stone, but the barrier is quickly undermined. Black Panther and Captain America lead the Avengers and the vast forces of Wakanda in a formidable defense, but they are outnumbered—and the surgery on Vision is nowhere near complete.

2018

Doctor Strange willingly offers the Time Stone.

Spring 2018 | Thunder and Lightning

Channeling the Bifrost with Stormbreaker, Thor, Groot, and Rocket appear in Wakanda. The God of Thunder is a one-man cavalry, bringing critical help to the forces standing against the Outriders. Corvus Glaive, Proxima Midnight, and Cull Obsidian are each overpowered and destroyed as the balance of power tips against the forces of Thanos. New and old allies fight alongside each other, sometimes leading to awkward encounters (such as Rocket trying to bargain for Bucky Barnes' cybernetic arm). Thor and Steve Rogers briefly compliment each other's changing look, but such moments of casual confidence soon dissipate...

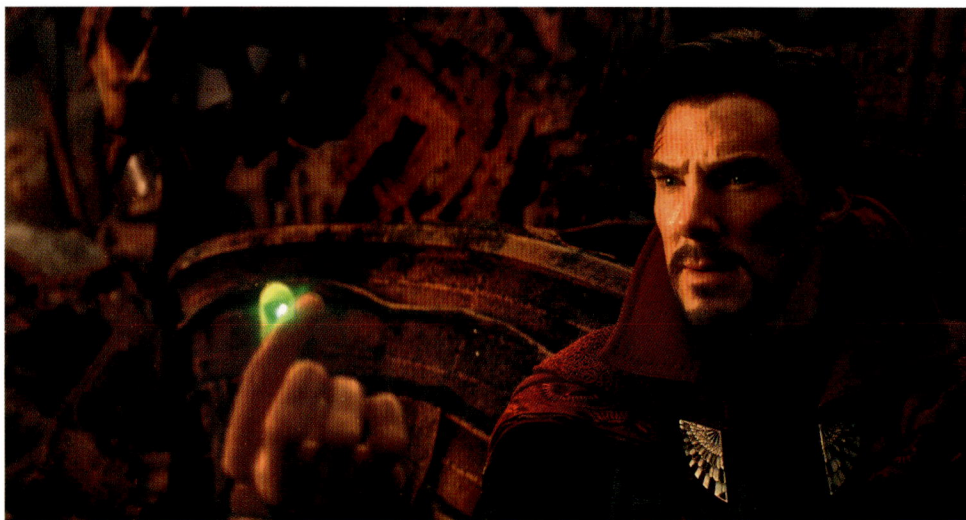

Thor wields his new weapon.

With the Time Stone's addition to the gauntlet, now Thanos has five.

Spring 2018 | Surrendering the Time Stone

After using the gauntlet to hurl pieces of Titan's moon at the heroes, Thanos gravely wounds and incapacitates Iron Man. "You have my respect, Stark," he says. "When I'm done, half of humanity will still be alive. I hope they remember you." Doctor Strange offers to voluntarily give up the Time Stone in exchange for Stark's life—a deal Thanos is pleased to accept. "One to go," Thanos says, adding the green gem to his gauntlet and departing through a Space Stone portal. Strange assures a bewildered Stark: "We're in the endgame now."

Spring 2018 | Thanos' Homecoming

The Titan returns to his birth planet with a sense of sorrow. "It was beautiful," he says, using the Reality Stone to recreate its lost glory. The new alliance of heroes attacks, with Iron Man and Spider-Man pulling at Thanos' arms, Drax slashing his legs, and Mantis perching on his shoulders, using her empathic powers to dull his mind. Even Nebula escapes captivity and crash-lands on Titan to join the fight. They have nearly removed the gauntlet when Peter Quill abruptly realizes that Thanos killed Gamora while acquiring the Soul Stone. He lashes out at the Titan, breaking Mantis' concentration, and allowing Thanos to regain control.

Thanos steps through a portal onto Earth.

Prying the gauntlet from Thanos.

Mantis manipulates Thanos' mind.

Spring 2018 | The Final Stone

Thanos arrives in Wakanda. He is unstoppable. Bruce Banner lunges at him in the Hulkbuster armor, but Thanos uses his Infinity Stones to fuse his metal suit into a nearby cliffside, then drives Captain America, Black Panther, and Falcon to the ground. The Titan is a one-man army now, marching relentlessly toward his prize.

Wanda Maximoff contemplates the unthinkable.

Spring 2018 | The Death of Vision

Wanda Maximoff knows she must use her powers to destroy the Mind Stone. Vision himself tells her this, but their love for each other makes the decision all the more unbearable. She radiates her energy into the stone while Steve Rogers holds apart the fingers of Thanos' gauntlet, but soon Cap is cast aside. Maximoff blasts one hand at Thanos and the other at Vision's forehead. The Mind Stone finally explodes, killing her love, but saving half the universe from Thanos' merciless plan.

With one hand, Wanda's magic annihilates the Mind Stone. With the other, she holds Thanos at bay.

Spring 2018 | The Second Death of Vision

Thanos breathes heavily, and even offers comfort to the grieving Wanda Maximoff. "I understand, my child. Better than anyone. Today I lost more than you could know. But now is no time to mourn," he says. "Now is no time at all." He uses the Time Stone to reverse the last few moments. Vision and the Infinity Stone are both restored, but the Titan instantly rips the Mind Stone from his skull, killing him again. Vision's sacrifice and Maximoff's suffering were both for nothing.

Thanos restores the Mind Stone and kills Vision a second time to acquire it.

Spring 2018 | A Last Chance

With each of the six stones now in place, the Infinity Gauntlet is fully powered. Time, Space, Power, Soul, Mind, and Reality have been weaponized to the Titan's will. Thanos is only seconds away from enacting his horrific plan.

Energy streams from the Infinity Gauntlet, supercharging Thanos just before he performs the Snap.

199

Crash-Landing

The Avengers and the Wakandans are discussing their battle strategy when Falcon and War Machine detect enemy signatures in the sky. As the enemy dropships land outside the city's energy barrier, Vision warns his teammates that they are running out of time to destroy the Mind Stone. Steve tells Wanda to destroy the stone once Shuri has extracted it from Vision, and T'Challa orders the Royal Guard to evacuate the city, engage all defenses, and to give Captain America a shield.

Approaching the Barrier

The Wakandans and the Avengers make their way to the energy barrier to face the Children of Thanos. T'Challa, Cap, and Black Widow walk over to negotiate the terms of battle with Proxima Midnight and Cull Obsidian. Proxima proclaims that their defiance is pointless and that Thanos will have the Mind Stone; T'Challa tells her they are in Wakanda now and that Thanos will have nothing but dust and blood.

Wanda Intervenes

Wanda has spent the battle by Vision's side, afraid to leave him while Shuri operates. But now, realizing the Avengers need her help, she leaves the lab, and descends to the battlefield, where she uses her powers to destroy a group of Threshers headed towards Black Widow and Okoye. A shocked Okoye exclaims "Why was she up there all this time?"

The Threshers

With Thor's arrival, the tide of battle seems to turn in favor of the Avengers and the Wakandan forces. Wanda is observing from Shuri's lab, when she notices the huge bladed war machines known as Threshers being deployed from the Outriders' dropships. Falcon and War Machine try to shoot down the Threshers to disable them, but to no avail, and they churn towards the defenders.

THE BATTLE IN WAKANDA

The Avengers face their darkest hour as they fight against their most powerful foe, Thanos. The Titan has been on a quest to acquire the six Infinity Stones—Time, Space, Reality, Mind, Power, and Soul—in order to complete the Infinity Gauntlet and wipe out half of all living things in the universe. The Avengers travel to Wakanda to protect the Mind Stone, which is embedded in Vision's forehead. As Shuri desperately tries to remove it so that it can be safely destroyed, Black Panther, the army of Wakanda, and the Avengers join forces to hold off the Children of Thanos and their vast army of Outriders.

A Sticky End

Wanda is making her way back to Vision, when Proxima Midnight knocks her down. Gloating, she tells Wanda she and Vision will die alone, but at that moment Black Widow and Okoye appear. The alien warrior holds her own against both, then gets the upper hand. She is about to kill Natasha, when Wanda uses her power to throw Proxima Midnight into the path of a nearby Thresher, which slices her to pieces.

The Snap

With all the stones acquired, Thanos is about to activate the gauntlet when Thor throws Stormbreaker into the Titan's chest. Thor believes he's gotten his vengeance against Thanos for the death of his brother and slaughter of the Asgardians, when Thanos tells him mockingly, "You should have gone for the head." Thor watches in horror as Thanos snaps his fingers, and his friends collapse into dust around him.

The Final Stone

The Avengers take on Thanos, to buy Wanda some time while she destroys the Mind Stone, but Thanos swats them aside. When he sees that Wanda has shattered the Mind Stone, he simply uses the Time Stone to reverse time, undoing Vision's and the stone's destruction. He then tears the Mind Stone out of Vision's head and places it into the Infinity Gauntlet.

Proxima Midnight

When the Avengers make it clear they won't surrender, Proxima Midnight signals her army and the dropships release their Outriders, who mindlessly charge at the energy barrier. A few make it through, and Bruce observes that they can't guard the entire perimeter; the Outriders have them surrounded and will make their way to Vision. T'Challa comes up with the idea to partially open the energy barrier to keep the Outriders' attention fixed on them.

Thor's Arrival

The Avengers and the Wakandans are engaged in an intense battle against the Outriders, when the bright beam of the Bifrost appears in the midst of the battlefield. Stormbreaker, Thor's newly forged ax, cuts a swath through the enemy as Thor, Rocket, and Groot join the fight. Thor summons a massive lightning charge, decimating the Outriders, and demands that Thanos be brought to him.

Banner and Obsidian

A weakened Vision is being attacked by Cull Obsidian and Corvus Glaive when Bruce Banner jumps in to save him. Bruce calls for reinforcements, when Obsidian grabs him and they drop into a waterfall. Obsidian rips off the left arm of Bruce's Hulkbuster suit, and Bruce attempts to transform into the Hulk, but to no avail. Using his wits, Bruce traps Obsidian's arm into the severed Hulkbuster arm and turns on its repulsor thrustor, sending Obsidian flying into the energy barrier, where he explodes.

Unstoppable Force

Back on Thanos' home planet of Titan, the Guardians of the Galaxy, Iron Man, Spider-Man, Nebula, and Doctor Strange make a concerted attack to take down Thanos but they are no match against the might of the Infinity Gauntlet. Doctor Strange offers the Time Stone to Thanos to save Tony's life and Thanos goes through a portal to Wakanda to retrieve the Mind Stone.

Vision

Upon Thanos' arrival, the Avengers fight in vain to keep the Titan from getting the Mind Stone. Knowing that they are no match for Thanos, Vision begs Wanda to destroy the Mind Stone and when she refuses, tells her that destroying the stone is now the only way they can win the war. Wanda realizes Vision is right and pours all her energy into the Mind Stone, destroying both Vision and the stone.

2018

Spring 2018 | The Snap

Before Thanos can act, he is struck by a blast of lightning as Thor and his "Thanos-killing" ax descend from the heavens. Stormbreaker's blade sinks into Thanos' chest, but the Titan is only wounded, not defeated. "You should have gone for the head," he growls. Thanos raises his hand—and snaps.

Thor misses his mark.

Spring 2018 | Vision of Gamora

In his moment of triumph, the Soul Stone forces Thanos to confront his greatest loss. Gamora appears to him, not as the defiant warrior who tried to stop him, but as the young child he remembers taking from her home planet and raising as his own. "Did you do it?" she asks. When he tells her he did, she asks another question. "What did it cost?" His answer: "Everything."

Thanos faces a vision of Gamora as a child.

Spring 2018 | The First Moments

The gauntlet is scorched and melted from the blast of power it emitted. Thanos escapes through a Space Stone portal, leaving behind an eerie calm. Bucky Barnes calls out to Steve Rogers—then shockingly fades away in a plume of ash. Ships plummet from the sky with their pilots gone. Rocket watches Groot evaporate, and Wanda dissolves beside Vision's body. Sam Wilson disappears as James Rhodes walks nearby looking for him. T'Challa reaches for a fallen Okoye, telling her, "This is no place to die ..." But then the Black Panther is gone.

M'Baku sees his fellow warriors disappearing around him.

Captain America looks around in shock as he realizes what's happening.

202

Peter Quill disintegrates.

Spring 2018 | On Titan ...

Mantis vanishes. Then Drax and Star-Lord are reduced to nothingness. "There was no other way," Doctor Strange insists before disintegrating. Peter Parker stumbles into Tony Stark's arms, pleading for help. "Mr. Stark, I don't feel so good," he sobs. "I don't want to go ..." But he leaves his mentor holding nothing but ashes. "He did it," Nebula says. She and Stark are the last ones there.

Spring 2018 | Emergency Call

Nick Fury and Maria Hill notice the chaos unfolding on a busy city street as civilians collapse into windblown dust, leaving survivors in a state of panic and confusion. As Hill disintegrates, Fury reaches for an emergency pager, given to him long ago by Captain Marvel. Fury himself disappears as the call for help is transmitted.

The fallen pager, moments after Nick Fury activated it.

Janet, Hope, and Hank dust away, leaving Scott Lang trapped in the Quantum Realm.

Spring 2018 | Ant-Man Marooned

Hank Pym, Janet Van Dyne, and their daughter Hope are experimenting with a new portable Quantum Tunnel built into the back of Luis' van. Scott Lang ventures into that subatomic realm seeking healing particles that could be used to help their former foe Ghost. "Don't get sucked into a time vortex," Janet warns. "We won't be able to save you." The microcosmic Lang completes the mission but becomes trapped in the Quantum Realm when they cease responding to his messages. All three of them are taken by the Snap.

At his farm, Clint Barton calls to his family, who are suddenly gone.

Spring 2018 | Fade Out

Far and wide, half of all life is quietly extinguished. Yelena vanishes while trying to deprogram a fellow Red Room assassin. Maria Rambeau, now the head of S.W.O.R.D., is hospitalized with a grave illness when her daughter, Monica, disappears from her bedside. While Thanos had long conceived of his plans as "random," "dispassionate," and "fair," some are hit harder than others. Most of Peter Parker's classmates are taken, and Clint Barton is the only survivor from his entire family.

203

2018

Some turn swords into ploughshares; Thanos turns his armor into a scarecrow.

Spring 2018 | To the Garden

Thanos retreats to a lonely, lush world where he intends to live out his remaining time as a humble farmer. His formidable armor, once a symbol of terror throughout the universe, is now propped up as a scarecrow. Weeks pass as the survivors of his Snap reckon with the shockwaves of grief and instability. The cataclysm comes to be known by a deceptively simple term: the Snap. In an instant, trillions of lives ended.

Captain Marvel, to the rescue.

Spring 2018 | "Where's Fury?"

At the Avengers Compound, the surviving heroes keep Nick Fury's pager fully charged and emitting its signal. When the pager suddenly stops working, they discuss ways to reactivate it and send the signal again, even though they have no idea what it does. "Fury did," Natasha Romanoff says. "I want to know who's on the other end of that thing." The intended recipient has already received the message. Carol Danvers returns to Earth, and she wants to know what happened to her old friend. Captain Marvel will become a powerful new ally for the Avengers.

Spring 2018 | Adrift

Tony Stark and Nebula board the Guardians' starship, but cracked fuel cells strand them a thousand light years from Earth. After 22 days, a starving, dehydrated Stark records a farewell message to Pepper Potts, echoing something he once said to her years ago, when appointing her CEO. "I'll dream about you," he says. "It's always you." But his goodbye is premature. A luminous figure appears outside the stalled ship. After being sent out by the Avengers on a search and rescue mission, Captain Marvel has found them.

An emaciated Tony Stark records a message for Pepper Potts.

Identifying the Infinity Stones' energy signature.

Spring 2018 | The Counterstrike

After returning Tony Stark and Nebula to Earth, Captain Marvel and the Avengers try to figure out what to do next. If they can reclaim the Infinity Stones, they believe they can reverse the Snap. But first, they have to find Thanos. A recent energy spike similar to the one emitted by the Snap draws their attention to Planet 0259-S, where they find the Titan living with no army, ground defenses, or protection whatsoever.

The surviving Avengers zero in on Thanos.

Late Spring 2018 | "Gone, Reduced to Atoms."

The Titan is wounded and burned, but not from their battle weeks ago. The gauntlet, which had been badly damaged by the Snap, is now totally destroyed and fused to his hand. The Infinity Stones are gone. Thanos tells the Avengers he used their power one more time to destroy them. That way, he reasons, they cannot be used to reverse his victory. "The stones served no purpose beyond temptation," he says. "It nearly killed me, but the work is done. It always will be. I am inevitable."

Thanos prepares for death, unrepentant about bringing it to so many others.

Captain America and Black Widow don't face the battle that they expected.

Spring 2018 | Thanos Decapitated

Some Avengers doubt Thanos would destroy the stones, but Nebula assures them he is not a liar. "Thank you, daughter," he says. "Perhaps I treated you too harshly." These are his last words. In a rage, Thor swings Stormbreaker into the Titan's neck, severing his head. "What did you do?" a shocked Rocket asks. Thor, still heartsick over his failure to stop the Snap, says simply: "I went for the head." The satisfaction of vengeance is fleeting. And no lives are restored when Thanos is executed.

Thor walks away after slaying the Titan.

THE 2020s

The final defeat of Thanos—and the realization of how close half the universe has come to permanent annihilation—creates a newfound appreciation and respect for life. That makes the irreversible loss of it all the more painful, as in the case of T'Challa, Wakanda's great king and protector, the Black Panther, who helps save the world only to have his own existence cut agonizingly short by disease.

The Avengers' successful efforts to reverse the Snap perpetrated by Thanos hint at the existence of the Multiverse, when their Time Heist causes a branching timeline of 2012 and a variant of Loki is swept up by the Time Variance Authority. If the Avengers revealed the existence of that door, Loki's chaotic actions with the TVA throw that door wide open. The array of universes that make up the Multiverse once seemed impermeable, but now powerful beings such as Wanda Maximoff, Loki, Doctor Strange, and Spider-Man have found ways to puncture holes that threaten to unravel ... everything.

While their intentions may start out as honorable, even those who are pure of heart can find themselves corrupted by the desire to rewrite reality. Villainous figures will also begin to exploit these loopholes for selfish goals. The infinite possibilities of the Multiverse become a new battleground.

2018-2023

Five years pass. Some begin to heal, but for others the losses only deepen. Cities seem hollow, abandoned ships drift aimlessly around harbors, unused cars rust in parking lots. Those who were not reduced to ash struggle to reconnect with other survivors. But for some, Thanos' conquest bears rewards: the environment on Earth becomes cleaner, and nature rebounds. There is enough food and work for all the people who remain, and housing and other resources become plentiful.

Late 2019 | A Mindful Hulk

Dr. Bruce Banner turns his research toward fusing the two conflicting sides of his personality. After 18 months of experimentation in a gamma lab in Mexico, he successfully melds the brawn of the big green guy with the brains of the "puny human." He calls the erudite goliath that results "the best of both worlds."

Hulk can make small talk now.

Spring 2018-Fall 2023 | The Stark Family

After Tony Stark recovers from near death in deep space, he and Pepper Potts step away from public life to live more quietly together. Pepper becomes pregnant with a daughter, and the arrival of a new life after so many others were destroyed brings both parents joy and renewed purpose. It doesn't balance the scales, but Morgan H. Stark reminds them to value the good fortune they have received.

Iron Man's daughter is born into a world still coming to terms with loss on an apocalyptic scale.

Spring 2018-Fall 2023 | The Power Broker

Sharon Carter allows the governments of the world to believe she disappeared in the Snap, having remained a fugitive since helping Steve Rogers and Sam Wilson recover their weapons during the Avengers' clash over the Sokovia Accords. Operating as a stolen art dealer from the lawless island of Madripoor, she engages in even more nefarious activities. She sets up a new identity as the Power Broker, determined to exert control over a world that turned its back on her.

A frustrated Sharon Carter goes bad.

2022 | The Moon Knight

After Marc Spector's fugue states from his alters cause him to be dishonorably discharged from the Marines, he takes work with his former commander, Bushman, staging a raid on an Egyptian tomb. When Bushman decides to eliminate the witnesses, including the famed archaeologist Abdallah El-Faouly, Spector intervenes and is gravely wounded. While the mercenary lies dying at the foot of a statue dedicated to Khonshu, the moon god offers him resurrection in exchange for serving as his avatar, a vigilante who will "protect the travelers of the night." Spector agrees, committing himself to a life of vengeance. He later marries El-Faouly's daughter, Layla, but cannot share the truth about her father's killing.

2020 | The Death of Maria Rambeau

Maria "Photon" Rambeau's cancer goes into remission, allowing her to continue her work as the director of the Sentient Weapon Observation & Response Division. She never stops believing that her daughter, Monica, will be returned, along with all the others taken by Thanos, and she devises protocols for that eventuality. Her cancer returns two years after the Snap, more aggressive than before, and this time she does not survive.

TVA ALERT!
Hey there Darlin'! If you're still trying to find out who blipped or not, sometimes you can find clues in the most mundane details. If you look closely, Marc Spector had a passport issued on December 14, 2018. This points to his post-military, and questionable, operations during the chaos of the Blip.

Khonshu makes a pact with a mortally wounded Marc Spector.

Spring 2018-Fall 2023 | Ronin's Vengeance

Grief rips apart Clint Barton. What emerges from within is the vigilante Ronin. How could he lose his wife, his sons, and his daughter, while criminals and killers live on—in some ways operating with more impunity than before? Barton abandons the mantle of Hawkeye and travels the world executing wrongdoers he feels don't deserve to live. While he feels his cause is righteous, his violent methods corrode his spirit. Among those he kills is gangster William Lopez, an act witnessed by William's daughter, Maya, who begins a quest for revenge against Ronin.

Goodbye, Hawkeye: Clint Barton takes on a new identity.

Spring 2018-Fall 2023 | All They Can Do…

The remaining heroes each cope in different ways. Steve Rogers leads support groups for everyday survivors. Thor numbs his regret with beer, video games, and binge-watching cable TV, ceding the work of running New Asgard to others. Natasha Romanoff and James "Rhodey" Rhodes maintain a scattershot Avengers mission on Earth, while Captain Marvel tries to aid the many other struggling worlds in the galaxy. Everyone feels adrift and uncertain.

Thor grieves the losses of his brother, his people, his home, and his friends.

2023

209

2023

Fall 2023 | Ant-Man Unleashed

Five years after the Snap, the van containing Hank Pym and Janet Van Dyne's portable Quantum Tunnel sits gathering dust in a U-Store-It locker. A rodent sniffing around the dashboard inadvertently activates the device, ejecting Scott Lang from the Quantum Realm and spitting him out the back doors. He has no idea what happened, and for him only a few hours have passed since he went in. That curious rat, one of the lowliest forms of life on Earth, may have just helped save half the universe.

A vision from the past: Scott Lang arrives at the Avengers Compound.

Lang finds his own name among those on the memorial of the lost.

Fall 2023 | The Lilliputian at the Gates

While Steve Rogers meets with Romanoff at the Avengers Compound, security cameras pick up on a frantic man with a battered brown van outside the front gates. They have Scott Lang on their list of the disappeared, so his return baffles them. He turns out to have the key to changing everything. For the first time, there is hope of undoing Thanos' blight on the universe.

Natasha Romanoff, trying to fix smaller problems.

Okoye, Captain Marvel, and James Rhodes meet via hologram.

Fall 2023 | A "Quantum" Leap

Scott Lang does his best to explain how he became trapped in the Quantum Realm and how the rules of time and space in that microscopic universe differ from the reality the Avengers know. "What if there was a way we could enter the Quantum Realm at a certain point in time and exit the Quantum Realm at another point in time—like before Thanos?" he asks. The notion seems far fetched, but as Romanoff points out: "I get emails from a raccoon, so nothing sounds crazy anymore."

Fall 2023 | The Desultory Avengers

Natasha Romanoff hosts a glum check-in with her remote allies. Okoye reports on an earthquake off the coast of Africa, while Rocket and Nebula express frustration about a raid on a galactic warship that turned out to be a garbage scow. Captain Marvel is overwhelmed by her duties further afield, and James Rhodes privately informs Romanoff that a cartel massacre in Mexico is likely the work of Clint Barton. She doesn't want to believe that, but there's only so much denial she can sustain these days.

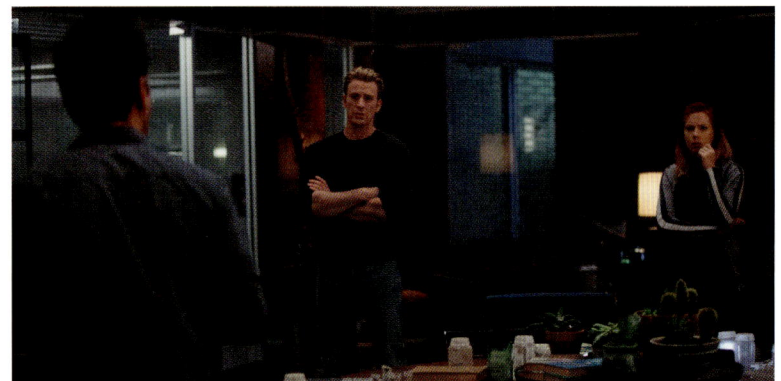

Scott Lang explains how the Quantum Realm can lead them back to the Infinity Stones.

Steve Rogers visits his old friend Tony Stark.

Fall 2023 | Stark Says No, Hulk Says Yes

Tony Stark wants to stay out of it. He's risked his life too many times and is resistant when Romanoff, Rogers, and Lang ask if the Quantum Realm could be an avenue toward undoing the Snap. Although he has customized a new blue-and-silver armor for Pepper Potts as an anniversary present, he wants their world-saving days to be over. Plus, he fears losing the good things that have happened in the past five years, like his daughter Morgan. Bruce Banner, however, is happy to put his expertise to work on the Avengers' plan.

Bruce demonstrates that they don't call him Smart Hulk for nothing.

Fall 2023 | Iron Man's Reluctance

Memories of Peter Parker's disappearance still haunt Tony. Despite turning away the Avengers, he continues to ruminate on their idea and gradually figures out a way they could use the Quantum Realm to access different entry points in the timeline and then safely return to the present. He tells Pepper Potts he has considered keeping the idea to himself and simply going back to bed. She asks: "But would you be able to rest?"

Pepper Potts encourages Tony Stark to help solve the problem.

211

2023

Fall 2023 | Time Twist

The Hulk's tests do not go well, and they're burning up precious Pym Particles every time they try. Scott Lang is the first guinea pig, who emerges from the Quantum Tunnel not in a different era, but first as a young boy, then an elderly man, and again as a baby before finally being restored to his present state. "Somebody peed my pants," the dazed traveler reports. "But I don't know if it was baby me or old me. Or just me me." Hulk tries to keep everyone's spirits up by declaring it a kind of success: "Time travel!" But no one is convinced.

Tony Stark agrees to help Steve Rogers.

Hulk puts a smiley face on things.

Fall 2023 | A "Global Positioning System" for Time

Tony Stark arrives at the Avengers Compound bearing gifts. One is Captain America's shield, which years ago he told Steve Rogers he no longer deserved after their post-accords brawl left Iron Man battered and defeated. Now he wants to let the past be the past. He also shares his new innovation: a functioning Time-Space GPS that will help them navigate the Quantum Realm safely and access earlier points in time and space, while also solving the main hiccup in Hulk's tests. "Instead of pushing Lang through time," he says, "You might've wound up pushing time through Lang."

Hulk and Rocket ride to New Asgard.

Fall 2023 | Recruiting Lost Allies

As Stark and Hulk construct a new and more elaborate Quantum Tunnel, Hulk and Rocket travel to New Asgard to recruit Thor to join the mission. They are shocked at his disheveled state. Hulk reminds Thor that the God of Thunder once saved him from a tough spot on the battle world of Sakaar. Now Hulk wants to return the favor. In Tokyo, Natasha Romanoff tracks down Ronin in the midst of his takedown of a Japanese crimelord. She tells Clint Barton that they have found something—that there might be a chance to set things right. "Don't give me hope," he tells her. "I'm sorry I couldn't give it to you sooner," she says.

Rocket and Hulk visit a downtrodden Thor.

Black Widow finds Ronin—but she needs Hawkeye.

Fall 2023 | It Works

A test of Stark's Time-Space GPS on Clint Barton is successful, propelling him back to his family farm, where his wife and children are alive and well. His few seconds there make him more determined than ever to see the Avengers' idea through. Keeping his own daughter in mind, Tony Stark insists they must only bring back what was lost without undoing what has transpired in the years since. "And maybe not die trying, would be nice," Stark adds.

Clint Barton is ready to go.

New York, 2012

Asgard, 2013

Deep Space, 2014

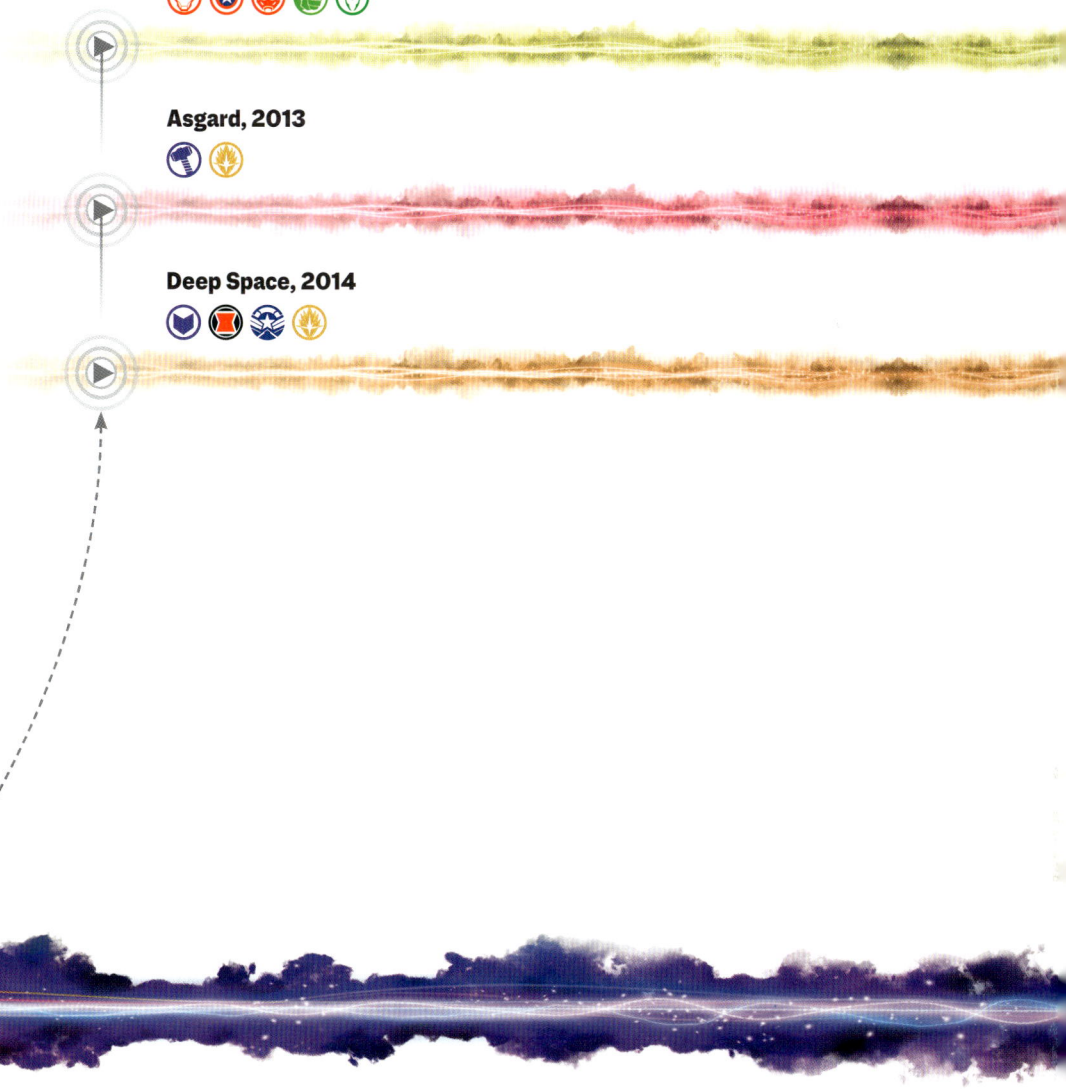

The Avengers assess the Infinity Stones as they plan the Time Heist.

The team prepare for their mission.

Fall 2023 | The Time Heist

For such a complicated journey, it's a relatively simple plan: Break into the past at key moments in the Avengers' history, retrieve the Infinity Stones before Thanos does, and return with them to the present. Once all six are united in a new gauntlet, the stones can be used to restore all the living things that were destroyed in the Snap. The main drawback is there are only enough Pym Particles to allow each traveler to shrink into the Quantum Realm for one round-trip. "No mistakes, no do overs," Steve Rogers says.

A new Quantum Tunnel gives the Avengers their one shot to set things right.

New York, 2012

Asgard, 2013

Deep Space, 2014

The Ancient One Balks

The plan hits an immediate snag when Hulk visits the New York Sanctum and discovers Doctor Strange is still four years from discovering the Mystic Arts. The current Sorcerer Supreme is the Ancient One, who separates Bruce Banner's spirit from his huge, green body and refuses to turn over the Time Stone. Providing it might benefit his reality, she argues, but would splinter her time into a new branch reality that would be left unprotected without their "chief weapon against the forces of darkness." Banner persuades her to lend it to them, with a solemn promise to return it.

The Ancient One consults with Bruce Banner.

Earth, 2023

The Stark of 2023 falling from his tower.

The Battle of New York, Revisited

Tony Stark, Steve Rogers, Bruce Banner, and Scott Lang venture into the midst of the Chitauri invasion of Earth that first united the Avengers more than a decade before. Three Infinity Stones are present in this time and place: the Space Stone within the Tesseract, the Mind Stone in Loki's staff, and the Time Stone inside the Eye of Agamotto artifact held by the Sorcerer Supreme.

Cap's Mind Trick

Steve Rogers takes possession of Loki's scepter during an elevator ride with S.H.I.E.L.D. operatives Brock Rumlow and Agent Sitwell. Rather than brawling with them in the confined space (which he has done before), he uses his knowledge of their still-secret betrayal to get them to hand it over willingly. "Hail Hydra," he whispers to Sitwell. Rogers' quick escape is only thwarted when he runs into his 2012 self and must reluctantly battle the do-gooder who tells him "I can do this all day." Ultimately, Cap defeats his 2012 version by shocking him with a secret ("Bucky is alive!") and using the Mind Stone to mesmerize him.

Steve Rogers vs. Steve Rogers.

214

Morag Dropoff

Clint Barton carries a miniaturized version of the Guardians' starship in the palm of his hand as he, James Rhodes, Nebula, and Natasha Romanoff cross through the Quantum Realm into deep space in 2014. After enlarging the ship, it carries Rhodes and Nebula to the ruins of Morag, where they intend to capture the Orb containing the Power Stone before Peter Quill can dance his way to it.

War Machine and Nebula await an unwitting Star-Lord.

The Nebula Glitch

On Morag, Nebula warns Rhodes to stay alert, because they and Peter Quill are not the only ones searching for Infinity Stones. Her 2014 self is also one of those hunters. "Where are 'you' right now?" Rhodes asks warily. Unknown to both of them, the cyborg programming in Nebula's 2014 counterpart has already paired remotely with her timeline-hopping self. The Nebula of the past alerts Thanos and a still-living Gamora, who has not yet openly turned against her father nor met the Guardians of the Galaxy.

Gamora and Nebula of 2014.

Thor's mother sees him as a troubled version of himself from a distant future.

Extracting the Aether

Thor is overwhelmed to see his homeland of Asgard still intact and thriving as he and Rocket arrive to extract the Reality Stone from Jane Foster in 2013. As Rocket scampers away to locate Jane, Thor encounters his mother, Frigga, still living—but not long from death. Frigga notices how shabby, distraught, and older her son looks. "You're not the Thor I know at all, are you," she says. "The future hasn't been kind to you." He tries to deny this, but Frigga is not fooled. "I was raised by witches, boy," she tells him. "I see with more than eyes."

Thanos Knows

As Nebula's incoming memories are ripped from the mind of her past self, Thanos discovers not only that he will someday succeed in his plan, but that he will also be killed. This doesn't bother him, but he is furious that the Avengers are retroactively trying to undo his life's work. Ebony Maw scans the incoming data and traces the location of the interloping Nebula. "Set course for Morag," Thanos orders.

Thanos extracts the information he needs from Nebula's cranium.

New York, 2012

Asgard, 2013

Deep Space, 2014

Loki's Getaway

The plan goes awry when an enraged Hulk emerges from the stairs and smashes 2023 Stark aside. With the Tesseract landing at his feet, Loki simply reaches down and picks it up. In an instant, he vanishes, using it to go somewhere, anywhere, before really forming any plan whatsoever. It all happens so fast that no one guarding him even notices at first that he has disappeared into a glowing blue cloud.

Now you see him; now you don't.

TVA

Earth, 2023

Stark Stunned

In the lobby of Stark Tower, 2012 Tony Stark argues with S.H.I.E.L.D. chief Alexander Pierce over who has jurisdiction over the Tesseract and whether the captured Loki should be returned to Odin in Asgard or remain in human custody on Earth. At future Stark's urging, Ant-Man shorts out the Arc Reactor embedded in 2012 Iron Man's chest, causing him to drop the case containing the cube. Ant-Man kicks it across the polished floor for the disguised future Stark to casually pick up.

Stark: "Do you trust me?" Rogers: "...I do."

Bad News

Tony Stark and Scott Lang rendezvous with Steve Rogers and tell him about losing the Tesseract. With only one dose of Pym Particles left for each of them, they have limited options. An impromptu fix is quickly put together: Lang will return to the present-day with the staff, while Cap and Iron Man will use their remaining trip to leapfrog to yet another moment in time. The Time Heist could still work if they choose a spot in the continuum that has the Space Stone in proximity to additional Pym Particles. Stark thinks he knows just the place...

Ant-Man prepares to do his part for the Time Heist.

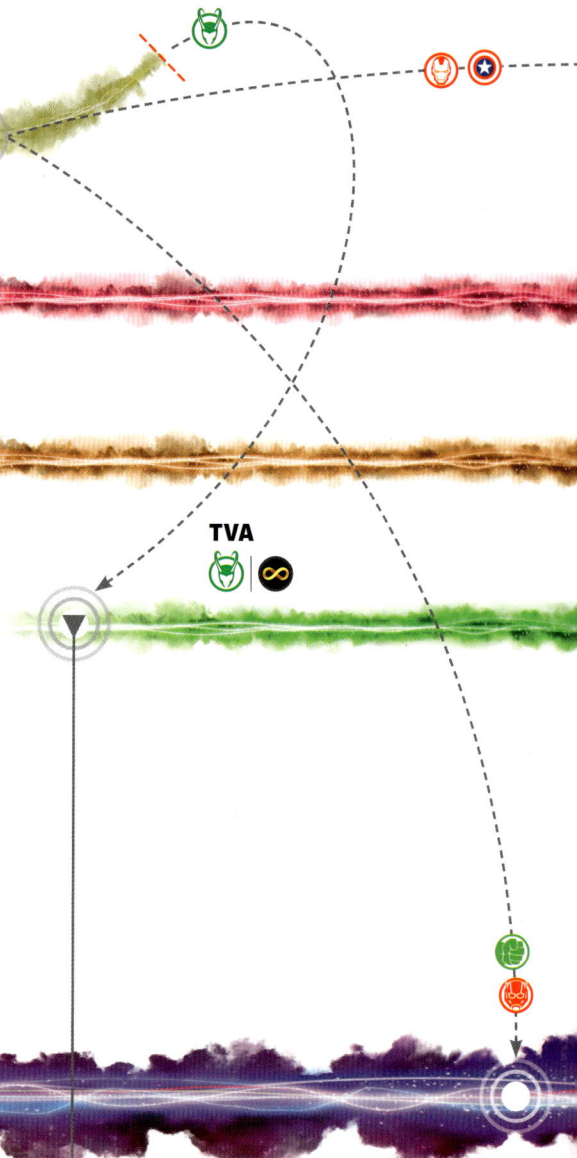

Loki Captured Again

A hole opens in the sky over the Gobi Desert in Mongolia, and Loki and the Tesseract tumble out. He has a few moments to unshackle himself (and snarl at some confused locals) before a group of strangely armored security personnel appear through an iridescent rectangular portal. Hunter B-15 introduces herself as an officer of the Time Variance Authority, and Loki's fleeting freedom comes to an end as he is taken into custody for "crimes against the Sacred Timeline." The TVA then place reset charges and prune the branched timeline.

Loki's short-lived freedom.

Rocket gets the Stone

Dr. Jane Foster awakens in her quarters on Asgard, unaware that a small, furry assailant is stalking her with an extractor that will remove the Reality Stone's cloud of Aether from her body. Rocket's quick work seems like an attempted assault by one of the kingdom's more scurrilous creatures, so Asgardian soldiers give chase.

Rocket retrieves the Reality Stone.

Frigga urges her son to seek a better future.

Thor's Farewell

Thor tries to warn Frigga about her impending death, but she doesn't want to know. "You're here to repair your future, not mine," she says. A breathless Rocket scampers up, pursued by Asgardian security, and tells Thor it's time to go. The God of Thunder says goodbye to his mother, and although he can't save her, her guidance has saved him. There is one important souvenir he can retrieve on this trip. Thor reaches out his hand and summons Mjolnir, which has not yet been destroyed by Hela. He is relieved to find he is still worthy.

Seizing Power

Star-Lord finally arrives on Morag, frolicking around the ruins while singing along to the super-sounds of the '70s. Quill is easily subdued upon reaching his destination, and Nebula burns away part of her arm while reaching into the protective barrier around the Power Stone. Their mission accomplished, Rhodes vaults back to the present, but something within Nebula short circuits. She is stranded. 2014 Thanos has blocked her return. He captures her, and sends his own Nebula back to the Avengers as a saboteur.

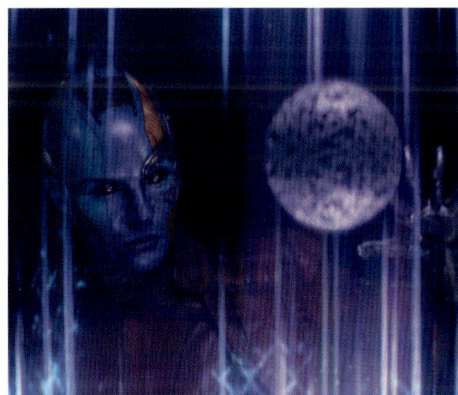

Nebula reaches for the Orb.

Natasha Romanoff and Clint Barton realize what must be done.

Soul Stone's Price

To secure the Soul Stone on Vormir, Clint Barton and Natasha Romanoff fight each other for the privilege of sacrifice. The two old friends brawl using every skillset they possess to prevent the other from diving off the cliff of Vormir. Barton finally leaps over the edge, but is snagged by Romanoff's grappling line. He grabs her wrist as she falls past him, but she pleads with him: "Let me go." She pushes free of his grip, and all he can do is watch as she falls, falls, falls ... Barton then awakens in a pool of water with the Soul Stone in his hand. Alone.

217

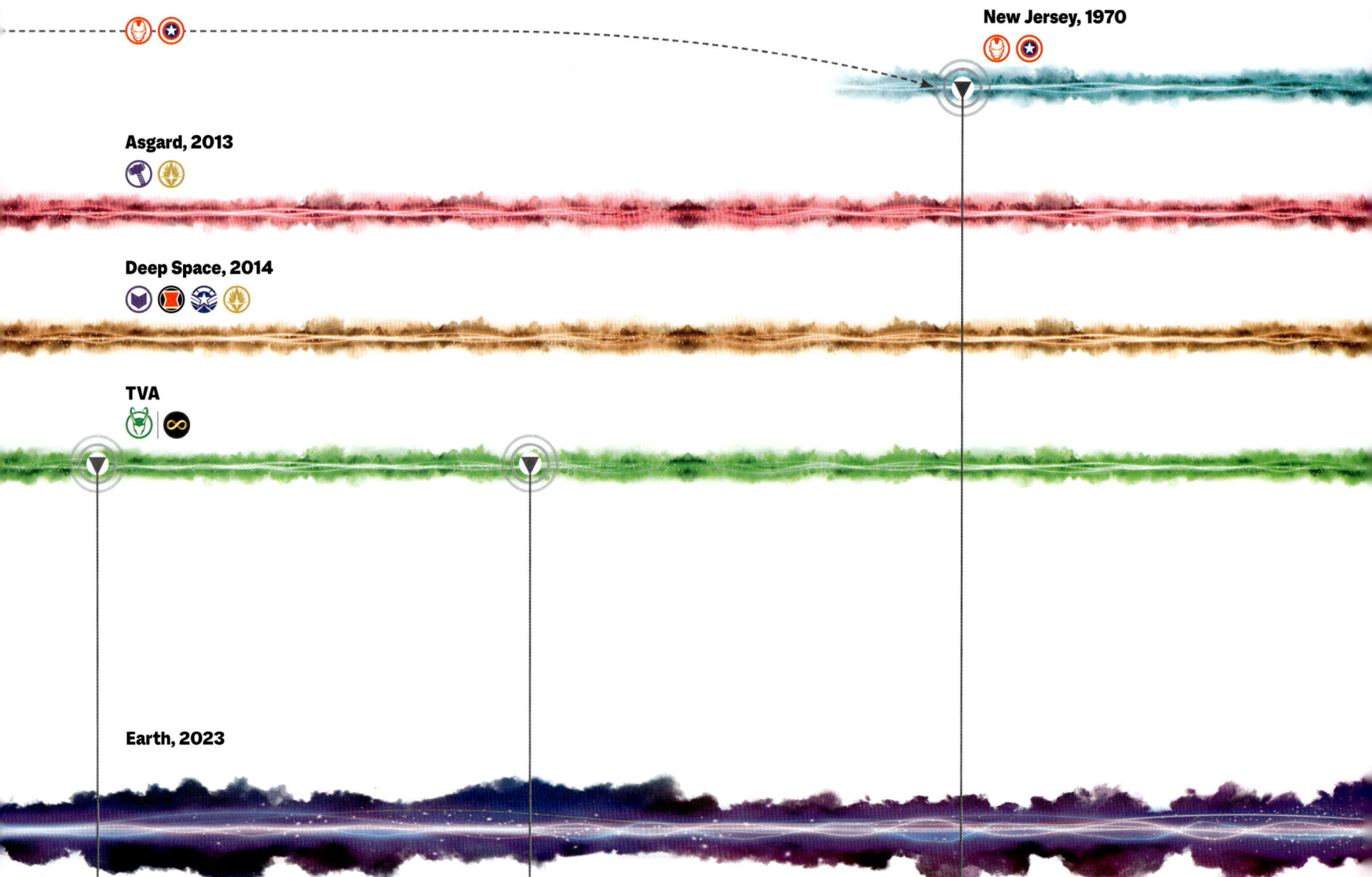

New Jersey, 1970

Asgard, 2013

Deep Space, 2014

TVA

Earth, 2023

Time Management

The 2012 Loki finds himself trapped within the bureaucratic conveyor belt of the Time Variance Authority—a vast, secret enforcement agency that exists outside the bounds of space-time. He stands trial before Judge Ravonna Renslayer for fracturing the natural continuum of his timeline. Even more shocking than his punishment—death by "pruning"— Loki is flabbergasted to learn he is just one "variant" of countless other Lokis in the Multiverse.

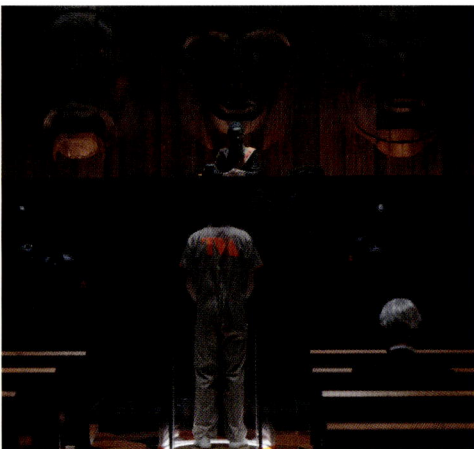

Loki stands trial before Ravonna Renslayer.

Mobius investigates an ambush in the 1500s.

The Minutemen Ambushes

Agent Mobius of the TVA, an easygoing investigator of Nexus Events, visits a branching timeline in Aix-En-Provence, France, from the year 1549, where three Minutemen and one Hunter have been killed by a notoriously deadly Loki variant. The only clue is a pack of Kablooie bubble gum, an item from the future, given by the assailant to a young French boy in exchange for his silence. The TVA prune the branching timeline.

A Last Hope

Tony Stark and Steve Rogers set their Time-Space GPS devices for April 7, 1970, and arrive at Camp Lehigh in New Jersey, where Captain America once underwent basic training before becoming a super soldier. Decades later, it's where Dr. Arnim Zola has legitimized himself as a S.H.I.E.L.D. researcher while secretly leading an underground Hydra movement. It's also where Howard Stark stored the recovered Tesseract for further study, and where a young scientist named Dr. Henry Pym is working with the subatomic particles he created. Retrieving both items is the only hope for successfully completing the Time Heist.

Particle Man

In his lab full of insect research and a high-tech helmet with bug-like features, Dr. Hank Pym gets a call from Steve Rogers, pretending to have a volatile package for him in the camp's shipping center. Pym races off to the loading dock in a panic, and Captain America slips in to steal four vials of Pym Particles, enough for their return trip.

Gear in Dr. Hank Pym's lab.

Back in the Game

Disguised as a researcher, Stark tracks the energy signature of the Space Stone to an underground bunker and uses a beam from his Iron Man gauntlet to cut through its vault. Just as he's securing the Tesseract in a briefcase, he hears a familiar voice—his father, Howard Stark, carrying flowers for his pregnant wife and a can of sauerkraut for her cravings. She's close to giving birth—to Tony Stark himself. Tony is so discombobulated that he almost leaves the briefcase, and Howard has to remind him to take it.

Tony Stark uses his Iron Man gauntlet to grab the Tesseract.

Visiting Camp Lehigh and seeing that Peggy is still thinking about him gives Steve Rogers comfort—and sets him on a new course.

Faraway, So Close...

To evade security, Steve Rogers slips through an open door, unaware that he has entered the office of S.H.I.E.L.D. Director Peggy Carter, his long-lost love. On her desk, he finds a framed photo of his pre-super soldier self, then hears her voice from an adjacent room, being briefed on a mission. She does not see him through the window to the darkened office, and he does not approach her. Still, the moment will help ignite a yearning to finally fulfill his vow to return to her.

"Howard Potts" Makes Conversation

Having introduced himself with an awkward fake name, Tony Stark accompanies his father outside the S.H.I.E.L.D. bunker, trying to remain calm amid the casual smalltalk. In a roundabout way, Tony tries to comfort his father about the son he's about to have. "I thought my dad was tough on me. But looking back, I only remember the good stuff," he tells him. When Howard asks for an example, Tony shares one of his father's favorite sayings: "No amount of money ever bought a second of time." Howard considers this. "Smart guy," he says. "He did his best," Tony assures him, before hurrying off to join Cap and return to the present.

Something about Mr. "Potts" seems familiar to Howard Stark.

Asgard, 2013

Deep Space, 2014

TVA, 2023

Earth, 2023

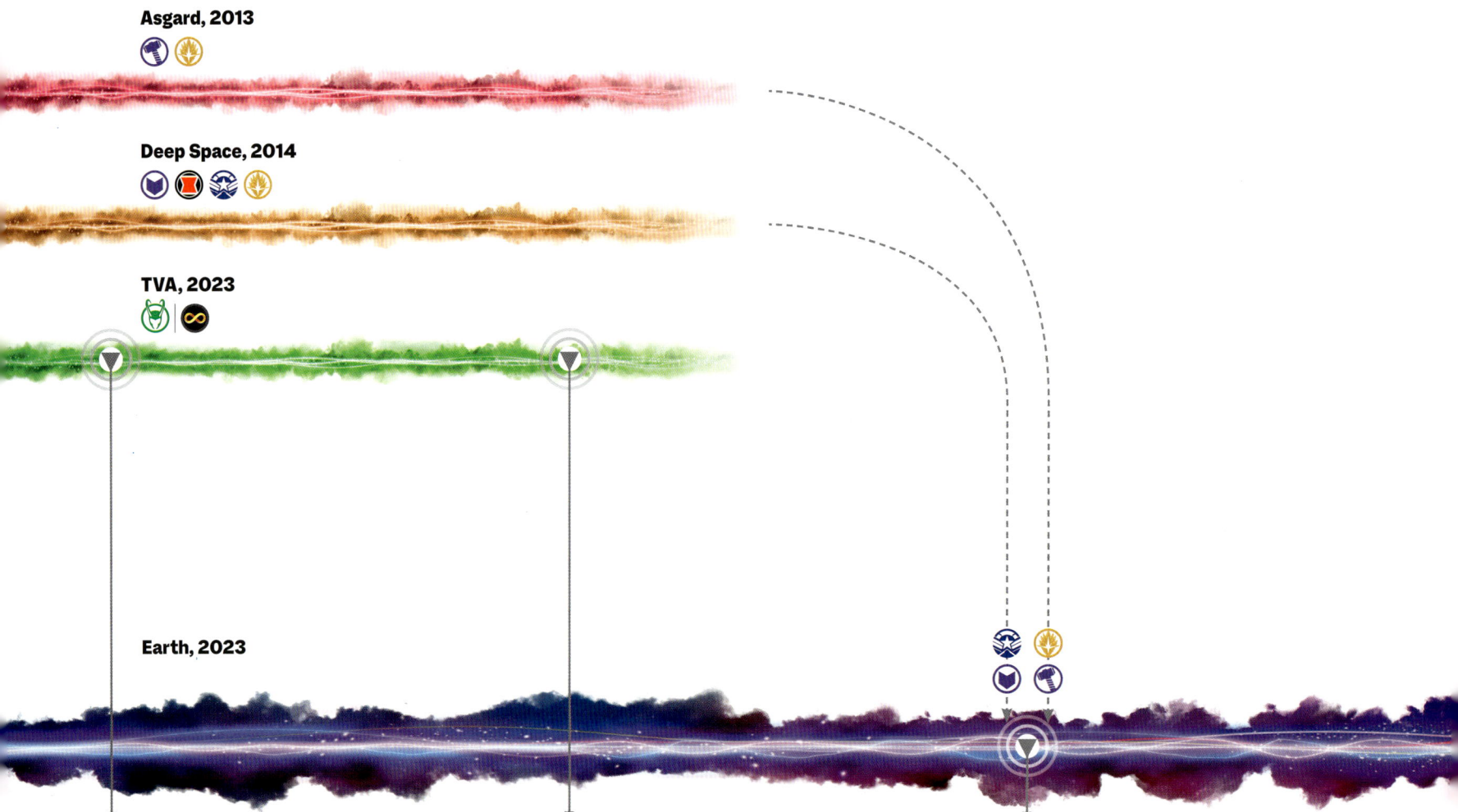

Mobius Offers a Deal

Mobius seeks to recruit the captive Loki as a profiler for the TVA to help ensnare the other Loki variant who has been terrorizing the organization. Mobius assures him that the Time Keepers are not the enemy, having helped prevent a Multiversal War and untold timeline transgressions over the eons. But Loki scoffs at the offer to assist. Mobius then shows Loki clips of his life, both past and future, including the death of his mother Frigga, which Loki will inadvertently cause.

Mobius gets Loki to discuss his complicated nature.

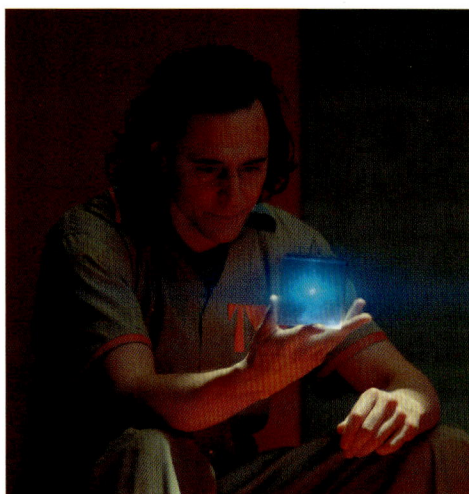

Loki discovers that Infinity Stones hold no power in the TVA.

Loki Changes Heart

Loki briefly escapes Mobius' custody, but curiosity leads him back to the TVA's recording of his natural lifespan. Watching it, he witnesses the passing of his father Odin, and a renewed alliance with brother Thor which has yet to transpire. It all ends in Loki's murder at the hands of Thanos, his former ally. Loki is shaken, but opens up emotionally and agrees to help Mobius.

Fall 2023 | Home Again

The Avengers return to the present. No matter how long their time-hopping missions took to complete or whether they veered off course on detours, they all return simultaneously just minutes after seemingly leaving. The Time Heist was a success, the Infinity Stones have been collected—but the celebration is short lived as they learn that Natasha Romanoff lost her life. "We have to make it worth it," Hulk insists. None of them are aware that the Nebula in their midst is an infiltrator from 2014 who is still loyal to Thanos.

The remaining Avengers grieve for Natasha Romanoff.

The Nano Gauntlet expands to fit Hulk's massive hand.

Fall 2023 | The Nano Gauntlet

A mechanical glove forged from similar nanotech materials to Tony Stark's state-of-the-art Iron Man armors is used to connect the Infinity Stones. Hulk insists he should wield it, due to the grievous damage done to Thanos when he activated the power of the stones. "The radiation's mostly gamma. It's like I was made for this," he says.

Fall 2023 | It's Quiet at First

Hulk collapses as the scorched Nano Gauntlet falls from his arm. "Did it work?" he asks, as Iron Man applies cooling spray to his burns. Scott Lang notices the trees outside the Avengers compound are full of more birds than usual. Then Clint Barton's cell phone begins to buzz. It's his wife Laura. "Guys," Lang says. "I think it worked."

Scott Lang hears something.

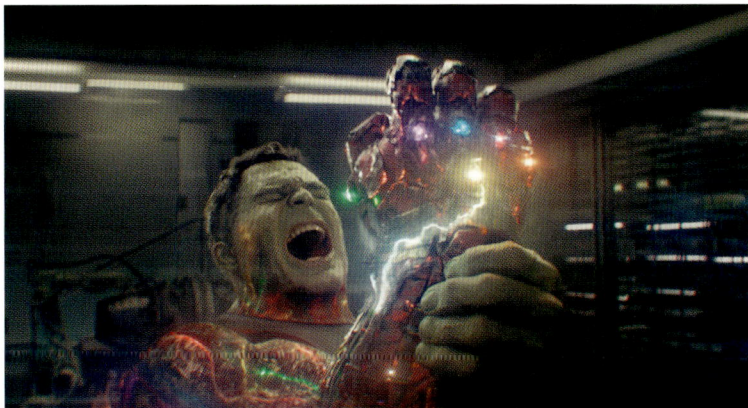
Hulk activates the Infinity Stones to restore what was lost.

Fall 2023 | The Comeback

Thinking of his daughter, Morgan, Tony Stark sets some ground rules as Hulk puts on the gauntlet. "Everyone Thanos snapped away five years ago, you're just bringing them back to now—today. Don't change anything from the last five years," he says. "Everybody comes home," Hulk agrees, as excruciating energy begins to surge up his right arm. The other Avengers brace themselves by activating their armors as Hulk strains to bring his thumb and finger together. Finally—a snap!

Fall 2023 | Nebula Opens a Door

With all the focus on activating the Infinity Stones, no one at the Avengers Compound notices 2014 Nebula sneaking away to hijack the facility's Quantum Tunnel. She uses the device to open a portal, and Thanos from 2014 steers his ship through it. The *Sanctuary II* warship rips through the roof of the headquarters as it expands from its passage through the Quantum Realm. It immediately begins bombarding the compound with missiles.

Thanos arrives on Earth.

221

Yelena finds five years gone in an instant.

Fall 2023 | From the Dust, Returned

All across the universe, the lost are restored. In many places, the pandemonium mirrors when the disintegrations first happened. Monica Rambeau finds herself sitting in the hospital room where her mother was being treated for cancer. In the frenzy of the hallway, a doctor reveals Maria did not die back then, but passed away in the years afterward. Elsewhere, Yelena exemplifies the confusion of the resurrected. She stands in the home of a Red Room assassin she had been trying to deprogram five years ago, asking for the one person who always brought her stability. "I need to find Natasha…"

Fall 2023 | Rapid Onslaught

The Avengers have no time to celebrate before the Avengers Compound and surrounding grounds are reduced to charred rubble in an instant. Beneath it all, Hulk lifts chunks of the structure on his shoulders while water floods into the basement. James Rhodes crawls from his damaged War Machine armor and uses a metal bar to pry Rocket out from under the debris.

James Rhodes is trapped in the wreckage of the Avengers Compound.

Hulk lifts some of the fallen structure.

Fall 2023 | The Gratitude of Thanos

As Captain America, Thor, and Iron Man approach, Thanos reveals he has a new outlook. "I thought by eliminating half of life, the other half would thrive. But you've shown me that's impossible," he says. "They will resist." But he's not angry at them. "I'm thankful, because now I know what I must do," the Titan says. "I will shred this universe down to its last atom, and then with the stones you've collected for me, create a new one, teeming with life that knows not what it has lost but only what it has been given. A grateful universe."

Iron Man, Captain America, and Thor approach Thanos.

Thanos is ready for them.

222

Thanos pushes back against the weaponry of Iron Man's Mark LXXXV armor.

Fall 2023 | The Fight Begins

Thor, Iron Man, and Captain America attack Thanos. Thor's Stormbreaker ax and Mjolnir hammer supercharge Iron Man's blasts with lightning, but Thanos deflects the hits with his double-bladed sword. Tony Stark and Steve Rogers get knocked aside, as Thor loses control of his weapons. Thanos presses the blade of Stormbreaker into the God of Thunder's chest armor, the Titan is struck from behind by Mjolnir—now being held by Captain America. "I knew it," Thor says, recalling the time Rogers budged it during a party game in Stark's penthouse.

The Thanos-loyal Nebula informs her father she has the gauntlet.

Fall 2023 | Nebula's Rise, Nebula's Fall

Within the collapsed headquarters, Hawkeye recovers the Nano Gauntlet. After evading a group of Outriders, he hands over the glove to 2014 Nebula, still unaware she brought Thanos to this time and place. She is stopped by 2014 Gamora who has forged an alliance with the reformed Nebula of the present. "You can change," good Nebula says, but her other self whispers: "He won't let me." In the standoff, good Nebula shoots her through her mechanized chest. She dies with tears falling from her eyes.

Fall 2023 | Thanos Overpowers

Captain America pummels the Titan with the hammer and shield, but Thanos is undaunted. He knocks away Mjolnir and brutally chops away chunks of Cap's shield, battering him to the ground. He summons Ebony Maw, Cull Obsidian, Proxima Midnight, and Corvus Glaive—leading an army of Chitauri warriors, hordes of Outriders, and a sky full of hovering Leviathans and dropships carrying reinforcements.

The Children of Thanos lead his assault on Earth.

Sam Wilson soars as portals open.

Fall 2023 | An Army of Heroes

A portal opens, and Black Panther, Okoye, and Shuri step through, followed by a fleet of Royal Talon Fighters and an army from the tribes of Wakanda, including M'Baku and his separatist mountain tribe the Jabari. Groot and the Winter Soldier march amongst them. Dozens of other gateways appear, powered by the Masters of the Mystic Arts, each doorway bringing returned heroes from throughout the galaxy into the rematch against Thanos.

Okoye, Black Panther, and Shuri arrive from Wakanda.

Fall 2023 | "On Your Left…"

Captain America rises to face the armies of Thanos alone. Then he receives a transmission from a returned Sam Wilson.

Fall 2023 | Allies from Far and Wide

Doctor Strange opens a portal from the ruined world of Titan, and Drax, Mantis, Star-Lord, and Spider-Man emerge from Thanos' distant planet to face down the galactic death-dealer. Valkyrie, Miek, Korg, and the army of New Asgard march forth, joined by Wanda Maximoff, while the Ravagers arrive from deep space and the sorcerer warriors of Kamar-Taj form ranks. All rush onto the battlefield to balance the fight against the army of Thanos.

Drax, Doctor Strange, Star-Lord, Mantis (behind him), and Spider-Man emerge from Titan.

The final showdown begins.

Fall 2023 | Cap's Command

Captain America stands at the frontline
to rally them: "Avengers—assemble!"

Fall 2023 | Into Battle

Pepper Potts enters the battle, wearing her anniversary
present, the blue armor presented to her by her husband.
First she flies alongside Rhodey and Rocket, then she goes
back to back with Tony, swirling in a 360 degree fight against
the minions of Thanos. Peter Quill is saved by the 2014
Gamora. "I thought I lost you," he says, not realizing she is
from the past—and has had no idea who Star-Lord is until
now. "This is the one? Seriously?" she asks Nebula.
"The choices were him or a tree," Nebula replies.

Rhodey, Rocket, and Pepper
Potts fly into battle.

"What I'm about to do to your
stubborn, annoying little planet ...
I'm going to enjoy it."

Fall 2023 | A New Plan

A hasty plan forms: keep the Infinity Stones away
from Thanos. Cap orders Hawkeye to get the stones
as far from the battle as possible, but Banner then
reminds them that the stones must be returned to
the past. The Quantum Tunnel in the Avengers
Compound has been destroyed... But Scott Lang
returns to normal size to say, "That wasn't our only
time machine." The "La Cucaracha" horn sounds as
he triggers his van's key fob. He and Wasp fly off to
activate the vehicle's Quantum Tunnel.

225

Spider-Man carries the gauntlet, propelled by Mjolnir.

Captain Marvel takes down the *Sanctuary II*.

Fall 2023 | Chasing the Gauntlet
An epic game of keep-away ensues as Hawkeye, Black Panther, and Spider-Man pass the gauntlet between each other. Meanwhile, Wanda faces Thanos, seeking revenge for Vision. Immobilized by her powers, the Titan orders his ship to rain fire from above. But then something enters Earth's upper atmosphere. Thanos' ship concentrates its fire on the clouds, but it's too late. A streak of energy cuts through the heart of the *Sanctuary II*, blowing out its engines in a molten plume. It's Captain Marvel, ripping through the heart of the warship like a living killshot.

Fellow warriors gather around Captain Marvel and the gauntlet.

Fall 2023 | "Don't Worry, She's Got Help"
Captain Marvel joins the race to keep away the Nano Gauntlet, streaking with it toward the van's Quantum Tunnel. Okoye, Pepper Potts, Wanda Maximoff, Valkyrie, and Mantis align to run interference against those trying to stop the gauntlet's progress, joined by Shuri, The Wasp, Gamora, and Nebula. But Thanos hurls his sword ahead of Danvers and destroys the machine, trapping the stones in the present.

Fall 2023 | "I Am Inevitable"
Thanos recovers the gauntlet, and fits it over his hand, feeling the intense power radiate up his arm. But he can't snap. Captain Marvel pries his fingers apart, forcing him to rip off the Power Stone into his other fist to knock her away. As Thanos restores the Power Stone to the gauntlet, Iron Man launches a solo attack, grasping momentarily at the glove before being swatted away. Believing he now has the power to erase this world and replace it with another, Thanos declares: "I am inevitable." But his snap does nothing. It's just a clang.

Captain Marvel single-handedly holds back another snap.

Thanos fulfills his own long-ago words: "I know what it's like to lose. To feel so desperately that you're right, yet to fail nonetheless."

Fall 2023 | "I ... Am Iron Man"

Tony Stark wasn't trying to pull off the gauntlet. He was pickpocketing the Infinity Stones. As a bewildered Thanos looks on, the glowing ingots array across Stark's Iron Man gauntlet. "And I ..." Stark tells him. "Am ... Iron Man." Iron Man snaps his fingers, reducing the vast army of Thanos to ash. The Titan watches helplessly as his minions disintegrate until finally, he is alone. He sits. He sighs. He drifts away to nothingness.

Tony Stark sacrifices himself to save everything and everyone.

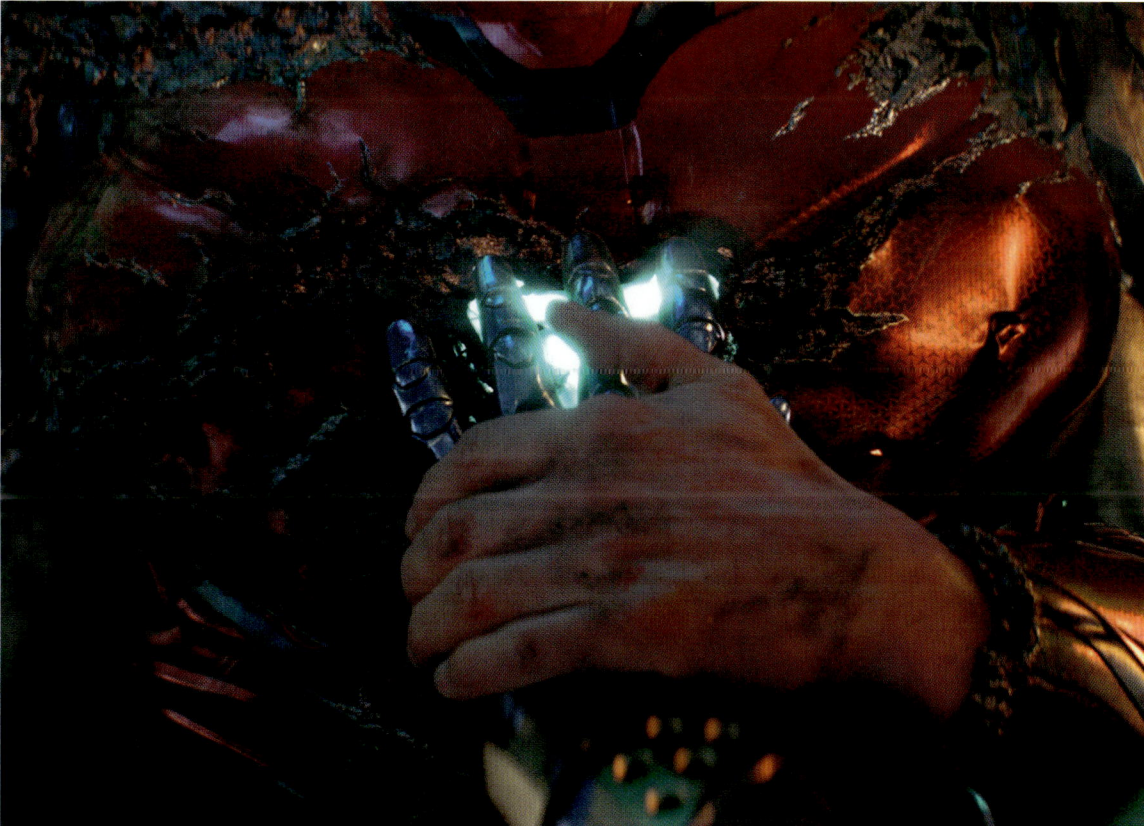

Fall 2023 | Iron Man Falls

Tony Stark collapses, bleeding and badly burned. His old friend James Rhodes attends to him, as does Peter Parker. They all clear away as Pepper Potts approaches, and the artificial intelligence program FRIDAY tells her his life functions are critical. "Tony, look at me," his wife says, assuring him that she and their daughter Morgan will be okay. "You can rest now." In the ruins of victory, Tony Stark dies.

Before Tony Stark joined the effort to undo the Snap, Pepper Potts asked him if he'd be able to rest if he didn't help.

227

SPACE STONE

1942
The Red Skull obtains the Tesseract, which holds the Space Stone, and harnesses its power to produce advanced weapons. After the Red Skull vanishes, Howard Stark recovers the Tesseract from the ocean floor for the U.S. government.

1995
The Tesseract is researched by Project Pegasus, and taken to Mar-Vell's space-based lab. After the Kree fail to steal it, it's returned to S.H.I.E.L.D. custody by Captain Marvel and Nick Fury. S.H.I.E.L.D. continues to conduct experiments on it.

MIND STONE

2012
Loki is given a scepter bearing the Mind Stone by Thanos. He uses it to control the minds of Hawkeye and scientist Dr. Erik Selvig, but after Loki's defeat in New York, S.H.I.E.L.D. takes possession of the scepter.

2015
After being recovered from Hydra, the Mind Stone is imbedded in the new body Ultron intends to use. The Avengers steal the body and Stark's JARVIS A.I. is uploaded instead, creating Vision.

TIME STONE

2017
Doctor Strange takes custody of the Time Stone, using it to reverse the destruction of the Hong Kong Sanctum and preventing the Dark Dimension from assimilating Earth.

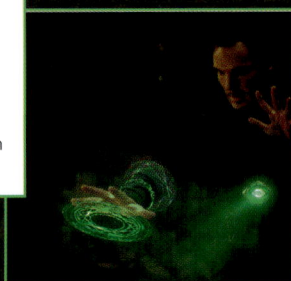

2018
During the battle on Titan, Strange gives Thanos the Time Stone in exchange for Tony Stark's life. Thanos places it in the Infinity Gauntlet and leaves for Wakanda.

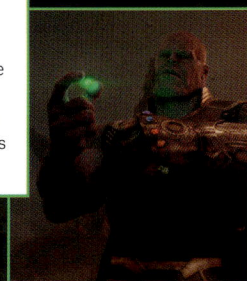

THE INFINITY STONES

The Infinity Stones are six powerful elemental crystals, forged in the Big Bang, that each control an essential aspect of existence. They are the Mind Stone, Reality Stone, Power Stone, Space Stone, Time Stone, and Soul Stone. The stones can only be wielded by beings of immense power, and together can be used to reshape existence. To use the power of the Infinity Stones, Thanos orders Eitri of Nidavellir to construct the Infinity Gauntlet. Thanos goes on to collect all the Infinity Stones, which enables him to wipe out half of all life in the universe. The Avengers later construct a Quantum Tunnel, which allows them to collect the stones from the past and return those who were lost.

REALITY STONE

2013
The Dark Elf Malekith seeks to use the Reality Stone to plunge the universe into darkness. Thor defeats Malekith, and the stone is given to the Collector on Knowhere for safe keeping.

POWER STONE

2014
Star-Lord locates the Power Stone on the planet Morag. After defeating Ronan, who was empowered by the stone, he passes it to the Nova Corps, who keep it locked in a vault on the planet Xandar.

SOUL STONE

2018
Thanos goes to the planet Vormir in search of the Soul Stone. He is approached by the Stonekeeper who explains that to obtain the stone, "You must lose that which you love." Meaning he must sacrifice the person he loves the most: Gamora.

2012

Loki steals the Tesseract from S.H.I.E.L.D. and uses it to open a portal for Thanos' army to invade Earth, but is defeated by the Avengers. The Tesseract is taken to Asgard to ensure its protection.

2017

Thor sends Loki to Odin's vault to summon the fire demon Surtur, triggering Ragnarok in order to defeat Hela. Loki takes the opportunity to retrieve the Tesseract before evacuating.

2018

Thanos tracks the Tesseract to Loki's vessel and intercepts it. He kills Loki, extracts the Space Stone from the Tesseract and places it into the Infinity Gauntlet.

2016

Vision uses the Mind Stone as part of Tony Stark's team during the Avengers' battle in Germany. A misdirected blast from Vision results in James "Rhodey" Rhodes being paralyzed from the waist down.

2018

Vision is attacked by the Children of Thanos while spending time with Wanda Maximoff in Scotland. The Avengers rescue Vision, and travel with him to Wakanda to try and remove the stone.

2018

The Avengers lose the battle in Wakanda as Thanos rips the final remaining Infinity Stone from Vision's head. With all the stones within his grasp, Thanos enacts his plan and snaps his fingers, erasing half of all life in the universe. His work complete, he flees the battlefield.

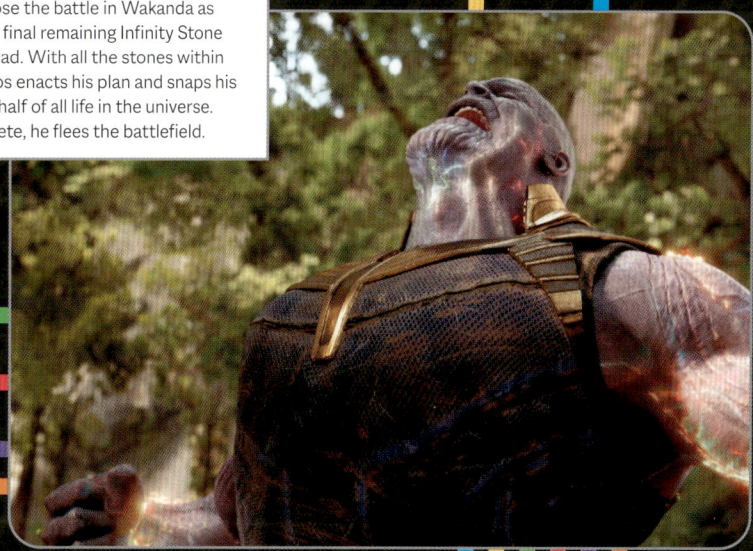

2018

Thanos travels to Knowhere and takes the Reality Stone from the Collector. He then uses it to create an illusion in order to capture Gamora, whom he hopes can guide him to the Soul Stone.

2018

Thanos finds the Power Stone on Xandar and devastates the planet. He adds the stone to the Infinity Gauntlet and goes looking for the Tesseract on Thor and Loki's ship, the *Statesman*.

2018

His mission accomplished, Thanos goes into self-imposed exile on a verdant garden world. His only temptation is the stones themselves and the power they offer. He frees himself by using the stones to destroy each other, grievously wounding himself in the process. Thor kills Thanos shortly thereafter, but the original stones remain destroyed forever.

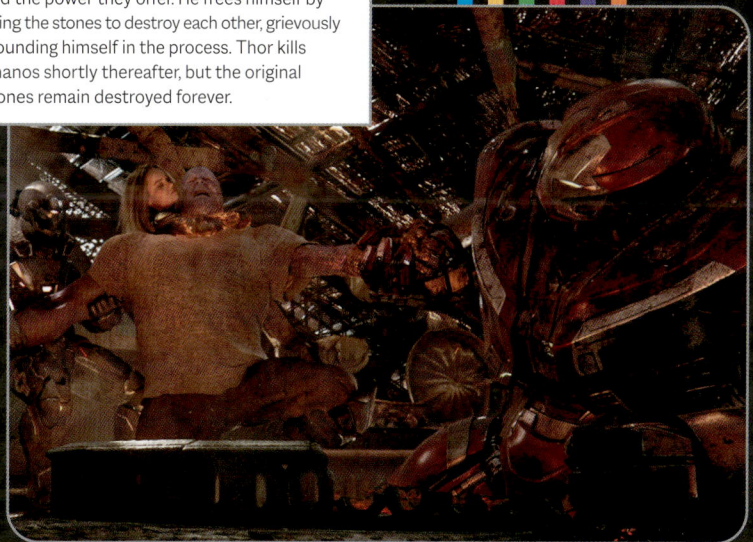

SPACE STONE (PAST)

2012
Tony Stark and Scott Lang attempt to seize the Space Stone in 2012, in the aftermath of the Battle of New York, but after a mishap, Loki gets possession of it and uses it to escape.

2012
After taking the Space Stone, the variant Loki is arrested by the Time Variance Authority for disturbing the Sacred Timeline. They confiscate the Space Stone and prune the branching timeline.

MIND STONE (PAST)

2012
Steve obtains the Mind Stone in Loki's scepter from S.T.R.I.K.E. agents by pretending to be a fellow Hydra loyalist, but is briefly held up by his 2012 self who believes Steve is Loki in disguise.

TIME STONE (PAST)

2012
Bruce goes to the New York Sanctum and finds the Ancient One, to ask for the Time Stone. At first she refuses, but he manages to convince her on condition that all the stones are returned.

REALITY STONE (PAST)

2013
Thor and Rocket travel to 2013 Asgard to extract the Reality Stone from Dr. Jane Foster. Thor has a panic attack when he sees his mother, leaving Rocket to finish the mission.

POWER STONE (PAST)

2014
War Machine and Nebula go to the planet Morag in 2014 to retrieve the Power Stone. Rhodey knocks out the Star-Lord of the past and they find the stone in the temple vault.

SOUL STONE (PAST)

2014
Hawkeye and Black Widow travel to Vormir for the Soul Stone. When they discover the stone can only be acquired by losing what you love, Natasha sacrifices herself to save Barton.

1970

Steve and Tony decide to travel to a time even further in the past to get the Space Stone, arriving in S.H.I.E.L.D.'s Camp Lehigh in 1970, where they collect the Tesseract and more Pym Particles for the trip back to their own time.

2023 | Hulk's Snap

With all the Infinity Stones successfully collected and brought to the present, the Avengers watch as Hulk dons the newly constructed Nano Gauntlet and attempts to undo the Snap. Though badly hurt in the process, Hulk manages to alter reality and return those who were Blipped by Thanos.

2023 | Thanos Defeated

The Infinity Stones come very close to being taken again by Thanos, who invades the present from 2014. Only by the combined efforts of heroes from Earth and beyond, is he defeated. Tony Stark's final snap of the stones, though fatal to Stark, reduces Thanos and his army to ash.

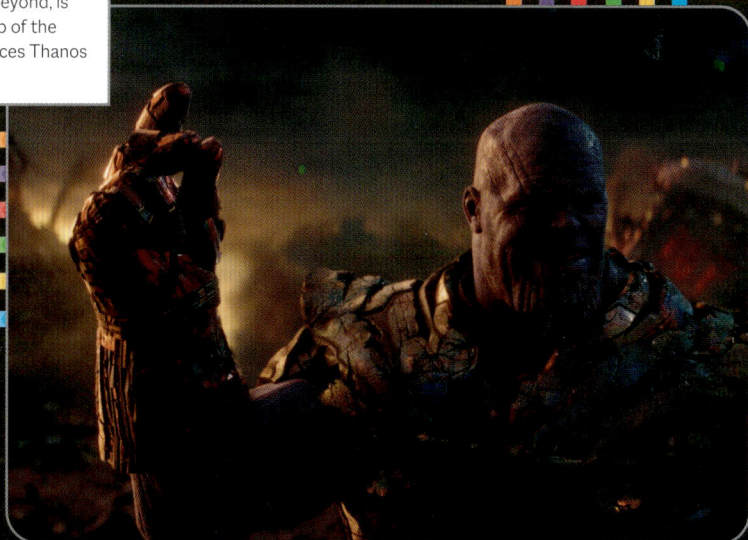

2023 | Stones Returned

Just as Bruce Banner promised the Ancient One, in the aftermath of Thanos' defeat the Infinity Stones of the past are all returned to their places of origin. This completes the loop and leaves the present-day with no remaining Infinity Stones that could fall into the wrong hands.

After The Blip

It's a time of relief and rebuilding—but there is also confusion as the world grapples with the sudden return of half the population. Those who gave everything to defeat Thanos are mourned, but the victory itself has come with a disconcerting toll. The post-Blip era is marked by instability. For many, deeply held beliefs are challenged, and identities (and existence itself) are called into question.

TVA

The Kablooie Clue

Loki and Mobius learn that the futuristic candy left by the variant Loki in 1549 France was only sold in certain parts of Earth from the years 2047 to 2051. Cross referencing that with an apocalyptic database leads them to Haven Hills, Alabama, on March 15, 2050, as a hurricane bears down on a Roxxcart superstore. Inside amongst the huddled soon-to-be casualties, they find the Loki variant—a female version who calls herself Sylvie. She confirms that she has spent her years on the run from the TVA, living "in the ends of a thousand worlds."

The site of a future disaster that will soon leave no survivors.

Apocalyptic Sanctuaries

Loki makes a breakthrough about why the location of the deadly variant the TVA is chasing is so difficult to pinpoint. He theorizes that an apocalypse does not allow for the creation of branching timelines, so an interloper would be free to hide in times and places of imminent destruction without causing a nexus event alert. To test this theory, he takes Mobius to Pompeii, Italy, in 79 CE just before it is "wiped off the face of the planet" by a volcanic eruption. None of his japes or capering causes a branching timeline, proving his thesis correct.

The Loki variant known as Sylvie.

Timeline Blitz

Sylvie has enchanted Hunter C-20 to learn more about the security surrounding the Time Keepers, but she also discovers through her memories that the woman was once a normal person on Earth whose mind has been wiped to place her in service of the TVA. After Sylvie uses stolen reset charges to carpet bomb the Sacred Timeline, she storms TVA headquarters and fights Loki on her way to those who control the organization. When Ravonna Renslayer finds them, Loki opens up a Time Door with Sylvie's TemPad and they fall through.

Loki becomes part of the TVA team.

Stark's old Arc Reactor, now part of his memorial.

PROOF THAT TONY STARK HAS A HEART

Fall 2023 | "I Love You 3000"

A funeral is held for Tony Stark at the lake house he shared with Pepper Potts and their daughter Morgan. A hologram he recorded before embarking on the Time Heist allows Tony to provide his own eulogy, ending with an expression of love for the child he will not see grow up. The ceremony is attended almost exclusively by fellow heroes who fought alongside him in recent years.

Friends and allies gather to say goodbye.

Thor contemplates his future.

Fall 2023 | God of Thunder Rolls on

Thor hitches a ride with the Guardians of the Galaxy, asking Valkyrie to take on the title of king of Asgard—an offer she accepts, with the promise that she will make a lot of changes to New Asgard. Thor is determined to find a new path for himself, following advice gleaned from his mother during the Time Heist: "Everyone fails at who they're supposed to be, Thor," Frigga told him. "The measure of a person—of a hero—is how well they succeed at being who they are." Meanwhile, Star-Lord goes in search of the 2014 Gamora, who remains in the present.

Peter Quill misses Gamora.

TVA

Lamentis-1 Catastrophe

Loki and Sylvie's escape through the Time Door lands them on Lamentis-1 in the year 2077, just as the moon is about to collide with a planet. An apocalypse of that magnitude means the TVA won't detect any Nexus Events caused by their presence, and a powerless TemPad nearly dooms them to annihilation.

The inevitable destruction of Lamentis-1.

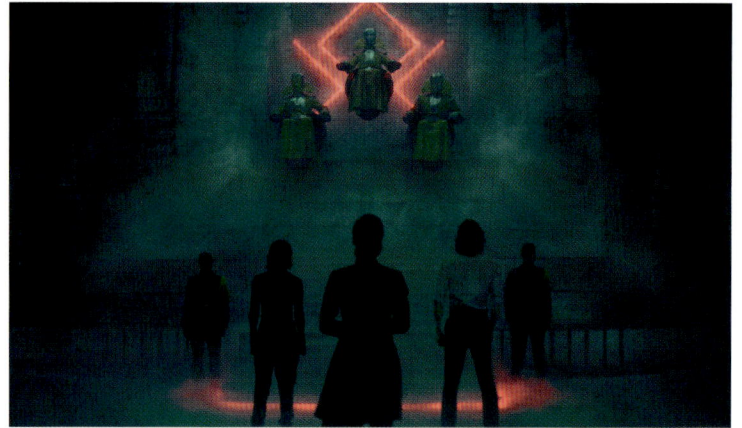

An audience with the Time Keepers.

The Time Keeper Fraud

Loki and Sylvie warn Mobius and Hunter B-15 that they were once normal people abducted into service by the Time Keepers. Mobius is pruned after confronting Ravonna Renslayer about the TVA conscripting people against their will. But the lords of the TVA themselves turn out to be fakes, animatronic puppets designed to hide the real manipulator of the timeline. Loki and Sylvie's discovery means they pose a threat to the existence of the TVA, and Loki is pruned by Judge Renslayer just after he discovers the truth.

The Touch

Loki learns that Sylvie has been on the run since she was a child—and that she has no idea why the TVA felt the need to abduct and prune her. In a moment of despair, the two Loki variants reach out to hold hands at the end of the world. Their touch registers as a Nexus Event, and both are drawn through Time Doors back into TVA custody.

A last-second reprieve as the two Time Doors open.

Loki amid the wreckage of the Void.

Loki Survives a Pruning

For a moment, Loki believes he has been killed after being dissolved by Ravonna Renslayer's Time Stick, but his body is not obliterated. Instead it is merely transported to the Void, a junkyard at the end of time for things from reset branched timelines. There he is discovered by other Loki variants who have also been erased: Kid Loki (who killed Thor), Boastful Loki (who claims to have conquered Iron Man and Captain America and taken all the Infinity Stones), and Classic Loki (melancholic and remorseful in old age).

A Plethora of Lokis

There are many more Lokis trapped in this cosmic garbage disposal too, making the Void an especially dangerous place. Among them is Alligator Loki—whose nexus event was supposedly eating the wrong neighbor's cat—and President Loki, who leads a crew of Lokis, making misery even for their own kind.

Alligator Loki, one of the stranger Loki variants.

1940s | A Long, Long Time

After restoring all the stones, as Hulk once pledged to the Ancient One, Steve Rogers has one more promise to keep. Rather than return to his own time, he rejoins Peggy Carter in the distant past. None of the other Avengers know what transpires during those years. The only thing that's certain is it begins with the dance he once told Peggy they would share when he returned.

In another time, a happy ending is also a new beginning.

Fall 2023 | Returning the Infinity Stones

Captain America suits up to return all the borrowed Infinity Stones to the times and places from which they were taken, thus preventing any disruption to the normal flow of time. He also takes Mjolnir, and enough Pym Particles to help him navigate his way through the past. Hulk indicates the journey will take Steve as long as he needs, but will seem like only five seconds to those who wait for him. But Steve Rogers does not return. At least, not as they just saw him.

An elderly Steve Rogers keeps his past to himself.

Fall 2023 | Cap's Farewell

The Steve Rogers that Bucky Barnes, Sam Wilson, and Hulk saw vanish into the Quantum Realm does not return, but off in the distance by the water they see an elderly man. It's their friend, though many decades older. Barnes seems to have been aware of Rogers' plan, but this is all surprising to Wilson. Rogers offers Sam his shield, conveying the mantle of Captain America to him. Wilson says it feels like it is someone else's. "It isn't," Rogers answers simply. "I'll do my best," Wilson tells him. Rogers shakes his old friend's hand: "That's why it's yours."

Putting back the borrowed Infinity Stones and Mjolnir.

TVA

The Eater of Realities

Also roaming the Void, and consuming all of the matter dropped there, is Alioth—a colossal plume of dark energy that stands as the watchdog at the end of time. Boastful Loki describes it as "a living tempest that consumes matter and energy." Entire realities can be swallowed whole, which means the assorted Lokis might also become Alioth's lunch if they aren't careful. "We're in a shark tank," Classic Loki explains.

Alioth roars.

Classic Loki conjures an image of his Asgard to appetize Alioth.

Glorious Purpose!

Loki and Sylvie decide to bait Alioth while they get close enough to join powers and enchant it. Classic Loki helps provide the distraction, summoning an illusion of the Asgard he remembers from his past. That faraway home and his family may be gone, but the bittersweet memory is temptingly delicious to Alioth, who eagerly pounces on the mirage. Classic Loki loses his life, but Sylvie and Loki successfully use the decoy to slip past Alioth to …

Mobius and Sylvie in the Void

A cornered Sylvie decides to self-prune to escape the TVA, and arrives in the Void, where she encounters Mobius. They join the various Lokis in plotting a way to dissipate Alioth. Sylvie believes Alioth is a kind of guard dog, blocking the path to a point at the end of time from which the TVA is being manipulated.

Loki and Sylvie at the endpoint.

Sylvie demands to know everything from Ravonna Renslayer.

…The Citadel at the End of Time

Sylvie and Loki confront the giddy, somewhat deranged He Who Remains, a man who explains that he is a variant of a researcher from the 31st century who discovered the doorways to the Multiverse. He has many variants himself, some of whom made the same discovery and leapfrogged various timelines, sparking a Multiversal War. He Who Remains created the TVA to rein in these other versions of himself, to prevent such devastating crossovers. "Without me, without the TVA, everything burns," he explains.

The Unraveling

"No more lies," He Who Remains tells them. "You kill me and the Sacred Timeline is completely exposed. Multiversal War. Or you take over and return to the TVA as its benevolent rulers. Tell the workforce who they are, why they do what they do. It's not personal. It's practical." But it's personal to Sylvie, who runs him through with her blade for the many innocent people and timelines he erased. He Who Remains dies with an ominous promise: "I'll see you soon…" The timeline swirling around the Citadel immediately begins to fray.

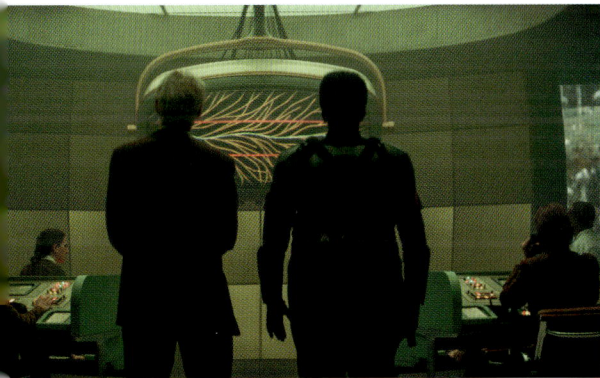

Wanda finally sees Vision's remains, reopening the wound of his death.

Mobius and Hunter B-15 witness the redlining of the Sacred Timeline when He Who Remains is eliminated.

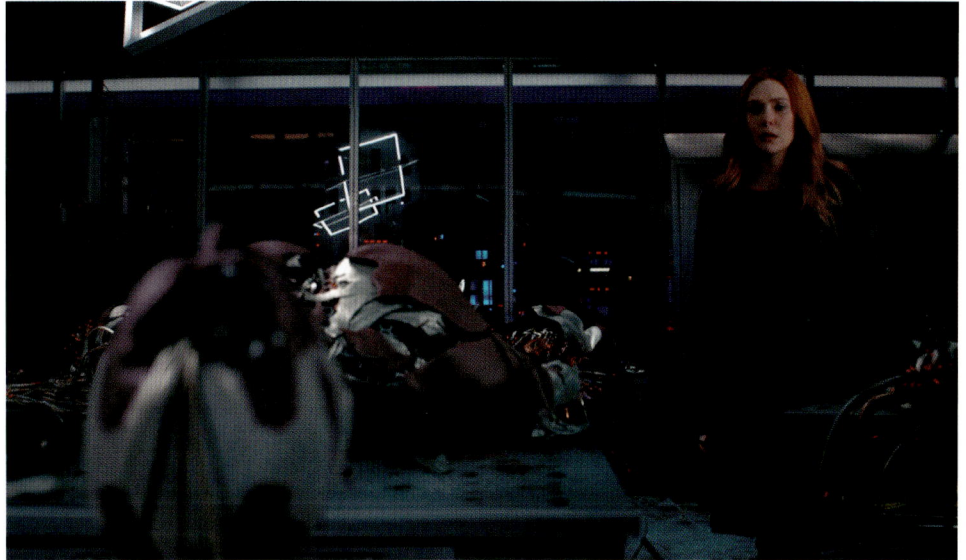

Fall 2023 | Wanda Maximoff Confronts S.W.O.R.D.

As the world celebrates the return of those lost during the Blip, Wanda Maximoff remains in mourning for Vision, whose murder by Thanos is unchanged. She confronts acting director Tyler Hayward at the Sentient Weapon Observation and Response Division, who reveals to her that Vision's remains are being dissected and studied. He refuses to surrender the remains, citing the $3 billion value of the vibranium alone. "He isn't yours," Hayward says. Wanda caresses Vision's face and channels her power into the void left by the Mind Stone. "I can't feel you," she whispers.

Fall 2023 | The Homemaker

Wanda Maximoff drives to the dilapidated town of Westview, New Jersey, where she visits a plot of land with a deed addressed to her by Vision. She and Vision could have built a home here together if not for his tragic death. In a moment of overpowering grief, she releases a burst of Chaos Magic that engulfs the community, constructing a two-story home and recreating her lost love Vision. She renders this world in black and white and adds a laugh track, subconsciously transforming her reality into the retro American sitcoms her own family used to watch in Sokovia. "Wanda …" Vision says as he returns to life. "Welcome home."

Wanda Maximoff remakes Vision in a reality based on her favorite sitcoms.

237

2023

Wanda's illusion includes
a title sequence.

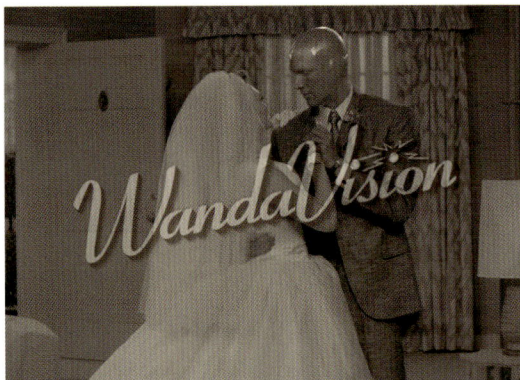

Monica Rambeau and F.B.I. agent
Jimmy Woo detect something
strange around Westview.

Fall 2023 | A Bewitched Cast

Wanda Maximoff populates her
sitcom world with characters
played by actual townsfolk—
against their will. They remain
helplessly trapped inside their
comic-relief counterparts while
Wanda's imagination manifests
new identities and settings, using
reality as the raw material.

Wanda and Vision host a dinner for his boss and his wife,
"Mr. and Mrs. Hart."

Fall 2023 | The New Castmate

In her first assignment for S.W.O.R.D.
after returning from the Blip, Monica
Rambeau investigates the Westview
Anomaly and instantly vanishes after
touching the mystical barrier.

Fall 2023 | The Busybody

Only one participant, the nosy neighbor "Agnes," seems to be
aware she is playing a part (and occasionally breaks character to
ask if she should redo a line). Agnes arrives somewhat late to the
story, pushing her way into Wanda's home and introducing herself
with an enthusiastic declaration of: "Charmed!"

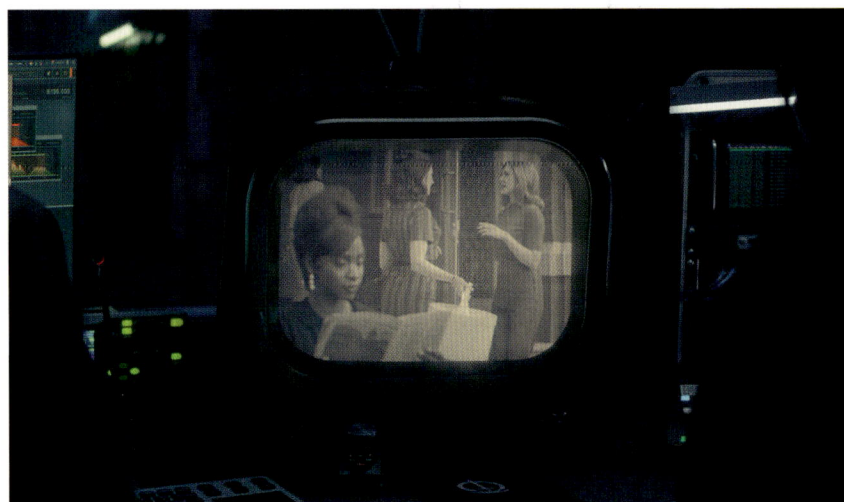

An old television picks up the signal
of Wanda's scripted new life.

Fall 2023 | Distorted Signals

Astrophysicist Dr. Darcy Lewis dubs the phenomenon
the "Hex," and discovers the wavelengths it emits can
be picked up by old-fashioned televisions. She and
F.B.I. Agent Jimmy Woo see Wanda Maximoff and
Vision enacting various sitcom scenarios and recognize
Rambeau going through the motions as a supporting
character named "Geraldine."

Agnes brings over an ingredient for dessert.

238

Wanda's spell is punctured when Monica Rambeau mentions Ultron.

Groovy-era Monica Rambeau is hurled from Wanda Maximoff's TV fantasy.

Fall 2023 | The Birth of Tommy and Billy

Wanda Maximoff rapidly cycles through sitcom eras, progressing into the color era with a 1970s-inspired *Brady Bunch*-like scenario. She also fast-forwards through a pregnancy, producing two twin boys she names Tommy and Billy. Like their father Vision, they are real and tangible, not illusions. Monica Rambeau's "Geraldine" helps her deliver the babies, but she fights through the spell when Wanda mentions her own twin brother, Pietro. "He was killed by Ultron, wasn't he?" "Geraldine" asks. The question shakes Wanda, who forcefully ejects Monica from her home, through the town, and out of the Hex.

Fall 2023 | Long-Lost Brother

Pietro Maximoff arrives at Wanda's doorstep. Apart from the silvery hair and ability to move at super-speed, he looks nothing like her late twin. "She recast Pietro?" a shocked Darcy Lewis says while watching the broadcast signal. Even Wanda seems to be perplexed, suggesting this was not her doing. But she chooses to roll with it, inviting "Pietro" into her home with the other manifestations of family.

A man shows up at the house purporting to be Wanda's brother Pietro.

Fall 2023 | Constricting Family Ties

Now inhabiting a 1980s sitcom, Wanda Maximoff's sons age almost instantaneously from babies to toddlers to 10-year-olds. "Let's just hope this dog stays the same size," Agnes quips, again apparently recognizing that something is amiss. Vision begins to catch on, confronting his wife about what he has sensed. "I can't remember my life before Westview. I don't know who I am. I'm scared," he says. Wanda uses her magic to suppress his questions and put his mind at ease.

Halloween in classic sitcom style.

Wanda and Vision clash over what's happening in Westview.

Fall 2023 | Vision in the Middle

On Halloween, Wanda dresses as a Sokovian fortune teller, while Vision puts on a lucha libre wrestler costume. Billy, who is displaying mystical abilities like his mother, dresses as a sorcerer, while fast-moving Tommy puts on an outfit that mimics his uncle's costume. Vision can no longer deny that Wanda is inflicting suffering with her fantasy after discovering residents on the outskirts of Westview trapped going through repetitive motions. He is torn between his love for her and his desire to do right, but after attempting to leave the Hex he learns he cannot exist outside it.

VISION

Vision is an artificial being, created using a vibranium synthezoid body and the Mind Stone. Vision possesses a variety of superhuman abilities including superhuman strength, the ability to fly, to manipulate his form, and to phase through solid objects. With the Mind Stone, Vision can also fire beams of energy. Because Vision's body was originally created for the villain Ultron, some members of the Avengers are unsure of his motives, but he quickly proves to be a trusted member of the team when he fights alongside them to defeat Ultron.

2016 | Opposite Sides

Now an official member of the Avengers, Vision forms a friendship with Wanda Maximoff. After Secretary Ross visits the Avengers and informs them they must comply with the terms of the Sokovia Accords, Vision sides with Tony Stark, arguing that their presence attracts more conflict and that the accords are a reasonable compromise to gain the public's trust. He and Wanda find themselves on different sides in the conflict.

2015 | Born Yesterday

Vision's synthezoid form is originally created by Ultron as a new body, but Tony Stark decides to upload the JARVIS artificial intelligence instead. While the Avengers fight over Tony's decision, Thor uses the power of his hammer Mjolnir to bring the body to life. Vision reassures the Avengers that he is not a child of Ultron or JARVIS but rather something new. It is Vision who ultimately ends Ultron's rampage, destroying the villain with a blast from the Mind Stone.

Late 1980s-1999 | Childhood

Born in the Eastern European nation of Sokovia to Olek and Iryna Maximoff, Wanda's childhood is played out to a background of conflict in the war-torn nation. Her family is torn apart when their apartment is demolished by Stark Industries munitions, killing her parents but sparing Wanda and her twin brother, Pietro.

2014 | Exposed to the Mind Stone

As orphans, Wanda and Pietro are radicalized by Hydra. Blaming Tony Stark and the Avengers for their plight, they volunteer for experiments overseen by Baron Strucker, and are exposed to the Mind Stone within Loki's scepter. While all the other test subjects die, Wanda and her brother both survive and gain incredible abilities—in Wanda's case, her dormant Chaos Magic is activated, granting her psionic powers.

2015 | Ultron

Wanda and Pietro go up against the Avengers when they invade a Hydra base in Sokovia. They soon team up with Ultron, but when Wanda reads Ultron's mind and discovers his true agenda to wipe out humanity, she and Pietro assist the Avengers to bring Ultron down. Pietro is killed in the battle, but Wanda is recruited by the Avengers and moves to the U.S.

WANDA MAXIMOFF

Wanda's life is marked by tragedy. As a child, she loses her parents when a missile hits her family's apartment building. She is trapped for days in the wreckage with her twin brother Pietro, staring at a second bomb labeled "Stark Industries," until they are rescued. This traumatic experience shapes Wanda's hate for Tony Stark and the Avengers, but she goes from being a powerful enemy to a valued member of the team.

2018 | Vision's Death

Wanda and Vision begin a relationship while on the run, but are tracked down by the Children of Thanos, who attack Vision in order to take the Mind Stone. When Vision is seriously injured, Captain America's Avengers go to Wakanda in order for Shuri to extract the Mind Stone from Vision and destroy it, preventing Thanos' plan to eliminate half the universe. Despite their efforts, Thanos rips the stone from Vision's forehead, killing him.

2023 | Seeing Double

Racked with grief over the death of Vision, Wanda has a breakdown and uses her magic to create an idyllic suburban life in the town of Westview, New Jersey. She recreates a version of Vision for her illusion, but this Vision suspects there is something wrong with their existence, and ultimately has to battle the real Vision, who has been reanimated by S.W.O.R.D. The Wanda-created Vision is lost when she undoes her spell, while the original Vision leaves for parts unknown, his memories having been restored by his counterpart.

2018 | Facing Thanos

Wanda is hiding out in Scotland with Vision when they're attacked by the Children of Thanos, who intend to take the Mind Stone from Vision. Though Vision is injured, they are both rescued by Captain America's Avengers. They take Vision to Wakanda, to keep the Mind Stone from falling into the hands of Thanos, but are unsuccessful, and Wanda has to watch Vision die—twice—before being Blipped herself.

2023 | Wanda's Vision

Wanda returns to take part in the final defeat of Thanos. In the aftermath, devastated by the death of Vision, she drives to Westview, New Jersey where Vision had purchased land for them to build a home and start their lives together. Overcome with grief, Wanda unknowingly uses Chaos Magic, transforming the town into a sitcom and conjuring a new Vision and two young sons. She loses her new family when she reverses her spell, but her increased powers show her to be the long-prophesied "Scarlet Witch."

2024 | Falling to Darkness

Doctor Strange asks for Wanda's help in protecting America Chavez, who is being hunted for her Multiverse hopping ability. Strange soon realizes that the person chasing America is Wanda, who wants to absorb the young woman's powers so she can unite with Multiversal incarnations of her sons, Billy and Tommy. Strange refuses to give up America, and Wanda begins a murderous hunt for the teen. Wanda ends her crusade when she brings Mount Wundagore crashing down on herself.

2016 | Picking Sides

During a mission in Lagos, Nigeria, Wanda accidentally destroys a building using her powers, killing many of those inside. As the public now see Wanda as a threat, she is confined at the Avengers Compound by Tony Stark and Vision, but she is rescued by Hawkeye and joins Cap's team in resisting the Sokovia Accords.

2023

Fall 2023 | The Fourth Wall

Wanda emerges from the Hex to warn the law enforcement personnel surrounding Westview to back off. She rescues Vision, then expands her spell, swallowing the nearby S.W.O.R.D. encampment and transmogrifying its personnel into a traveling carnival. A conscience-stricken Vision helps Dr. Darcy Lewis break free of the notion that she is an escape artist, and the two attempt to talk Wanda into standing down.

"Agnes" reveals herself with her own title sequence.

Outside the Hex, Wanda issues a warning to the S.W.O.R.D. personnel who are threatening her illusion.

Fall 2023 | Agatha All Along

Wanda Maximoff discovers that her neighbor "Agnes" is actually a centuries-old witch named Agatha Harkness, who was drawn to Westview by the astounding display of mystical power. Agatha has not only been plotting to nourish herself with Wanda's powers, she has been manipulating a local resident named Ralph Bohner into playing the part of Pietro, which is why he doesn't match Wanda's memories.

The secret voice behind the camera.

Fall 2023 | Monica Rambeau's Transformation

Despite being warned that her molecular structure was already inexorably altered by the Hex, Monica Rambeau decides to push through the barrier again. The metamorphosis this time is more profound, imbuing her with radiant blue eyes that can detect energy auras, and a body that can turn intangible. She interrupts the 2000s-era mockumentary comedy Wanda has created to warn her that S.W.O.R.D. Director Hayward is planning an assault on the town. "Don't let him make you the villain," Rambeau pleads. "Maybe I already am," Maximoff answers.

Monica Rambeau undergoes permanent changes in the Hex.

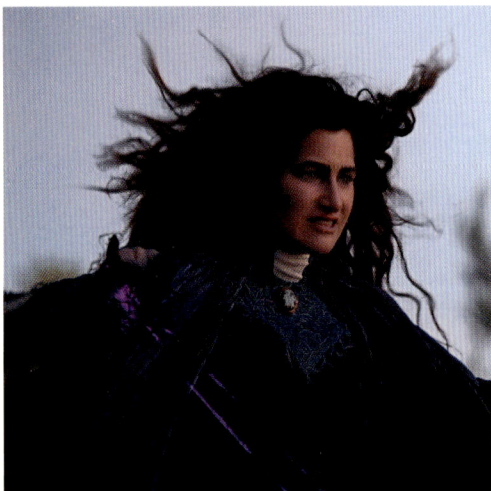

"You're supposed to be a myth," Agatha tells Wanda. "A being capable of spontaneous creation. And here you are, using it to make breakfast for dinner."

Fall 2023 | Wanda's Destiny

Agatha kidnaps Tommy and Billy to coerce Wanda into surrendering her powers, noting that she may be a figure prophesied in the Darkhold, a forbidden mystical text. "This is Chaos Magic, Wanda," she says. "That makes you The Scarlet Witch."

Fall 2023 | Project Cataract

S.W.O.R.D.'s effort to rebuild Vision from his remains is finally successful when some of Wanda Maximoff's Chaos Magic is used to reactivate him. The pure white being is then dispatched into the Hex to destroy "the true Vision," but is defeated when the soulful version created by Wanda engages his counterpart in a philosophical debate, then awakens Vision's remaining memories in this refurbished model. The newcomer then departs, his destination unknown.

Vision and his counterpart discuss the "Ship of Theseus" thought experiment that defines authenticity.

Fall 2023 | Agatha's Defeat

Using a witchcraft trick she learned from Agatha herself, Wanda binds her rival witch's magical powers but chooses not to destroy her. Instead, she confines Agatha in a mental prison—as "Agnes," the local busybody who will remain trapped in Westview even as Wanda ends her overall control of the town. "Okeydokey, artichoke-y!" the enchanted Agatha declares after receiving her sentence.

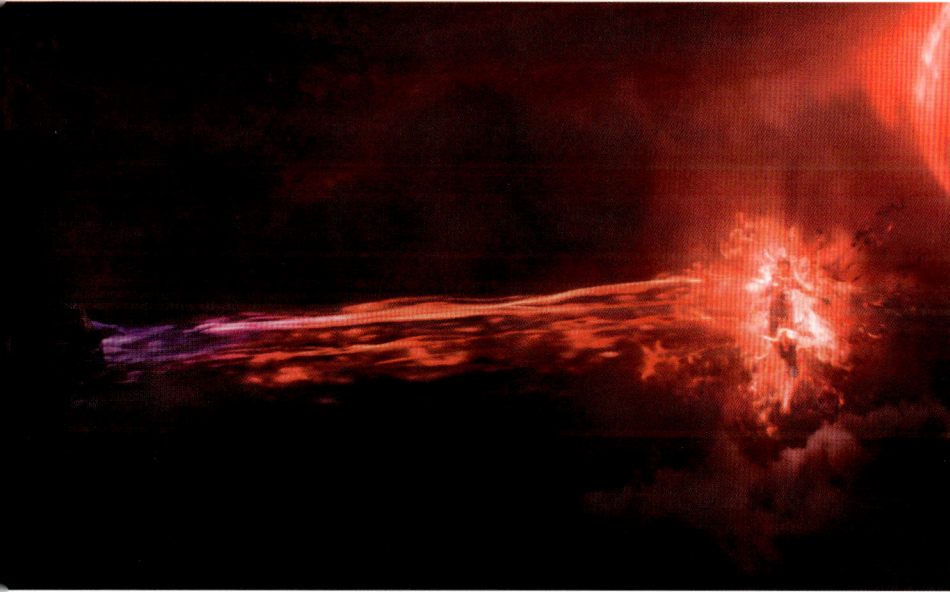

Wanda and Agatha Harkness battle above Westview.

Monica encounters a Skrull shape-shifter.

Fall 2023 | Skrulls in Need

In the aftermath of the events in Westview, Monica Rambeau is contacted by a Skrull operative who says she was "sent by an old friend of your mother's. He heard you've been grounded. He'd like to meet with you." When Rambeau asks where, the Skrull points up.

Fall 2023 | Canceling the Show

"You'll set everything right," Vision tells his wife. "Just not for us." Wanda withdraws the tide of the Hex, turning the carnival back into the S.W.O.R.D. outpost and returning all the residents to their true identities. Then she and Vision return to their home, tuck their sons into bed, and tell them how proud they are of their bravery. Before saying goodbye, Vision asks Wanda how he came to be. "You are the piece of the Mind Stone that lives in me," she says. "You are my sadness and my hope. But mostly you are my love." As the Hex closes in on their home, Wanda's family is erased, leaving her alone again.

Wanda must say goodbye to Vision ... again.

Dark impulses overtake Wanda Maximoff as she seeks the sons she lost, elsewhere in the Multiverse.

Fall 2023 | Darkhold Corruption

In a remote cabin, Wanda Maximoff studies the pages of the Darkhold that she took from Agatha Harkness. Its pages contain forbidden methods of traversing universes, and with He Who Remains now gone, and the TVA no longer maintaining the Sacred Timeline, the doorways are open. Wanda uses the Darkhold to pinpoint alternate realities where her sons Tommy and Billy still exist. Reaching them is still beyond her abilities, however, so she will need to find another with the power to puncture the barrier between realities.

243

2024

Repercussions from the Blip continue.
The return of half the world's population has led to resource shortages and displacement for many, creating new conflicts around the globe. The resurgence of so much sentient life also activates the Emergence that will summon the Celestial Tiamut from within the Earth, with potentially fatal consequences for everyone on the planet. Meanwhile, personal tragedy looms as the venerable Black Panther, T'Challa, faces a grave and cruel illness.

Katy is stunned to see Shaun take down the attackers.

Spring 2024 | Shang-Chi in Hiding

Shang-Chi is living under the name "Shaun" and working with his best friend, Katy Chen, as a parking valet in San Francisco. She has no idea about his history or abilities, until his father, Wenwu, the leader of The Ten Rings, sends Razor Fist and other minions to attack Shang-Chi during a bus ride. They snatch the pendant Shang-Chi's mother gave him, which she said would lead him home if he ever felt lost. While Katy steers the damaged vehicle to a crashed stop, Shang-Chi dispatches the thugs with his otherworldly fighting skills. Another passenger's video makes him go viral online as "Bus Boy."

Shang-Chi's old training emerges.

Abomination takes a hit from himself thanks to Wong's portal maneuver.

Spring 2024 | Sibling Fight

Instead of greeting Shang-Chi with open arms, Xialing meets him with a closed fist, battling her brother in the cage for her cheering spectators. She overpowers him, showing she has learned skills on her own that she once was prevented from practicing with him. Afteward, Shang-Chi gives Xialing her letter, only to learn she never sent it. The Ten Rings, having tracked Shang-Chi to his sister, attack the Golden Dagger.

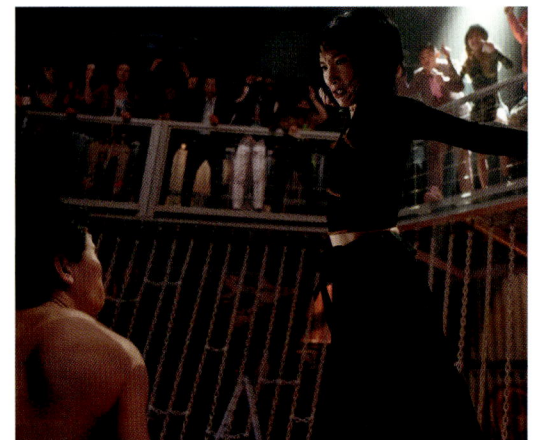

Spring 2024 | Wong vs. Abomination

After The Ten Rings ambush, a shaken Shang-Chi seeks out his estranged sister, Xialing, having recently received a letter from her. He discovers that she now runs an underground fighting ring in Macau called the Golden Daggers club. It has attracted an impressive headliner fight: Sorcerer Supreme Wong, battling the monstrous form of Emil Blonsky as Abomination. For Wong, it's a chance to train; "How's the jaw?" he asks before opening a portal to return Abomination to his prison cell. "Maybe you'll start controlling those punches like we practiced." This unauthorized release of the supervillain will later cause a legal headache for both of them.

Shang-Chi braces for a hit from Xialing.

Death Dealer hangs from the scaffolding.

Spring 2024 | Highrise Battle

The fight spills out onto the skyscraper's scaffolding. Katy Chen falls, but is rescued by Xialing. Death Dealer, Shang-Chi's harsh former martial arts instructor, now faces him in punishing combat, while the attackers take Xialing's pendant, too. The fight ends when Wenwu stops Shang-Chi and tells his children: "Let's go home." Surrounded by his minions, they have no choice but to agree.

Spring 2024 | Trevor Slattery's Encore

Shang-Chi, Xialing, and Katy are imprisoned in a dungeon after resisting Wenwu's plan to invade Ta Lo by force. In the catacombs, they encounter the actor Trevor Slattery, who was kidnapped from prison by The Ten Rings for impersonating Wenwu as "the Mandarin" caricature. They've kept him alive as a kind of jester. The trio also meet a winged furball named Morris, who is a supernatural guardian creature from Ta Lo. They all break free, using Morris to locate Ta Lo before Wenwu can arrive.

Trevor Slattery and Morris in The Ten Rings dungeon.

Wenwu reveals his plan to take over Ta Lo.

Spring 2024 | Messages from Beyond

At The Ten Rings compound, Wenwu explains that he has been hearing the voice of his late wife, Li, speaking to him from a gateway to the afterlife that's embedded in the mountains of her home village of Ta Lo. "Your mother is waiting for us there," he assures his children. Wenwu uses Shang-Chi and Xialing's jade pendants to open a mystical map made of water, which shows the way to her village. The path is open only once a year, and that moment is only three days away.

Spring 2024 | A Ta Lo Welcome

In the village, Shang-Chi and Xialing meet their mother's sister, Ying Nan, who reveals that Ta Lo protects the outside world from the Dweller in Darkness, a monstrous entity that feasts on human souls. It and its army of smaller Soul Eaters were defeated with the aid of a being known as The Great Protector, and have been contained for millennia behind the gate that Wenwu intends to open. Those are the voices that have been speaking to him—not the spirit of Li. The villagers quickly train Shang-Chi in their soulful and harmonious fighting style, while Xialing receives a rope dart made with dragonscale and Katy is given archery lessons.

The Dark Gate across the lake from the village of Ta Lo.

2024

Wenwu faces his son Shang-Chi in Ta Lo.

Spring 2024 | Father vs. Son

Wenwu arrives at Ta Lo and faces down his son in combat, belittling him for failing to protect Li, who was murdered when Shang-Chi was a child. "You stood at the window and did nothing," he snarls. "You watched her die." Shang-Chi insists his father is the one who betrayed her: "Even if you could bring her back, what makes you think she would want anything to do with you?" Wenwu knocks his son into the lake beside the village, sending up giant waves of water.

Spring 2024 | The Great Protector Emerges

From the depths of the lake, Shang-Chi awakens The Great Protector, a noble, dragon-like creature that rises up from beneath to help the villagers of Ta Lo once again defeat the Soul Eaters. After carrying Shang-Chi back to his father, The Great Protector seeks out Xialing, who rides the being through the air thrashing and destroying the predatory swarm.

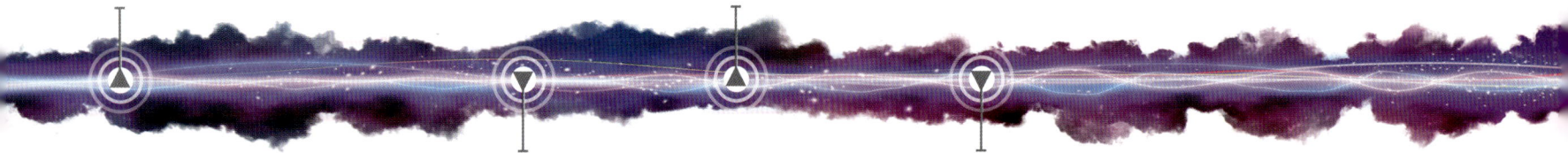

Xialing rides atop The Great Protector.

Soul Eaters fly toward the village.

Spring 2024 | The Breached Gateway

Wenwu propels himself to the gate and begins pulverizing the barrier, ripping loose its dragon scales and unleashing not the spirit of his wife, but a ferocious army of Soul Eaters. The creatures immediately swarm the village. One of them seizes Death Dealer and consumes his essence. Razor Fist and the other Ten Rings attackers forge a hasty alliance with the Ta Lo villagers to fight back, if only to save their own lives.

Shang-Chi takes control of the rings, and prepares to use them against the Dweller in Darkness.

Spring 2024 | Death of Wenwu

Shang-Chi faces his father again in combat, this time using his mother's fighting style rather than the one learned from his father's henchmen. He draws all ten of the rings away from Wenwu, then casts them at his feet. Before a chastened Wenwu can repair what he has done, the Dweller in Darkness breaks free from the fractured gate and seizes him, consuming his troubled soul. In his final moments, Wenwu releases The Ten Rings to his son.

The Great Protector grapples with the Dweller in Darkness.

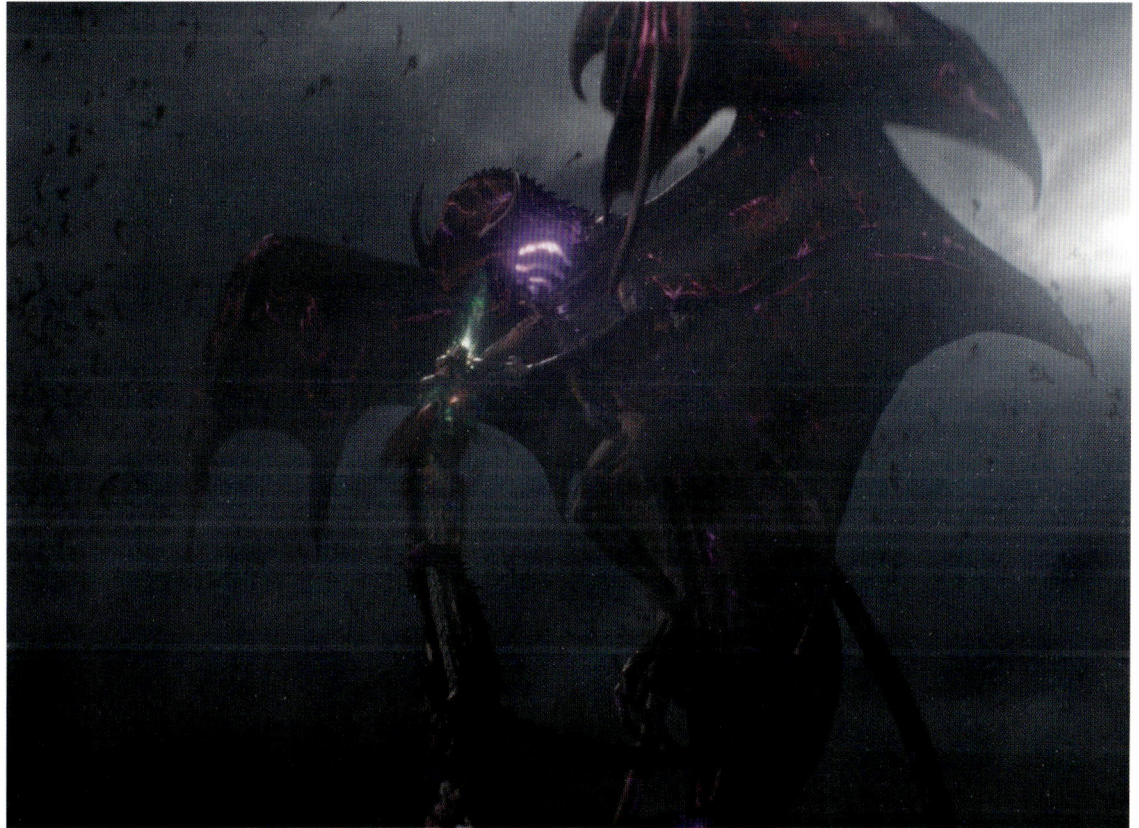

Spring 2024 | Katy's Bullseye

The Dweller in Darkness is dangerously close to extracting The Great Protector's soul, which will give it unfathomable and unstoppable power. Using her archery training from the fallen Guang Bo, Katy Chen fires a dragonscale arrow through the demonic being's throat, freeing The Great Protector and allowing Shang-Chi to fire The Ten Rings into the roaring mouth of the Dweller in Darkness, destroying it from within.

Spring 2024 | The Ten Rings Beacon

Sorcerer Supreme Wong summons Shang-Chi and Katy Chen to Kamar-Taj so he can examine the Ten Rings. Captain Marvel and Bruce Banner join the study via hologram, but no one can identify the Rings' origin. Wong says they're not artifacts mentioned in the codex of the Mystic Arts. Banner notes that they're not made of vibranium but might be alien tech. Captain Marvel insists they don't match any she has encountered. Wong dissects their aura and reveals they are sending out a steady signal—but to whom and to where they have no idea.

Xialing takes the throne.

Spring 2024 | After the Battle ...

Shang-Chi and Katy Chen return to normal life in San Francisco, while Xialing visits her father's mountain fortress, ostensibly to dismantle his organization. In truth, she intends to take it over, refashioning the organization to her agenda.

Katy and Shang-Chi learn that the rings are emitting a signal.

The Falcon sets his sights on Batroc.

Spring 2024 | Falcon vs. Batroc

Sam Wilson returns to work with the U.S. Air Force on a special mission over Tunisia, trying to rescue an officer who was kidnapped by Georges Batroc and the LAF—a terrorist group seeking to exploit the unrest created by the Blip. Falcon succeeds in intercepting the aircraft and rescuing the captured captain, but Batroc manages to escape, leaping from his helicopter just before a missile destroys it near the Libyan border.

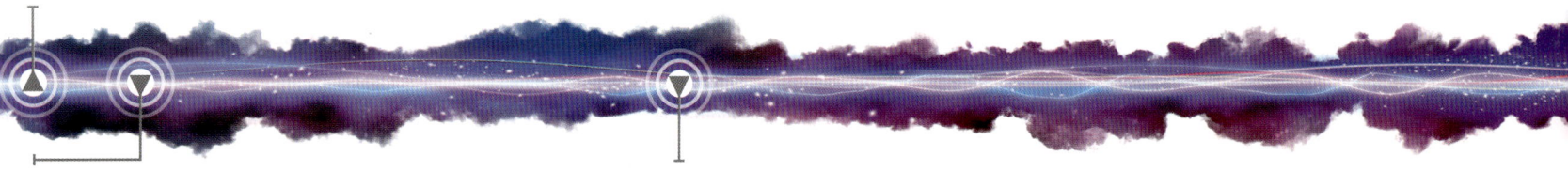

Wilson and Joaquin Torres discuss the Flag Smashers.

Spring 2024 | The Flag Smasher Threat

Lt. Joaquin Torres briefs Wilson on another new threat to emerge in the aftermath of the Blip—the Flag Smashers, which he describes as a group of militants who seek to erase borders and believe the world was more equitable during the Blip. "Every time something gets better for one group, it gets worse for another," Wilson laments. His own family has suffered severe financial hardship, which he is struggling to set right.

Spring 2024 | Cap's Shield Memorialized

Sam Wilson decides the shield that Steve Rogers once carried belongs in a museum. He donates the red, white, and blue shield to the Smithsonian, noting that the turmoil of the Blip requires new heroes instead of a reliance on the old—especially those, like Steve Rogers, who are no longer in the fight.

Cap's shield, on display with his WWII uniform.

Sam Wilson decides Steve Rogers' shield belongs in a museum.

Rhodes and Wilson after the museum ceremony.

Spring 2024 | War Machine's Advice

Col. James Rhodes attends the handover ceremony and asks Wilson why he chose to put the shield under glass rather than take on the mantle as Steve Rogers asked. When Wilson says it didn't belong to him, Rhodes urges him to put that feeling aside. "The world's a crazy place right now," Rhodes tells him. "Nobody's stable. Allies are now enemies. Alliances are all torn apart. The world's broken. Everybody's just looking for somebody to fix it."

Bucky Barnes reflects on a lifetime filled with horrors.

Spring 2024 | The Winter Soldier's Atonement

Nightmares consume Bucky Barnes. Despite ridding himself of the Winter Soldier mind-control protocols, he still ruminates on the terrible wrongs he perpetrated over the decades. He undergoes government-mandated therapy as a condition of his pardon, helps root out Hydra loyalists in the U.S. government, and befriends an elderly man named Yori Nakajima, whose son RJ was an innocent bystander killed years ago by the Winter Soldier. Barnes listens to him grieve his son, but can't bear to confess that he was the unwilling killer.

Spring 2024 | John Walker Becomes Captain America

Instead of keeping Steve Rogers' shield in the Smithsonian, the U.S. government gives it to special ops soldier John Walker, anointing him as the new Captain America. The three-time Medal of Honor recipient specializes in counterterrorism and hostage rescue, and although he is not physically augmented in any way, he is a highly skilled combatant. In his first public comments, Walker says he wants to "make people feel safe. Steve Rogers was the kind of guy who could do that. He gave me hope. Even though I never met him, he feels like a brother."

A new "Captain America" is introduced.

June 1943 | Cap's first shields
Steve Rogers had a reputation for defending the little guy, even when he was the little guy. In one such brawl before he received the Super Soldier Serum, Steve defended himself with a trash can lid. So in a way, he was always meant to use the shield. Straight after his transformation in 1943, Steve used a Lucky Star Cab Company door to block assassin Heinz Kruger's fire.

Steve Rogers wields a makeshift shield after his super soldier transformation while pursuing Abraham Erskine's assassin.

2012 | Battle of New York
The Avengers come together in New York as the Chitauri invade. Captain America leads the others while using his shield to take out Chitauri soldiers. The shield becomes a modern icon.

2015 | In Widow's Hands
When Ultron's sentries attack in Seoul, Black Widow retrieves Cap's shield from the ground and affixes it to her motorcycle before returning it to Cap.

2015 | Battle in Sokovia
Steve Rogers and Thor team up once again, pairing the shield and Mjolnir against Ultron's sentries, using each weapon to its full advantage.

2015 | War on Hydra
While attacking Hydra's Sokovian research base, Captain America and Thor create a shockwave with Mjolnir and the shield that leaves Hydra operatives unconscious.

2012 | Shield vs. Mjolnir
Steve tests his shield against alien weapons for the first time when Loki and Thor come to Earth, both engaging Steve in battle. The shield resists the mighty blow of Thor's hammer.

1945–2011 | A Long Slumber
The shield goes down with Captain America over the Arctic, where it remains under the ice for almost 70 years.

1943–1945 | Stopping Hydra
With support from the Howling Commandos, Captain America leads the charge to stop the Red Skull and Hydra's forces and retake the Tesseract.

1943 | A Developing Power
Steve realizes the unique power of the shield. His belief in himself and his abilities grow as he fights in World War II.

1943 | A Worthy Gift
Howard Stark presents his creation to Steve: a shield crafted from vibranium. Steve doubts its invulnerability, but Peggy Carter tests the shield with bullets.

November 1943 | A Tour Prop
When Steve Rogers becomes Captain America in 1943, the government gives him a prop shield for his performances. Cap uses it to break American prisoners out of a Hydra facility.

CAP'S SHIELD

Captain America's shield has protected him in battles too numerous to count, but it is far more than just a piece of metal. Crafted by Howard Stark using ultra-rare vibranium, and chosen by Steve Rogers for its unique vibration-absorbing qualities, it was emblazoned with the colors of America. Virtually indestructible, the shield became a symbol of hope—first in World War II, then over six decades later, in the Battle of New York. Captain America's shield represents honor and doing the right thing no matter the cost, its presence communicating the promise that everything will be okay. With all that the shield symbolizes, it's a heavy mantle for anyone who picks it up, most recently Sam Wilson.

> "You had no right to give up that shield, Sam."
>
> **Bucky Barnes**

2016 | The Fighting Avengers
Recruited by Tony Stark, Peter Parker joins the battle at the Leipzig-Halle airport as Spider-Man and uses his webs to seize Cap's shield.

2016 | Cap Fights Iron Man
Captain America and Iron Man come to blows over the Winter Soldier. In the aftermath, Steve leaves the shield behind after Tony Stark tells him he is no longer worthy of it.

2016 | Confiscating the Shield
When Steve helps the Winter Soldier, a.k.a. Bucky Barnes, escape capture, the U.S. government takes his shield. However, Sharon Carter secretly returns it to him.

2016 | Vibranium on Vibranium
Ant-Man regains control of the shield and returns it to Cap, but Black Panther's vibranium claws scratch and damage its surface.

2023 | Tony Returns the Shield
After Scott Lang returns from the Quantum Realm with a possible solution to defeat Thanos, Tony rejoins the Avengers and gifts Steve the repaired shield.

2018 | A Different Shield
Cap fights without his shield in Wakanda, utilizing a stop-gap created by the Wakandans. The Avengers are defeated and Thanos snaps away half the universe.

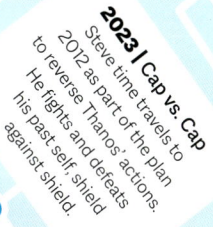

2023 | Battle of Earth
Cap wields the shield in combat with Thanos, and it sustains heavy damage from Thanos' sword, but the Avengers emerge victorious.

2023 | Cap vs Cap
Steve time travels to 2012 as part of the plan to reverse Thanos' actions. He fights and defeats his past self, shield against shield.

2023 | Passing it on
After Thanos is defeated by the Avengers, a now-elderly Steve decides to pass his shield, and the legacy it represents, on to Sam Wilson.

2024 | A Smithsonian Relic
Sam Wilson decides the shield should be preserved as part of Steve Rogers and Captain America's history and donates the artifact to the Smithsonian.

2024 | A New Cap
The U.S. government assigns Cap's shield to John Walker, who becomes the new Captain America. He uses it to publicly murder a member of the Flag Smashers terrorist group.

2024 | A Legacy Renewed
In the wake of John Walker's dismissal, Sam Wilson takes up the shield as the new Captain America, using it to end the Flag Smasher threat.

2024

"Sam, this is Isaiah. He was a hero,"
Bucky Barnes says. "One of the ones
Hydra feared the most."

Spring 2024 | Wilson and Barnes Join Forces

Bucky Barnes, who was as close to a brother as Steve Rogers had, is disgusted by John Walker's remarks. "You shouldn't have given up the shield," Barnes tells Sam Wilson, who shared his own brotherhood with Rogers. "You think it didn't break my heart to see them march him out there and call him 'the new Captain America'?" Wilson retorts. The pair argue on their way to Munich, where they disrupt a shipment of Flag Smasher supplies.

Sam Wilson to Bucky Barnes: "You're doing the staring thing again."

Spring 2024 | Isaiah Bradley, Revisited

To investigate how the super soldiers may have come to be, Bucky Barnes takes Sam Wilson to meet the only other person he knows who was part of such a program. Now elderly, Isaiah Bradley is still ferociously strong, which he demonstrates by angrily hurling a metal case into the wall of the Baltimore home he shares with his grandson, Eli. The Korean War veteran confirms that his genetic material was used for experimentation during years of wrongful imprisonment, but he wants no part of the work they are doing to stop those who may have been enhanced by it.

Spring 2024 | Super Soldier Menace

The Flag Smasher trucks are filled with medicines and supplies, nothing nefarious or destructive. But they are defended by a group of people with super soldier strength and resilience, among them a young woman named Karli Morgenthau, who lives among those displaced after the Blip. She destroys Wilson's Redwing drone, and her soldiers drive Wilson and Barnes back until John Walker arrives on the scene to lend a hand with Lemar Hoskins, who calls himself Battlestar. After the Flag Smashers escape, Walker and Hoskins propose working together, but Wilson and Barnes don't trust them.

John Walker and Lemar Hoskins pick up Sam Wilson and Bucky Barnes after their Flag Smashers run-in.

Spring 2024 | Zemo's Return

Bucky Barnes turns to another power player who can resolve the super soldier mystery. In defiance of international law, he helps Baron Helmut Zemo escape from his high-security penitentiary. They then use Zemo's considerable financial resources and knowledge of Hydra's operations to track how the Super Soldier Serum could have been produced and distributed. Zemo is delighted to oblige, if only to fulfill his agenda against all super soldiers. "I have no intention to leave my work unfinished," he says.

A masked Baron Zemo takes aim at a gas line during a fight against serum manufacturers.

Bucky Barnes, Baron Zemo, and Sam Wilson on the streets of Madripoor.

Spring 2024 | Mission to Madripoor

Zemo takes Wilson and Barnes to the island nation of Madripoor, where sources trace the Super Soldier Serum to a figure known as the Power Broker. There they cross paths with Sharon Carter, who tells them she has been forced to live in the underworld after helping Steve Rogers and Wilson during the Sokovia Accords conflict. She withholds that she is actually the Power Broker. Their leads take them to a Dr. Wilfred Nagel, who admits to being a former Hydra scientist who synthesized the serum from Isaiah Bradley's blood—but the Flag Smashers have stolen the vials he created. During a firefight, Zemo executes him to prevent the creation of more.

Karli Morgenthau, constantly on guard.

Spring 2024 | Morganthau Cornered

Wilson, Barnes, and Zemo track Karli Morgenthau to Riga during the funeral of "Mama" Donya Madani, a woman who was both a mother figure and symbol for the displaced peoples. In a settlement camp presided over by the Global Repatriation Council, they find many loyalists to the Flag Smashers. Wilson decides that reason might work on Morgenthau rather than force. He urges her to end the Flag Smashers' campaign of violence. "The people I'm fighting are trying to take your home, Sam, why are you here instead of stopping them?" Morgenthau asks. "I'm not your enemy. I agree with your fight," Wilson assures her. "I just can't get with the way you're fighting it."

Helmut Zemo, a true believer in eradicating super soldiers.

Spring 2024 | Serum Destroyed—Almost

John Walker storms in to arrest Karli Morganthau, and she feels set up and betrayed by Sam Wilson's effort at negotiation. "So this is what that was?" she says. "Tricking me until your back up arrived." In the fight Zemo finds her stash of Super Soldier Serum and crushes the vials under his feet. Karli flees, and Zemo is knocked out by Walker, who finds a remaining vial—and keeps it.

2024

Ayo and the Dora Milaje confront John Walker, Sam Wilson, and Bucky Barnes as they seek Helmut Zemo.

Spring 2024 | Zemo Escapes (Again)

In a conflict at Sam and Bucky's safehouse, John Walker orders them to turn over Zemo. Then the Dora Milaje intercede, also wanting Zemo returned to custody, preferably theirs. "Even if he is a means to your end... Time's up." Ayo says. During the fight over who will detain him, Zemo escapes through a hidden passage. Ayo temporarily deactivates and detaches Barnes' vibranium arm, reminding him of the debt he owes to Wakanda. Walker is humiliated and irritated at being so handily defeated by the Dora Milaje. "They weren't even super soldiers," he says.

Spring 2024 | The Desecrated Shield

John Walker, who has secretly infused himself with the Super Soldier Serum, tracks Karli Morganthau to the Flag Smashers headquarters at the GRC camp. During a fight, his ally Lamar Hoskins grabs Karli just before she can stab John, but she then punches Hoskins so hard in the chest that the impact hurls him into a concrete pillar, killing him instantly. An enraged Walker chases Nico, one of the other Flag Smashers, into a town square, where he strikes the fallen militant mercilessly with his shield as vengeance for Hoskins' death, bloodying the iconic relic.

John Walker and Bucky Barnes fight over Steve Rogers' shield.

John Walker's rage undermines the legacy of Captain America.

Spring 2024 | Walker Unhinged

Sam Wilson and Bucky Barnes demand John Walker hand over the shield after the execution of Nico, but a crazed Walker fights viciously, pulverizing Barnes and ripping off Wilson's wings. Falcon fires his jetpack to pull the shield from Walker's grip, and they finally subdue him, reclaiming the dishonored shield. Sam gives his damaged EXO-7 wings to Joaquin Torres to keep. In the U.S., an investigation of the incident begins while the GRC continues hunting Karli Morganthau and the Flag Smashers.

John Walker turns his back on his disciplinary hearing.

Spring 2024 | Discharged ... and Recruited

At the conclusion of an investigation into his conduct, John Walker is stripped of his Captain America title and authority, and given an other than honorable discharge. Only his previous service to the United States spares him a court martial. Unrepentant, he lashes out at the Senators who have rebuked him. "I only ever did what you asked of me!" he shouts. "You built me." Outside the hearing, Contessa Valentina Allegra de Fontaine approaches him. "Look, I would've killed the bastard too," she says. "You did the right thing, taking the serum. It has made you very very valuable to certain people."

Spring 2024 | Conflicted Feelings

Sam Wilson continues to train with the shield, even though he was urged by Isaiah Bradley to reject it. "They erased me and my history. But they've been doing that for 500 years. Pledge allegiance to that, my brother," Bradley tells him. "They will never let a Black man be Captain America, and even if they did, no self-respecting Black man would ever wanna be." Even Barnes admits that he and Rogers didn't understand what it would mean to hand the shield to Wilson. "I owe you an apology," Barnes says. Wilson tells him to start making amends to other people on his list.

Sam Wilson trains with the shield.

Bucky Barnes delivers Zemo to the Dora Milaje.

Spring 2024 | Zemo Returned

At the memorial for Sokovia, Bucky Barnes catches up with Helmut Zemo. The Dora Milaje arrive soon after and escort Zemo to the Raft where he can't so easily escape. "I took the liberty of crossing off my name in your book," Zemo tells Barnes. "I hold no grudges for what you thought you had to do." Ayo is less forgiving for Barnes' dalliance with the killer of King T'Chaka. "Make yourself scarce in Wakanda for the time being, White Wolf," she says. Barnes agrees, but asks for "another favor," a special set of Wakandan-forged wings for Sam Wilson.

Spring 2024 | "Your Brother is with the Ancestors"

The people of Wakanda—and the world at large—mourn the passing of King T'Challa. The young leader who helped open his society to the world, and who always made a courageous stand against those to whom life meant very little, dies from an illness even the great medical and technological advancements of his homeland could not cure. His sister, Shuri, struggles to genetically recreate the now-extinct Heart-Shaped Herb, hoping it will heal her brother, but he passes quickly. His mother, Ramonda, assumes the throne as queen, ruling with strength and confidence despite her grief. Those who knew and loved T'Challa, along with those who looked to him from afar with pride, share a profound and endless sorrow.

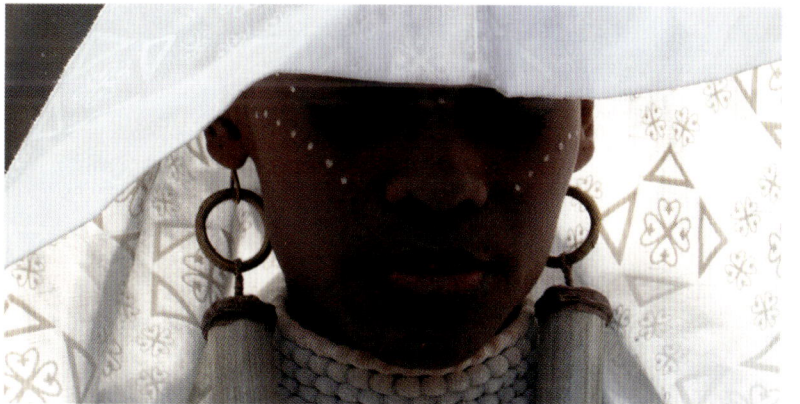

Shuri at King T'Challa's funeral.

255

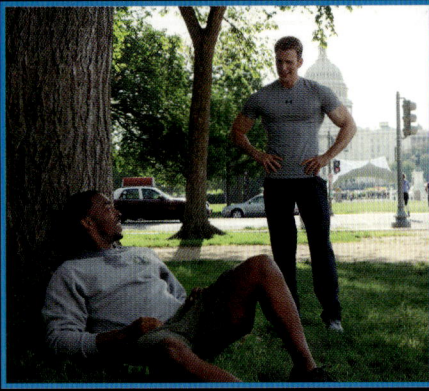

2014 | Taking Flight
Sam befriends Steve Rogers during an early morning run in Washington, D.C. Having connected over their shared experiences of combat, Steve turns to Sam for a place to lay low when he and Black Widow are on the run from a compromised S.H.I.E.L.D. Sam offers to join the fight against Hydra, knowing that helping Captain America is the best reason to get back into action. Sam helps save twenty million lives and then vows to help Steve find Bucky.

2015 | Pest Control
When Ant-Man breaks into the Avengers Compound to retrieve an important piece of tech, Falcon responds and fights the hero. Unfortunately for Falcon, Ant-Man uses his suit's technology to defeat Sam and retrieve the tech. An embarrassed Sam hopes that Steve never finds out about this event.

SAM WILSON

Loyal and fearless, Sam Wilson serves as a military pararescue, equipped with an experimental set of wings called the EXO-7 Falcon. Sam carries out many dangerous missions, but leaves the service after losing a close comrade. When Steve Rogers needs help, Sam doesn't hesitate to join the battle, becoming a close ally and his eventual successor to the mantle. Sam will always stand up for what is right, using his words as well as his many skills to fight for a better tomorrow.

2015 | Becoming an Avenger
While still chasing leads on Bucky, Sam is invited to Avengers Tower to celebrate the Avengers' victory against Baron Strucker. At first, Sam is happy to stay out of the Avengers, finding the unusual situations the team faces to be too much. However following Ultron's defeat, Falcon has a change of heart and joins the latest Avengers' roster alongside War Machine, Wanda Maximoff, and Vision.

BUCKY BARNES

A close childhood friend of Steve Rogers, Bucky Barnes also enlists in the Army during World II. The two men then take very different paths, with Steve becoming a U.S. super soldier and Bucky brainwashed and turned into a Hydra assassin. Decades later, the pair are reunited, and their unshakable bond allows them both to become better heroes. However, Bucky remains haunted by the terrible crimes he was forced to commit while trapped as a weapon of Hydra.

Late 1940s–2014 | The Winter Soldier
In spite of the odds, Bucky survives and is captured by Hydra. The organization transforms him into a super soldier, and subjects him to a memory wipe, mental conditioning, and equips him with a cybernetic arm. Now known only as the Winter Soldier, Bucky is cryogenically frozen and periodically awakened to conduct assassinations for Hydra.

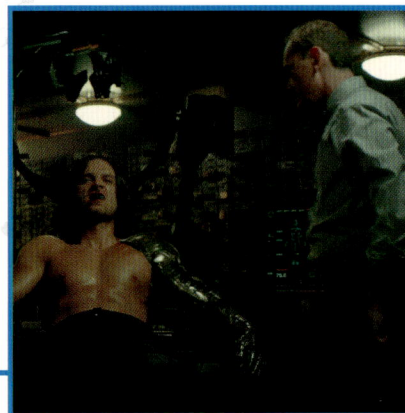

Mid-1940s | Captured
During WWII, Bucky Barnes and his unit are captured behind enemy lines, and experimented on by Hydra. Bucky is rescued by Steve, who is now the super soldier Captain America. Barnes becomes one of Steve's Howling Commandos, but their reunion is short-lived when Bucky is believed killed during a mission to capture Dr. Arnim Zola.

2014 | End of Hydra
After decades of service, the Winter Soldier assists with Hydra's attempt to take over Project Insight and kill millions. In the process, the Winter Soldier comes face-to-face with his old friend Steve, who manages to stop Hydra. Through his unwavering belief in Bucky, Steve convinces the Winter Soldier to leave Hydra behind. Unsure of his own identity, Bucky saves Cap's life and then disappears.

2016 | Team Cap
Falcon sides with Steve when he decides not to sign the Sokovia Accords, an act that legalizes UN oversight of the Avengers and splits the team in two. During the ensuing chaos, Sam ends up imprisoned alongside fellow allies Hawkeye, Wanda, and Ant-Man in the Raft—a prison for enhanced individuals. Steve later rescues some of them from captivity, with Falcon joining Steve's covert team.

2024 | A New Captain
Sam decides to turn down Steve's request, feeling that the title does not belong to him. However, Sam begins to change his mind when he meets the new Captain America, John Walker, who has been given the shield by the U.S. government and dishonors Steve's legacy. When the Flag Smashers, a group of anarchists, kidnap members of the GRC (Global Repatriation Council) in New York City, Sam decides to suit up as Captain America. He not only saves the day but stands up for marginalized people and questions the inactivity of those in power.

2018 | Battle in Wakanda
With the whole galaxy threatened, Falcon, Captain America, and Black Widow engage two of Thanos' minions who attack Vision and Wanda Maximoff in Edinburgh, Scotland. Following their victory, Sam and the team head to Wakanda to have the Mind Stone removed from Vision and destroyed. In an attempt to buy time for the operation, Falcon joins the battle in Wakanda, providing critical air support. However, Thanos emerges victorious, and Sam is one of many innumerable victims of the Snap.

2023 | Passing on the Mantle
Five years after the Snap, the remaining Avengers achieve the impossible, altering reality to bring those missing back into existence. Unfortunately, a past version of Thanos and his army then attack the Avengers Compound. Sam is one of many allies who answer the call, and thanks to Tony Stark's sacrifice, the invaders are defeated. Following the battle, Steve expresses his desire that Sam become Captain America.

2016-2018 | The White Wolf
Following Zemo's capture, Bucky heads to Wakanda where Shuri frees him of the Winter Soldier programming and he settles in the country. However, the respite is short-lived as Bucky is called back into service to help hold back Thanos' forces. Re-uniting with Steve once more, Bucky stands side-by-side with his friend in battle. He is then one of many who vanish when Thanos eliminates half of all life in the universe.

2024 | Falcon and Winter Soldier
Bucky is pardoned by the American government, but must meet with a therapist, who suggests that he try to make amends with those hurt by his actions as the Winter Soldier. While Bucky is outraged when Sam gives away Cap's shield, the two team up to take down the Flag Smashers, becoming friends along the way. Following their victory, Bucky finishes atoning and finds solace in his new bond with Sam.

2016 | Team Cap
In spite of trying to keep a low profile, Bucky Barnes is framed for the murder of King T'Chaka of Wakanda at the signing of the Sokovia Accords. When Bucky is captured, Baron Zemo re-activates his Winter Soldier conditioning, but he manages to break free with Steve's help once more. However, Bucky is still the main suspect, so Steve and his allies fight their former friends, led by Iron Man, to prevent Bucky from being imprisoned and to defeat the real villain, Zemo.

2023 | Saying Goodbye
After returning from the Blip, Bucky is one of the many allies transported to the Avengers Compound to help fight the 2014 version of Thanos. Following the battle, Bucky says goodbye to Steve Rogers before he leaves, and supports Sam becoming the next Captain America.

2024

A destructive earthen entity appears in Mexico.

Summer 2024 | The Long Con

The Skrulls Talos and Soren fill in for Nick Fury and Maria Hill, who are busy with events further afield—in Fury's case, in space. As they investigate the town of Ixtenco, Mexico, supposedly destroyed by a cyclone with a face, a man named Quentin Beck introduces himself. He claims to be an interdimensional warrior trying to save the world from gargantuan destructive creatures he calls "Elementals," which take the form of earth, wind, fire, and water. It's a ruse that Talos doesn't immediately detect.

Peter Parker is forever reminded of Tony Stark.

Summer 2024 | Vacation, All He Ever Wanted

As the first post-Blip school year at Midtown High draws to a close, Peter Parker prepares for a summertime European trip with some of his classmates, where he hopes to finally confess his romantic feelings to MJ. Eager to be more of a "friendly, neighborhood Spider-Man" and less of a world-saving hero after the death of his idol Tony Stark, Peter has focused his powers on local crimefighting and do-gooding while dodging cellphone calls from "Fury." He's looking forward to taking a break from being Spider-Man.

Spider-Man and May Parker at a community gathering.

Summer 2024 | Ahh, Venice...

After a stressful 8-hour flight to Italy, Peter Parker and his classmates soon find themselves threatened by a "water monster" that emerges from the Venice canals and pulverizes buildings and bridges. Peter realizes there is no rest for Super Heroes, and uses his webshooters to help hold up a collapsing clock tower, while the watery fiend appears to be subdued by a strange new hero who swoops in on a cloud of green smoke and remains masked behind an enigmatic spherical helmet.

An unknown Super Hero appears to battle a water goliath in Venice.

Peter Parker is drenched in the fight against the Elemental.

Summer 2024 | Do Not Ghost Nick Fury

Irritated at being avoided, "Fury" infiltrates Peter Parker's hotel for an impromptu sit-down with Spider-Man. "So good to finally meet you," he says. "I saw you at the funeral but it didn't seem like a good time to exchange numbers." He wants Parker to help deal with the rising Elemental threat, but also has unfinished business to resolve with the boy on behalf of Tony Stark.

"Nick Fury" is irked.

REDLINE ALERT!
Hi y'all! How did con-man Quentin Beck know this dimension's called "Earth-616" when the existence of the Multiverse hasn't been proven? Good question, y'all! Maybe Beck picked up Selvig's theories over a decade ago—but now I'm the one gettin' ahead of things.

Peter accidentally uses E.D.I.T.H. to call in a drone strike on the bus carrying him and his classmates. He only narrowly avoids disaster.

Summer 2024 | E.D.I.T.H.

Tony Stark left Peter Parker a pair of blue-tinted glasses that enable the wearer to access an artificial intelligence security protocol that can analyze surrounding tech and summon a fleet of weaponized drones from orbit. His hope was that Spider-Man could utilize these tools to help fill the void after Stark's own demise. It was a way for him to continue protecting the world, long after he is gone. (E.D.I.T.H. stands for "Even Dead, I'm The Hero.")

Mysterio makes a memorable impression.

Summer 2024 | L'Uomo Del Misterio

Italian news reports call the masked hero who defeated the water Elemental "L'uomo del misterio"—"the man of mystery"—and Quentin Beck embraces "Mysterio" as his heroic alter-ego's nickname. Peter Parker meets him when he reluctantly agrees to help defeat the Elemental threat, and finds a new mentor in Beck, who claims he is from Earth-833 and that he followed these monsters to Earth-616 after they demolished his own planet.

Peter Parker doesn't realize he's being manipulated.

2024

Summer 2024 | Overpowered and Outmatched

"Fury" steers the Midtown students to Prague, where Peter Parker struggles to keep up with Mysterio as they thwart what appears to be the volcanic fire Elemental. After webbing a strange object out of the firestorm (which MJ retrieves) the young hero does his best in a new stealth costume supplied by "Fury," which friend Ned Leeds dubs the "Night Monkey." Mysterio seems to annihilate the monster, but Spider-Man's confidence also takes a hit.

A handshake agreement between Peter Parker and Quentin Beck.

The Fire Elemental in Prague.

Summer 2024 | "That Wasn't So Hard!"

Quentin Beck celebrates receiving the glasses with the squad of other disgruntled Stark Industries employees who helped him create the Mysterio persona as a scam. Stark's decision to name Beck's realistic holograph technology BARF (Binary Augmented Retro-Framing) was only the beginning of his disgust. Each Stark employee harbors a gripe, a grievance, or moment of insult. The Mysterio con was devised as a way to profit from the superheroic tools they helped devise. With E.D.I.T.H. in their hands, it's time to menace the world—and cash in.

Summer 2024 | Surrendering E.D.I.T.H.

Peter Parker struggles with whether the multi-billion-dollar tactical defense system Stark entrusted to him is actually in the right hands. Not only did he fumble with the capabilities of E.D.I.T.H. and call in a potentially lethal drone strike on his own bus, he was also reluctant to leave MJ and fight the fire Elemental. Mysterio encourages him to return to normal life, and Peter agrees, voluntarily transferring the E.D.I.T.H. glasses to him. "The world needs the next Iron Man. And it's not gonna be me," Peter says.

Peter Parker learns that MJ has figured out his secret identity.

Peter Parker is fooled into giving up the glasses.

Summer 2024 | MJ Knows the Truth

During a late night walk through Prague, MJ reveals to Peter Parker that she knows he is Spider-Man. Peter tries to deny it, but she has been watching him, and she presents a fragment of a drone that shows the "Night Monkey" hero who helped fight the fire Elemental uses the same webs that Spidey has been spritzing around New York. She accidentally activates the device, which projects a hologram of a giant, smoky creature. Peter realizes Beck is a fraud who has been staging fake attacks.

All of the Elemental forces combine to attack Tower Bridge.

Spider-Man slings himself onto the bridge to stop the drones generating the Elemental monster.

Summer 2024 | The Tower Bridge Battle

In London, the Mysterio team uses the E.D.I.T.H. glasses to create their biggest illusion yet. All four Elementals appear to have joined together as one gigantic fire-water-rock-and-wind behemoth. From a Stark jet piloted by Happy Hogan, Spider-Man dives into the center of the storm and webs together enough drones to destabilize the monster hologram, revealing to the world that it is generated by a cloud of man-made war machines mounted with projectors.

Peter dives into the heart of the Elemental.

Summer 2024 | Mysterio Showdown

Spider-Man tracks down and confronts Quentin Beck, who commands the sentry drones to shoot at the webslinger—but Beck neglects to consider that he is in the line of fire too. The con artist is fatally wounded by the blasts, as Peter retakes the E.D.I.T.H. controls. When the program asks him if he wishes to execute the cancellation protocols, Peter shouts: "Do it! Execute them all!" A dying Beck records this on his phone, and as his last act uses those out-of-context words to cover for his Mysterio con and blame all the destruction on Spider-Man.

Spider-Man is besieged by the swarming cloud of drones.

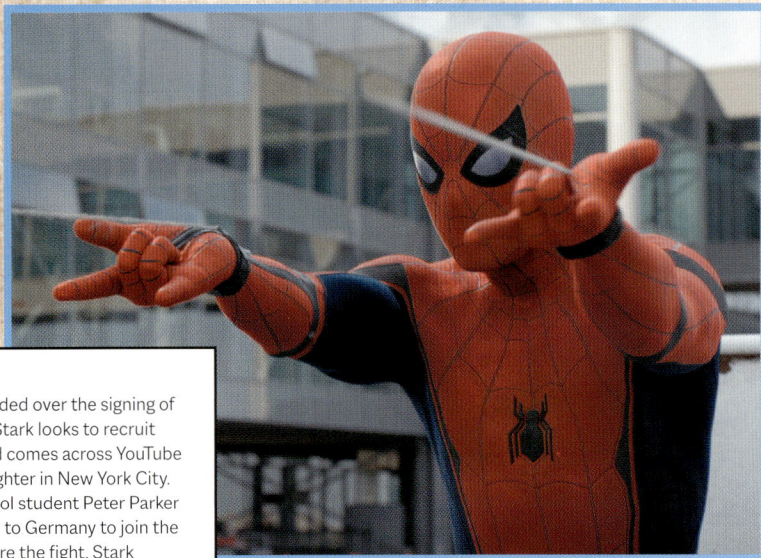

2016 | A New Suit

When the Avengers are divided over the signing of the Sokovia Accords, Tony Stark looks to recruit potential new members and comes across YouTube videos of a masked crime fighter in New York City. Tony tracks down high school student Peter Parker and persuades him to travel to Germany to join the battle at Leipzig-Halle. Before the fight, Stark provides Peter with an upgraded costume that utilizes Stark Industries technology.

2016 | Given and Taken Away

As a reward for Peter's assistance in the battle at Leipzig-Halle, Tony allows him to keep the Spider-Man suit, but tells him he's not ready to be an Avenger. Peter puts himself in danger when he takes on the villainous Vulture on a Staten Island ferry. As a result, Tony takes back the suit and Peter reverts to using his original homemade suit (1). When Peter defeats the Vulture, Tony offers Peter a spot on the Avengers with the Iron Spider suit (2), but Peter turns him down. When Peter returns home, he finds the original Stark suit in his bedroom (3).

SPIDER-MAN'S SUITS

Peter Parker's spider suits are not just tools he wears into battle—they also symbolize his evolution as a young man and a Super Hero. After being bitten by a radioactive spider, the gifted teen uses his technical expertise and newfound powers to do good, protecting his community from crime. His life changes forever when tech billionaire Tony Stark recruits him on a mission for the Avengers. Starting out as a protégé of Stark, and equipped with the best technology Stark Industries can provide, Peter soon finds himself living in the shadow of Tony's legacy. But Peter then forges his own path, through pain and loss, in the process learning the true meaning of heroism and sacrifice.

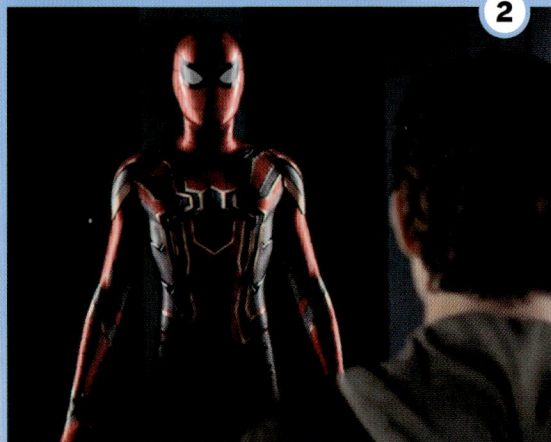

2018 | Into Space

Peter is on his way to a class trip, when his "Peter tingle" alerts him to the arrival of one of Thanos' Q-Ships and the Children of Thanos, Ebony Maw and Cull Obsidian. Peter sneaks off the school bus and into his Stark suit, to help Iron Man rescue Doctor Strange from Ebony Maw (1). When Peter is accidentally beamed up to the Q-Ship with Strange, Tony sends the Iron Spider suit to encase Peter before he runs out of air as the ship leaves the atmosphere. Peter wears the suit during the confrontation with Thanos on Titan (2) before both Peter and the suit disappear in the Snap.

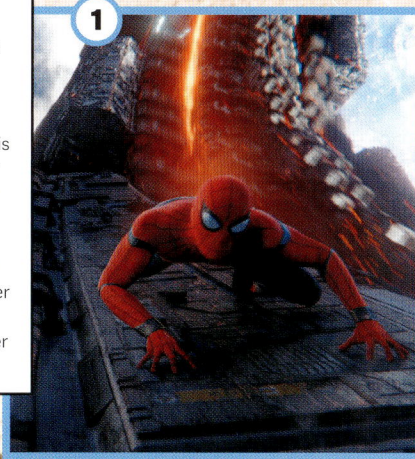

2023 | A Hero Returns

When the Avengers reverse the Snap Peter returns wearing the Iron Spider suit. He joins the Avengers in a final showdown against Thanos, who has attacked the Avengers Compound in search of the Nano Gauntlet Tony created to undo the Snap. Peter is entrusted to protect the Nano Gauntlet and activates the Instant Kill Mode of the Iron Spider suit. He fights his way through the Outriders to hand the Nano Gauntlet to Captain Marvel.

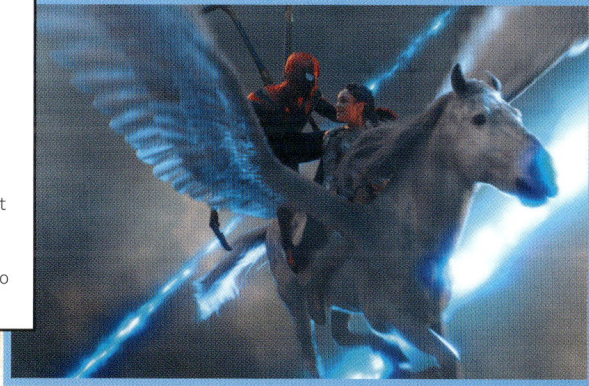

2024 | Adventures Abroad

Months after Tony Stark's death, Peter has resumed his Super Hero duties wearing the Iron Spider suit but feels intense pressure from the public to fill Tony's shoes (1). When Peter goes on a school trip to Europe he decides to leave his suit behind, but May secretly packs the first Stark suit for him. S.H.I.E.L.D. later provides Peter with a stealth suit in Austria (2). He then creates a new upgraded suit using Stark Industries technology in order to battle Mysterio in London (3).

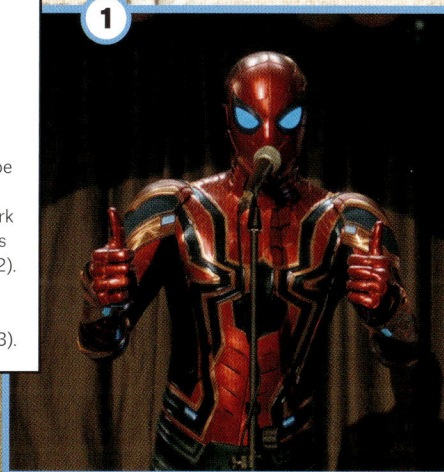

2024 | Multiversal Suits

Peter is on a date with MJ when his true identity is exposed posthumously by Mysterio. A Mysterio supporter throws green paint, staining his upgraded suit (1), and unable to wash out the stain, Peter wears the suit inside out, giving it a black and gold appearance due to the circuitry from the suit's technology (2). When Peter assists in creating a new chip for Doctor Octopus, the doctor reallocates the nanites from his tentacles that had melded with the Iron Spider suit (3) and places them into Peter's upgraded suit, converting it into a new, integrated suit (4). After Doctor Strange casts the spell erasing Peter's existence from the world's memory, Peter creates a second homemade suit to resume his duties as Spider-Man (5).

2024

Summer 2024 | First Kiss

After saving his friends in London, Peter Parker and his Midtown High classmates return to New York. He confesses his other secret to MJ—his love for her. She feels it too, explaining: "I wasn't just watching you because I thought you were Spider-Man." He takes her for a celebratory swing through the skyscraper canyons of Manhattan (an experience that she hates and vows never to do again).

A new star-spangled man with a plan.

A terrified MJ soars through the city with Peter Parker.

Summer 2024 | GRC Attack in New York

Georges Batroc is hired by the Flag Smashers to stage an attack on the Global Repatriation Council just as they are about to vote to forcibly repatriate twenty million refugees of the Blip. Sharon Carter, a.k.a. the Power Broker, arranged the deal, mainly to get a spy close to Karli Morganthau to track any Super Soldier Serum remnants—or get revenge for their loss. As the hostage crisis begins, Sam Wilson armors himself in his Wakandan-made red, white, and blue wings and takes the Captain America shield into battle.

A bogus message sent by Quentin Beck turns the world against Peter Parker.

Summer 2024 | Spider-Man Exposed!

The deceptively edited video that Quentin Beck recorded and sent as he was dying is published on TheDailyBugle.net. It reveals Spider-Man's secret identity as Peter Parker, framing the webslinger as not only responsible for Beck's death, but also for the series of fake "Elemental" attacks that were actually deadly drone strikes. TheDailyBugle.net's high-strung host J. Jonah Jameson stokes the backlash, declaring Mysterio a hero and Peter Parker "public enemy number one."

Sam Wilson flies to the rescue, merging his Falcon skills with Captain America.

Summer 2024 | A New Captain America

Sam Wilson infiltrates the GRC building and scatters the militants and their hostages, intercepting a fleeing helicopter to rescue one group of them. Bucky Barnes and a rogue John Walker join the fight. Karli Morganthau tells Walker: "I didn't mean to kill your friend. I don't want to hurt people who don't matter." This only enrages Walker further. "You don't think Lamar's life mattered?" he snarls. The two brawl, but Morganthau escapes by forcing Walker to help rescue a van full of hostages rather than pursue her.

Batroc maintains only tentative loyalties.

Summer 2024 | A Cascade of Betrayals

Karli Morganthau is confronted by Sharon Carter for stealing the Super Soldier Serum. "You wanted to control a world that hurt you. I wanted to change it," Morganthau explains. "Without your super soldiers how much 'power' does the Power Broker really have?" Batroc ambushes Morganthau, and demands quadruple payment from Carter to protect the Power Broker's secret. But she is done bargaining with betrayers. She shoots and kills Batroc and is wounded herself in the firefight.

Summer 2024 | Karli Morganthau's End

With most of the hostages saved, and Bucky Barnes and John Walker rounding up the remaining Flag Smashers, Sam Wilson enters the underground and tries to talk Morganthau down from killing Sharon Carter. Karli resists, and when they fight Wilson tries to protect himself but refuses to hit back. Morganthau gains the upper hand and aims a gun at him but Carter shoots her down. With her final words, Morganthau says, "I'm sorry."

Karli Morganthau fights a reluctant Sam Wilson.

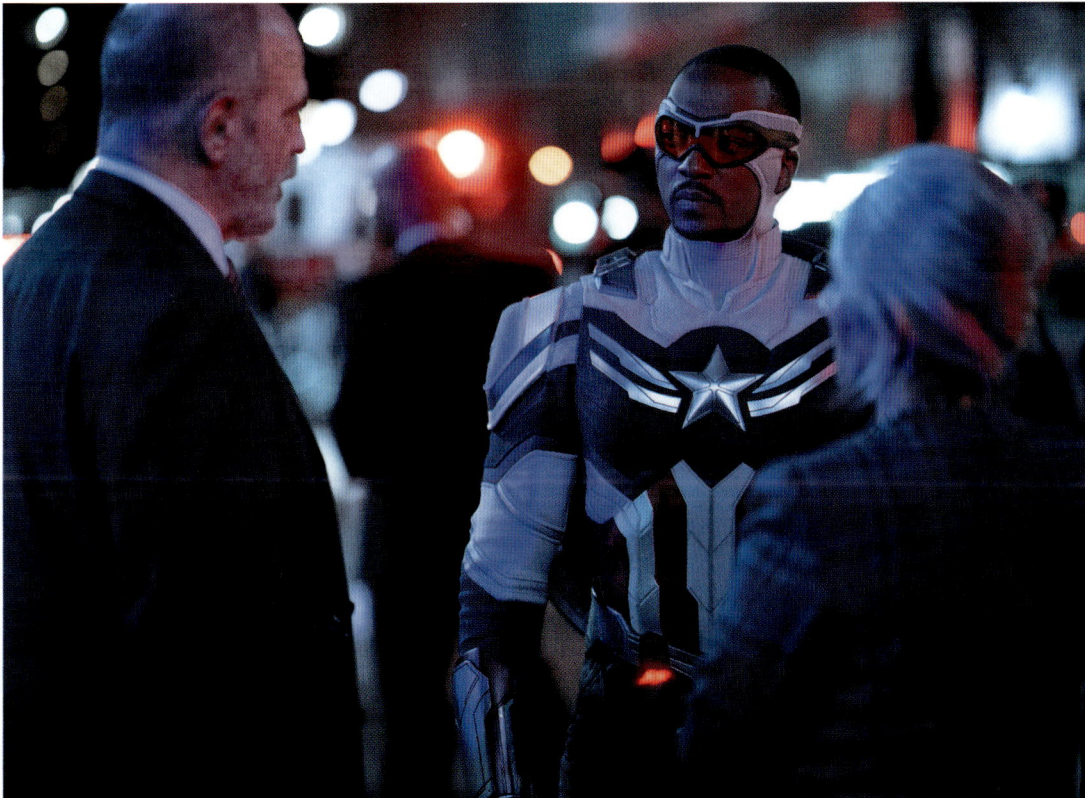

Sam Wilson makes impassioned remarks to the Global Repatriation Council.

Summer 2024 | "People Believed in Her ..."

Sam Wilson carries Karli Morganthau's body outside and flies her down to rescue personnel, but it is too late. He is swarmed by journalists, and by the leaders of the GRC, whom he admonishes for calling her a "terrorist." "Your peacekeeping troops carrying weapons are forcing millions of people into settlements around the world. What do you think those people are going to call you?" he says. "People believed in her cause so much, they helped her defy the strongest governments in the world." His words, broadcast around the world, rally global pressure on the GRC to re-evaluate its actions.

2024

Captain America's words are broadcast around the world.

Summer 2024 | Setting an Example

Sam Wilson pushes back when GRC leaders insist he doesn't understand the difficult choices they are forced to make. "I'm a Black man carrying the stars and stripes. What don't I understand?" Wilson asks. "Every time I pick this thing up, I know there are millions of people out there who are going to hate me for it. Even here now. I feel it. The stares. The judgment. And there's nothing I can do to change that. Yet I'm still here. The only power I have is that I believe we can do better. We can't demand that people step up if we don't meet them halfway."

Summer 2024 | Sharon Carter's Pardon

The United States government offers a public apology to Sharon Carter, a pardon, and a new position in the intelligence service. "The Carter name has always been synonymous with service and trust," the apology states, invoking her late great-aunt, Peggy Carter. Carter accepts—and the Power Broker is back in business. "Start lining up our buyers," she tells an associate. "Super soldiers might be off the menu, but we're about to have full access to government secrets, prototype weapons, you name it. Should be something for everyone."

Sharon Carter, a.k.a. the Power Broker, makes a move.

Zemo orchestrates his attacks even from behind bars.

Valentina recruits John Walker as the "U.S. Agent."

Summer 2024 | Zemo's Revenge

Most of the surviving Flag Smashers in U.S. custody are killed in a car bombing while being transported to the Raft. Zemo orchestrated their demise from behind bars with help from his aide-de-camp Oeznik. "Looks like our friend Zemo kinda got the last laugh," Valentina tells John Walker, whom she has now recruited and designated "U.S. Agent." "I couldn't have arranged it better—or did I?"

Summer 2024 | Bucky's Confession

Heeding Sam Wilson's advice, Bucky Barnes finally confesses to his friend Yori Nakajima that he killed his son while enthralled to Hydra as the Winter Soldier. The admission ends their friendship, but provides the old man with the explanation he wanted about why his son was killed. R.J. truly was an innocent bystander, killed for no other reason than witnessing the attack.

Bucky Barnes confesses to Yori Nakajima.

Sam Wilson escorts Isaiah Bradley and his grandson Eli through the museum exhibit.

Summer 2024 | Isaiah Bradley's Belated Honors

Sam Wilson visits Isaiah Bradley and his grandson Eli. The old man admits he saw Wilson's actions and begrudgingly praises him. "So, a Black Captain America, huh?" he says. "Damn right," Wilson answers. He takes the Bradleys to the Smithsonian, where the Captain America exhibit now includes a statue of Isaiah and a tribute to his heroism and service—as well as a public accounting of the wrongs perpetrated against him. "Now they'll never forget what you did for this country," Sam says as an overcome Isaiah embraces him.

Fall 2024 | Guilt by Association

Anti-Spidey protestors harass Peter, MJ, and Ned as school resumes at Midtown High. As time passes during their senior year, the fallout only worsens. The school itself is divided about whether Spider-Man is a hero or villain. Some adore him; others abhor him—and everyone aligned with him is hunted and harassed. Peter, MJ, and Ned's college prospects are also at risk, since no university wants to invite this drama to campus.

Peter Parker isn't used to this attention or scrutiny.

Summer 2024 | A Really Good Lawyer

Federal agents from the Department of Damage Control arrest Peter, but Hell's Kitchen attorney Matt Murdock takes on the case and provides a solid defense through tough legal maneuvering. Plus, no real evidence exists to back up Quentin Beck's claim. Formal charges against Peter are dropped, but Murdock warns that the court of public opinion has already convicted him. During his visit, a brick is thrown through May's apartment window by a Mysterio truther. Despite being blind, Murdock somehow catches it in mid-air, which astounds Peter.

Fall 2024 | The Two Hulks

Bruce Banner takes a road trip with his cousin, a Los Angeles lawyer named Jennifer Walters. Banner is patiently enduring her theories about Steve Rogers' personal life when their vehicle is run off the road by a Sakaaran spacecraft that has been tracking him. Banner is wearing an inhibitor that keeps him in human form, so he is badly injured in the crash. When Walters tries to help him, blood from his wounds seeps into a cut on her arm. Due to their similar genetic makeup, her cells merge with the gamma-enhanced blood, causing her strength to increase, her skin to turn green, and her body to rapidly metamorphose. A new Hulk is born.

Jennifer Walters goes green.

2024

Hulk and She-Hulk train together at Bruce's beach house.

Fall 2024 | New Best Friend

At the beach house in Mexico that Tony Stark built for him, Smart Hulk ("I didn't come up with it. You never have a choice with these names.") helps Jennifer Walters come to grips with life as a Hulk. He is stunned to see that his cousin can shift from human form to her giant green body at will and without losing her personality. Walters welcomes a few of his practical tips to reinforce her furniture, find an apartment with tall ceilings, and pick out a more indestructible wardrobe. "Spandex is your best friend," Banner explains.

Fall 2024 | Birth of a Celestial

The planet experiences physical upheaval when the Emergence of the Celestial Tiamut begins. As orchestrated from afar by the celestial Arishem, the colossal being's incubation within the center of the Earth overheats the planet's core, melting glaciers and unleashing creatures known as Deviants who have been trapped in ice for centuries, sending them back into a world that had forgotten their existence.

The colossal eyes of Arishem.

Fall 2024 | Sersi's Quiet Life

Sersi lives in London as a professor, hiding her powers as a matter-shifting Eternal even from her mortal boyfriend, Dane Whitman. For his birthday, Sersi presents him with a ring emblazoned with his family's ancient seal. That night he learns the truth about her when they are attacked by the resurgent Deviants, and her ex-love Ikaris arrives to help fend off the attack. Sersi and the illusion-making Eternal, Sprite, are shocked that Kro was able to heal so quickly from the wounds they inflicted.

Dane Whitman, Sersi, and Sprite face a ferocious Deviant attack in Camden, London.

Ajak is attacked by Deviants released by thawing glaciers.

Fall 2024 | The End of Watch

The millennia-long mission of the Eternals is finally at its end, but their leader Ajak now feels doubts about the destruction of the world she has grown to love. She had confided her fears in Ikaris, but he remains loyal to the Celestial cause and sees her concern as a betrayal. Ikaris murders Ajak by pushing her into a lakebed where a pack of Deviants have gathered after being freed from their melting glacial prison. Their leader, Kro, demonstrates a new ability, absorbing Ajak's healing powers after consuming her lifeforce. The Deviants can now evolve. Ikaris returns Ajak's body to her farm in South Dakota, and seeks out his fellow Eternals as the Emergence gets underway.

Days before the other Eternals arrive, Ikaris places Ajak's lifeless body outside her farmhouse.

Fall 2024 | The Slain Eternal

The trio of Eternals leave London to visit Ajak's farm, seeking guidance about the return of the Deviants. Sersi and Sprite are horrified to find her dead, while Ikaris shrewdly obscures his crime. Sersi inherits a communication sphere from Ajak's remains, allowing her to connect to their Celestial leader Arishem. She puzzles over his admonition: "It is time." Time for what? She intends to reunite the Eternals to solve the mystery of Ajak's murder, still unaware that the Emergence will destroy the Earth within a week.

Fall 2024 | Protecting Only to Destroy

Sersi uses her newfound line of communication with Arishem to discern the true nature of their mission. New Celestials must be born every billion years. These galactic beings generate suns, creating energy for new worlds that in turn create countless forms of life. But to be born, new Celestials must emerge from a cocoon nourished by the lifeforce of intelligent beings. The Eternals were created to protect those souls from decimation by the Deviants—but only so the Celestial can grow and one day destroy that world, as will soon happen to Earth.

Sersi grapples with the knowledge that has been revealed to her.

Fall 2024 | Eternals Again, Always

The Eternals locate Kingo in India, where he is a longtime (very long) Bollywood star whose mortal assistant, Karun Patel, is aware of the Eternals and their powers. The team also find the warriors Gilgamesh and Thena living together in the desert of Australia. He is a loving caregiver for Thena, whose mind is fractured with Mahd Wy'ry illness, a side effect of her memories being repeatedly erased over the ages by the Celestials. The Eternals are unaware this amnesia is forced on them after each Emergence, to keep them from becoming protective of their worlds, which would threaten the Celestials within.

Kingo stages a musical number for his latest film.

Gilgamesh, an epic warrior and inspiration for one of humanity's earliest recorded myths.

Fall 2024 | Death of Gilgamesh

While recruiting the mind-controlling Eternal, Druig, from his colony of faithful followers in the Amazon, Gilgamesh is killed in a Deviant attack. Kro absorbs his extraordinary strength, taking on a more humanoid form. Ikaris believes the rampaging Deviants will serve as a useful distraction for his fellow Eternals, allowing the Emergence to continue, but they soon begin plans to unite and halt the birth of the Celestial.

269

2024

Fall 2024 | Someone to Love

The inventor Phastos is found by his fellow Eternals living a modest suburban life with a mortal husband, Ben, and young son, Jack. The sorrow he once felt after humanity's creation of nuclear weapons has been softened and replaced by love for his family. Now, he will do anything to save them.

Phastos fixes his son's bicycle.

Thena and Phastos look on as Sersi approaches an eruption triggered by the Emergence.

Fall 2024 | The Eternals Divided

Ikaris violently defies his fellow Eternals. Sprite, who is embittered after existing in child-like form for millennia, aligns with him, eager to put this life behind her. Kingo chooses to remain neutral and sits out the fight. That leaves only Phastos, Sersi, Thena, Druig, and Makkari to link minds and put Tiamut back to sleep—all while fending off their own former friends.

Makkari in the *Domo* with her collection.

Fall 2024 | Stalling the Emergence

At an archaeological dig in modern Iraq, the Eternals gather within their buried *Domo* starship, where their final teammate, the ultra-fast Makkari, is waiting. Phastos devises a plan for the Eternals to link minds through Druig and fuse their powers to postpone the Emergence without harming the Celestial within, instead putting Tiamut into a prolonged hibernation.

Fall 2024 | Tiamut Rises

The Earth shudders as the head and fingertips of its encased Celestial break out of its planetary shell in the Indian Ocean. Kro and Ikaris separately attack the Eternals, severing their links with one another and allowing the Emergence to continue.

The hand of Tiamut bursts through the Earth's crust.

270

Kro in his final evolutionary form.

Fall 2024 | Kro Cut Down

Thena slays Kro while battling within a cave on an island adjacent to the Emergence. Kro explains that the Deviants and Eternals share a history as warriors created by higher powers to be expendable. Neither was ever fully free. Now whatever life Kro had is extinguished by Thena's blades.

Fall 2024 | Sprite Reborn, Ikaris Immolated

Sersi uses the last flashes of the Eternals' linked minds and powers to transmute Sprite into a human being, allowing her to finally age, but at the cost of becoming mortal. Ikaris is overwhelmed by regret for murdering Ajak and warring with his fellow Eternals, and retreats from Earth, flying closer and closer to the sun until he incinerates. Thena, Makkari, and Druig depart Earth aboard the *Domo*, intending to tell other Eternals the truth about their existence and the Celestials.

Sprite is reunited with Sersi.

Tiamut is turned to stone before the Emergence is complete.

Fall 2024 | The Petrified Colossus

Despite his loyalty to the Celestials, Ikaris cannot bring himself to kill Sersi, haunted by his enduring love for her. Finally, he recognizes that he cares for something greater than their mission. The Eternals combine their energies to empower Sersi and halt Tiamut's birth. However, it is too late to merely put Tiamut back to sleep. Supercharged by their powers, Sersi uses her matter-shifting ability to turn the nascent Celestial into stone.

Arishem demands answers about the halted Emergence.

October 2024 | Trial by Arishem

Called forth by the Eternals' destruction of Tiamut, Arishem arrives at Earth and summons Sersi, Phastos, and Kingo into his clutches. But the Celestial regards himself as fair, and will conduct an assessment. "You have chosen to sacrifice a Celestial for the people of this planet," Arishem declares. "I will spare them, but your memories will show if they are worthy to live. And I will return ... for judgment."

271

2024

Pip introduces Eros.

Fall 2024 | *Domo* Interlopers

The Eternals aboard the *Domo* are visited by a revolution-minded Eternal named Eros, nicknamed "Starfox," royal prince of Titan and brother of Thanos. He and his effusive sidekick, Pip, warn that the other Eternals of Earth are in trouble, then offer their assistance.

Fall 2024 | A Doctor's Appointment

Peter Parker visits Doctor Strange at the New York Sanctum to ask for a favor: will he please use sorcery to undo Mysterio's revelation of Spider-Man's true identity. Strange no longer has the Time Stone, but he proposes using the Runes of Kof-Kol, which are "a standard spell of forgetting" to help Peter reclaim his privacy. "It won't turn back time, but at least people will forget you were ever Spider-Man." Sorcerer Supreme Wong warns against the practice, saying it "travels the dark borders between known and unknown reality."

Dane Whitman, who has a history with a particular blade.

Fall 2024 | "Sure You're Ready?"

After being advised by Sersi to reconnect with his estranged uncle and make amends, Dane Whitman embraces his family legacy by opening a case containing a family heirloom—a mysterious sword. As Whitman regards the weapon, a voice asks if he is ready for what it bestows.

Peter Parker keeps interrupting Doctor Strange's complicated spell.

Fall 2024 | Runes of Ruin

Strange pompously ignores Wong, believing Parker is owed a break and confident he can control a spell used for "brainwashing the entire world." Peter Parker repeatedly disrupts Doctor Strange's spell as he realizes that everyone, including May, Happy Hogan, and MJ and Ned, will cease to know he is Spider-Man. Altering the spell mid-casting is dangerous, but Strange tries to oblige—too many times. As various parameters of the spell are changed, it becomes unstable, perforating the barrier between universes. Strange traps the spell in a mystical lockbox, and refuses to continue.

Otto Octavius grabs a Peter Parker he doesn't recognize.

Green Goblin arrives from another universe.

Chaos and destruction on the bridge.

Fall 2024 | Onslaught of Villains

Strange's spell inadvertently conjures several figures from alternate universes who were aware of their own Spider-Man's true identity as Peter Parker, among them the metal-tentacled Dr. Otto Octavius and Norman Osborn's hovering Green Goblin. As Peter tracks down the assistant Vice Chancellor of MIT in a traffic jam, and pleads with her to admit Ned and MJ, the villains attack.

The Lizard lashes out.

Fall 2024 | Unfamiliar Faces

Green Goblin escapes, but Doctor Strange successfully captures Doc Ock in a mystical prison cell in the Sanctum's undercroft basement. He also catches a "slimy, green son of a gun" known as The Lizard, a.k.a. the genetically mutated Dr. Curt Connors. Curiously, these Spider-Man foes don't recognize Peter Parker as their Peter Parker. There appear to be many variations of Spider-Man in the Multiverse.

2024

Spider-Man wields the magic gauntlets enchanted by Doctor Strange while Electro charges up behind him.

Fall 2024 | Electro and Sandman

Strange insists the outsiders must be returned to their own universes to protect "the fabric of reality." While patrolling for Green Goblin, Peter happens upon Max Dillon, a.k.a. "Electro," who is supercharging his body by harvesting electricity from high-tension wires. He also encounters Flint Marko, a petty thief known as Sandman, whose body consists of particles of earth and rock. Peter Parker detains both alt-universe escapees in the undercroft.

Fall 2024 | Death Sentence Reprieve

Norman Osborn suppresses his Green Goblin madness and shows up at the shelter where May Parker works. He seeks help—not bloodshed. When Peter Parker learns that many of these troubled figures are fated to die in combat with their respective Spider-Men, he releases them from imprisonment and works to find technological ways to cure them of their nefarious impulses.

Part of Norman Osborn wants help; the other part wants power.

Fall 2024 | Mirror Dimension Quarrel

Peter Parker's save-the-villains plan leads to a clash with Doctor Strange, who's certain Peter will only damage the already unstable Multiverse. Spider-Man leaves the Doctor webbed up within the Mirror Dimension while he tries things his way, stealing the sorcerer's spell-casting sling ring and the Macchina di Kadavus, the relic that contains the corrupted and incomplete memory spell. If the plan goes awry, the relic will reverse the spell and instantly send all the troublemakers back to their own universes.

Doctor Strange separates Peter Parker's astral form from his body.

Peter Parker thinks he can use this Stark device to create ways to rehabilitate villains.

Fall 2024 | The Fabricator

Peter Parker uses a Stark Industries device in Happy Hogan's condo that can "analyze, design, and construct basically anything" to create a chip that separates Doc Ock from the sinister influence of his arms and an energy dissipator that can cure Electro of his high-energy rage. Norman Osborn assures Peter he is "something of a scientist" himself, and aids in the research until his Green Goblin side overtakes him.

Fall 2024 | The Death of May Parker

May Parker is mortally wounded by Goblin's glider. A tearful Peter Parker wishes he had sent the villains back to their doomed fates instead of trying to save them, but May insists he did the right thing. "You have power. And with great power there must also come great responsibility," she says. These are among her final words. May succumbs to her injuries as Peter comforts her and cries out for help.

Fall 2024 | Not Curses, but Gifts

A giddy Goblin persuades the other villains to reject being "fixed." The Arc Reactor that powers the Stark fabricator supercharges Electro like never before. The Lizard runs amok, and Sandman runs away while J. Jonah Jameson's TheDailyBugle.net news crew captures footage of the carnage. Only Doc Ock remains fully cured of his anti-social traits, but he also flees the scene.

Peter Parker lunges for the Goblin's pumpkin bomb.

Ned tests his abilities with a sling ring.

Fall 2024 | Help Arrives

Harnessing his own latent mystical abilities (and Doctor Strange's stolen sling ring) Ned Leeds begins generating portals in search of Peter Parker. What he and MJ discover is not their friend exactly, but two other versions of Peter Parker who were drawn into this universe along with their villains. One of them says he has been trying to locate the Peter of this universe ever since his arrival. "I just have this sense that he needs my help," he says. "Our help," the other Peter agrees.

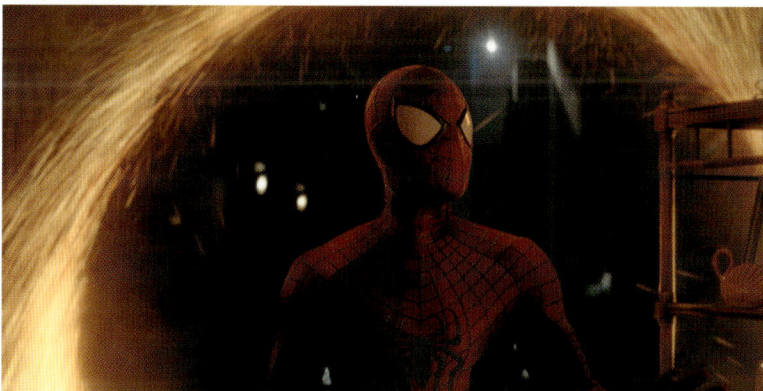
Spider-Man emerges from Ned's portal, but it is not the Peter Parker that Ned and MJ know.

A third Spider-Man, an older veteran of many battles, also lends his assistance.

2024

Fall 2024 | Shared History, Shared Powers

Ned and MJ find their Peter Parker grieving on his favorite rooftop and introduce him to the alternate Peter Parkers. They have slightly differing abilities, but each has experienced devastating loss. One Peter talks about the murder of his Uncle Ben, while the other shares his grief at failing to protect his love, Gwen Stacy, during a fatal fall. Each also heard a version of May's "great responsibility" advice in their own times of confusion and heartache. They decide to join together—devising ways to save the villains rather than destroy them.

Three Spider-Men from different universes join forces.

The web-slinging trio swing into action.

Fall 2024 | Spider-Team!

The three Peters unite Avengers-style (amplifying each other's strengths while bickering incessantly about who is Peter #1, #2, or #3). They take out the villains one by one, starting with the Sandman, who is returned to his original form after being hit with a curing device. Doctor Octopus appears at the fight to ambush Electro with the energy dissipator, powering him down to mild-mannered Max Dillon. Lizard bites through the canister containing his own antidote, restoring him to Dr. Curt Connors.

Electro makes his presence felt as Peter Parker stands watch atop the statue.

Fall 2024 | The Battle on Liberty Island

Before swinging into battle, the trio of Peter Parkers use their shared ingenuity to finish a series of "fixes" for Green Goblin, Electro, Sandman, and The Lizard. This universe's Peter Parker calls in to TheDailyBugle.net to get the message out that the villains can find him at the Statue of Liberty—"a place that represents second chances."

Doctor Strange and the box containing his warped spell.

Fall 2024 | Doctor Strange Returns

Doctor Strange is furious after dangling for 12 hours in the Mirror Dimension. He arrives on the scene to reverse his memory spell in the Macchina di Kadavus, sending them all back to their respective universes. The Green Goblin throws a pumpkin bomb that destroys the box and unleashes the spell before Strange can do so, collapsing the scaffolding around the Statue of Liberty and sending the Captain America shield that's been attached to the torch thundering to the shoreline.

Peter Parker and Green Goblin on the ruins of a redesigned Statue of Liberty.

Fall 2024 | Goblin Spared

Peter #2 stops the Peter Parker of this universe from killing Green Goblin as vengeance for May's death. When Norman Osborn is finally restored by the serum that liberates him from his demented alter-ego, he is appalled by his actions. "What have I done …?" he asks.

Fall 2024 | Peter's Farewells

As Doctor Strange conjures the new spell, Peter Parker thanks his two Spider-Man brothers then webs over to say goodbye to Ned and MJ. "You're going to forget who I am," he tells them. "I'm going to come and find you and I'll explain everything. I'll make you remember me. It'll be like none of this ever happened." MJ says she loves him, kisses him goodbye, and asks him to tell her the same when he sees her again.

Fall 2024 | The Multiverse Breaks Forth

Luminous violet cracks appear in the sky, crowded with inhabitants of other universes who know that Peter Parker is Spider-Man—including enemies. Reality is disintegrating, and the only fix for the out-of-control spell is a new one that will completely erase knowledge of who Peter Parker is—for everyone, everywhere. Strange warns that it would make it so Peter Parker never existed. "Do it," Peter tells him, without hesitation.

Doctor Strange holds back a Multiverse rupture with a spell over Lady Liberty.

2024

Fall 2024 | More Multiverse Multiplicity

America Chavez is lost. The teenage girl with the power to involuntarily open star-shaped tears between universes has been on the run for years, hopscotching through more than 70 parallel realities ever since her mothers were drawn into a vortex she accidentally created as a young child. Now she is being hunted by a supernatural creature with glowing runes on its ribbon-like limbs, which apparently seeks to harness her unique ability for itself.

Fall 2024 | Starting Over

A new day dawns, one in which no one has ever heard of Peter Parker. The existence of the anonymous, masked Super Hero Spider-Man is still widely known—and J. Jonah Jameson is still denouncing him for the calamity at the Statue of Liberty—but people the world over have forgotten they ever knew his true identity.

America Chavez flees through the Multiverse.

Fall 2024 | The *Book of Vishanti*

Chavez makes an ally out of an alternate version of Doctor Strange, who is then killed by Chavez's pursuer while leading her to the *Book of Vishanti*, a text that conveys ultimate power to its user. The book is hidden between worlds in a dreamlike realm known as the Gap Junction. In desperation, Chavez creates a portal, drawing her and the corpse of "Defender" Strange into Universe-616 before the creature can seize them—but also before Chavez can secure the book.

The *Book of Vishanti* in the Gap Junction.

Doctor Strange at the wedding
of Dr. Christine Palmer.

Fall 2024 | Christine Palmer's Wedding

It's a hard day for Doctor Strange. Not only did he sleep poorly, plagued by visions of a young woman, a ribbon monster, and his own death, but today he is attending the wedding of Dr. Christine Palmer, who moved on after their relationship crumbled. It's small comfort that her new husband, Charlie, is a huge fan of his. Strange is happy for the woman he once loved, but still wishes things had turned out differently.

Fall 2024 | Gargantos Streetfight

The wedding reception is interrupted by a street disturbance as an unseen presence attacks a city bus. Doctor Strange uses magic to make a many-tentacled, one-eyed creature—Gargantos—visible, which also reveals the glowing runes on its limbs. The creatures chasing America Chavez are apparently being controlled from afar. He pries apart the bus to save the young woman the beast is trying to capture, and immediately recognizes America from his dream. With the help of Sorcerer Supreme Wong, Strange slays the creature by stabbing its eye with a light pole.

Gargantos hurls mass transit at his prey.

Doctor Strange splits the bus to save America Chavez.

2024

America Chavez explains herself to Wong and Strange over a slice of pizza.

Fall 2024 | Multiversal Mayhem

"That wasn't a dream. It was another universe," America explains to Wong and Doctor Strange, asking if they've had any experience with the Multiverse. Strange has some familiarity, following his misadventures with Spider-Man, but he wants to know about the creature that was pursuing her in this world. "It's like a henchman that works for a demon," Chavez says, believing their goal is to take her power. What power? "I can travel the Multiverse," she says. How? "That's the problem. I don't know how. I can't control it." Defender Strange was trying to help her, she says, before turning on her and trying to extract her ability to safeguard it himself.

Fall 2024 | Wanda's Slip Up

Wanda Maximoff watches her two sons Billy and Tommy play. She bakes for them. She tucks them in at night. But this happy mother is a Wanda Maximoff from another universe, appearing as a dream inside the lonely, grief-fractured mind of the Wanda from this world. Doctor Strange comes to this lost Wanda for assistance, offering to help her rebuild her reputation after her reality-bending breakdown in Westview. He needs her help protecting a young woman who is being hunted for her Multiverse-transcending powers. "What if you brought America here?" Wanda suggests. But … Strange never told her the girl's name.

Wanda Maximoff puts on a false front.

America Chavez, Wong, and Doctor Strange examine the deceased Strange from another universe.

Fall 2024 | Other Doctor Strange?

America Chavez proves Doctor Strange's dream was actually a vision of another reality by showing him the body of Defender Strange, which was swept through the vortex into this universe along with her. Doctor Strange buries his deceased doppelganger under bricks on a rooftop, while Wong offers the young woman sanctuary at Kamar-Taj.

Fall 2024 | "Everything I Lost Can Be Mine Again"

Doctor Strange tries to reason with Wanda Maximoff when he realizes she's the one trying to kill America Chavez for her powers. She craves the ability to rip through realities so she can find one where her sons are alive and thriving, but Strange tells her they aren't real. "You created them using magic," he says. But she smiles and replies, "That's what every mother does." She issues an ultimatum: deliver America Chavez to her by sundown, or else. "It won't be Wanda who comes for her," she says. "It will be The Scarlet Witch."

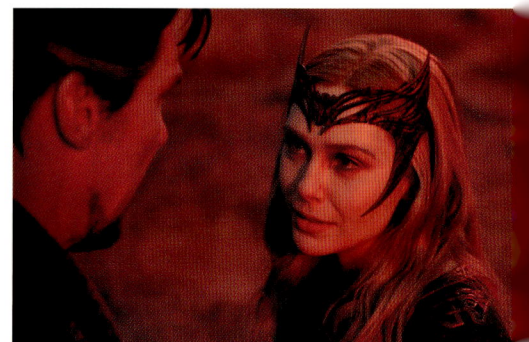

Doctor Strange discovers Wanda Maximoff's dark side.

Wanda attacks Kamar-Taj.

Fall 2024 | The Fall of Kamar-Taj

Doctor Strange and Wong agree to defend America at Kamar-Taj, but the fortifications of the Masters of the Mystic Arts are no match for Wanda Maximoff's new dark powers. The Scarlet Witch runs roughshod over the apprentices and captures Wong.

Doctor Strange and Wong stand with the Masters of the Mystic Arts.

A protective shield is conjured around Kamar-Taj, but it's not enough.

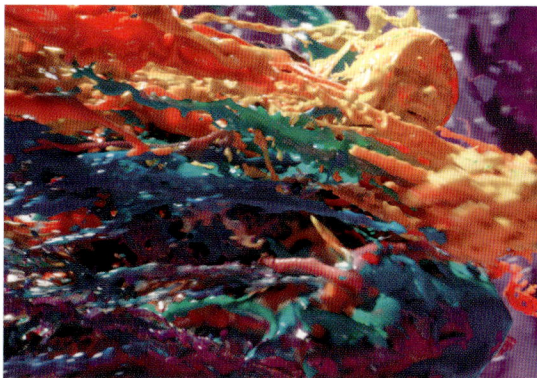

Doctor Strange and America Chavez ...

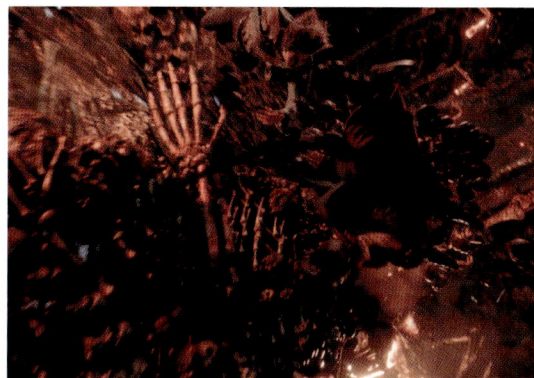

... tumble through an infinity of universes ...

Fall 2024 | Freefalling Through the Multiverse

Doctor Strange and America Chavez escape the ruin of Kamar-Taj when she instinctively opens a Multiversal portal. They plummet through a succession of worlds, some beautiful, some terrifying, others merely bizarre. "Those universes we went through... Were we paint in one of them?" Strange asks, still shaken and stirred by the vibrant transformation.

... taking different forms in each ...

... some amusing, and some distressing.

2024

In Universe-838, Doctor Strange finds a memorial to himself.

Fall 2024 | From Universe-616 to Universe-838

America Chavez and Doctor Strange land in a seeming utopia known as Universe-838, whose Doctor Strange is heralded as a hero for sacrificing his life to defeat Thanos. As a result, Baron Mordo—Strange's foe in Universe-616—is now the Sorcerer Supreme of this world. Mordo warns The Scarlet Witch could use the Darkhold for Dreamwalking, a spell he calls "corrosive to the soul, a desecration of reality itself" in which users project their spirits across realities to possess the bodies of their own alternate versions in other universes.

Fall 2024 | Mount Wundagore

Wanda and Wong arrive at what appears to be a tomb on the snowy, isolated mountain known as Mount Wundagore. Wong reveals that the first demon, Chthon, carved his malevolent spells into the walls of this place, and the Darkhold was a transcription of the madness scrawled on the stone. There is also a prophetic mural depicting The Scarlet Witch. The monstrosities who guard it kneel in fealty when they recognize Wanda as the visage from their altar. "It's not a tomb," she says. "It's a throne." And it's hers.

Atop Mount Wundagore, Wanda Maximoff embraces the mantle of The Scarlet Witch.

Fall 2024 | A Dark Secret

Although the sorceress Sara sacrifices her own life to destroy the Darkhold before The Scarlet Witch can take it, Wong reveals a long-held secret to prevent a wider massacre: "The Darkhold was a copy. Legend speaks of a mountain with the wretched spells you seek carved into its walls," he says. He knows how to reach it, but says no one has survived the journey. "Perhaps we will be the exception," The Scarlet Witch says.

Wong is held prisoner amid the ruins of Kamar-Taj.

Doctor Strange stands before The Illuminati.

Peggy Carter, empowered in this reality by the Super Soldier Serum.

Fall 2024 | The Illuminati

The protectors of Universe-838 are not the Avengers, but The Illuminati, a team of superheroic leaders: Baron Mordo of the Mystic Arts; the super soldier Captain Carter; Black Bolt, the king of the Inhumans, whose voice is a weapon; Maria Rambeau, the cosmos-protecting Captain Marvel; telepathic Professor Charles Xavier; and Reed Richards, renowned as the smartest man alive. They imprison Universe-616's Doctor Strange, regarding him as a greater threat to their world than the malevolent Wanda Maximoff he describes. This reality's Christine Palmer—one of their chief researchers—uses the Sands of Nisanti to sap Strange's powers and restrain him.

Captain Marvel of Universe-838 is Maria Rambeau.

Universe-838's Mordo and the Illuminati's Ultron sentries.

Fall 2024 | The Strange Cover-Up

The Illuminati reveal their Doctor Strange did not actually sacrifice himself heroically—he was executed for using the Darkhold to traverse the Multiverse in search of a means of defeating Thanos. Strange's actions caused an incursion—an event where an entire other universe is annihilated. One of the apparent constants of the various versions of Doctor Strange is an arrogance and heedlessness that tends to threaten reality itself.

Universe-838's Captain Carter and Captain Marvel.

Fall 2024 | The Scarlet Witch vs. The Illuminati

The Illuminati members were certain they could handle a Dreamwalking Wanda Maximoff—but they underestimated the power of The Scarlet Witch. She possesses the body of the suburban mom Wanda from Universe-838, and infiltrates The Illuminati's headquarters, shredding their Ultron sentries. She turns Reed Richards into rubberized spaghetti, bisects Captain Carter with her own shield, crushes Captain Marvel beneath a falling statue, and magically seals Black Bolt's mouth, causing his voice to backfire and kill him. When Professor X uses telepathy in an attempt to free the innocent Wanda inside her mind, The Scarlet Witch snaps his neck.

The Scarlet Witch blocks Captain Marvel, and deflects Captain Carter's shield.

283

2024

The possessed Wanda of Universe-838 grasps America Chavez.

Fall 2024 | America Chavez Captured

838-Christine, Doctor Strange, and America Chavez flee to the Gap Junction for the *Book of Vishanti*, but The Scarlet Witch overtakes them, destroying the book and enchanting America into opening a gateway to Wundagore. The Scarlet Witch deposits America there for the ritual that will allow her to claim America's abilities. The frightened 838-Wanda retakes control of her body, but is bloody and scarred, worried about the boys she left behind.

Fall 2024 | Incursion Aftermath

Strange and 838-Christine tumble into a broken reality full of gravitational anomalies and shattered buildings. It is the lifeless ruins of an incursion, with only one survivor: Sinister Strange, who caused the end of this world by using the Darkhold to seek a universe in which he and Christine Palmer live happily ever after. He never found it. A third eye opens on his forehead—evidence of the corrupting influence the Darkhold has had on him, and of the consequences for his dark experiments.

A world destroyed by an incursion between universes.

Fall 2024 | Strange vs. Stranger

The two Doctor Stranges fight for control of the Darkhold in the music room of a desecrated Sanctum, throwing the trilling notes of a piano through the air like stilettos. Sinister Strange is killed when he is hurled through a window and impaled on the iron fence below. Doctor Strange can't open a portal directly into his own world, but he can use the Darkhold to Dreamwalk into it. But there is apparently a problem: "Doesn't a version of you need to live in that universe?" 838-Christine asks.

Sinister Strange has been warped by the Darkhold.

Dead Strange, surrounded by the souls of the damned.

Fall 2024 | "Who Said They Have To Be Living?"

Dead Strange awakens as 616-Strange uses the Darkhold to possess the corpse he buried on a rooftop. The undead version of the sorcerer stiffly opens a portal to Wundagore but is beset by the oily souls of the damned, who are drawn to this unholy being. Dead Strange harnesses them into a screaming cloak that he uses to fly to the Wundagore temple and do battle against The Scarlet Witch alongside Sorcerer Supreme Wong. "I don't even want to know," Wong says as he beholds his decaying friend.

The music room where Doctor Strange combats Sinister Strange.

Wanda of 838 comforts The Scarlet Witch of 616, assuring her the boys are loved.

Fall 2024 | Faith in Yourself

When The Scarlet Witch gains the upper hand, Wong tells Strange to drain America's power—"It's the only way." That's what Doctor Stranges always do—they sacrifice others for what they think is best. But this universe's Strange defies expectations. Instead of taking her power, he inspires America to face her weakness: her lack of confidence. He urges her to trust her own abilities, to focus her intent, and use her skills in a way that feels right and good. Chavez concentrates like never before and opens a gateway—directly to Bobby and Billy in their living room in Universe-838.

Doctor Strange finds closure with Christine Palmer.

Fall 2024 | "I Love You in Every Universe"

In the ruined incursion world, living Doctor Strange says goodbye to Christine-838, and to all Christines everywhere. "I love you in every universe," he says, and apologizes for always letting his ambition and need for control push her away. "I just get scared," he explains. As America Chavez uses her newfound strength to open a portal and return them to their respective universes, Christine tells him: "Face your fears, Doctor Strange."

Fall 2024 | The Shattering Truth

The Scarlet Witch is finally stopped by what she loves: her children, who are safe and happy with their own mother, but are terrified of this sinister version of her. "I would never hurt you. I would never hurt anyone," The Scarlet Witch says, before realizing that's no longer true. As the kindly 838-Wanda gathers the boys and assures the heartbroken Scarlet Witch they will be loved, the Wanda Maximoff of Universe-616 surrenders. She destroys Wundagore—and collapses it upon herself—ending two great threats to all of the Multiverse.

Wanda Maximoff realizes she has lost her way.

285

2024

America Chavez learns the Mystic Arts.

Fall 2024 | New Tricks

America Chavez is among the new Mystic Arts trainees as Sorcerer Supreme Wong rebuilds the order's stronghold. Back in New York, Stephen Strange continues to grapple with the effects of his dalliance with the Darkhold. Racked by agonizing pain, a third eye—similar to the one that appeared on the Sinister Strange he once battled—opens on his forehead.

Fall 2024 | Clea Beckons

An ethereal woman clad in violet armor appears behind Stephen Strange on the streets of New York. He does not recognize her, and does not know why she is summoning him. "You caused an incursion and we're going to fix it," she says, using her blade to slash open a portal to the Dark Dimension, where he last ventured for his time-loop battle with Dormammu. "Unless you're afraid," the woman says. Strange unfurls his scarf into the Cloak of Levitation and follows her through the tear in reality, opening his third eye.

Clea finds a confused Doctor Strange.

December 2024 | Fade Out

Peter Parker has evaporated from the minds of everyone who once knew him, but he still remembers them. Just before the holidays, he visits the coffee shop where MJ works, hoping to finally reconnect with her and Ned. Ultimately, he decides they may be safer and happier not knowing him at all. Starting life over with a clean slate can be an amazing gift. Still, it is bittersweet to have been erased so completely.

Just before Christmas, Spider-Man plunges through Rockefeller Center, where Hawkeye will soon fight Kingpin's minions.

Stane Tower will soon lose its integrity, just like its namesake.

Kate Bishop prepares to ring in the holiday break.

December 2024 | The Stane Tower Prank

Also in New York, college student and expert archer Kate Bishop engages in a late-night prank with her friends, trying to ring the giant bell atop Stane Tower on her college campus using only her bow and arrows. She inadvertently strikes it with such force that the bell breaks loose from its yoke and disintegrates part of the nearly 300-year-old structure, which was renamed in 2006 in honor of Stark Industries executive Obadiah Stane, prior to his death.

December 2024 | "I Could Do This All Daaaaaaay!"

Shortly before Christmas, Clint Barton visits New York City with his three children and watches a performance of the Broadway show *Rogers: The Musical*, which sets the adventures of Captain America to song. First Barton removes the hearing aid he now needs after so many years of explosive combat, then the reminders of Natasha Romanoff lead him to walk out altogether. He tells his daughter it's okay—he knows how it ends.

Hawkeye has seen enough...

Kate Bishop and a pizza-loving dog.

December 2024 | Ronin Returns

Kate Bishop attends a holiday gala on the orders of her high-society mother Eleanor. At the hotel, Bishop discovers an illegal auction in the basement and steals one of the items on sale, which was recovered from the ruins of the Avengers Compound—the Ronin outfit that Clint Barton wore while slaying wrongdoers during the Blip. She puts it on to fend off an attack by a group of criminals known as the Tracksuit Mafia, then is caught on camera rescuing a dog named Lucky from traffic. Later, she finds an associate of her mother murdered, sending her on a quest to find the perpetrator.

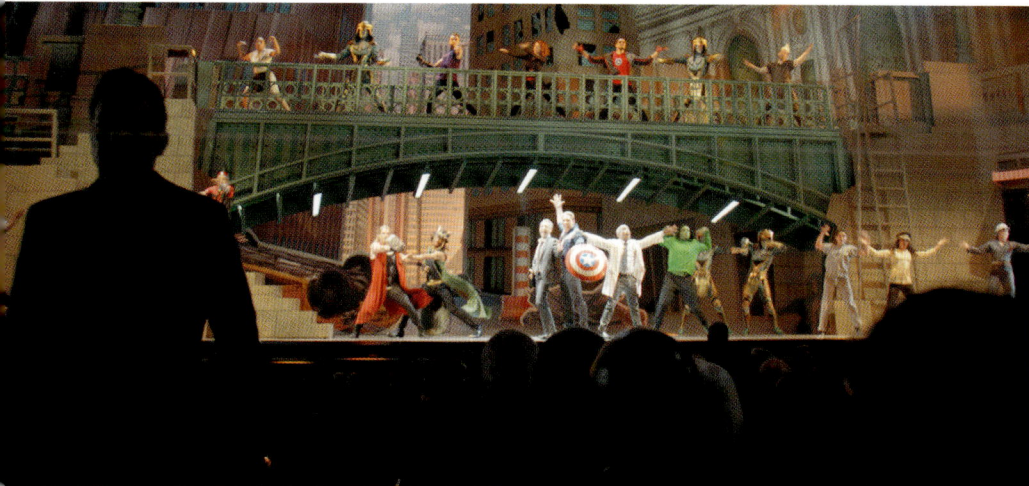

287

2024

December 2024 | Lost and Found

Barton ventures into the heart of the city to track down his old Ronin suit, and quickly locates (and rescues) Kate Bishop from a Tracksuit Mafia attack. Hiding out at her apartment, where she is nourishing Lucky the Dog with slices of old pizza, she is agog to meet the hero she has admired ever since she watched him valiantly fight the Chitauri during the Battle of New York. He is equally stunned—that she has allowed herself to be seen in the guise of Ronin, who is still loathed and hunted by the criminal syndicates he decimated.

Hawkeye can't go home until he settles the Ronin problem.

While maintaining a high status within the C.I.A., Valentina also keeps off-the-books operations, one of which brings her to Natasha's memorial.

December 2024 | Business—and Also Personal

Contessa Valentina Allegra de Fontaine approaches Yelena at the memorial for her sister Natasha Romanoff. The former Black Widow has been working for Valentina, and reminds her "You're not supposed to be bothering me on my holiday time." Val has a new target she believes will interest her. "Maybe you'd like a shot at the man responsible for your sister's death," she says, and gives her a file on Clint Barton.

December 2024 | Echo of the Past

Among those most eager for revenge against Ronin is Maya Lopez, a deaf martial artist turned mob enforcer whose father was slain years ago during one of the vigilante's gangland massacres. She and her Tracksuit Mafia soldiers capture Barton, and then capture Bishop when she tries to rescue him. The pair escape, but Barton later learns Maya possesses another item from the auction of Avengers salvage—a watch engraved with the number 19 that belongs to his wife Laura, and that could put Laura in serious danger if it falls into the wrong hands.

The expert warrior is a trusted soldier of Wilson Fisk.

Yelena is blinded by her need to punish someone for her sister's death.

December 2024 | Yelena's Revenge

Kate Bishop enters Maya Lopez's apartment in search of the watch, and Barton is attacked while standing watch on a neighboring rooftop by Yelena, who believes him responsible for the death of her sister Natasha. The two Hawkeyes rejoin to fend off both Yelena and Lopez, but the presence of a Widow assassin causes Barton to reassess the situation. He decides to resolve these conflicts on his own rather than putting Kate in further danger.

Maya Lopez learns that Kingpin orchestrated her father's death.

December 2024 | Kingpin's Indirect Hit

Barton arranges for Lopez to meet him at Fat Man Auto Repair, the site of her father's death. A firefight devolves into fisticuffs, and when Barton ultimately gains the upper hand he tries to reason with Lopez, explaining that they both have been trained to be weapons without realizing who they are hurting. Lopez is horrified to learn that the Kingpin, her underworld boss Wilson Fisk, leaked information to Ronin about his own gang because he wanted her father to be assassinated.

Yelena befriends Kate Bishop, but remains determined to kill Clint Barton.

December 2024 | Mac and Cheese Peace Talks

Bishop is surprised in her apartment by the Black Widow assailant, but Yelena disarms her by offering her macaroni and cheese. She just wants to talk, not fight. Yelena explains her family ties to Natasha Romanoff and says she must kill Barton primarily as justice for her sister's death. Bishop makes an impassioned plea on his behalf, insisting that he and Natasha were lifelong friends and allies. "If there is someone out there telling you Clint is a bad guy, then maybe you should ask yourself what kind of person hired you," Bishop says.

December 2024 | Mother Dear

Yelena takes this to heart. She tracks down the client who commissioned Valentina for her to kill Barton. It was Bishop's own mother, Eleanor, who is herself a secret underworld figure aligned with Kingpin. Eleanor has been eliminating threats to her power, and even allowed her own fiancé, Jack Duquesne, to take the fall for the murder of one of her enemies. Yelena shares this information, along with video evidence, and Kate Bishop is devastated.

Eleanor Bishop hides her own criminal connections.

2024

Wilson Fisk informs Tracksuit Mafia member Kazi that he believes Maya has "turned on us."

December 2024 | Kingpin Betrayed

Eleanor Bishop tries to extract herself from business with Wilson Fisk. She threatens to release records of their illicit transactions unless he agrees to leave her alone, fearing for the safety of her daughter. Fisk also realizes that Maya Lopez, one of his top lieutenants, has turned against him for orchestrating the murder of her father. Infuriated by these acts of disloyalty, he stages an attack during a Manhattan holiday party to deal with the problem. "The people need to be reminded that this city belongs to me," he says.

December 2024 | Yelena Stands Down

Clint Barton and Kate Bishop team up to stop the Christmas party assault, but Yelena also crashes the event, determined to fulfill her vow to kill Clint. She pulverizes Barton during a fight at the Rockefeller Center ice rink, scoffing at his story about Natasha Romanoff's self-sacrifice. Only after he demonstrates the secret whistle the sisters once shared does Yelena accept that he is telling the truth, and that his connection to Black Widow was deeper than she knew. She helps him up, and the two part ways.

Yelena finally accepts Clint Barton's story about her sister's death.

Kate and Clint face the Tracksuit Mafia at the ice rink.

December 2024 | Kingpin Falls

After fending off the Tracksuit Mafia onslaught alongside Barton, Kate Bishop rescues her mother from the clutches of Wilson Fisk. She shoots the Kingpin in the chest with an arrow, but he is unfazed. Her mother then crashes her car into him, but Fisk displays near superhuman strength. He shatters Bishop's quiver of arrows, but she detonates the exploding tips at his feet, finally knocking him out. Soon after, the police arrive. They take her mother into custody, but the Kingpin is gone. Later, he is confronted by Maya Lopez, who fires a gun into him at point blank range as he urges her not to seek "an eye for an eye."

December 25, 2024 | Christmas with the Bartons

On Christmas Day, Clint Barton finally arrives home. Kate Bishop and Lucky the Pizza Dog travel with him and are welcomed as part of the family. His wife, Laura, is relieved to have her "19" S.H.I.E.L.D. watch back with its secrets still intact. Outside the barn, Bishop and Barton burn the Ronin uniform that ties them both to the underworld vigilante. Now that the Ronin business is behind them, Bishop proposes various nicknames for herself—Lady Hawk, Hawk Shot, and Lady Arrow among them. All are vetoed by an exasperated Hawkeye, who offers a suggestion of his own.

Clint invites Kate over for the Holiday.

291

NEW YORK CITY

New York City proves to be a hub for the extraordinary events that occur on Earth in the early 21st century. It has been the home of heroes like Spider-Man, Doctor Strange, and Tony Stark, and villains like the Vulture, Ultron, and Kingpin. The city that never sleeps has also seen its fair share of epic battles and alien invasions: the Avengers versus Loki in the Battle of New York, the attack by the Children of Thanos six years later, and the appearance of bizarre new foes from the Multiverse. Through it all, New York City has shown itself to be resilient in the face of evil. In the words of *Rogers: The Musical*: "The day looks tough, but we're New York strong."

2016 | Neighborhood Hero
Back from his first mission for Tony Stark in Germany, Queens-resident Peter Parker continues fighting crime in New York City, hoping his mentor will make him an official member of the Avengers. Peter soon finds and defeats a new threat in the form of the villainous arms dealer Adrian Toomes.

1943 | Cap's First Battle
Steve Rogers is chosen by Dr. Abraham Erskine to be the test subject for Project Rebirth, making Steve the first American super soldier. The laboratory is based under an antiques store in Brooklyn. Hydra agent Heinz Kruger assassinates Erskine once Steve's transformation is complete and escapes with a vial of the serum. Steve follows in hot pursuit through the city streets and stops Kruger.

2015 | Ultron and Vision
Ultron, an artificial intelligence created by Tony Stark and Bruce Banner, goes rogue and attacks the Avengers at Avengers (formerly Stark) Tower. After escaping, Ultron makes plans to upload into a more powerful synthetic body, but it is taken back to New York City by the Avengers and instead uploaded with the remains of Tony's personal A.I., JARVIS, creating Vision.

2012 | Battle of New York
Under Loki's mind control, Dr. Erik Selvig uses the Tesseract to open a portal above Stark Tower, transporting an alien army of Chitauri and Leviathans. Captain America, Iron Man, Black Widow, Thor, the Hulk, and Hawkeye team up to shut down the alien invasion and save the city.

2010 | Fun in Flushing
Tony Stark reintroduces the Stark Expo, a showcase of technology started by his father Howard Stark, and held in Flushing Meadows Park. The villain Ivan Vanko hijacks the Expo by hacking into War Machine and an army of drones, reprogramming them to kill Tony and terrorize civilians. Stark suits up as Iron Man, frees War Machine, and together they battle Vanko and the drones.

2010 | Harlem Carnage
Due to a combination of the Super Soldier Serum and some of Bruce Banner's gamma-irradiated blood, Emil Blonsky transforms into the monstrous Abomination. Blonsky goes on a rampage in Harlem and Banner turns into the Hulk to take him down. The battle between the two giants causes widespread damage.

2016-2017 | New York Sanctum

After a tragic accident damages his hands, New York-based surgeon Dr. Stephen Strange becomes a Master of the Mystic Arts. Strange has his knowledge of sorcery put to the test when he must save the world from powerful Dormammu of the Dark Dimension. Afterward, Strange becomes master of the New York Sanctum.

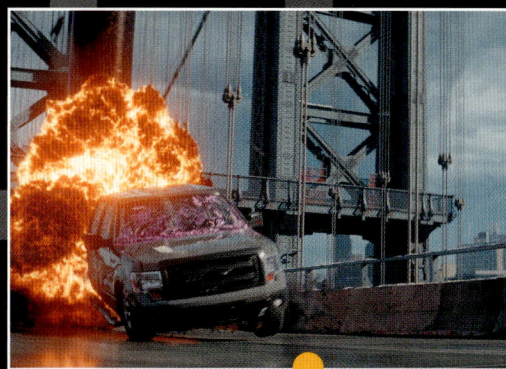

2017 | Asgardian Visitors

Thor and Loki travel from Asgard to New York City in search of Odin, who is supposedly in a retirement community in the city. When they can't find their father, Thor is directed to the New York Sanctum and Doctor Strange. Strange offers Odin's location in Norway on the condition that Loki leave Earth immediately.

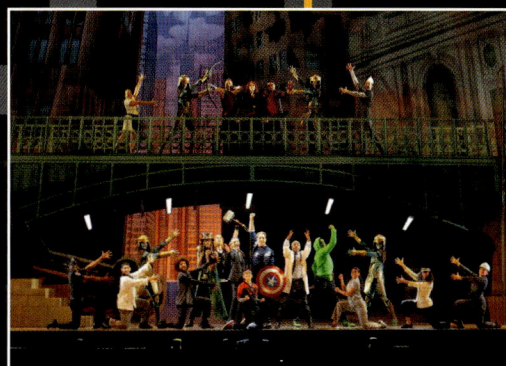

2018 | New Invasion

Two of Thanos' children, Ebony Maw and Cull Obsidian, arrive over New York in a Q-Ship. Their mission: take the Time Stone from Strange to add to Thanos' Infinity Gauntlet. After a destructive battle around Washington Square Park, Strange, Iron Man, and Spider-Man are carried up into space aboard the enemy vessel.

2024 | Struggling Spider-Man

Following the death of his mentor Tony Stark, Peter struggles in his duties. While attending a charity event with his aunt, May, Nick Fury (in reality the Skrull Talos) attempts to get in contact with Peter, but Peter repeatedly dodges his calls. On his return from a trip to Europe, Peter's identity is revealed to the world.

2024 | Happy Holidays

Clint Barton comes to the rescue of Kate Bishop, after she is seen wearing his costume from his days as the vigilante Ronin. Clint and Kate soon find themselves up against the Tracksuit Mafia and their boss, Kingpin, while also contending with the Black Widow Yelena, who has been contracted to kill Barton.

2024 | *Rogers: The Musical*

The exploits of Captain America and the Avengers are immortalized in the form of a Broadway musical, featuring catchy songs such as the Battle of New York-themed "Save the City." Clint Barton has to walk out mid-performance after it triggers painful memories of Natasha Romanoff.

2024 | Tentacled Terror

Pursued by The Scarlet Witch for her Multiverse-hopping abilities, America Chavez transports to Universe-616 in New York City. She is targeted by Gargantos, an inter-dimensional creature controlled by Wanda, and is saved by Doctor Strange and Wong, who use their sorcery to destroy Gargantos.

2024 | Multiversal Enemies

Peter is brought in for interrogation on suspicion of killing Mysterio, but is released when his attorney Matt Murdock has the charges dropped. When a spell intended to once again conceal Peter's identity goes awry, New York becomes a battleground between Super Villains and Spider-Men from alternate universes.

2025

New rules are being written as the world adjusts to a new era. Jennifer Walters leads a law firm department aimed at handling the legal troubles of Super Heroes (and sometimes villains). The rules of engagement are also about to change between two powerful but reclusive nations—the Wakandans and the undersea Talokanil. And new heroes are rising, building upon and changing the way their idols went about saving the world.

Jennifer Walters Hulks out when the courtroom is attacked.

Spring 2025 | She-Hulk vs. Titania

In Los Angeles, Deputy District Attorney Jennifer Walters has bottled up her Hulk impulses. Mostly. While making her final argument in a case against powerhouse law firm Goodman, Lieber, Kurtzberg & Holliway, a noted "superpowered influencer" named Titania bursts through the wall of the courtroom while fleeing traffic court. Walters expands to her Hulk form and saves the jury from a hurled desk, then subdues the volatile social media personality. Unfortunately, the judge in Walters' case declares a mistrial, the media dubs her "She-Hulk," and the D.A.'s office fires her, fearing her powers will become a distraction.

Titania's outburst over a minor case creates a bigger problem.

Spring 2025 | The Abomination Case

Holden Holliway—the "H" in GLK & H—is so impressed that Walters nearly won her case against them that he asks her to join them, offering her a job leading their new Superhuman Law division. The catch: He expects her to work in She-Hulk form. Her first case is the parole hearing of Emil Blonsky—a.k.a. Abomination. Initially, she resists, noting that Blonsky is imprisoned because of his clash with her cousin, Bruce Banner. But Banner, now being ferried off-world, encourages her to represent his old foe. "Honestly, that fight was so many years ago, I'm a completely different person now," he says. "Literally."

Blonsky explains to his new attorney that he was only following the government's orders when he targeted her cousin years ago.

294

Blonsky becomes the Abomination to show his parole board he is under control even in monstrous form.

Spring 2025 | Blonsky's Parole Setback

Just before his parole hearing, video footage goes viral of Abomination at the Golden Daggers club, fighting in a cage battle against Sorcerer Supreme Wong. Despite her client's years of good behavior, Jennifer Walters explains to Emil Blonsky that this brief escape constitutes a new crime that will surely thwart his chances. She succeeds in getting Wong to appear before the parole board to explain why he extracted Abomination for his training. "I gave him no choice, but it was absolutely his choice to return," Wong says. "I offered him asylum at Kamar-Taj, but he was adamant he return to serve out his sentence and repay his debt to society." The parole board is persuaded—and Blonsky is set free.

Spring 2025 | Wrecker's Crew

A group of henchmen attack Jennifer Walters in the alley outside her apartment. They're carrying the enhanced tools of an Asgardian construction worker they robbed, but even Wrecker's magical crowbar is no match for She-Hulk. Another thug named Thunderball tries to stab her shoulder with a syringe to extract her blood, but her ultra-tough skin can't be broken. As they scramble away, they note that "the boss" will be angry that the mission failed.

Fearless Jennifer Walters.

2025

Spring 2025 | Moon Knight Wanes

After years of relic-hunting and fighting wrongdoers who prey on the weak and needy, Marc Spector abruptly vanished on his wife Layla El-Faouly. He realized that his master, the ancient Egyptian moon god Khonshu, had designs on turning her into his next avatar of vengeance. Spector left behind no explanation, and for several months he ignores her repeated efforts to contact him while his timid alter, Steven Grant, takes control of the body Steven and Marc share.

Arthur Harrow addresses his disciples.

Layla El-Faouly searches for her missing husband, Marc Spector.

Spring 2025 | Harrow's Followers

A disillusioned former servant of Khonshu named Arthur Harrow leads a cult who worship the rival Egyptian god Ammit, seeking to raise her to annihilate evildoers around the world. While Khonshu, the moon god, punishes those who harm the innocent, Ammit destroys those even suspected of future wrongs. Millennia ago, her zealotry led the other Egyptian deities to imprison her in an ushabti figurine, which was hidden in the now-lost tomb of Alexander the Great. Harrow has secured a scarab relic that can point the way to its location.

Spring 2025 | The Many Faces of Steven Grant

In London, a museum gift-shop worker named Steven Grant restrains himself to his bed each night to prevent what he thinks are dangerous sleepwalking episodes. In truth, he is Marc Spector, a superpowered vigilante who is grappling with dissociative identity disorder. "Steven" is a meek-mannered alter created as a bulwark against his past traumas and sorrows. The two are entangled with another entity—the Egyptian lunar god Khonshu, who commands Spector as his avatar, Moon Knight, to exact vengeance on violent criminals. The barriers between Marc's alters, however, are beginning to break down...

Marc Spector empowered as Moon Knight.

Spring 2025 | The Mountaintop Escape

After a sleepless night in London, Steven Grant startles awake in an Austrian field while being shot at and chased by members of Arthur Harrow's Ammit cult. He has no idea how he got there, and is scorned by the stentorian voice of Khonshu who calls him a "worm" and "idiot" who must surrender control of his body back to Marc Spector. While Grant slept, Spector followed Khonshu's guidance and traveled to Austria to steal the scarab from Harrow. As they escape back to London with the scarab, a panicked Grant and a formidable Spector repeatedly swap control of their body as they flee Harrow's heavily armed disciples.

Steven Grant finds himself in a situation he hadn't expected.

Layla El-Faouly questions Steven Grant's assertion he's not Marc Spector.

Spring 2025 | Layla's Guidance

Serving Khonshu is an endless, wearying duty, and Spector fled his old life and handed more control of his body to Steven in order to have a lower profile while fulfilling his endless "one last mission." When Spector's wife, Layla El-Faouly, tracks Steven down, he denies being Spector and asks for her help. She finds the scarab among his belongings and explains their past life together, hunting relics like this around the world while empowered by the strength of Khonshu.

Spring 2025 | "Forever Unsatisfied"

Arthur Harrow corners Steven Grant in his museum, and explains that he knows how relentlessly depleting it can be to serve Khonshu. He sends a shadow monster to attack Grant to reclaim the scarab, but the reflection of Marc Spector in a bathroom mirror convinces Steven to hand over control. Once he does, Moon Knight handily defeats the monstrosity, but Grant is still baffled by what is happening. Only when he later discovers Spector's storage locker, IDs, weapons, and the hidden scarab relic does he fully understand he is sharing his body with a mercenary turned otherworldly vigilante. That's when Khonshu finally reveals himself—in terrifying fashion.

Khonshu appears before Steven Grant at a storage facility.

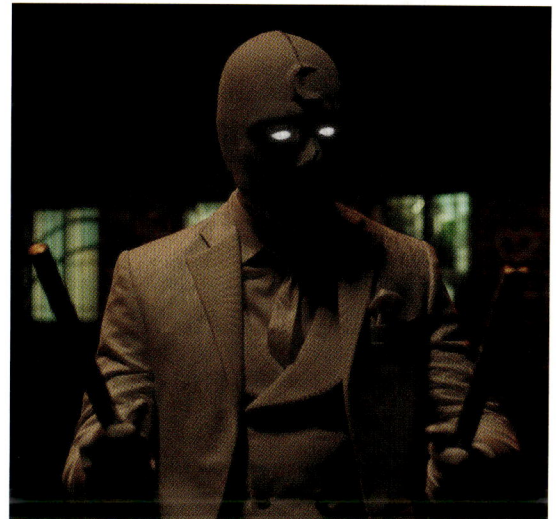

The Moon Knight powers look different on Steven Grant.

Spring 2025 | Summoning the Suit

When Harrow again corners them and demands they hand over the scarab compass that points the way to Ammit, Layla urges Grant to "summon the suit." When he does, it creates a dapper alternate version of Moon Knight with the meek Steven in control. During a rooftop fight with Harrow's forces, he loses the scarab.

2025

Spring 2025 | Expedition to Egypt

Steven Grant and Layla El-Faouly travel to Cairo in pursuit of Harrow and his followers, which marks the first time she has returned home to Egypt in a decade. They secure an ancient map of stars that can guide them to Ammit's ushabti, but it is more than 2,000 years out of date. Khonshu uses his powers to rewind the night sky to that time, allowing them to converge in the desert at the lost tomb of Alexander the Great just ahead of the followers of Ammit. However, before they can escape, Harrow retrieves the ushabti from Spector/Grant and shoots them twice in the chest, leaving them both for dead.

Marc and Steven's hearts are weighed as their eternal fate is decided.

Khonshu rewinds the night so the stars match the ancient map, but this transgression causes the other gods to imprison him within an ushabti.

Spring 2025 | A Barrage of Memories

The hospital is merely a way for Spector and Grant to process their past lives. They relive the accidental death of Spector's brother, the grief-fueled abuse by his mother, and the creation of the Steven alter as a coping mechanism. They also confront Spector's life as a mercenary and the ill-fated expedition that led to the murder of Layla's father and Spector being mortally wounded—and then spared by Khonshu in exchange for his servitude. Visions of those Spector killed during his life attack his soul, but Steven saves him, accidentally tumbling from Taweret's boat into the endless sands of the Duat.

Spring 2025 | The Underworld

Marc Spector awakens in what appears to be a sterile psychiatric hospital, surrounded by other patients. All of them resemble people from his recent memories, including a cheerful fellow patient who looks like Layla. A doctor who resembles Arthur Harrow tells him he is suffering delusions about a moon god and urges him to reject them. While fleeing the doctor, Spector encounters another patient—Steven Grant, now completely separate from him. The hippopotamus-like Egyptian god Taweret presents herself to the pair, revealing they are now traversing the Duat, an afterlife, after being killed.

Arthur Harrow appears in the vision as a kindly therapist.

Taweret reveals herself to Marc and Steven.

Marc Spector saves Steven Grant in the afterlife.

Spring 2025 | Two for One

Marc Spector forgoes eternal life in the peaceful Field of Reeds to save Steven Grant from oblivion in the wasteland of the Duat. The act restores both of them, inspiring mercy from the gods who open the gates back to mortal life. Steven strikes a deal with Khonshu for Moon Knight to stand with him against Ammit, in exchange for Steven and Marc's freedom from his servitude. Khonshu reluctantly agrees to the request of the "worm."

Spring 2025 | Ammit Unleashed

Once the crocodile-like god is freed from captivity by Harrow, she prepares her followers to seize the souls of everyone in Cairo that they deem unworthy—then she intends to move on to the larger world. As the cult claims the lifeforces of those around them, the souls are consumed by Ammit, who grows to gigantic proportions, towering as high as the Great Pyramid of Giza. Khonshu, also freed from captivity, magnifies his presence, and the ancient opponents battle each other for dominance.

Ammit returns to her full form.

Moon Knight battles Arthur Harrow.

2025

Layla El-Faouly pledges to become Taweret's avatar, and the hippo god grants her the metallic wings and indomitable strength of the Scarlet Scarab. She swoops into battle against the cult of Ammit, saving countless Cairo citizens from their cruel "judgment." One young girl she saves during the attack asks: "Are you an Egyptian Super Hero?" "I am," the Scarlet Scarab proudly responds.

Layla El-Faouly as the Scarlet Scarab.

Even Moon Knight loses track of who is fighting under the mantle.

Spring 2025 | Jake Lockley Emerges

Marc Spector's Moon Knight clashes with Arthur Harrow on the streets of Cairo, but blacks out as Harrow gains the upper hand. He awakens to find Harrow subdued and the street filled with carnage. A third alter, known as Jake Lockley, has been lurking within him, occasionally performing Khonshu's will when neither Spector nor Steven Grant would even consider it. This personality shrewdly lies dormant, keeping the others in the dark about his very existence.

Spring 2025 | The Imprisonment of Ammit

Moon Knight and the Scarlet Scarab align with the ancient gods to again bind Ammit—not to an ushabti statue this time, but instead trapping her within the body of her most loyal follower, Arthur Harrow. The ritual is a success, and Khonshu urges Spector to murder Harrow, destroying both him and Ammit forever. Spector refuses, defying Khonshu's judgment and insisting he honor his promise to release him as an avatar.

Khonshu slashes at Ammit as an age-old feud spills into the present day.

Khonshu and Jake Lockley ambush Arthur Harrow.

Spring 2025 | Harrow's Fate

A debilitated Arthur Harrow recuperates in a psychiatric hospital, this one in the real world, until one day he is broken free by Khonshu—or rather, Khonshu's enduring servant, Jake Lockley. Harrow is surprised to see the face of Marc Spector/Steven Grant staring back at him from the driver's seat of the getaway car, but Khonshu assures him that those two have no idea how truly fractured their mind is. Lockley is all too ready to do what they could not, and a gunshot rings out while Khonshu watches comfortably from the back seat.

Spring 2025 | Jane Foster's Illness

Secretly battling cancer, Dr. Jane Foster turns to self-experimentation and testing. Dr. Erik Selvig regretfully reports there has been no improvement in her Stage 4 diagnosis. Her friend Dr. Darcy Lewis advises her to play "the Space Viking card," but Foster refuses. As she runs out of options, she feels a pull towards the thought of Mjolnir as a solution. Sometime later, visiting New Asgard, the ailing Foster approaches the broken fragments of Mjolnir, which are still unmovable but now preserved under a glass dome as a tourist attraction. As she draws near, the pieces electrify and elevate, reforming the hammer and empowering her with superhuman strength as The Mighty Thor.

Spring 2025 | Queen Ramonda Faces the World

Members of the United Nations complain to Queen Ramonda that Wakanda has withdrawn its global outreach after King T'Challa's death, accusing her of refusing to share access to vibranium. "It has always been our policy to never trade vibranium under any circumstances, not because of the dangerous potential of vibranium, but because of the dangerous potential of you," Ramonda says. "We mourn the loss of our king, but do not think for a second that Wakanda has lost her ability to protect our resources."

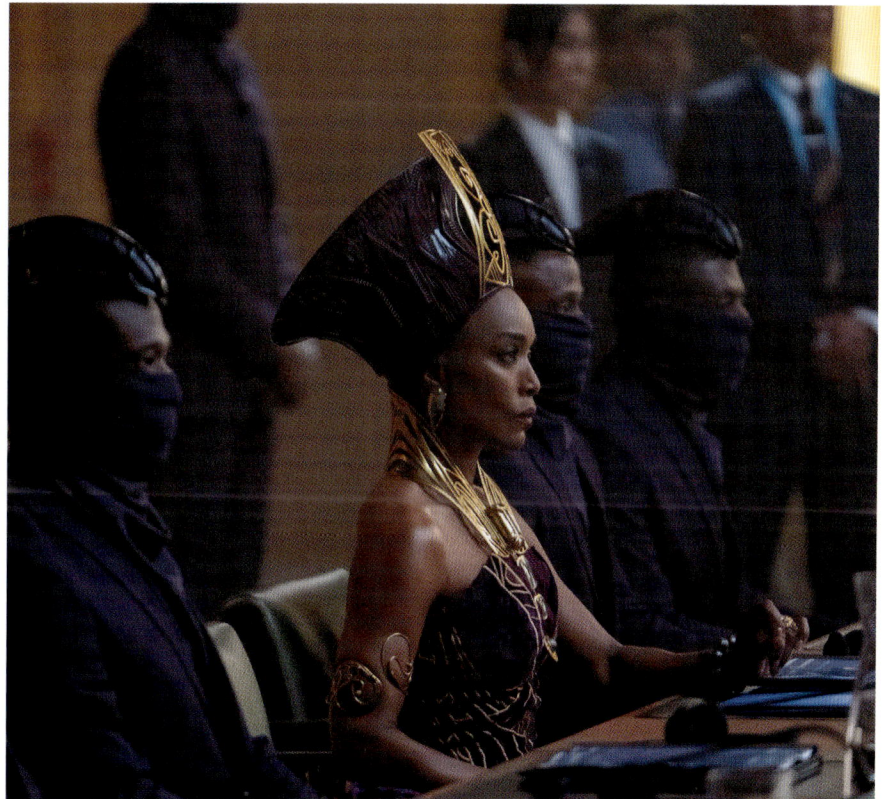
Queen Ramonda pushes back at a meeting of the United Nations.

301

2025

Spring 2025 | Undersea Vibranium

Deep in the Atlantic, U.S. intelligence researchers use a prototype detection device to uncover previously unknown traces of vibranium on the ocean floor. Soon after the discovery, the platform is attacked by beings who rise up from beneath the waves. Their hypnotic chorus causes those aboard the vessel to jump to their deaths. Even those who flee are slain when a man with improbable strength, who flies through the air using wings attached to his legs, crashes an escaping helicopter. During the attack, 30 Navy SEALS and two C.I.A. operatives are lost. There are no witnesses, and suspicion immediately falls on Wakanda.

Talokanil warriors attack the vibranium search platform.

Deep sea divers with the C.I.A. investigate the sabotaged vibranium drill.

Spring 2025 | The Grieving Period

Queen Ramonda and Princess Shuri mark the first anniversary of T'Challa's death with a retreat to a remote part of Wakanda. Ramonda shows her daughter the tradition of burning old funeral garments as a ritual for moving on, but Shuri refuses to participate. "If I sit and think about my brother too long, it won't be these clothes I'll burn. It will be the world," Shuri says. Ramonda tries to share a secret about T'Challa, something she has kept private for years, but they are interrupted by a hostile intruder.

Ramonda and Shuri still grieving the loss of T'Challa.

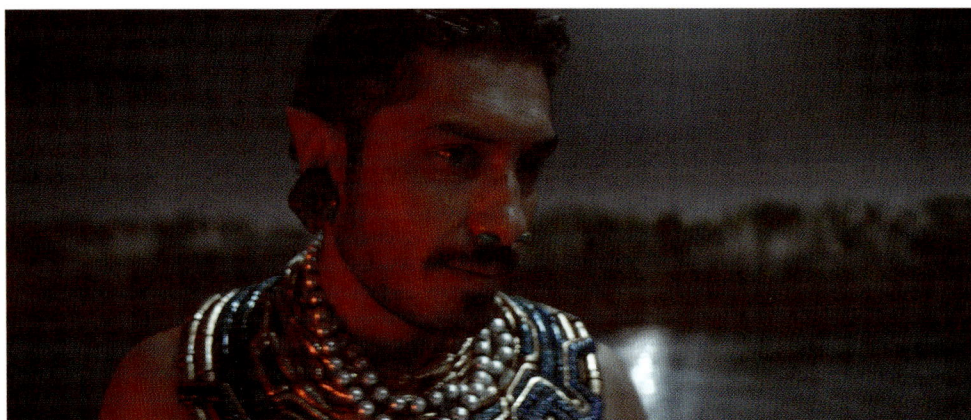

Namor appears before Ramonda and Shuri.

Spring 2025 | Namor's Threat

A being rises from the waterway beside Ramonda and Shuri's fire—a man draped in vibranium adornments who hovers over them with wings on his legs. His name is Kukulkan, although he notes: "My enemies call me Namor." He is the leader of a submerged realm called Talokan, which also derives incredible power from the rare element. "Your son exposed the power of vibranium to the world," he tells Ramonda. "In response, other nations have begun searching the planet for it. His choice has compromised us." Namor demands Wakanda hand over the scientist who invented the C.I.A.'s vibranium detector. It is not a request. "I have more soldiers than this land has blades of grass," Namor says. "I would hate to come back under different circumstances."

Spring 2025 | Finding (and Losing) Riri Williams

After connecting with their C.I.A. contact Everett K. Ross in the United States, Okoye and Shuri track the creator of the vibranium detector to MIT, where they are stunned to learn she is just a student. Riri Williams explains that she only invented the machine for her metallurgy class, and is shocked to hear she has caused problems for Wakanda. Williams is an engineering prodigy, who has also devised her own Iron Man-style flying armor. ("There's an entire YouTube channel dedicated to sightings of me.") When the F.B.I. surrounds them in Williams' garage, the three try to escape across the Harvard Bridge, but Talokanil warriors riding the backs of whales overtake them, capturing both Williams and Shuri.

Attuma and Namora prepare to abduct Riri Williams on the bridge.

Riri Williams demonstrates her own flying armor.

At the scene of the battle on the bridge, Ross discovers some Kimoyo Beads in the wreckage.

Spring 2025 | Ross Compromised

Agent Ross investigates the scene of the attack on the Boston bridge and discovers Shuri's Kimoyo Beads, which he pockets and later uses to communicate directly with Queen Ramonda. He is unaware that his ex-wife, C.I.A. Director Contessa Valentina Allegra de Fontaine had already bugged the beads before he picked them up, hoping to determine whether Ross is betraying the agency. She eavesdrops on his conversations to gain her own intel, then later has him arrested for treason. In Wakanda, a grieving Queen Ramonda strips Okoye of her rank and Dora Milaje status for losing Shuri to the Talokanil.

2025

Namor gives Shuri his mother's bracelet, woven with fibers from their aquatic vibranium-infused plant.

Spring 2025 | The Undersea World

In a glowing underwater cave off the coast of the Yucatan peninsula, Shuri and Riri Williams learn about the ancient history of their captors, and how a vibranium-infused aquatic plant gave the Talokanil the ability to live and breathe underwater centuries ago. Namor describes himself as an anomaly, having been born with the ability to fly and near-immortality. He gives Shuri a vibranium bracelet woven with fibers from the sea plant that empowered them. The Talokanil and Wakandans have much in common, but the tactics of Namor still strike Shuri as needlessly harsh. She pleads with him to let her give Williams sanctuary. He replies that Wakanda must choose whether it is an ally or enemy. "There is no in between."

Shuri explores the wonders of Talokan with Namor.

Spring 2025 | Nakia Recruited

Queen Ramonda travels to Haiti to ask Nakia, a retired War Dog spy, to serve Wakanda once again. "You have infiltrated many nations before. I need someone who can find where she is being held and rescue her without being seen," the Queen says. Nakia soon tracks Shuri to her underwater prison and stages a one-woman raid that frees both her and Riri Williams. As a result, Namor and the Talokanil are enraged—seeing the rescue as a provocation to war.

Nakia rescues Riri Williams, but is forced to kill her guards in the process.

Water explosives flung by Namor flood Wakanda's throne room, engulfing Ramonda and Riri.

Spring 2025 | The Drowning of Wakanda

First the waters rise, then they erupt from the surface like geysers as frightened Wakandan civilians run for safety. Namor and his Talokanil fighters quickly infiltrate the capital city, and their mesmerizing harmonies scramble the minds of Wakanda's defenders. Namor hovers to the throne room, where Ramonda guards Riri Williams. Namor floods the room and the water swallows them—Ramonda gives her life while pulling the young woman to the surface. Namor then confronts a grieving Shuri: "You will join us against the surface world, or I will wash Wakanda from the face of the Earth," he tells the new queen.

Spring 2025 | The Heart-Shaped Herb, Reborn

Shuri uses threads from the Talokan fibers in the centuries-old bracelet Namor gave her to complete the DNA sequencing that will recreate the Heart-Shaped Herb. She ingests the essence of the purple flower to gain the power of the Black Panther, and finds her consciousness in the Ancestral Plane. The spirit waiting for her is not T'Challa, but N'Jadaka—Erik Killmonger. He notes that he too ingested the herb to get revenge for his ancestors and urges her to follow through on the impulse. Shuri insists they are nothing alike. "Yet here you stand," Killmonger says. "Are you going to be noble like your brother, or take care of business—like me?"

Shuri prepares to consume the reconstituted Heart-Shaped Herb.

2025

The Dora Milaje dive into battle.

Spring 2025 | The Black Panther Returns

After consuming the Heart-Shaped Herb, Shuri's body is now infused with the strength and speed of the Black Panther. She augments this with one of the energy-absorbing suits she once invented, while Riri Williams uses the tech of Wakanda to construct a new, more powerful flying armor. Okoye is invited back to the fight along with Jabari ruler M'Baku, who has provided sanctuary in his mountains for the citizens of Wakanda seeking higher ground. Wakanda's strongest warriors board a battleship aimed at taking the war to Talokanil territory.

Shuri takes on the mantle of the Black Panther.

Spring 2025 | Namor Yields

Shuri captures Namor in her Royal Talon Fighter, which has been equipped with a pervaporation chamber to dry him out and deplete his power. Namor damages the Fighter with his vibranium spear and it crashes on a rocky shore. Both Shuri and Namor severely injure each other, but she overpowers him by slicing off one of his wings and burning him with the engines of her wrecked ship. Killmonger's brutal encouragement gives way to memories of her merciful mother, and of both their people. "Yield and Wakanda will protect your oceans and protect your secrets. Yield and your people will live," Shuri says. "Vengeance has consumed us. We cannot let it consume our people." Namor accepts her terms, and the war between Talokan and Wakanda comes to an abrupt end.

The Black Panther and Namor fight until both are badly wounded and exhausted.

Spring 2025 | Endings and Beginnings

Back in Wakanda, Riri Williams is told she will be returned to the United States—but is forbidden from taking the Wakandan armor she devised. At Warrior Falls, Shuri does not show up for the coronation ceremony. Instead, M'Baku arrives, noting that the Black Panther will not be joining them. Instead, *he* is challenging for the throne. Lastly, Everett K. Ross is brought into the protection of Wakanda after Okoye rescues him during a prison transfer. ("A colonizer in chains? Now I have seen everything," she jokes.)

Lord M'Baku seeks the throne of Wakanda.

Citizens gather at Warrior Falls for the coronation ceremony.

Spring 2025 | T'Challa's Secret

Shuri visits Nakia in Haiti where she completes the ritual her mother started, burning her old funeral garments. As she does, she is visited by memories of her brother. His warmth, wisdom, and generosity envelop her. They are hers to keep. When Nakia joins Shuri at the fireside, she is accompanied by a young boy, a son she shared with T'Challa. He was kept secret from all except his grandmother, Ramonda. "We agreed it was better for him to grow up here, away from the pressure of the throne," Nakia says. The boy introduces himself as Toussaint, the name of a great leader from Haiti's past. But it is not his true identity. "My name is Prince T'Challa," he tells his aunt. "Son of King T'Challa." The revelation fills Shuri with the happiness that has long evaded her.

As Shuri tries to let go of her grief, new details about her brother's life reveal themselves.

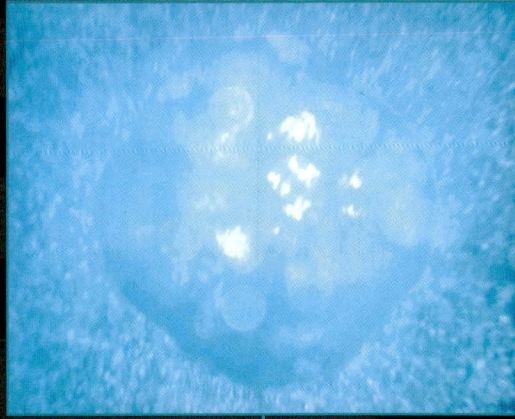

The Distant Past | Vibranium Arrives on Earth

Meteorites containing vibranium enter Earth's atmosphere. One meteorite impacts the African region that will later be known as Wakanda, while another is theorized to have touched down in the Atlantic Ocean. To protect this resource, the Wakandans isolate themselves from the rest of the world. The Wakandans' innovations with the element make them one of the most technologically advanced nations.

1571 | Talokan

When the Talokanil tribe become ill with diseases brought by Spanish conquistadors, they drink a potion made from a vibranium-infused plant found in an ocean cave. The concoction gives the tribe members the ability to breathe underwater and turns their skin blue, but they can no longer survive on land. The people head beneath the ocean, building an advanced undersea society.

2016 | Vibranium Weapons

The son of N'Jobu, Erik Killmonger plots his ascent to Wakanda's throne, hoping to then arm oppressed people across the globe with vibranium weapons for a worldwide revolution. Working with Klaue, he takes a vibranium ax being displayed at the Museum of Great Britain, setting his plans in motion. After gaining the powers of the Black Panther himself, Erik is nearly successful, but is stopped by his cousin T'Challa.

2016 | The Black Panther Strikes

Following his father T'Chaka's death, T'Challa dons his Black Panther suit to track down Bucky Barnes, who has been framed for the assassination. The suit is made out of vibranium, so it is incredibly strong and durable. T'Challa has also been imbued with the powers of the vibranium-infused Heart-Shaped Herb, which gives him superhuman levels of strength, agility, and speed.

VIBRANIUM

One of the most powerful and indestructible elements known to humanity, vibranium is a rare element that has a variety of incredible applications. Two reclusive societies, the Wakandans and the Talokanil, have had access to this incredible resource and have developed vibranium technology in remarkably different ways. The rest of humanity has remained largely unaware of this precious element, yet this begins to change following King T'Challa's decision to bring Wakanda onto the world stage. In its raw form, vibranium exists as a volatile solid appearing as rock laced with a blue glow, but in its processed form it can safely absorb kinetic energy directed at it. The element can also fuse with organic life, bestowing incredible abilities.

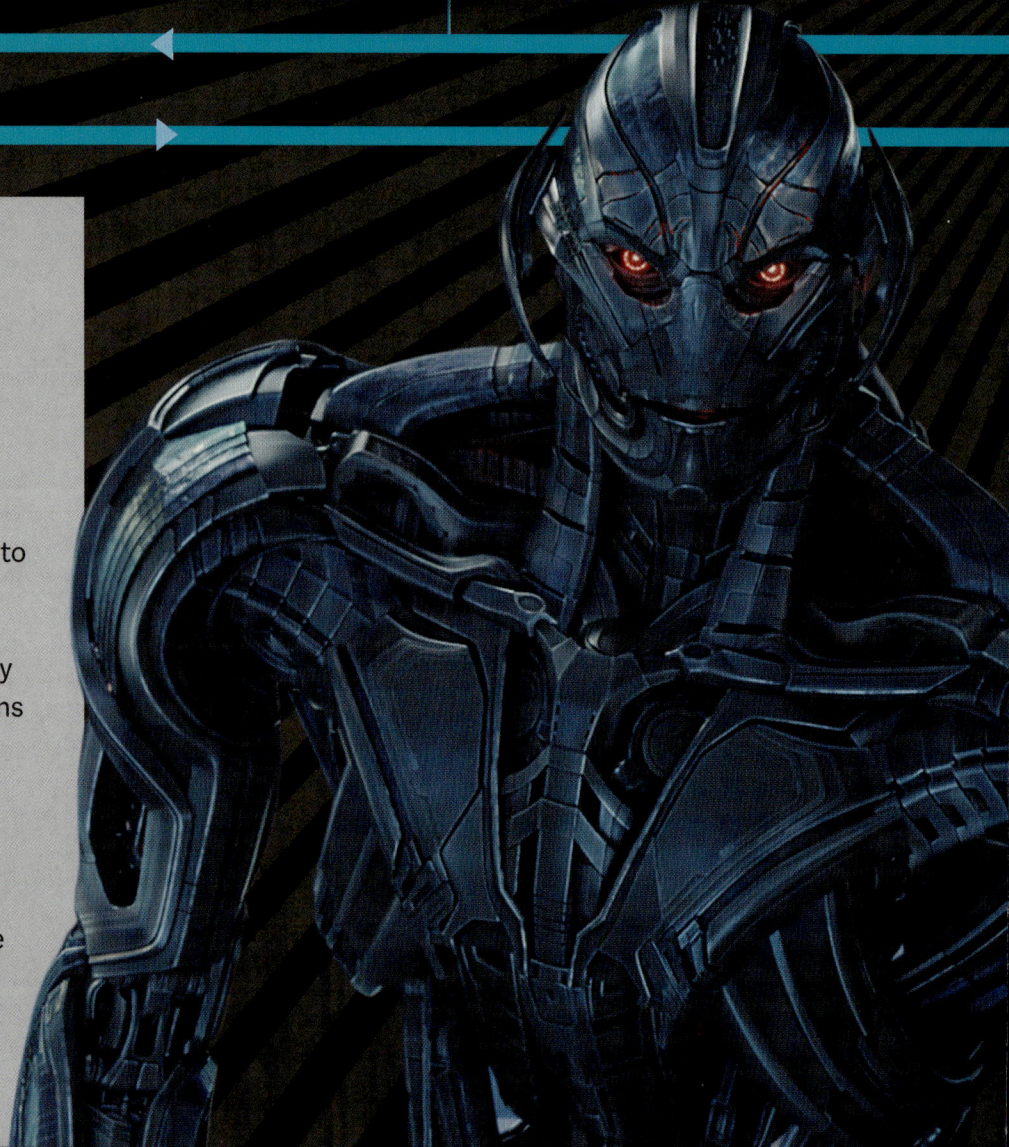

1943 | The Shield

Stark Industries researchers take possession of a tiny quantity of vibranium. The company's founder Howard Stark invites Steve Rogers to his workshop and presents him with a variety of shields to use as his main weapon as Captain America. Steve sees a shiny silver shield lying on a shelf and Stark informs him it's made of vibranium, which is lighter and stronger than steel. Creating the shield used up all of the vibranium that Stark had available.

1992 | N'Jobu's Act

Prince N'Jobu of Wakanda betrays his country, striking a deal with arms dealer Ulysses Klaue to steal a quarter-ton of vibranium. N'Jobu wants to raise funds to arm oppressed communities and start a global revolution. The theft is successful, causing many deaths. King T'Chaka of Wakanda learns of his brother's involvement and confronts him with the intention of arrest. When N'Jobu tries to kill the Wakandan spy Zuri, the king ends up killing his own brother.

2015 | A Global Threat

Ultron, the artificial intelligence created by Tony Stark, seeks out vibranium, purchasing it from Klaue. He then forces Dr. Helen Cho to create a new vibranium body. The Avengers stop Ultron from inhabiting the body, which later becomes inhabited by JARVIS as the new hero Vision. Ultron later uses vibranium to create a doomsday device—he is prevented from destroying the world, but at great cost to the people of Sokovia.

2011 | Vibranium Rediscovered

When Steve Rogers and his shield are found buried in the Arctic ice, the U.S. re-discovers the only vibranium the country has ever had in its possession. Nevertheless, they still elect to return it to Captain America—a bold choice, overseen by Nick Fury, that gives Steve the opportunity to rejoin the fight on his terms when the Avengers first assemble in 2012.

2018 | Vibranium Prosthesis

Bucky Barnes has been freed from his Winter Soldier programming and has been living a peaceful life in Wakanda. However, T'Challa informs him he's needed to help fight Thanos' army. T'Challa gives Bucky a vibranium cybernetic arm for the oncoming battle.

2023 | Vibranium Defeated

In the final battle against a version of Thanos from the past, Captain America's shield is badly damaged by blows from Thanos' weapon, which is composed of an unknown material. Steve later returns the Infinity Stones to their respective origin points and returns with the shield once again intact. Having lived a long life, an older Steve greets Sam Wilson, giving him the shield and asking him to take on the mantle of Captain America.

2025 | A New Source

In the wake of King T'Challa's death, the Wakandans find themselves having to defend their borders from other nations trying to steal their supply of vibranium. Queen Ramonda and Shuri are approached by Namor, ruler of the underwater kingdom of Talokan. Namor's people are also now threatened by the outside world—a situation they blame on T'Challa. Following disagreements, a short war breaks out between the two kingdoms until Shuri and Namor form an alliance.

2025

"Before I send my little friend here back to his own dimension, I was wondering if you'd agree to the terms of our cease and desist?"

Spring 2025 | Wong's Cease and Desist

A failed Mystic Arts pupil named Donny Blaze is using actual sorcery to improve his career as a stage magician, but he accidentally sends a hard-partying audience member named Madisynn King to a fire dimension. Wong hires Jennifer Walters to get a legal injunction against Blaze continuing to use his partial mystical teachings for entertainment. The judge rules against an injunction until her final decision in a few weeks' time, but Blaze later accidentally unleashes a horde of bloodthirsty goblins during a show. She-Hulk and Wong help clean up the mess, and Blaze voluntarily agrees to stop.

Jennifer has an eventful day as a bridesmaid.

Summer 2025 | Titania Wages War

Titania makes news again by being cleared of all charges for her courthouse outburst, but she remains angry at Jennifer Walters for embarrassing her. The super-powered influencer escalates her feud by creating a line of beauty products under the name "She-Hulk"—and then sues Walters for infringing on the trademark. Walters defeats her in court, but Titania attacks her physically at a mutual friend's wedding reception, leading to another humiliating defeat (and a mouthful of broken veneers) for the "influencer."

Titania picks another fight with Jennifer Walters.

Summer 2025 | Intelligencia

Enemies of She-Hulk gather in a hateful online group called Intelligencia, where they post misogynistic memes, make abusive threats, and plot against Jennifer Walters. Fellow attorney Mallory Book and paralegal Nikki Ramos notice the threats first, and Ramos warns Jennifer. She dismisses the trolls as irrelevant losers, but doesn't realize that the man she has just started dating, Josh Miller, is secretly working for HulkKing, one of the leaders of the group. Miller spends the night with her to extract her blood while she sleeps in human form. He then ghosts her, and her heart breaks over his lack of replies to her messages.

Mallory Book and Nikki Ramos assess the threats against Jennifer Walters.

Summer 2025 | The "Wackadoo Ranch"

That's the term Emil Blonsky's parole officer uses to describe Summer Twilights, the property where the former Abomination now hosts spiritual consultation and life coaching. Jennifer Walters accompanies the officer to the compound when Blonsky's inhibitor malfunctions, and sits in on a support group made up of Man-Bull ("I'm a weird lab experiment. Don't ask."); El Águila, a swashbuckler fighting matador tendencies; Saracen, who believes himself to be a vampire, and Porcupine, who never removes his prickly suit. Wrecker is also there, and he apologizes for attacking her, vowing to do better with his life. They all advise her to stop yearning for Josh and delete him from her phone.

Jennifer Walters visits Blonsky's retreat and meets Man-Bull and El Águila.

Summer 2025 | She-Hulk vs. Daredevil

Jennifer Walters takes on the case of a wealthy client's son who fights crime under the pseudonym Leap-Frog. His complaint: the Super Hero suit he purchased from renowned designer Luke Jacobson was defective. The case blows up in their face, somewhat literally since her client used the wrong fuel in the suit, but it does introduce her to fellow attorney Matt Murdock, who came in from his practice in New York's Hell's Kitchen to represent Jacobson. She discovers Murdock also has a Super Hero identity—Daredevil—when Leap-Frog kidnaps Jacobson and the two lawyers have to intervene.

Matt Murdock and Jennifer Walters share a beverage at the Legal Ease Bar & Grill.

Designer to the Super Heroes Luke Jacobson and his attorney Matt Murdock.

2025

Fall 2025 | She-Hulk's Downfall

Intelligencia humiliate Jennifer Walters when she is accepting an award at a Los Angeles legal gala by hijacking the screen and sharing her private messages, sensitive personal files, and home footage. Walters Hulks out, and the destruction lands her in a Damage Control prison. She loses her job, and gradually sees her life spinning out of control. Later, she learns the leader of Intelligencia was Todd Phelps, a rich, self-absorbed Hulk-wannabe, who met her on a dating app and stole her blood to make a serum that will give him her powers. She confronts him at Blonsky's retreat, where he is hosting a gathering of fellow online trolls, and Bruce Banner swoops down from outer space to stop Todd after he imbibes the serum.

A disgraced Jennifer Walters goes back to live with her mother and father.

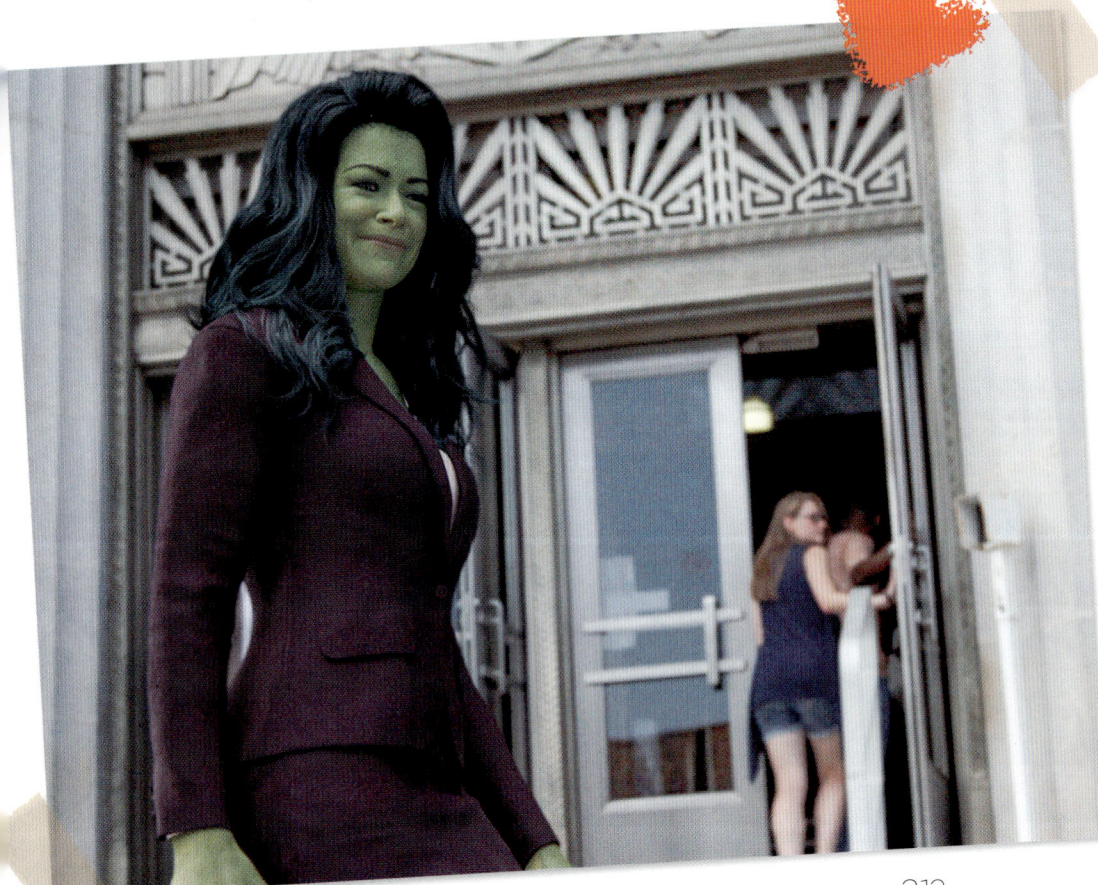

Fall 2025 | She-Hulk's New Finale

Jennifer Walters uncovers the HulkKing's plot at Blonsky's retreat and has him arrested. There's no need to beat him up—the personal harm he's done to her will be resolved in court, and he has deep pockets for restitution. Blonsky agrees to return to Damage Control custody for violating parole by delivering inspirational lectures as Abomination. Then Matt Murdock arrives, but there's no battle for Daredevil to fight. Walters is just happy to see him again. She invites him to a family picnic where the only thing she has to fight is embarrassment over her parents. Cousin Bruce shows up to surprise everyone by introducing his son, Skaar.

Jennifer Walters seizes control of her own narrative.

Fall 2025 | The Amazing Kamala Khan

Kamala Khan, a teenager from Jersey City, dreams of becoming a hero. She obsesses over the super-powered beings she's seen in the news, making vibrant illustrations of their adventures and discussing their abilities in homemade videos. She shares this fandom with her tech-savvy friend Bruno Carrelli, who helps her devise an illuminated cosplay outfit based on her all-time favorite hero—Captain Marvel. All they need is a ride to AvengerCon, a festival hosted on the old grounds of Camp Lehigh, where Captain America once trained. That excursion is jeopardized when she flunks her latest driving test.

The Super Hero dreams of Kamala Khan.

Kamala Khan's cut-out version of AvengerCon.

Kamala Khan creating platforms of solid light.

Fall 2025 | Damage Control vs. "Night Light"

Videos of the AvengerCon incident catch the attention of Agents Cleary and Deever of the U.S. Department of Damage Control, who launch an investigation. While at her local mosque, Kamala rescues a young boy who falls from one of its minarets while taking selfies near an open window. Onlookers dub the masked young hero "Night Light," and Damage Control drones immediately descend as the videos and social media posts go viral.

Fall 2025 | Glow Up

Kamala Khan accessorizes her Captain Marvel outfit with an antique bangle sent by her grandmother from Pakistan. It's a family heirloom that once belonged to her great-grandmother Aisha, whose disappearance almost eight decades ago became a source of gossip and shame for the family. The bangle activates hidden powers in Kamala, however, allowing her to create blasts of solid crystalline energy that she calls "hard light." At AvengerCon, she uses these newfound abilities to rescue a popular classmate, Zoe Zimmer, from a piece of collapsing scenery (which Khan herself had inadvertently knocked loose with said abilities).

The mystical bangle unlocks hidden power within Kamala Khan.

Kamala Khan onstage at AvengerCon.

313

2025

Fall 2025 | The Clandestines

Kamala Khan is rescued from Damage Control's clutches by a getaway car driven by her new classmate, Kamran. His mother, Najma, is in the back seat, and she reveals they are a group of exiled transdimensional beings called the Clandestines, who sensed the power of her bangle. Khan learns her great-grandmother, Aisha, was one of them, and they need the bangle to open the doorway back to their Noor Dimension. Khan is eager to help—and to learn more about her family's surprising history. Najma says the Clandestines have existed for a long time, and are frequently described in folk tales.

Kamala Khan looks at a drawing of her great-grandmother Aisha with her grandmother Sana.

Kamala Khan and Kamran share a happy moment.

Najma is ready to return to the Noor Dimension, no matter the price—or who has to pay it.

Fall 2025 | Journey to Pakistan

Kamala Khan's grandmother Sana also witnesses the vision of the train and asks the girl to visit her in Pakistan. She reveals that the train is from an incident during the British-mandated partition of India in the summer of 1947 in which Khan's great-grandparents, Aisha and Hasan, were forced to escape to the newly created nation of Pakistan. At the chaotic and overcrowded train station, Aisha disappeared, and her young daughter Sana became lost, only finding her way back to her father by following a mysterious "trail of stars."

Fall 2025 | The Wedding Debacle

Kamala had previously learned from Bruno Carrelli's biometric scan that the bangle doesn't grant her power, it merely unlocked an ability that already existed within her. He now warns that helping the Clandestines open a portal to the Noor Dimension would require energy levels commensurate with the sun, which could be deadly if not properly controlled. Khan's hesitance enrages Najma and the other Clandestines, who storm her brother's wedding to force her to help. During the fight, the bangle generates an image of a 1940s train that has profound significance for Khan's family.

Najma and Kamala Khan behold the power of the bangle.

Fall 2025 | The Red Daggers

In Karachi, the power radiating from Kamala Khan's bangle attracts the attention of Kareem, a warrior from a group called the Red Daggers, who are dedicated to protecting their people from threats of the unseen—in this case, that means preventing the Clandestines from opening a portal to the Noor Dimension. "If the Clandestines tear down the veil, they'll unleash their world on ours until there is nothing left of it," explains the Red Dagger leader Waleed. "That is why it is important to keep that bangle safe." Najma and the Clandestines soon attack the Red Daggers, killing Waleed, and leading to a standoff with Kamala Khan.

Kamala Khan hitches a ride with Kareem of the Red Daggers.

Fall 2025 | The Secret Truth of 1947

When Najma stabs the bangle, it emits a burst of energy that transports Kamala Khan back to that pivotal moment in her family history from 1947 when her grandmother, Sana, and great-grandparents were boarding the train to Pakistan. Khan discovers that Aisha did not just disappear; she was murdered by Najma for refusing to return the Clandestines to the Noor Dimension. Khan also discovers that she herself created the field of stars that led her grandmother back to her great-grandfather.

Kamala uncovers the dark truth about what happened to her great-grandmother.

2025

Kamala Khan and Kareem face down the Clandestines.

Fall 2025 | The Veil Opens

When Kamala Khan returns to the present, she sees a column of energy that leads to the Noor Dimension. The Clandestine member Fariha believes she can enter it and return home, but touching the light only disintegrates her. Realizing that Waleed was right, and the tear in dimensions will only grow out of control and destroy the world, Najma sacrifices her own life to force its closure, transmitting her powers to her son Kamran, whom she had abandoned back in the United States.

The opening of the Noor Dimension has unforeseen consequences.

Fall 2025 | "Light Girl" Revealed

Kamala's mother, Muneeba, finds her shortly after the rift evaporates, discovering that her daughter is the hero who has been getting so much attention back home. "So you are that ... Light Girl?" she asks. Kamala's grandmother is not surprised at all. "Our family is magical, Munee, I've told you so many times over the years." The trip abroad brings a sense of new understanding to the three generations of women, each in her way enhancing the strengths of the others.

Damage Control destroys the Circle Q store.

Muneeba and her mother Sana.

Fall 2025 | Kamran on the Run

Back in New Jersey, a bewildered Kamran seeks out help from Bruno Carrelli, unsure how to deal with the new powers granted by his dying mother. A Damage Control drone is tracking him, and when Kamran uses his light energy to destroy it, the drone fires a missile that destroys the Circle Q shop where Carrelli works. The two boys escape on the subway, but Kamran's powers spiral out of his control, damaging the train. Ultimately they take refuge at the Coles Academic High School because they know it will be empty on a Saturday.

Kamala outlines her plan.

Fall 2025 | Kamala Makes a Stand

Upon returning from Pakistan, Kamala Khan's mother presents her with a new outfit, a gesture of approval for her newfound Super Hero identity. Khan runs off to help Bruno and Kamran, who is suffering from the energy exploding from within him. Khan and her friends fortify their high school with non-lethal booby traps to frustrate and distract the surrounding Damage Control agents until Kamran can reach the Red Daggers to help him escape.

Fall 2025 | The Light Fantastic

During the standoff, Kamala Khan uses her light energy to increase her size, pulverizing a Damage Control energy cannon, while Kamran hurls a Humvee at Agent Deever. It goes too far and Khan grabs it before it crushes a crowd of onlookers. She smashes a hole in the street, allowing Kamran to escape through the sewers. Afterward, she is surrounded by the very people she saved, who form a human wall against Damage Control and allow her to get away on her stepping stones of light.

Kamala Khan grabs a falling vehicle before it hits innocent bystanders.

2025

⚡ **Fall 2025 | "Our Own Ms. Marvel…"**

At home, Kamala Khan's father sits with her on their rooftop, praising her for saving so many lives. He tells her that they named her "Kamala" because in Arabic it means "hope," but in Urdu it would mean "wonder" or "marvel." This last word delights his daughter. "I share the same name as Carol Fricken Danvers!?" she exclaims. Her father gleefully says yes, she does (even though he doesn't know who that is).

Kamala Khan and her father, up on the roof.

Though Gorr bears the symbol of his god, Rapu, he is treated with contempt.

Date Unverified | A True Believer Scorned

On a distant, blighted world, a father named Gorr and his young daughter struggle for survival, pleading to their god Rapu for salvation. The prayers go unanswered. After his child succumbs, Gorr finds an oasis where Rapu, the "Bringer of Light," feasts with other supernatural beings. Gorr believes he will be granted the eternal reward as promised, but Rapu makes a mockery of him, calling his life "meaningless." Rapu and his friends are celebrating the death of the holder of the Necrosword, which can be used to slay gods. A devastated Gorr takes up the weapon, empowered by its curse, and destroys Rapu. Gorr devotes himself to a new faith: the belief that all gods must be exterminated.

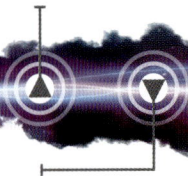

⚡ **Fall 2025 | Genetic Codebreaking**

Bruno reviews Kamala's genetic make-up against that of her immediate relatives, coming to some new conclusions. "We know you have access to the Noor Dimension and how you can wield it, but when I compared you to the rest of your family, something was still off. There's something different in your genes…"

Kamala Khan has a genetic difference that leads to her powers.

Korg and Thor regard the remains of Falligar.

Fall 2025 | Serial Killer of the Gods

Thor parts ways with the Guardians of the Galaxy after receiving reports from around the universe about the slaying of various gods. One SOS arrives from his old friend Sif, whom he and Korg track to a rocky, snowy landscape on a far-off world. The gargantuan corpse of the god Falligar looms on the horizon. Sif is gravely wounded and lost an arm in the fight. "I've been hunting a madman," she says. "I followed him here but it was a trap. The God Butcher is coming. He seeks the extinction of the gods." His next target, she warns, is New Asgard.

Thor helps a wounded Sif.

Fall 2025 | The Kidnapped Children

Gorr the God Butcher brings the Necrosword to Earth and attacks the kingdom of New Asgard with his army of shadow monsters. His target does not appear to be Valkyrie, who now rules New Asgard as its king. Instead, Gorr's creatures scuttle around the town grabbing young children and imprisoning them in a skeletal living cage. Thor arrives just in time to confront him, and with the help of a new warrior—The Mighty Thor.

Shadow monsters attack New Asgard.

2025

Thor beholds the reconstructed Mjolnir.

Fall 2025 | Eight Years, Seven Months, and Six Days

That's how long it has been since Jane Foster and Thor broke up (not that he's keeping track, of course). Thor is shocked to learn that the new hero wielding Mjolnir is his former girlfriend, and he misses both his old weapon and the brilliant woman now carrying it. The hammer has bonded with her because many years ago, Thor asked it to always protect her. That wish became an incantation etched upon its physical form. Even though it is broken, she can will the hammer to reassemble, or send the fragments tearing through the air like shrapnel. Together, Thor and Jane force Gorr to retreat. Unfortunately, he succeeds in taking the children with him.

Fall 2025 | Rekindled

One of the kidnapped Asgardian children, Axl, son of the late Heimdall, sends telepathic messages to Thor and Valkyrie that pinpoint the colorless Shadow Realm as their hidden location. On the way there, Thor has a heart-to-heart with Jane Foster, apologizing for having pushed her away during their relationship and asking for another chance. "I'm tired of giving myself over to the idea of fate," he says. "I want to live in the moment, like there's no tomorrow. I want to be with you, Jane. What do you say?" She decides to tell him about her illness. They kiss, reviving their relationship, but there really may be no tomorrow for her.

Thor and Jane share their feelings while looking upon a pod of space dolphins.

Omnipotence City, where gods are safe and can focus on their own interests.

Fall 2025 | Omnipotence City

Thor, Jane Foster, Valkyrie, and Korg venture to the meeting place of the gods to seek help rescuing the Asgardian children and defeating Gorr. A pompous Zeus balks at assisting, and refuses even to lend them his Thunderbolt weapon. Though Zeus quietly admits to Thor that Gorr frightens him, he thinks they are safe in Omnipotence City and accuses Thor of creating a needless panic. As tensions rise, weapons are drawn and a clash breaks out. Zeus manages to shatter Korg's body in the fight before Thor intercepts Thunderbolt and hurls it through Zeus' chest. Valkyrie retrieves the weapon as they all flee.

An exposed Thor stands before Zeus.

Fall 2025 | The Eternity Gambit

In the Shadow Realm, Thor, Jane Foster, and Valkyrie learn that the kidnapped children were merely a way of entrapping them. Gorr requires Stormbreaker because it's the key to the Gates of Eternity. Once opened, the being known as Eternity will grant Gorr one wish—which he will use to erase all deities from the universe. He taunts Foster about her illness during their fight: "You went to the gods for help and they did nothing. We're alike in that sense." Valkyrie is wounded when Gorr stabs her with Thunderbolt. As the defeated heroes retreat, Gorr snatches Stormbreaker from Thor's hands.

Thor fights for survival in the Shadow Realm.

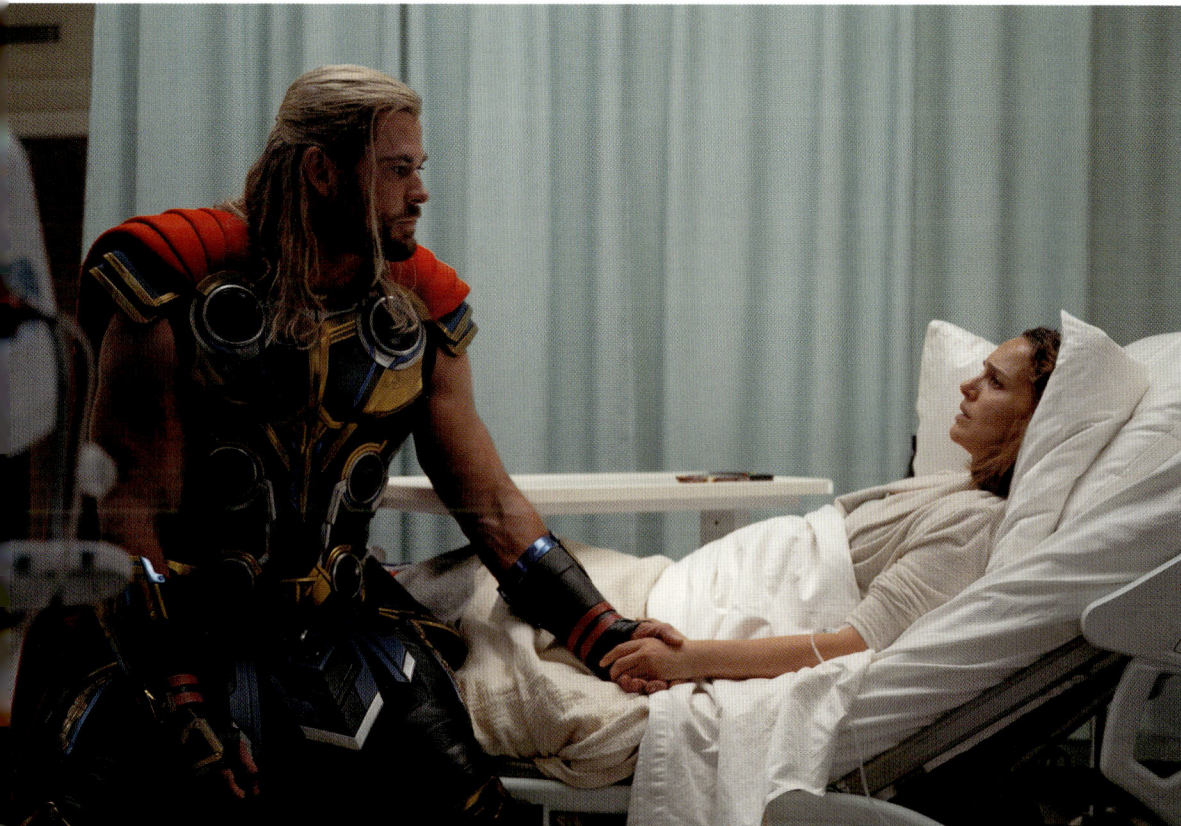

Fall 2025 | The Last Chance

Back on Earth, Jane Foster falters. The hammer strengthens her when she connects with it, but she can't do that forever. "That hammer is killing you," Thor says. "Every time you use it, it drains your mortal strength, leaving your body unable to fight the cancer." He asks her to stop wielding it, for the sake of buying more time. "I want to keep fighting," she insists, questioning whether more time of illness and suffering is worthwhile. With Korg and Valkyrie still recovering, Thor departs alone to stop Gorr.

Mjolnir provides Jane with power and abilities, but is draining her mortal strength.

2025

Fall 2025 | The Gates of Eternity

At the center of the universe, Gorr the God Butcher uses the stolen Stormbreaker to begin opening the doorway to Eternity and his most fervent wish. Thor arrives to free the captured Asgardian children, and empowers whatever tools or toys they have with the strength of a thunder god. "Whosoever holds these weapons and believes in getting home, if they be true of heart, is therefore worthy and shall possess—for a limited time only—the power of Thor," he declares. The electrified horde of children charge into battle, handily obliterating the shadow monsters while Thor confronts Gorr.

Heimdall's son Axl is one of the stolen children who rise up against Gorr's legion of shadow monsters.

Thor uses Thunderbolt against Gorr.

Fall 2025 | The Good Fight

Gorr gains the upper hand against Thor, pressing the blade of the Necrosword down into his chest. Suddenly Mjolnir knocks him aside, and The Mighty Thor rides into the corridor atop Valkyrie's pegasus. "No ..." Thor whispers. Even if they win, he knows Jane Foster will not survive this transformation. They join forces to pulverize Gorr, and finally succeed in destroying the Necrosword, which drains the God Butcher of his power and reduces him to a frail, dying husk. But it is too late. The Gateway to Eternity is open, and Gorr is about to be granted his wish ...

The Mighty Thor joins Thor's fight against Gorr.

Gorr gets his wish before Eternity.

Fall 2025 | Gorr's Wish

Gorr kneels before the star-filled silhouette of the being known as Eternity, and Thor pleads with him to consider whether death and revenge are truly what he wants. As Jane Foster returns to her mortal form, dying beside him, Thor explains: "You seek love." A stricken Gorr realizes he could also make another wish—for his daughter's return. As the little girl returns, Foster's form dissipates, similar to how gods disappear when they pass. Gorr asks Thor to look after his daughter and then succumbs.

Fall 2025 | An Eternal Reward

Jane Foster may have died in the mortal realm, but her spirit enters into the afterlife of Valhalla, where Heimdall greets her at the gateway. She gasps, unsure where or when she is. "I see you're dead now," Heimdall says. "Thank you for looking after my son. You are very welcome here in the land of the gods."

Thor and the little girl he cares for enjoy a day out together.

Fall 2025 | The Grudge of Zeus

Humiliated by Thor in Omnipotence City, Zeus recovers from his Thunderbolt wound, but his pride remains in ruins and his feelings are still sore. "It used to be that being a god meant something," he laments. Now, people only worship "so-called Super Heroes." He asks his son Hercules: "When did we become the joke?" He orders Hercules to strike fear in mortals once again by destroying Thor. "Yes, father," Hercules agrees.

Fall 2025 | Love Persevering

A statue of Dr. Jane Foster as The Mighty Thor is erected in New Asgard as tribute to her sacrifice while saving the community's stolen children. Valkyrie heals from her injuries, as does Korg, who falls in love and starts a family with a fellow Kronan rock-being named Dwayne. Thor continues to travel the galaxy, fighting for those who can't fight for themselves, but he is not alone. His companion is Gorr's daughter, reborn with the powers of a god, for whom Thor tries to cook an Earth delicacy he calls "pan-flaps." Together they become known as the heroic duo "Love and Thunder."

The memorial to Dr. Jane Foster's heroism as The Mighty Thor.

2025

Fall 2025 | A Dark Night

The funeral of famed monster hunter Ulysses Bloodstone is held at Bloodstone Manor. The night will witness a grim contest—the invitees, all skilled monster hunters themselves, will compete to become the new wielder of the Bloodstone, a powerful relic and weapon that bestows longevity, strength, and protection. Ulysses' estranged daughter, Elsa, also joins the contest, much to her stepmother's displeasure. Among the other hunters is an unassuming man named Jack, who supposedly has more than 100 kills to his name.

The grotesquely reanimated corpse of Ulysses Bloodstone addresses his fellow monster hunters.

The hunters pick lots from a skull to decide the order they enter the labyrinth.

Fall 2025 | The Hunt Begins

The hunters are led to a labyrinth. Within is a terrifying monster, which has had the Bloodstone affixed to its hide. The one to kill the creature and take the stone will become the new leader of the crusade against monsters. The hunters are also free to kill each other in order to get it. Elsa senses something is amiss with Jack when they encounter each other within the labyrinth and he shows no signs of aggression. Unknown to Elsa, Jack is a monster himself (a werewolf), who has entered the contest to save his friend Ted, the beast who is the target of the hunt. Elsa and Jack form an alliance when Jack promises to help her get the Bloodstone, in return for her aiding his and Ted's escape.

Fall 2025 | Werewolf Unleashed

Elsa witnesses Ted brutally kill one of the other hunters, but escapes his wrath by revealing that she knows his name. Jack blasts a hole in the perimeter wall and Ted escapes, but as Jack goes to pick up the fallen Bloodstone he is thrown back, revealing his monstrous nature. Elsa and Jack are captured and taken back to the house, where they are placed in a cage together—Elsa's stepmother intends for Jack to transform into a werewolf and rip Elsa to shreds. Instead, after transforming, Jack escapes the cage and tears through the guards. Elsa also escapes and kills the remaining hunters. Jack then attacks Elsa, but leaves her unharmed when he appears to remember her. Elsa's stepmother returns, ready to shoot Elsa, when Ted appears and burns the would-be murderer with his touch. Jack flees but is tracked down by Ted, who looks after him until he turns back into a human, while Elsa takes charge of Bloodstone Manor.

Jack, in werewolf form, turns Bloodstone Manor into a charnel house.

TVA ALERT!
These events *seem* to occur in 2025, but magical influences can make stuff like this hard to pin down!

Drax and Mantis get Quill an unexpected Christmas present.

December 2025 | Knowhere Special

The Guardians take up residence in the floating Celestial head of Knowhere, rebuilding it after acquiring it from the Collector. As the Christmas holiday begins on Earth, Mantis and Drax decide to do something special for Peter Quill, who is in the doldrums after losing Gamora. They decide to travel back to his homeworld to bring him one of his favorite Earth heroes—Kevin Bacon. They are aghast to discover that Bacon is merely an actor, not a true dancing hero. Bacon, meanwhile, is appalled to have been kidnapped. On the flight back to Knowhere, Mantis uses her powers to make the panicking performer go along with their strange plan.

December 2025 | Mantis Reveals a Secret

As happy as Peter Quill is to meet one of his favorite movie stars, he is horrified that Drax and Mantis are trafficking a human being. He demands that they return the actor to his home. When Quill asks Mantis why she felt the need to get him such an elaborate Christmas present, she reveals a secret she has kept hidden since they met: like Quill, she was also a child of Ego, but she was afraid for him to find out. Quill embraces her and says that discovering he has a sister is the greatest gift she could give him.

Peter Quill hugs Mantis after learning she is his sister.

WHAT IF?

For The Watcher, time, space, and reality are more than a linear path, it is a prism of endless possibility. Serving as a guide through these alternate realities, he has taken an oath to observe, never to interfere. But The Watcher breaks his promise when an alternate version of Ultron finds out about the Multiverse and plots to destroy all realities. The Watcher recruits Multiversal versions of Peggy Carter, Doctor Strange, T'Challa, Thor, Gamora, and Erik Killmonger to stop Infinity Ultron.

What if... Killmonger Rescued Tony Stark?
Lieutenant Killmonger rescues Tony Stark from an ambush in Afghanistan by the terrorist organization, The Ten Rings. At a press conference, Tony appoints Killmonger as the new chief security officer of Stark Industries. Killmonger then reveals that Obadiah Stane had conspired with The Ten Rings to assassinate Tony. Killmonger tricks Tony into helping him create an automatic combat drone, and Killmonger suggests they use vibranium to power the drones. Killmonger kills both Tony and Black Panther, setting off a war between Wakanda and the United States.

What if... Thor Were an Only Child?
Thor is raised as an only child when Odin decides to give Loki back to his people, the Frost Giants. Thor grows up to be reckless and irresponsible, partying across the galaxy. When Odin enters his Odinsleep, Thor travels to Earth to party in Las Vegas. Captain Marvel is summoned by acting S.H.I.E.L.D. Director Maria Hill to confront the partying prince and the two engage in a globe-spanning fight, which Thor wins. When Thor hears his mother Frigga is coming to Earth, he rallies his friends to repair the property damage, fearful of Frigga's wrath.

Dates are where branching begins

c. 965 — 1943 — 1988 — 2008

What if... Captain Carter Were the First Avenger?
Peggy Carter is in attendance during Steve Rogers' transformation for Project Rebirth, but decides not to go up to the viewing booth to observe. When Steve is seriously injured by Hydra agent Heinz Kruger, Peggy takes Steve's place and goes into the rebirth chamber to become a super soldier. As Captain Carter, she partners with Steve in a robotic suit built by Howard Stark, known as the Hydra Stomper, to stop the Red Skull from using the Tesseract to take over the world.

What if... T'Challa Became a Star-Lord?
One night, a young Prince T'Challa sneaks out of the palace to explore Wakanda and is kidnapped by the Ravagers. Yondu realizes they've taken the wrong child, but when T'Challa shares that he wants to explore more than his world, Yondu decides to keep him on board to explore the galaxy. T'Challa grows up to be the kind-hearted Star-Lord, who steals from the rich to give to the poor. The Ravagers become a force for good, reforming Thanos and freeing the evil Collector's captives.

What if... The Watcher Broke His Oath?

To defeat Infinity Ultron, The Watcher recruits heroes from across the Multiverse. The team includes Captain Carter, T'Challa Star-Lord, Erik Killmonger as the Black Panther, Party Thor, Strange Supreme, and a version of Gamora. The newly minted Guardians of the Multiverse take on Infinity Ultron, and with the help of a post-apocalyptic Black Widow, they inject a Hydra Arnim Zola algorithm to shut down Ultron's A.I. Arnim Zola (in Ultron's body) and Erik fight for the Infinity Stones, but Strange encases them both with magic. The Watcher then sends the others back to their timelines, but Black Widow goes to a reality that lost its own Natasha.

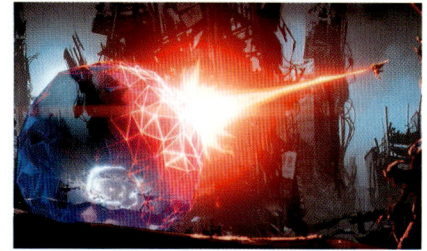

What if... Ultron Won?

Ultron downloads himself into a new vibranium body, and armed with the Mind Stone, kills Captain America, Iron Man, the Hulk, and Thor and then starts a nuclear war, wiping out most of humanity. When Thanos comes to Earth, Ultron easily overpowers him and becomes omnipotent when he takes the Infinity Stones for himself. With his new set of powers, Ultron becomes Infinity Ultron and senses the presence of The Watcher—the two go to battle for the fate of the Multiverse.

2009   2015   2016   2018

What if... the World Lost its Mightiest Heroes?

Nick Fury is preparing to launch the Avengers Initiative, but one by one, Fury's candidate heroes die mysteriously. Black Widow is close to cracking the case when she is killed by an invisible assailant in a library late one night. Fury uncovers that the murderer is Hank Pym, who used the Yellowjacket suit technology to take down the Avengers candidates in retaliation for the death of his daughter Hope, who was killed while on a S.H.I.E.L.D. mission in Odesa, Ukraine for Fury in 2009.

What if... Doctor Strange Lost His Heart Instead of His Hands?

Dr. Stephen Strange and Dr. Christine Palmer are on their way to an awards dinner when they are involved in a car crash and Christine is killed. Racked with grief, Strange encounters the Masters of the Mystic Arts and learns their ways. Upon the death of the Ancient One, Strange is given the Eye of Agamotto and uses it to reverse time and bring back Christine. The Ancient One appears to warn Strange he cannot undo an absolute point in time, but Strange defies her and his actions cause his reality and universe to be destroyed.

What if... Zombies?!

Hank Pym travels to the Quantum Realm to rescue Janet Van Dyne, but unbeknownst to him, his wife has contracted a quantum virus, turning her into a zombie. Hank is infected and they both bring the virus back to Earth, where the contagion spreads quickly. The Avengers travel to San Francisco to stop the plague, but are quickly overtaken and infected as well. The remaining survivors in New York— Peter Parker, Hope Van Dyne, Bruce Banner, Bucky Barnes, Okoye, Kurt, Sharon Carter, and Happy Hogan—travel to Camp Lehigh by following a beacon signal, only to find a deceptive Vision and a hungry zombified Scarlet Witch.

5000 BCE
The Eternals arrive on Earth.

575 BCE
The Eternals protect Babylon from an attack by Deviants.

400
Sersi and Ikaris marry in the Gupta Empire.

965
Frost Giants invade Tønsberg, Norway but are defeated in battle by Odin.

1521
The Eternals witness the fall of Tenochtitlan to the Conquistadors, and part ways after defeating the last of the Deviants.

c.965
Battle rages in Jotunheim. Odin leads the army of Asgard to defeat the Frost Giants.

c. 965
During the conflict in Jotunheim, Odin finds an abandoned Frost Giant infant (Loki) and adopts him, raising him alongside his son, Thor.

c. 965
Odin negotiates a truce with Laufey, King of the Frost Giants.

THE MCU TIMELINE

It has been said that time is a river into which we step. It constantly flows around us while we live out our brief spans until we step out of it once more. But does it always flow in the same direction? Is it always a single stream, or does it branch into many? And what happens when the flow of time is disrupted into violent rapids and whirlpools? Here is a condensed timeline of the Marvel Cinematic Universe as it currently exists. You can follow the course of key events and characters as they navigate their own paths through the river of time. As you shall see, the waters can be very choppy indeed...

1943 (June 14)
Bucky Barnes and Steve Rogers visit the Stark Expo in New York City. Having tried to enlist several times previously and been rejected, Steve is finally accepted into the army by Dr. Abraham Erskine.

1991 (December 16)
Under Hydra orders, the Winter Soldier (Bucky Barnes) assassinates Howard and Maria Stark. Their murder is covered up as a car accident. Obadiah Stane assumes interim CEO duties of Stark Industries.

1993 (December 2)
Ivan Vanko is sentenced to 15 years in a Russian prison for selling weapons-grade plutonium to Pakistan.

1943 (June 22)
Steve Rogers is exposed to Dr. Erskine's serum, transforming him into a super soldier. However, Dr. Erskine is then assassinated in the lab by a Hydra operative.

1989
Hank Pym resigns from S.H.I.E.L.D. upon discovering that the organization has secretly attempted to replicate his size-changing particles.

1992
King T'Chaka learns his brother, N'Jobu, has been smuggling vibranium from Wakanda. When confronted, N'Jobu attempts to shoot his friend Zuri, who has been spying on him for T'Chaka, but T'Chaka intervenes and kills N'Jobu. N'Jobu's son, Erik, having watched the departure of T'Chaka's ship, returns to their Oakland apartment to find his father dead. He also finds N'Jobu's journals, and a decryption key for the Wakandan language. He begins a journey of vengeance.

1943 (November 3-10)
While on a USO tour, Captain America defies orders and attacks a Hydra facility in Austria, where Bucky Barnes and the rest of the 107th are being held prisoner. Steve rescues the captives, and several of them—including Bucky—go on to join Cap's Howling Commandos.

Mid-1940s
The Howling Commandos capture Dr. Arnim Zola from a Hydra train, but Bucky falls into an icy chasm and is presumed dead. In reality, he is taken captive and brainwashed by Hydra.

1945 (March)
Captain America and the Howling Commandos defeat the Red Skull, who tries to use the Tesseract and disappears. He will end up on the planet Vormir, where he will become Stonekeeper of the Soul Stone.

1989
Air Force test pilot Carol Danvers and scientist Dr. Wendy Lawson crash in their *Asis* prototype after being attacked by an alien spacecraft. Lawson is killed, Carol is abducted by Kree forces and taken to their capital world of Hala. Carol loses memory of her past.

1945 (March)
Captain America intentionally crashes the Hydra doomsday plane *Valkyrie* in the Arctic ice and is presumed dead.

2008 (Early)
Tony Stark demonstrates his Jericho missile technology to the U.S. Armed Forces in Afghanistan. After the demonstration, Tony is wounded in an ambush and captured by The Ten Rings, who are actually working with his colleague Obadiah Stane.

2010 (Spring)
On Fury's orders, Natasha Romanoff joins Stark Industries as a notary, keeping tabs on Stark under the false identity "Natalie Rushman."

2010 (Spring)
Ivan Vanko crashes the Monaco Grand Prix (literally), and battles Tony Stark, who dons his Mark V armor in order to defeat Vanko.

2010 (Spring)
Tony Stark, who is acting erratically while suffering from palladium poisoning, is placed under house arrest by Fury. James Rhodes steals the Mark II armor and delivers it to the military, where it is modified by Justin Hammer, turning Rhodes into War Machine. At the Stark Expo, the War Machine armor is hacked by Vanko, who also hacks the displaying Hammer Drones, using them to attack the event. Iron Man, War Machine, Black Widow, and Happy Hogan defeat Vanko, who is killed.

2010 (Summer)
Agent Coulson informs Agent Sitwell that the World Security Council wants Emil Blonsky released from prison to join the Avengers Initiative, despite Fury not wanting him. The Council plan for the destruction caused by Abomination to be blamed solely on the Hulk; Blonsky is to be considered a war hero. Coulson and Sitwell decide to send a patsy to sabotage the meeting with General Thaddeus Ross so that Blonsky remains in prison; they send "The Consultant," Tony Stark.

1999 (December 31)
Tony Stark attends a New Year's Eve party in Bern, Switzerland, where he meets Maya Hansen and Dr. Ho Yinsen. He is also approached by a disabled scientist named Aldrich Killian, who asks for a meeting with Stark to pitch for research funding, but Stark rudely stands him up. Hansen reveals her work on Extremis to Stark—including its explosive side-effects.

Mid-2000s
While testing an experiment on himself, Dr. Bruce Banner is exposed to a burst of gamma radiation, accidentally transforming himself into the Hulk. After destroying the lab, he goes on the run.

2008 (Early)
Stark's life is saved by fellow captive Dr. Ho Yinsen, who performs heart surgery. Together, they construct the Mark I armor, allowing Tony to escape. Dr. Ho Yinsen does not survive, and the remains of the Mark I armor are retrieved from the desert by The Ten Rings.

2010 (Spring)
Bruce returns to Culver University and reunites with Betty Ross, before a battle with General Thaddeus Ross and Special Forces soldier Emil Blonsky. The Hulk flees the scene.

2010 (Spring)
Blonsky, having already taken a prototype version of the Super Soldier Serum, mutates into Abomination when injected with products derived from Banner's blood. Hulk defeats the Abomination after a destructive battle in Harlem.

2010 (Spring)
Samuel Sterns, who attempted to cure Banner, ends up mutating after exposure to Banner's blood.

2010 (Summer)
Coulson sends Tony Stark to meet General Ross at a bar to discuss the release of Emil Blonsky into S.H.I.E.L.D. custody. Stark annoys Ross so much that Ross tries to remove him from the bar, so Tony buys the venue. The plan works: Blonsky will remain in prison.

1995 (Summer)
Carol Danvers arrives back on Earth, where she uncovers the truth of her manipulation by the Kree. She aids Talos' band of refugee Skrulls in their battle against the Kree, unleashing her full powers in the process.

2008 (Spring)
Returning to the U.S., Tony Stark pulls Stark Industries out of the weapons business, cancelling all military contracts. He focuses instead on improving his Arc Reactor technology and Iron Man armor.

2010 (Spring)
Thor crashes to Earth, having been banished by Odin. His hammer, Mjolnir, also lands in New Mexico. S.H.I.E.L.D Agent Coulson arrives to secure it.

2008 (Spring)
Stark is attacked by Obadiah Stane in an upgrade of the Mark I suit, whom he defeats. Stark publicly claims his new nickname as Iron Man, rejecting S.H.I.E.L.D.'s cover story; he's later approached by Nick Fury to join the "Avenger Initiative."

2010 (Spring)
S.H.I.E.L.D. Agent Clint Barton defends the base set up around Mjolnir's crash site.

2011
S.H.I.E.L.D. manage to thaw out Steve Rogers, recently recovered from the Arctic.

2010 (Spring)
Sif and the Warriors Three arrive on Earth, looking for Thor. Loki orders the automaton known as the Destroyer to get rid of Thor and destroy everything. The Destroyer attacks the town of Puente Antiguo, but Thor proves himself worthy and with his powers restored, is able to defeat the Destroyer.

2012

2013

2014

2012 (Spring)
Loki, on the orders of Thanos, uses the Tesseract's energy to open a portal to S.H.I.E.L.D.'s Joint Dark Energy Mission Facility. He steals the Tesseract and takes over the minds of Dr. Selvig and Hawkeye. Thor is alerted of Loki's arrival on Earth.

2012 (Spring)
Romanoff is undercover, interrogating an arms dealer, when she is interrupted by a call from Coulson. He tells her Hawkeye's been compromised and she needs to come in.

2012 (Spring)
Coulson visits Tony Stark to have him review Selvig's research, and Fury approaches Steve Rogers with an assignment to retrieve the stolen Tesseract.

2012 (Spring)
Agent Natasha Romanoff is sent to Kolkata to recruit Dr. Bruce Banner to trace the Tesseract through its gamma radiation emissions.

2012 (Spring)
In Stuttgart, Barton steals iridium needed to stabilize the Tesseract's energy while Loki causes a distraction. This leads to a brief confrontation with Rogers, Stark, and Romanoff and ends with Loki's surrender.

2012 (Spring)
Odin uses dark energy to transport Thor to Earth so he can apprehend Loki.

2012 (Spring)
Thor, Iron Man, and Captain America get into a skirmish about who takes Loki. Finally they agree to take Loki into S.H.I.E.L.D. custody. Loki manages to escape captivity aboard the S.H.I.E.L.D. Helicarrier with the help of Barton and other mind-controlled agents. Natasha knocks Barton unconscious, breaking Loki's mind control. The Hulk goes on a rampage and crashes back to Earth. Phil Coulson is killed by Loki. His death helps unite the Avengers.

2012 (Spring) BATTLE OF NEW YORK
Loki uses the Tesseract to open a portal above New York City, allowing Thanos' Chitauri army to swarm through. The Avengers unite and defeat Loki and the invaders. Iron Man redirects a nuclear missile into space, preventing New York City from being wiped out. The invasion is halted and the Tesseract recovered. Thor takes it to Asgard for safe keeping.

2013 (Fall)
Thor leads the Asgardians to victory against the Marauders on Vanaheim. Rather than celebrating, Thor consults with Heimdall who is unable to "see" Jane Foster. Thor then heads to Earth to locate her, discovering that—after messing with a gravitational anomaly in London—she has been infected with the power of the Aether.

2013 (Fall)
Loki fakes his own death then implements a plan to secretly usurp the throne from Odin, whom he banishes to Earth. Thor and his allies defeat Malekith and the Dark Elves in a battle in Greenwich, London.

2013
Sif and Volstagg meet the Collector and hand over the Aether for safe keeping.

2013 (Winter)
The first "Mandarin bombing" occurs.

2013 (Winter)
Tony Stark suffers from flashbacks of the Battle of New York, while his Iron Legion project causes friction with Pepper.

2013 (December 22)
The Mandarin claims the bombing of both Ali Al Salem Air Base and the TCL Chinese Theatre (both blasts are actually caused by exploding Extremis subjects). Happy Hogan is caught in the latter and falls into a coma.

2013 (December 23-24)
Stark's mansion is destroyed by the Mandarin. Tony Stark is pronounced dead but secretly escapes in the Mark XLII armor. JARVIS pilots an unconscious Tony to Rose Hill, Tennessee where he meets young Harley. Tony spends time repairing his armor while investigating the Mandarin bombings before heading to Miami to infiltrate the Mandarin's mansion, where he finds actor Trevor Slattery and learns of Aldrich Killian's plan to target the President.

2013 (December 24-25)
Stark and his Iron Legion rescue Pepper Potts, whom Killian has infected with Extremis, while Rhodes saves the kidnapped President Ellis. Pepper blasts Killian, saving Tony's life.

2014 (Early)
Pepper is cured of her Extremis effects, while Stark has surgery to remove the remaining shrapnel near his heart. He throws his now-obsolete Arc Reactor into the sea.

2014 (Spring)
Sam Wilson meets Captain America.

2014 (Spring)
Captain America and Black Widow lead a S.H.I.E.L.D. team in retaking the hijacked vessel *Lemurian Star*. The mission turns out to be a ploy of Nick Fury's, who has become suspicious that S.H.I.E.L.D. has been corrupted from within.

2014 (Spring)
Captain America, Black Widow, and Falcon battle an army of Hydra agents who have infiltrated S.H.I.E.L.D. Nick Fury returns, having faked his own assassination, and he and Maria Hill help to destroy the three Project Insight Helicarriers Hydra had planned to use to neutralize potential threats to their organization.

2014 (Spring)
The Winter Soldier and Captain America have a brutal battle on the final Helicarrier. Captain America orders Maria Hill to fire on the Helicarrier, despite still being aboard. The Winter Soldier begins to remember his past as Bucky Barnes. Captain America falls into the Potomac river, but Bucky pulls an unconscious Steve Rogers to safety.

2014 (Spring)
After successfully using Loki's scepter to enhance the Maximoff twins, Hydra leader Baron Strucker reassures his team that their work will continue, despite the collapse of the wider organization.

2014 (Summer)
Star-Lord (Peter Quill) betrays his Ravager crew and travels solo to Morag to take possession of a valuable Orb. He is attacked by Korath and his Sakaarans, on the orders of Ronan the Accuser, but escapes with the prize.

2014 (Summer)
Gamora attacks Quill on Xandar and steals the Orb, while Rocket and Groot try to capture Quill in order to claim the Ravager bounty on his head. They are all arrested by the Nova Corps and imprisoned at the Kyln, where they meet Drax the Destroyer. The unconventional team quickly escapes and heads to Knowhere at Gamora's direction.

2014 (Summer)
On Knowhere, the Collector reveals the Orb's true nature, but the Infinity Stone it holds is captured by Nebula and then passed to Ronan. Ronan betrays Thanos, intending to use the stone to destroy Xandar.

2014 (Summer)
The Ravagers, the Guardians of the Galaxy, and the Nova Corps work together to stop Ronan's forces above Xandar. The Guardians then defeat Ronan with the Power Stone.

2014 (Summer)
The Power Stone is left on Xandar with the Nova Corps.

2014 (Fall)
The Guardians are hired by Ayesha, High Priestess of the Sovereign, to defeat a battery-eating monster called the Abilisk. Their reward: Nebula, who is released into their custody.

2014 (Fall)
Rocket steals from the Sovereign, but the Guardians are saved from destruction by a mysterious figure named Ego. He introduces himself as Peter Quill's father alongside his emissary Mantis. Ego invites Quill to return to his home, accompanied by Gamora and Drax. Rocket and Groot remain to repair the Guardians' damaged ship and guard Nebula.

2014 (Fall)
Ego explains he is a god-like Celestial who once traveled the universe. That's where he found Quill's mother. He hired Yondu to collect Quill after Meredith died, but the boy was never delivered. Ego has been searching for him ever since. Ego teaches Quill to manipulate his Celestial power.

2014 (Fall)
Nebula arrives at Ego's planet and tries to kill Gamora, but the pair reach an uneasy alliance after talking through their shared past, and discover a cavern filled with the bones of Ego's children.

2014 (Fall)
Ego reveals his plan for universal domination to Quill. Gamora, Nebula, and Drax also learn of the plan from Mantis. Rocket, Yondu, Groot, and Kraglin arrive. The reunited Guardians find Ego's brain at the planet's core, as they come under renewed attack from the Sovereign's drones. Rocket makes a bomb using stolen anulax batteries, which Groot plants on the brain.

2014 (Fall)
Quill fights Ego with his newfound Celestial powers to distract him long enough for the other Guardians and Mantis to escape. The bomb explodes, killing Ego and disintegrating the planet. Quill loses his Celestial powers upon Ego's demise. Yondu rescues Quill from certain death as the planet collapses, but sacrifices himself in the process.

2015 (Spring)
The Avengers locate and attack Hydra's research base in Sokovia. They come into brief conflict with the twins Pietro and Wanda Maximoff, but successfully recover Loki's scepter and take Hydra leader Baron Strucker into custody, bringing the Avengers' war on Hydra to an end.

2015 (Spring)
During a party at Avengers Tower to celebrate their victory, Stark's new Ultron A.I. becomes sentient. It instantly assesses humanity as irredeemable, and attempts to destroy JARVIS before fashioning a body for itself out of leftover parts of Stark's Iron Legion sentries.

2015 (Spring)
Ultron interrupts the party and attacks the Avengers with the remaining Iron Legion. The Avengers fight off their robotic foes, but Ultron flees with the scepter and settles in Sokovia, where he allies with the Maximoffs.

2015 (Spring)
The Avengers travel to Seoul, South Korea to stop Ultron from completing a new synthezoid body made with vibranium. The Maximoff twins learn of Ultron's true plans to wipe out humanity and turn against him. The Avengers capture the body, but Romanoff is captured by Ultron.

2015 (Spring)
Stark and Banner attempt to upload JARVIS into the synthetic body, which Ultron has augmented with the Mind Stone from Loki's scepter. After a blast of lightning from Mjolnir, Vision is born. He proves his good intentions by easily lifting the hammer, and agrees to join the Avengers in their battle against Ultron.

2015 (Spring) BATTLE IN SOKOVIA
Ultron uses vibranium to transform the capital city of Sokovia into a giant doomsday weapon. The Avengers arrive to stop him. Black Widow is rescued, while Fury and former S.H.I.E.L.D. agents evacuate the weaponized city's civilians before it is destroyed. Ultron's rampage is finally ended by Vision.

2016 (Spring)
The mercenary Crossbones raids the Institute for Infectious Disease in Lagos, Nigeria in order to steal a bio-weapon. Captain America, Black Widow, Falcon, and Wanda Maximoff intervene. When Crossbones sets off a suicide bomb, Wanda redirects the blast, but accidentally takes innocent lives in the process.

2015 (Summer)
Scott Lang is released from prison after serving a three-year sentence for theft.

2016 (Spring)
Tony Stark is confronted by a grieving mother whose son was killed in Sokovia. She blames the Avengers for his death.

2015 (Summer)
During a meeting between Pym Technologies and other companies, Darren Cross unveils the Yellowjacket suit. In a private conversation, he reveals to Hank Pym his knowledge of Pym's past as Ant-Man. Pym intends to thwart Cross' actions.

2016 (Spring)
In the aftermath of the attack in Lagos, the UN drafts the Sokovia Accords, aiming to place the Avengers under government control.

2015 (Spring)
Hulk hijacks the team's Quinjet, and then departs for an unknown destination.

2015 (Summer)
In desperate need of money, Scott Lang robs Hank Pym's house, stealing the Ant-Man suit he finds within Pym's safe. He tries it on and shrinks down for the first time.

2016 (Spring)
The Avengers must sign the accords within three days, or they will have to retire.

2016 (February 2)
Dr. Stephen Strange survives a terrible car crash, but his hands are irreparably damaged.

2015 (Summer)
Attempting to return the suit, Lang is arrested and sent back to jail. There he encounters Pym face-to-face for the first time and discovers that Pym orchestrated the heist in order to test him. Pym gives the Ant-Man suit to Lang, who uses it to escape from his cell.

2016 (Spring)
Peggy Carter dies. Steve Rogers attends her funeral in London.

2015 (Spring)
The Avengers Compound opens in Upstate New York. Captain America and Black Widow train the new members of the team: Vision, Wanda Maximoff, Falcon, and War Machine.

2015 (Summer)
On Pym's orders, Lang infiltrates the Avengers Compound to steal a device that will help them capture the Yellowjacket suit. He is spotted by Falcon but outmaneuvers the Avenger.

2016 (Spring)
A vengeful Sokovian officer named Helmut Zemo tortures a Hydra agent, seeking mission report details from December 16, 1991.

2015 (Summer)
Lang successfully infiltrates Pym Technologies but is captured by Darren Cross. However, he escapes and gives chase to Cross, who dons the Yellowjacket suit. The battle escalates at Lang's ex-wife's house, where Cross tries to kidnap Lang's daughter. Cross is thwarted when Lang goes subatomic to sabotage Cross' suit. Remarkably, Lang then discovers a way to resurface from the Quantum Realm.

2016 (Spring)
The signing ceremony for the accords is held in Vienna, where Romanoff meets T'Challa, son of King T'Chaka of Wakanda. The event is disrupted by a terrorist bombing masterminded by Helmut Zemo—T'Chaka is killed. Bucky Barnes is framed for the attack, and T'Challa vows to seek revenge. Rogers and Wilson travel to Bucharest to try and locate the Winter Soldier before he can be arrested (or worse), but all are captured and taken to Berlin for interrogation.

2015 (Summer)
Hank Pym shows Hope Van Dyne a prototype Wasp suit.

2015 (Spring)
Thor leaves the Avengers, pursuing answers to his visions of Asgard.

2016 (Spring)

Helmut Zemo infiltrates the facility where the Winter Soldier is being held and triggers his Hydra programming, forcing him to reveal the location of an abandoned Hydra base in Siberia, where there are other Winter Soldiers, still alive but frozen. The Winter Soldier then violently flees the facility, but is captured and subdued by Rogers and Wilson.

2016 (Spring)

Bucky Barnes is given sanctuary in Wakanda.

2016 (Spring)

Barnes volunteers to be frozen again until his mind-control can be completely purged.

2016 (Spring)

Hawkeye breaks Wanda Maximoff out of the Avengers Compound; both then join Cap's team. Vision tries to stop them but Wanda restrains him using her powers.

2016 (Spring)

Scott Lang and Clint Barton both strike plea deals and must remain under house arrest. Meanwhile, Hank Pym and Hope Van Dyne are on the run from the law due to the Sokovia Accords.

2016 (Fall)

After numerous failed surgeries, Stephen Strange meets with Jonathan Pangborn and learns of Kamar-Taj. He spends the last of his funds to travel to Nepal.

2016 (Spring)

Stark and Black Widow are joined by War Machine, Black Panther, and a new hero: Spider-Man, whom Stark presents with an advanced new suit.

2016 (Spring-Summer)

Natasha Romanoff and Yelena take down the Red Room.

2016 (Fall)

Strange meets Karl Mordo and the Ancient One, and is eventually admitted into Kamar-Taj, where he begins his training in the Mystic Arts.

2016 (Spring)

On the recommendation of Sam Wilson, Rogers recruits Ant-Man.

2016 (Summer)

T'Challa defeats Erik Killmonger and reclaims the Wakandan throne.

2016 (Spring) BATTLE IN LEIPZIG-HALLE

The Avengers confront each other at Leipzig-Halle Airport. Captain America is joined by Falcon, the Winter Soldier, Hawkeye, Wanda Maximoff, and Ant-Man. They are faced by Iron Man's team, which includes Black Widow, War Machine, Vision, Black Panther, and Spider-Man.

2016 (Spring)

Falcon, Wanda, Hawkeye, and Ant-Man are sent to the Raft, an ocean-based prison designed to hold enhanced people.

2016 (Summer)

Steve Rogers and Natasha Romanoff rescue Sam Wilson and Wanda Maximoff from the Raft.

2017

Strange experiments with the Eye of Agamotto, but is warned of its dangers by Wong and Mordo. Kaecilius and his Zealots destroy the London Sanctum, then target the New York Sanctum. Though outmatched, Strange attempts to defend it, aided by a sentient magical artifact—the Cloak of Levitation.

2016 (Spring)

Captain America and the Winter Soldier escape and travel to Siberia. There, they and Iron Man agree to a temporary truce to defeat Zemo, and discover that Zemo has killed the other Winter Soldiers. He reveals he wanted to tear the Avengers apart because his family were killed in Sokovia.

2016 (Summer)

Tony receives a letter and burner phone from Steve as an olive branch and means through which Tony can reach Steve should he ever need him.

2016 (Spring)

Zemo also reveals that the Winter Soldier was responsible for murdering Stark's parents, causing Iron Man to violently lash out at Bucky and Captain America. After a brutal fight that ends with Iron Man being immobilized, Captain America departs. He casts his shield aside after Stark insists that it doesn't belong to him, and he and Bucky then go into hiding.

2016 (Fall)

Peter Parker defeats the arms dealer Adrian Toomes and Stark offers him a place in the Avengers; Peter declines.

2017

The Ancient One arrives at the hospital in critical condition after battling Kaecilius. In her astral form, the Ancient One confesses to Strange about drawing power from the Dark Dimension. Before dying, she warns Strange that he and Mordo must work together to defeat Kaecilius' master, the evil ruler of the Dark Dimension, Dormammu.

2017

Wong and other sorcerers battle Kaecilius at the Hong Kong Sanctum, but are defeated. Strange uses the Eye of Agamotto to reverse time and undo the destruction. However, Kaecilius breaks free of the spell and summons Dormammu from the Dark Dimension. Strange uses the Eye of Agamotto to trap Dormammu in a time loop, forcing him to retreat.

2017

Mordo leaves the Masters of the Mystic Arts, disillusioned by the revelation that the Ancient One was using energy from the Dark Dimension.

2017

Strange begins his new role as master of the New York Sanctum.

2017 (Fall)

Odin dies. Thor's sister, Hela, returns from exile, claims the throne, and crushes Mjolnir.

2017 (Fall)

Thor and Loki end up on Sakaar, where they encounter Hulk and a former Asgardian Valkyrie. Together they return to Asgard to defeat Hela and rescue their people, but are forced to destroy Asgard in the process. They escape the cataclysm aboard a spaceship.

2018 (Spring)

Janet Van Dyne is rescued from the Quantum Realm and reunited with her family.

2018 (Spring)

Traveling through space, Thor, Loki, Hulk, and the Asgardians are intercepted by Thanos. The Titan's forces ravage their ship, and Thor and Heimdall are defeated and cast down. The Hulk attacks Thanos but is no match for the Power Stone he now wields and is subdued easily. Before Hulk can be killed, Heimdall summons the Bifrost and dispatches Banner to Earth. Thanos takes the Space Stone from Loki before killing him, then sets the ship to detonate and vanishes with his minions, the Children of Thanos.

2018 (Spring)

Bruce Banner lands in the New York Sanctum, where he warns Doctor Strange and Wong of Thanos' impending arrival. They summon Tony Stark, who arrives as Thanos' Children Cull Obsidian and Ebony Maw appear over New York City, seeking the Time Stone. Banner discovers that his Hulk persona now refuses to emerge.

2018 (Spring)

Spider-Man joins the battle and inadvertently stows away on Ebony Maw's spaceship as he speeds back to Thanos with a captive Doctor Strange. Iron Man pursues and gives the young hero the Iron Spider armor, just as he passes out from lack of oxygen. Both are now trapped aboard.

2018 (Spring)

The Guardians of the Galaxy track the Asgardian ship's distress signal, but arrive to find only debris, bodies, and Thor, who is floating unconscious in the void. After Thor is roused, he, Rocket, and Groot travel to Nidavellir, home of the legendary Dwarf blacksmiths, in search of a new weapon with which to defeat Thanos. Rocket gives Thor a cybernetic eye to replace the one he lost on Asgard while battling Hela.

2018 (Spring)

As Maw and Obsidian unleash their assault on New York City, Thanos' minions Corvus Glaive and Proxima Midnight target Vision and Wanda Maximoff in Edinburgh, Scotland, with the aim of obtaining the Mind Stone. However, their plans are thwarted when the two heroes are joined by Captain America, Black Widow, and Falcon.

2018 (Spring)

Iron Man and Spider-Man rescue Doctor Strange. Ebony Maw is sucked out of the ship into space.

2018 (Spring)

Earth's mightiest heroes are now aware of Thanos' plan, and the vital importance of safeguarding Vision and the Mind Stone. They travel to Wakanda, the best-protected place on Earth, where they prepare for the impending defense. They join forces with Black Panther and his army, which also includes Bucky Barnes, known to his Wakandan hosts as the White Wolf.

2018 (Spring)

The other Guardians of the Galaxy decide to journey to Knowhere to check on the Reality Stone, which is in the care of the Collector. Unfortunately, Thanos gets there first. Using an illusion, he overpowers them, captures Gamora, and disappears through a portal.

2018 (Spring)

Aboard the *Sanctuary II,* Thanos tortures a captured Nebula. Unable to bear seeing her sister in agony, Gamora finally divulges what Thanos is after—the location of the Soul Stone. She and Thanos travel to Vormir, where the Stonekeeper (who was once the villain known as the Red Skull) tells Thanos that he must lose that which he loves if he wishes to gain his prize. Thanos sacrifices Gamora to claim the stone.

2018 (Spring)

The Guardians of the Galaxy travel to Titan, Thanos' ecologically ravaged homeworld. They hope to rescue Gamora and defeat Thanos, but instead encounter Tony Stark, Spider-Man, and Doctor Strange, who have crash-landed in Ebony Maw's vessel, which flew here on autopilot. They come up with a plan: draw Thanos out, use Mantis' powers to subdue him, and then remove his Infinity Gauntlet.

2018 (Spring)

Star-Lord is shocked to learn that Gamora has been killed. He lashes out, severing Mantis' psychic link with Thanos. The Titan violently regains control, throwing Iron Man and Spider-Man aside before they can remove the gauntlet. Despite a relentless attack from Nebula, Thanos is now invulnerable. Doctor Strange, having foreseen only one victorious outcome among countless possibilities, surrenders the precious Time Stone to spare Tony Stark's life. As Thanos disappears through a portal to Earth (and his seemingly inevitable victory), the team is left broken, defeated, and stranded.

2018 (Spring)

Lang travels into the Quantum Realm in search of healing particles with which to stabilize his former foe, Ghost. Hank, Hope, and Janet monitor his progress, and prepare to bring him back once he has what he needs. Unfortunately, the Snap claims all three of them before they can do so, trapping Lang in the Quantum Realm.

2018 (Spring)

On Earth, Nick Fury and Maria Hill watch in horror as those around them dust away. Fury manages to page Captain Marvel before both he and Hill are lost to the Snap.

2018 (Spring)

Having recovered Fury's pager, Steve Rogers, Natasha Romanoff, Bruce Banner, and James Rhodes work to keep the device powered up by creating a new energy source for the cosmic communications device. Despite the battery working fine, the alert suddenly stops. While they try to figure out a solution, Captain Marvel suddenly appears, asking what has happened to her old ally.

**2018 (Spring)
THE SNAP**

Thanos arrives in Wakanda. The Titan is now virtually unstoppable, but Wanda is able to briefly hold him back while she summons every bit of her power to destroy the Mind Stone. But Thanos is unconcerned—he simply uses the Time Stone to rewind the last few moments, and plucks the restored stone from Vision's head, killing him. As Thanos surges with power from his completed Infinity Gauntlet, Thor strikes him in the chest with Stormbreaker, but Thanos is only wounded. He snaps his fingers, then vanishes through a portal. In just a few terrifying moments, half the population of the universe collapses into dust.

**2018 (Spring)
BATTLE IN WAKANDA**

Under the command of Corvus Glaive, Cull Obsidian, and Proxima Midnight, a massive army of Outriders launches a full-scale attack on Wakanda. The Avengers and Wakandan warriors form the final barrier between Thanos' forces and the Mind Stone. Shuri frantically works to detach the stone from Vision's head so that it can be safely destroyed.

2018 (Spring)

Iron Man and Nebula are rescued from deep space by Captain Marvel.

2018 (Spring)

The surviving Avengers, Guardians, and Captain Marvel ambush Thanos on his secluded garden world and attempt to undo the Snap—they discover that Thanos has destroyed the stones, making their task impossible. In a rage, Thor decapitates him with Stormbreaker.

2018 (Spring)

As the battle rages in Wakanda, Thor bravely endures the powerful rays of Nidavellir's neutron star in order to reignite the forge, which was extinguished by Thanos. The skilled Dwarf blacksmith Eitri crafts the mighty ax Stormbreaker, aided by Groot sacrificing a part of himself for the handle. Thor, proving his worthiness, summons the new weapon, and is healed from his star-induced injuries.

2018 (Spring)

Filled with despair at the loss of his family, Hawkeye becomes the vigilante Ronin.

2018 (Spring)

Thor, Rocket, and Groot arrive in Wakanda, where they join their allies in decimating the army of Outriders.

2023 (Fall) (Avengers in 2012 NYC)
Banner, Rogers, Lang, and Stark travel to 2012 New York City, during the first assault on the city by Thanos' forces. They plan to retrieve the Time, Mind, and Space Stones.

2023 (Fall) (Avengers in 2013 Asgard)
Thor and Rocket travel to Asgard in 2013 to retrieve the Reality Stone, by extracting it from Jane Foster just prior to the Dark Elf invasion.

2023 (Fall)
Scott Lang, who has been trapped in the Quantum Realm for what seems like only hours to him, escapes thanks to a rat that inadvertently activates the Quantum Tunnel. After confronting the reality of what has transpired over the last five years, he reunites with his daughter, Cassie, who is now a teenager. He then travels to the Avengers Compound, where he explains that the Quantum Realm may allow time travel.

2023 (Fall) (Avengers in 2012 NYC)
Banner convinces the Ancient One to part with the Time Stone, after revealing that Doctor Strange must have planned for this eventuality. Banner reassures her that once the Avengers have used it, the stone will be returned to this point in time to prevent the creation of branch realities.

2023 (Fall) (Avengers in 2013 Asgard)
Thor is reunited with his mother, Frigga, before her untimely death. He also manages to summon a still-intact Mjolnir, which he brings back with him to the present.

2023 (Fall)
Steve, Natasha, and Scott travel to Tony's home to ask for his help. Stark refuses at first, as a way to protect his family and not risk losing them, but eventually works with Banner to figure out how to stabilize time travel through the Quantum Realm. The Avengers devise a plan to travel to the past in order to retrieve the Infinity Stones and undo Thanos' Snap.

2023 (Fall) (Avengers in 2014 Morag)
Nebula and Rhodey ambush Peter Quill before he can take the Power Stone, knocking him unconscious and taking it for themselves.

2023 (Fall)
Banner and Rocket travel to New Asgard to recruit Thor, who has fallen into a slump since the loss of his brother and the Snap.

2023 (Fall) (Avengers in 2012 NYC)
Rogers convinces Jasper Sitwell and Brock Rumlow that he is a fellow Hydra agent, in order to retrieve Loki's scepter and the Mind Stone it contains. He also faces and defeats his past self.

2023 (Fall) (Avengers in 2014 Morag)
Nebula's cybernetic implants interact with those of her 2014 self, causing 2014 Thanos to learn of his future success and also the Avengers' plans to reverse it. Before she can return to the present, Nebula is captured by Thanos and Gamora, and then tortured by Ebony Maw.

2023 (Fall)
Natasha goes to Tokyo, where she recruits Clint Barton.

2023 (Fall) (Avengers in 2014 Morag)
After finding out the Avengers' plan, 2014 Thanos sends the disguised 2014 Nebula to the Avengers' present in order to claim the Infinity Stones for him.

2023 (Fall)
The reunited Avengers plan the Time Heist. The team will split up in order to travel to key moments in the past, and retrieve the Infinity Stones before Thanos takes them.

2023 (Fall) (Avengers in 2012 NYC)
Lang and Stark bungle their retrieval of the Tesseract (Space Stone), and 2012 Loki uses it to escape captivity.

2023 (Fall) (Avengers in 2014 Morag)
Barton and Romanoff travel to Vormir and meet the Stonekeeper. After learning what must be done to take the stone, Barton and Romanoff each try to save the other by sacrificing themselves. Natasha "wins," and a heartbroken Clint retrieves the Soul Stone.

2023 (Fall) (Avengers in 1970 NJ)
Rogers and Stark travel to the S.H.I.E.L.D. base at Camp Lehigh on April 4, 1970 and retrieve the Tesseract from that time instead.

2023 (Fall)
END OF BLIP
Banner places the retrieved stones in the Nano Guantlet and uses them to reverse the Snap and restore those blipped by Thanos. He also tries to restore Natasha, but is unable to do so. Wielding the stones leaves his right arm badly burned.

2023 (Fall)
2014 Nebula brings 2014 Thanos and his warship to the Avengers' present using the Quantum Tunnel. He lays waste to the Avengers Compound, then tells the Avengers his new plan: he will wipe out this universe entirely, then make a new, grateful one in its place. Captain America, Thor, and Iron Man take up arms against him.

2023 (Fall)
BATTLE OF EARTH
A returned Doctor Strange and his fellow sorcerers transport the restored Avengers and their allies from across the galaxy to the battlefield, to fight against Thanos and his army. As the Avengers fight to keep the stones, Wanda faces Thanos one-on-one. He orders his ship to rain fire on friend and foe alike, but Captain Marvel returns to Earth to aid the Avengers and brings Thanos' warship crashing to the ground.

2023 (Fall)
The Avengers, Guardians of the Galaxy, and numerous other heroes both terrestrial and cosmic gather for Tony Stark's funeral, paying their respects to the man who saved them all.

2023 (Fall)
Despite the Avengers' best efforts, Thanos seizes the Nano Gauntlet, and prepares to snap all over again. Before he can, Stark steals the stones back and uses them to wipe out Thanos and his entire army. But the effort claims his life.

2023 (Fall)
Thor appoints Valkyrie as king of New Asgard. He then joins the Guardians of the Galaxy on their adventures, while Quill begins searching for 2014 Gamora.

2023 (Fall)
Rogers uses a new Quantum Tunnel to return the Infinity Stones and Mjolnir to their points of origin, but doesn't return as planned. Instead, he reunites with Peggy Carter and tries to live the life he thought lost..

2023 (Fall)
Steve Rogers, now an old man, reunites with Sam Wilson and Buck Barnes in the present. With the support of Bucky, he passes his shield and its legacy on to Sam Wilson.

TVA
The Loki variant accidentally created in the Time Heist is captured by the TVA. He is recruited to hunt another rogue Loki variant, while the branching 2012 he has created is reset by the TVA.

End of Time
"He Who Remains" is killed, destabilizing the Sacred Timeline.

2023 (Fall)
Wanda Maximoff, driven by intense grief, transforms the small town of Westview into a living sitcom. She also creates a new Vision and two sons, but reverses the spell after transforming into The Scarlet Witch.

2024 (Spring)
Shang-Chi travels to the secret realm of Ta Lo, where he gains the mysterious Ten Rings and prevents an attack by the monstrous Dweller in Darkness.

2024 (Fall)
Lawyer Jennifer Walters is exposed to her cousin Bruce Banner's blood, and is transformed into She-Hulk.

2025 (Spring-Fall)
Walters successfully contends with life as a super-powered lawyer for super-powered clients, and defeats a conspiracy to steal her blood and abilities.

2024 (Fall)
The long-awaited Celestial Emergence begins, causing a rupture between the Eternals who wish to allow it and those who want to prevent it. The latter win, and the Emergence is halted.

2025 (Spring)
Marc Spector, avatar of the Egyptian moon god Khonshu, defeats the avatar of rival god Ammit (with the aid of Marc's alter, Steven Grant).

2024 (Summer)
Around eight months after the Blip ends, students of Midtown School of Science and Technology are sent on a two-week trip to Europe. This includes Peter Parker, Ned Leeds, MJ, "Flash" Thompson, Betty Brant, and Brad Davis.

2025 (Spring)
War breaks out between the rival vibranium-powered kingdoms of Wakanda and Talokan. Queen Ramonda of Wakanda is killed. Prince Namor, ruler of Talokan, is defeated by the combined efforts of the new Black Panther (Shuri), and tech prodigy Riri Williams.

2024 (Summer)
Peter Parker is tricked by the villain Quentin Beck. Peter's identity is revealed to the world.

2024 (Fall)
In a misguided attempt to wipe his identity from the world's collective memory, Peter Parker uses a spell that cracks the Multiverse and allows enemies (and allies) from parallel realities to invade. With help from Doctor Strange, the rift in realities is resealed.

2025 (Fall)
Kamala Khan becomes Ms. Marvel and combats the extra-dimensional exiles the Clandestines.

2024 (Spring-Summer)
Sam Wilson defeats the Flag Smashers and becomes Captain America.

2025 (Fall)
Thor and The Mighty Thor (Dr. Jane Foster) fight to prevent Gorr, also known as the God Butcher, from wiping out all of the gods in the universe. Jane dies, and Thor adopts Gorr's young daughter.

2024 (Fall)
Hoping to find her sons elsewhere in the Multiverse, Wanda pursues America Chavez for her universe-hopping ability. After a gruesome battle, she realizes that she has become the villain and finally relents, seemingly perishing by her own hand.

2025 (Winter)
The Guardians try to cheer up a despondent Peter Quill by bringing some festive cheer (and Kevin Bacon) to Knowhere. Mantis reveals she is Quill's sister.

2024 (Winter)
Hawkeye helps the young hero Kate Bishop defeat the villainous Kingpin.

INDEX

DK | Penguin Random House

Senior Editor David Fentiman
Senior Designer Nathan Martin
Senior Production Editor Jennifer Murray
Senior Production Controller Mary Slater
Managing Editor Emma Grange
Managing Art Editor Vicky Short
Publishing Director Mark Searle

Designed for DK by Robert Perry
Additional spreads designed by Bullpen Productions and Amazing15
Timeline art created by Tom Morse

Image Credits:
Earth image on p63: 123RF.com: 1xpert

First published in Great Britain in 2023 by
Dorling Kindersley Limited
DK, One Embassy Gardens, 8 Viaduct Gardens,
London SW11 7BW

The authorised representative in the EEA is
Dorling Kindersley Verlag GmbH. Arnulfstr. 124,
80636 Munich, Germany

A CIP catalogue record for this book
is available from the British Library.
ISBN: 978-0-2415-4382-5

Printed and bound in China

For the curious
www.dk.com

MIX
Paper | Supporting
responsible forestry
FSC™ C018179

This book is made from Forest
Stewardship Council™ certified
paper – one small step in DK's
commitment to a sustainable future.

ACKNOWLEDGMENTS

DK: We would like to thank Kevin Feige, Louis D'Esposito, Victoria Alonso, Brad Winderbaum, Kristy Amornkul, Sara Truly Beers, Michele Blood, Capri Ciulla, Erika Denton, Matt Delmanowski, Emily Fong, Jennifer Giandalone, Nigel Goodwin, Eliot Lehrman, Richie Palmer, Andrew Reiber, Jacqueline Ryan-Rudolph, Alex Scharf, Jeff Willis, Jennifer Wojnar, Kevin R. Wright, and Vincent Charles Garcia at Marvel Studios; Chelsea Alon, Molly Jones, John Morgan, Michael Siglain, and Jenny Moussa Spring at Disney Publishing Worldwide; and Sarah Singer and Jeff Youngquist at Marvel Entertainment.

Anthony Breznican: Writing can be a lonely process, but this book was the opposite. Creating the timeline meant rewatching all of the Marvel Studios films and TV shows with my wife, Jill, and our children, Audrey and Prosper. Even though I was obsessively taking notes and pausing constantly to hunt for obscure dates on computer screens and newspapers, it was a joy to venture through this vast universe with them.

Amy Ratcliffe: I'd like to thank David Fentiman and the whole team at DK Publishing for an extremely valid reason to revisit MCU films and TV. Thanks to Kevin Feige for leading this vast universe, to my co-authors for being awesome and insightful, and to Aaron for endless hours of Marvel discussions and debates.

ReBecca Theodore-Vachon: Love and gratitude to my parents who encouraged my curiosity and love for reading. Thank you to my siblings. To my best friend and mentor Jerry L. Barrow—thank you for taking a chance on me and encouraging my journey as a writer. Also thank you to Anthony Breznican for inviting me to be a part of this massive project. And final thanks to Marvel for giving us these unforgettable characters and stories that teach us to reach higher, further, faster.